BLOOD ON THE TRACKS
ENGLAND IN AUSTRALIA
THE 1974/75 ASHES

BLOOD ON THE TRACKS
ENGLAND IN AUSTRALIA
THE 1974/75 ASHES

DAVID TOSSELL

Ashes to Ashes, Dust to Dust
If Thomson don't get ya, Lillee must
Cartoon caption, *Sydney Sunday Telegraph*

First published by Fairfield Books in October 2024

fairfield books

Fairfield Books
Bedser Stand
Kia Oval
London
SE11 5SS

Typeset in Garamond and Ridley Grotesk
Typesetting by Rob Whitehouse

The right of David Tossell to be identified as the author of this work has been asserted by him in accordance with sections 77 and 78 of the Copyright, Designs and Patents Act 1988

This book is printed on paper certified
by the Forest Stewardship Council

Every effort has been made to trace copyright and any oversight will be rectified in future editions at the earliest opportunity

All rights reserved. No part of this book may be reproduced, sold, utilised or transmitted in any form or by any electronic or mechanical means, including photocopying, recording or by any information storage and retrieval system, without prior permission in writing from the publishers

The views and opinions expressed in this book are those of the author and do not necessarily reflect the views of the publishers

© 2024 David Tossell
ISBN 978-1-915237-41-5
Ebook ISBN 978-1-915237-47-7

A CIP catalogue record for this title is available from the British Library

Printed by CPI Group (UK) Ltd

CONTENTS

	Introduction	13
1	Selection of the Likely Lads	19
2	In Sickness and in Health	47
3	Storm Warning	66
4	We Didn't Start the Fire	83
5	Fast and Furious	97
6	Flight of Fancy	118
7	The Wild West	127
8	Family Fortunes	149
9	Protect and Survive	156
10	Signs of Life	166
11	Captains at War	187
12	Ashes to Ashes	212
13	Advance Australia Fair	238
14	The Same Old Scene	253
15	The Day of Denness	267
16	Escape to Victory	287
17	Following On	299
	Acknowledgements	310
	Tour results	312
	Bibliography	316
	Scoresheets	318

INTRODUCTION

*I enjoy hitting a batsman more than getting him out.
It doesn't worry me in the least to see the batsman hurt
rolling around screaming and blood on the pitch.*
Jeff Thomson

*I try to hit the batsman and thus intimidate him. I
try to hit the batsman in the rib cage when I bowl a
purposeful bouncer and I want it to hurt so much
that the batsman doesn't want to face me anymore.
I want to be in complete control of the situation
and that's one way of keeping hold of the reins.*
Dennis Lillee

*Never in the ninety-eight years of Test cricket have
batsmen been so grievously bruised and battered
by ferocious, hostile short-pitched balls as were
those led conscientiously by Michael Denness.*
Wisden Cricketers' Almanack, 1975

'Come on, fellas. Let him have it.' Tony Greig's exhortation was a product of his frustration at the diffidence of England's seam bowlers. Time and again they afforded Dennis Lillee the courtesy of balls delivered close enough to his batting crease that he could concentrate on adding to the Australian total without concern for personal safety.

The first Test match of the 1974-75 Ashes series was into its second day and enough had been seen of the patchwork surface and ridges of the Brisbane pitch to know the tricks it might play. In losing their first eight wickets for 229, Australia had witnessed five batsmen[1] perish after ill-advisedly entrusting their existence to the hook shot on The Gabba's unpredictable surface. With Lillee now on 15 and having added 28 important runs in partnership with Max Walker, Greig could not understand his seamers' adherence to the unwritten custom of not bowling short to their opposition counterparts. At one point Peter Lever had announced, 'I am going to bounce this bloke,' but, according to Lillee's memory, 'I am pretty sure he didn't, or if he did it was nothing special.'

A product of his competitive sporting upbringing in South Africa, Greig was never one to put convention in the path of ambition. He urged captain Mike Denness to give him the ball. He might not be the quickest bowler in the team but, at almost 6ft 8in, he could certainly get the ball up to a threatening height. For the past year in Test cricket, Greig – the pre-eminent all-rounder in the world – had been mixing his medium pacers with a form of off-spin, and for his second delivery he approached the crease off an abridged run-up. It was a bluff. Greig bent his considerable back and pitched short. An unbalanced Lillee attempted to hook and succeeded only in gloving the ball down the leg side to wicketkeeper Alan Knott.

Lillee briefly stood his ground, his ire at Greig's effrontery as clear on his face as the dark, Zapata moustache he'd grown since England had last encountered him two years earlier. His exit route took him up the pitch past Greig, to whom he made his displeasure known and offered a warning of what to expect in return – various versions of which have been recounted over the years. The gist, however, was clear enough for England's opening batsman, Dennis Amiss, to ponder, 'Greigy, what have you done that for?'

Holding his bat dismissively by the toe, Lillee stalked back to the pavilion, the fury hovering about him like a dust cloud. On the Australian team's balcony, captain Ian Chappell noted his teammate's manner. 'We all looked at each other and thought, "Hello what is going on here? He is not too happy." So we all found a reason to go into the changing room and rummage around in our bags.'

Beyond the gaze of the TV cameras, Lillee hurled down his bat and saw teammates staring, wondering what he would do next. 'Just

---

1 In order to remain authentic to the period in which events take place, I will use the term 'batsman' throughout, rather than the modern 'batter'.

remember who fucking started this,' he barked, pausing to let the implication of that sink in before adding with menace, 'But we'll fucking finish it.'

Partnered by a new terrifying force in Jeff Thomson, Lillee made good on his promise. By the end of the first match of the series, two English batsmen had suffered broken bones and there was plenty more suffering to follow. Not one of the seven specialist batsmen who represented the tourists in the series escaped at least one significant blow and not one played in every game. Most suffered some kind of serious injury; or, in the case of Denness, the severest of indignities when he dropped himself for the fourth – and ultimately decisive – Test match in Sydney.

When Bob Dylan released his album 'Blood on the Tracks' a few days after the Ashes had been surrendered in that game it could have been timed deliberately to provide a future author with a book title that reflected events in Australia. Bob Willis, the fast bowler who'd added the American singer's stage name to his own legal identity by way of tribute, was excited by the album's release, but to anyone else in the England camp it sounded like a taunt. Instead of songs reflecting a 'bleak fatalistic view of love', as one reviewer described it, the album might have been expected to deliver stories of broken bones and frightening near misses. For that was the narrative of the doomed attempt by the England team – touring as usual under the banner of the Marylebone Cricket Club – to retain the urn in the face of a barrage of some of the most frightening fast bowling ever witnessed. Perhaps that same album reviewer wasn't so far off the mark when he described a tone of 'world-weary bitter survival'. After all, Denness remembered the mood among the team being 'relief that they had got out of there alive' as their plane took off after almost four months in Australia.

Even the great Australian all-rounder Keith Miller, who had bowled his share of bouncers at English batsmen over the years, argued, 'The Aussie fast bowlers are wild colonial boys trying to maim rather than defeat fairly.'

According to Sir Donald Bradman, the most successful Test batsman of all-time, 'Lillee and Thomson were probably the fastest and most lethal opening pair in Australia's history. They possessed remarkable physical strength and stamina and ability and a willingness to exploit the short-pitched ball to an extent which would have unnerved any side.'

Back home, the folks in a country feeling the impact of 12 months of industrial and political civil war – strikes, power cuts, two General Elections and IRA bombings – had been waking in the hope of having their winter days brightened by the BBC. But when Radio Three crackled into life at 6.30 each morning, live commentary of the closing stages of each day's play had to wait until after the latest tally of injuries and surrenders. It was more like dispatches from a battle zone than a sports bulletin.

Capturing the mood of the country and demonstrating the importance of radio in the days before overseas cricket tours were routinely televised live was songwriter Richard Stilgoe. One of the light-hearted ditties he penned to reflect the news on BBC One's evening current affairs show, *Nationwide*, began:

> *Every morning on the radio*
> *The news comes from Australia*
> *The English batsmen once again*
> *Have had a ghastly failure*

The song hailed 'Lilian Thomson' as 'the fastest lady bowler the world has ever seen', which was itself an indication of how the two tormentors of English batting had become inextricably linked in the public consciousness more than any previous pair of fast bowlers. What added to their ogrish personae was the fact that daily television highlights from Australia were being presented in colour for the first time, adding vividly bruised flesh to the bones of the statistics presented on the radio. And the half-hour of action on BBC Two meant that the British public saw little other than the wickets, the bouncers, the blows and the narrow escapes. On occasions it seemed surprising that the carnage was deemed suitable for airing before the 9 p.m. watershed. And when the *Sunday Express* asked comedian Eric Morecambe for some New Year's advice for the England team, he quipped, 'Keep off the grass.'

Such was the Australian duo's annexing of the nation's psyche that when they toured England several months later, renowned *Daily Mail* columnist Ian Wooldridge presented an occasional diary of events written by 'Terror Tompkins', a coarse, rambunctious character he had fictionalised out of the combined personalities of Lillee and Thomson. And when *Punch* featured a mickey-taking article on Australian culture – which it called a contradiction in terms – in its August 1975 edition it was the instantly recognisable cartoon depictions of the duo that the publication put on the front cover, alongside the heading, 'Life under the Aussies'. Yet the legacy of their contribution to a 4-1 series victory – the loss coming when both were injured – was cricketing as well as cultural. 'To my mind, Thomson and Lillee in harness sparked off the beginning of a change of era in Test cricket,' is the view of Knott, while Australian batsman Ross Edwards described it as 'cricket beyond anyone's experience'.

'That was the time in the mid-'70s after which it became very physical short-pitched bowling,' said John Edrich, England's vice-captain on the tour. 'It wasn't a lot of fun to play.'

Willis, whose ailing knees had impaired his ability to retaliate on behalf of his beleaguered batting colleagues, said, 'Test cricket had set out on its new, and some would say sinister, direction. From then on, the fast short balls were to be employed more and more frequently as the killer punches on wickets that had any semblance of life. Old timers will still insist that the fast bowlers of their day were just as swift as most of today's tearaways. Maybe they were, but it is the length of the fast delivery which has changed, ever since that Brisbane Test.'

'It was not pleasant,' said Brian Luckhurst, who opened the England batting at The Gabba at the tail end of his international career. 'But it gave me an insight into how Test cricket was changing.'

John Woodcock, cricket correspondent of *The Times*, wrote in a magazine article shortly after the tour, 'Fast disappearing are the days of flight and guile and the readiness to buy wickets rather than blast or bore away for them.'

When Lillee and Thomson dished out the same punishment to the West Indies tourists on the way to a 5-1 victory a year later, defeated skipper Clive Lloyd took careful note. Along with the subsequent inability of his motley collection of slow bowlers to defend a target of 400-plus against India, he had all the evidence he needed to unleash four fast bowlers at a time on helpless opponents – a method that led to almost two decades of dominance of world cricket.

Yet the two Aussies who had so enlightened the West Indies captain were to embark on different career paths. Lillee went on to become the marker by which all fast bowlers of his and subsequent eras were measured, retiring from Test cricket in 1984 with what was then a word-record total of 355 wickets, despite the years lost to injury and then to World Series Cricket. Thomson, meanwhile, was never the same force – at least not consistently – after dislocating his right collarbone in a fielding collision late in 1976. He took his 200th and final Test wicket during the 1985 Ashes tour of England.

Their indelible mark on the sport was assured, however, after the events of one terrifying Australian summer. As the MCC touring party gathered in high spirits amid England's autumn drizzle they had no idea what was about to hit them.

1
SELECTION OF THE LIKELY LADS

The cupboard is bare.
Alec Bedser, England chairman of selectors

If anyone thought it was a daft idea for a team picture, they kept it to themselves. They had already posed for the traditional pre-departure shot, grouped in two rows in their blue Marylebone Cricket Club blazers, grey slacks and tourists' ties – colour of shirts optional, but mostly white or pale blue. Now, the players who would soon be flying to Australia to defend the Ashes were asked by photographer Patrick Eagar to try something different.

Directing Mike Denness to stand closest to him, he instructed the other 15 players and three members of the touring management team to line up behind the captain, snaking back through the puddles in the car park of Heathrow Airport's Excelsior Hotel. Then each man in turn was encouraged to lean to his right so that faces emerged from behind the shoulder in front; giants such as Tony Greig and Bob Willis naturally sent to the back of the line. The end impression was that of a camp cruise-ship dance troupe about to engage in a soft shoe shuffle rather than a group of elite sportsmen carrying the hopes of a nation,

'To be honest, I don't recall taking the photo, it was just a press call of some sort,' admitted Eagar, who was as excited as any player at the thought that he would soon be embarking upon his first England tour. He had been taking pictures at cricket matches for a decade, but this was to be what he remembered as a 'ground-breaking' period on his way to becoming the sport's most renowned photographer.

The man Eagar stuck closest to his lens on this day in October had been destined to take his place at the head of the team to visit Australia and New Zealand for more than six months; ever since England's previous tour had ended with an against-the-odds Test triumph against West Indies in Trinidad. Having drawn that series in the Caribbean on his first engagement as England captain, only a disastrous summer could deny Denness, the Kent batsman from Lanarkshire in Scotland, the honour of attempting to emulate Ray Illingworth, who had led England to Ashes success four years earlier. Comprehensive victory over India followed by a rain-affected stalemate against a strong Pakistan team kept him on course for the southern hemisphere. He'd even managed to score his first two Test centuries against India. His appointment for the winter had been confirmed publicly at the close of the second day of the English season's final Test match.

The role of the man whose features poked out from the very back of Eagar's chorus line, Alec Bedser, was announced at the same time. An imposing figure, by way of size if not personality, Bedser had provided England with nine years of committed seam bowling, ending his playing career with a then-record 236 Test wickets, and had now served for 12 years as a selector – chairman of the panel since 1969. After three Ashes series in Australia as a player, one as a journalist and another as assistant manager, he was considered to have the knowledge, local profile and feel for diplomacy that made him the obvious choice as tour manager.

The appointments were announced shortly after Pakistan had declared with 600 on The Oval's scoreboard, hardly an auspicious backdrop for what had been intended as a moment of positivity, a maintaining of the impetus of a successful summer. 'It was perhaps a bizarre moment to choose, close upon Pakistan's vast score,' noted EW Swanton in *The Daily Telegraph*, 'but Mr Bedser is a down-to-earth fellow, not perhaps much influenced by psychological niceties.' Such a no-nonsense attitude would contribute to a perception of lack of empathy before the tour was over.

On an expedition that would last four and a half months and cover more than 35,000 miles, the manager-captain relationship was critical for the well-being of the venture. For one thing, with only an assistant manager and a physiotherapist to complete the support staff, there were few people to whom players could turn for advice, care and the opportunity to air problems and grievances. Everything would filter through Bedser and Denness, and if they were not fully synchronised it would make for a long period away.

The fact that Bedser was a bachelor, and considered somewhat unworldly by many, was always – as we shall see later – liable to create an environment where the players felt he was unable to understand their various predicaments. How Denness walked the potential tightrope of supporting his men if things came to a head, while sustaining a workable union with the manager, would be a test of his leadership every bit as arduous as setting the fields and managing his bowling changes in the cauldron of the Melbourne Cricket Ground.

Recent history had demonstrated the importance of the manager-captain relationship. The 1970-71 tour ended in triumph in spite of the ever-growing rift between Illingworth and manager David Clark, whom the captain felt rarely had the interests of the players as his priority. The most striking example of that was Clark agreeing to the Australian Cricket Board's suggestion of a seventh Test after the fourth match of the series in Melbourne had been washed out without a ball being bowled. Illingworth fought for his players' demand that they should receive additional payment for the new fixture, which would be played in front of a full house at the Sydney Cricket Ground. In the end, an extra £25 per man was all Illingworth could squeeze out of the MCC officials. That was far from being the only bone of contention. Illingworth was aggrieved that his team received little support or sympathy from the tour management as they dealt with criticism for the hard-nosed nature of their play and became increasingly dissatisfied at the umpiring in the series. They closed ranks, became reluctant to mix with media, and created an us-against-the-world mentality that probably did them no harm in the bigger picture of digging for victory on a long, exhausting tour but ran contrary to the missionary element that Lord's considered an important element of tours under the MCC Banner. Illingworth was clearly the dominant personality on the tour, with Clark, a Parachute Regiment war hero who went on to become captain of Kent, left feeling marginalised. There was little danger of the balance of power being skewed in a similar way on this trip. Not only was Denness nothing like the forceful character of Illingworth, but he was unlikely to do anything to set himself against Bedser, the man who controlled his future selectorial status.

Rounding out the management team for the tour were assistant manager Alan 'AC' Smith, the long-time Warwickshire captain, who played six Tests as a wicketkeeper, and physiotherapist Bernard Thomas, another man with Warwickshire ties. Thomas, chosen for his fifth MCC tour, had begun working with the county as physio in the 1960s after setting up the Edgbaston Health Clinic. One of his charges, the injury-prone Willis, commented, 'It was state of the art at the time. It was always full of the latest gizmos.'

Before Bedser could chair the meeting that would reach accord on the players forming the tour party, a letter – typed in green – arrived for him at Lord's from author Frank Hansford-Miller, chairman of the English National Party. Breaking off from his party's preparations for an increasingly inevitable second general election of the year, Hansford-Miller wrote, 'The English National Party wishes to protest at the choice by you and your Selection Committee of a Scotsman to lead England in the forthcoming cricket tour of Australia. We consider this most inappropriate and an insult to many outstanding English cricketers … and also an insult to our country of England.'

Suggesting that 'no other country but England is treated in this way by its own selectors', he added, 'Why limit your choice on your logic to a Scotsman? Why did you not choose Gary Sobers, Intikhab Alam or Barry Richards?' Noting that press pictures after his appointment showed Denness and his family wearing tartan, the letter continued, 'Have you informed Mike he is to be captain of ENGLAND in Australia?'[2] Joining Bedser and Denness in the committee room at Lord's after the final day against Pakistan closed across London were the three other regular England selectors, not one of whom had played a single day of Test cricket. Jack Bond was a modest county batsman who had made his name as an inspirational leader of the Lancashire team that had dominated limited-overs cricket in the late 1960s and early 1970s. Essex wicketkeeper-batsman Brian 'Tonker' Taylor had made one MCC tour as understudy to Godfrey Evans and had led his county for six years until his retirement in 1973. And former Cambridge University man Ossie Wheatley had taken more than 1,000 first-class wickets as a seamer and skippered Glamorgan for six seasons. Good chaps, the lot of them, but unable to put themselves in the shoes of the men whose careers they held

---

2 The letter concluded with what amounted to a summary of the ENP's argument for a devolved English parliament, which it had been campaigning for since forming as the John Hampden Freedom Party in 1966. In the October 1974 General Election, called by Labour Prime Minister Harold Wilson a couple of weeks later in the hope of strengthening his minority government, the ENP's two candidates combined for 1,115 votes.

in their hands. Or, as Swanton put it, they were 'as a body, an inadequate appointment'.

Also present was Cecil Paris, serving a second term as chairman of the Test and County Cricket Board, which had been established in 1968 to take the administration of the sport out of the hands of a private members' club, MCC. Paris was another journeyman county cricketer, his own career having ended almost three decades earlier, and within a year he would succeed Prince Philip, Duke of Edinburgh, as president of the MCC.

Although England tours still took place under the flag of the MCC – as they would until the start of the 1977-78 winter – responsibility for administration of those trips had transferred to the TCCB after 1968-69. Yet, as was to prove significant, there was still a place in the selection room for an MCC committee member. With Doug Insole away on holiday, it was treasurer Gubby Allen – like Insole, a former chairman of England selectors – who attended the meeting.

Pakistan's mountain of runs at The Oval had increased Denness's conviction that he could not afford to travel to Australia without fast bowler John Snow, an absentee throughout his term as England captain. 'From the time that I took over, my first port of call was to have John Snow in the team and the selectors said no,' he explained. 'We went through the West Indies and came back and played India and Pakistan and I still wanted Snowy.' Denness had made a point of checking with the Sussex man as the summer neared its end and found him pondering alternative employment for the winter months. 'I wanted to know how enthusiastic he was to be selected. In a roundabout way I got the answer that if selected he would go to Australia and give his utmost.'

If Snow betrayed any reticence about selection, one could hardly blame him. Even while he'd been taking 31 wickets as England won back the Ashes with a 2-0 win on Illingworth's tour, those in management were coming up with reasons to find fault. He might have been excused – although not by the Australian fans – when he hit tail-ender Terry Jenner with a short ball at Sydney, but tour manager Clark had never forgiven him for what he perceived as a lack of effort in the nets after he had just sent down more than 400 deliveries in the first Test.

John Edrich recalled Illingworth telling Snow he could do what he liked off the field as long he gave 100 per cent in the Test matches. 'He gave him a free rein. It's Snowy; you could not coach him. He was a natural.' And the bowler was unafraid of firing back when given a dressing down by Clark, telling the manager he didn't care if he lost his good conduct bonus and saying later that the tour 'emphasised the gulf between administrators and players'.

That rift, in Snow's case, was to grow the following summer when, with India batting in the fourth innings at Lord's, he collided with Sunil Gavaskar as he attempted a quick single and then tossed his dropped bat towards him. From a distance and from the television footage, it looked as though Snow had deliberately caused the contact. Back in the pavilion, he was preparing to visit Gavaskar to apologise when MCC secretary Billy Griffith entered the dressing room and announced that the incident was 'the most disgusting thing I've ever seen on the field.' Snow was dropped for one match as a punishment.

Ted Dexter, the former England captain who had skippered the young Snow at Sussex, was hardly alone in identifying the issue as being less about one specific incident and more about the philosophical and cultural chasm between the wild-haired fast bowler and the neatly-trimmed Bedser. 'Often there is no way of bridging the generation gap which divides them, there is no denying the antipathy between men of different convictions when giving instructions to their barber,' he wrote in the *Sunday Mirror*. 'There is still, for my likes, too much of the headmaster Bedser ticking off the schoolboy Snow.'

While managing to regain his place for the majority of home Test matches, Snow was one of several senior players, including England captain Illingworth, who chose to miss MCC's 1972-73 winter in India and Pakistan. When it came to selection for the 1973-74 trip to the West Indies, he was no longer considered a suitable character to take on tour. He had, however, travelled with the Derrick Robins XI to South Africa, where he had been dropped for not practising.

For the second year running he was invited to take part in the early-season Test trial between England and The Rest,[3] a fixture that he viewed as 'a bore and an insult' and felt should be used

---

3 The fixture had been reintroduced in 1973 and was ditched again after the 1976 season

simply for the selectors to look at promising young players. The 1974 match was staged at Worcester, where Geoff Boycott scored a century in each innings and Edrich secured a Test comeback with a hundred of his own. 'What the match proved I have no idea,' recalled Snow, who argued with Wheatley on the final day when the England selector urged Lancashire batsman Frank Hayes to 'make a game of it' by batting with abandon. Snow snapped, 'If any player needs to play decently and properly, building an innings in the right way to show he is Test material, it is Frank.' His card had been marked in black once more and he was not picked for England that summer.

Now Denness found himself going to bat again for a man who, despite being 33 by the time the plane was due to leave for Australia, was someone who could take with him a psychological edge over the home batsmen. 'We sat round the table at Lord's and I said, "We have got to have John Snow",' said Denness. But as he looked for a reaction, he could see few allies. Not only had Snow upset Wheatley at Worcester, but he knew that others felt he was not 'a good team man', while Bedser resented his progressive views on how players should be treated. Snow wrote in his autobiography, '[Bedser] is of a different generation, brought up in an era where the professionals were still the workhorses, accepting orders and not questioning their masters.'

According to Christopher Martin-Jenkins, BBC correspondent and chronicler of several MCC tours of the 1970s, 'Bedser's opinion, simply, was that there was no place for anyone inclined to be a prima donna.'

The manager even stressed the demands he would place on players to present themselves throughout the tour in a manner befitting MCC ambassadors. 'We don't want people turning up at the ground looking as though they are off to a jamboree on the beach,' he would say at the outset.

As Dexter wrote of Bedser in 1975, 'If you want him to react quickly and heatedly then you need only mention loafers, prima donnas and barrack-room lawyers – in something like that order – to draw his full firepower. If such people have the temerity to wander into first-class cricket and, furthermore, expect to play for England, then they inevitably become much more disagreeable to him.' Snow, of course, could be placed in all three categories as far as Bedser was concerned.

And then there was Allen, the man who lived behind the Lord's pavilion, whose blood pumped MCC scarlet and gold and whose role at the meeting appeared to be that of moral guardian and defender of the old amateur ethos. As a seam bowler under Douglas Jardine in the infamous 1932-33 'Bodyline' series he had boldly refused to follow orders to aim short-pitched deliveries at the Australian batsmen rather than the stumps. After the particularly combative third Test in Adelaide he had written to his father of 'a most unpleasant match', describing it as 'nothing but rows and barracking until I am fed up with everything to do with cricket.' When MCC set about rebuilding relations on their return four years later it was to Allen that they turned to captain the side.

'Gubby Allen regarded Lord's as his own fiefdom,' said England batsman Dennis Amiss. 'We heard that he was determined that the selectors should not pick Snowy to go to Australia and they went along with it.'

Denness was asked, 'How can you control him when no other England captain has been able to?' No matter that a supposedly uncontrollable Snow had effectively won them the Ashes that they still held after a drawn home series in 1972. 'He was not acceptable to the MCC, so he didn't come,' the captain explained. 'I had to ring Snowy up and say, "I am sorry. I fought for you, but I can't have you."'

According to Keith Fletcher, a previous tour teammate, Snow's bowling in Australia had been as fast as anything that would be served up by Australians and West Indians later in the decade. 'If only Snow and Willis could have bowled together regularly for England,' he lamented.

To Australians, the decision was unfathomable. 'If Snow isn't classified within the top five pacemen in England in the selectors' eyes, they need a doctor's test,' said Eric Beecher, editor of the nation's *Cricketer* magazine. Decades later, Australian skipper Ian Chappell suggested, 'Australia did some silly things in selection. For example, how you could not have Neil Harvey and Keith Miller as Australian captains is bloody ridiculous. But England was more likely to make what I would call a class-system decision than Australia, like leaving out John Snow.'

According to Dennis Lillee, Snow was 'at that stage the ultimate fast bowler in the world'. He said, 'He was certainly an inspiration. I didn't ever in my wildest dreams think I could achieve the level he was at.'

When Snow subsequently announced his intention to travel to Australia to work as a television analyst, he dismissed any thoughts of being called upon to play in an emergency. 'If the whole [squad] broke down tomorrow, they wouldn't send for me,' he said. 'The only way I'll ever be selected to play for England is to shoot all the selectors. And I wouldn't waste my money on the cartridges. Perhaps I should be angry seeing everyone going off to Australia without me. It's every cricketer's dream and I think I helped win the Ashes last time. When the Australian captain says he's relieved I'm not going, well, that's all very flattering, very nice, but my not being selected has got nothing to do with my cricket.'

The MCC seamers who were selected felt weakened by Snow's absence. Yorkshire's Chris Old recalled, 'As a group of bowlers we talked during that summer about how several of us would have been quite happy to go out there and play all the state games and have John in the right frame of mind and fitness to be firing in the Test matches, which was the key thing. Two or three of us would have been quite happy to fill that role for him.'

Time and again as the touring party took shape – both on this night and in enforced subsequent meetings – previous success in Australia was an important criterion for selection. Yet that had been ignored when it came to Snow. It was the main reason that Lancashire fast bowler Peter Lever, soon to be 34, was recalled after a gap of two years. He had played in five matches of the 1970-71 series, proving himself a willing worker who could maintain his pace throughout the day.

Chosen to spearhead the attack was Willis, another who had been on the last Australian tour, since when he had switched counties from Surrey to Warwickshire and seen his Test career make staccato progress because of injuries. 'I remain convinced that when he is 100 per cent fit and firing on all cylinders he is one of the quickest bowlers in the world,' said Denness, who'd had Willis with him in the Caribbean, along with three other right-arm fast-medium bowlers selected again: Geoff Arnold of Surrey, Mike Hendrick of Derbyshire, and Old, about whom the hopes that he could develop into a genuine all-rounder were countered by fears that he was too physically fragile to become a long-term force in Test cricket.

The selection of five seam bowlers for a long tour that would encompass 31 matches of all descriptions raises no eyebrows when viewed with the perspective of a modern age in which England routinely name six of them for a two-match series and workloads are micro-managed through a system of central contracts. It seems remarkable, then, to look back on the widespread criticism the selectors attracted and the assumption that there would not be enough overs to keep all five men gainfully employed, especially when you consider the injury record of Willis and Old.

'Keeping them fit will be like having too many horses in the yard,' argued John Woodcock in *The Times*. 'The middle is the place for that, not the nets.' Later, he added, 'It really is a gruesome prospect having to watch three fast bowlers at work in each match, up-country and down-town.'

Another typical comment was that of Swanton in *The Daily Telegraph*. 'By over-weighting this overrated form of bowling the selectors have almost ruined the prosect of fielding a balanced attack,' he wrote. 'The more I think about it, the more thoroughly foolish in all circumstances I think this aspect of the selection to be.'

Yet a different view was offered by the man who had brought the Ashes into England's possession, former captain Illingworth, who remembered that he was 'condemned time and again for using too much pace'. He called the selection of five seamers 'the most positive step they have taken towards keeping the Ashes', although he could not fathom the absence of Snow. 'He should top the list of anybody who saw him open the bowling in Australia on the last tour. For the first five or six overs he was virtually unplayable in four of the Tests. Snow in County Championship matches is one thing. Snow in Test matches before a huge crowd is another, especially when there is an Australian in his sights.'

Among the nation's slow bowlers, Kent's Derek Underwood was an automatic choice to provide the left-arm variety, but there was much discussion around the table over the identity of the off-spinner. Neither of the men who had been on the most recent tour,

Surrey's Pat Pocock and Leicestershire's Jack Birkenshaw, made the cut. Instead, it was another name from the past, Middlesex's Fred Titmus, who was brought back for the first time since he'd lost four toes in a boating accident in the West Indies in 1968.

Much of the media focus when the team was revealed the following day fell on the unlikely figure of the six-toed almost-42-year-old who had been playing first-class cricket since the 1940s. His Middlesex wicketkeeper, John Murray, reckoned he had bowled better than ever in 1974, getting through 941 overs, while he had achieved three 100-wicket seasons since his trauma in Barbados. But with another off-spinner, Illingworth, skippering the team, there had always been a considerable obstacle barring his way back to Test cricket.

John Arlott suggested in *The Guardian* that 'no one knows cricket and cricketers better than he does', while Bedser explained, 'Although Titmus's age and lack of toes have always been a factor against him we decided that proven ability counts most.' For his own part, Titmus assured everyone that he was fit enough to stand up to the rigours of the tour, although he did admit that his lack of speed might cause Denness to think hard about where to place him in the vast Australian outfields.

It was another selection that surprised observers in Australia. Frank Tyson, the former England fast bowler who had become a respected writer and broadcaster in that country, noted, 'When he first learned of his inclusion ... Titmus declared that there would be people in Australia who would fall over themselves laughing at his selection. It was a shrewd observation.'

These being the days when the players heard about the squad at the same time as the public, it proved ironic when Titmus found himself bowling at his selection rival Birkenshaw as the Lord's tannoy revealed his place on the tour. Two balls later, he got him out. 'I thought my chance had gone,' admitted Titmus, who had planned to spend his winter coaching in South Africa. 'Some members of the press had rooted for me and I think that helped.'

When it came to the batting, the preoccupation for those same journalists had been the likelihood of Yorkshire opener Geoff Boycott being included among the men selected. Boycott's runs– 657 at an average of 93.85 – had done almost as much as Snow's wickets to wrest back the Ashes four years earlier and he had been the foundation stone of England's batting for the best part of a decade. But the summer of 1974 had found him battling personal demons and fighting a civil war in a Yorkshire changing room over which he had presided since 1971. Down the road from Headingley, his friend Brian Clough, the former Derby County manager, was facing a similar summer of bitterness and rancour after taking over from the beloved Don Revie as manager of Leeds United, a team for which Clough had always professed hatred and contempt. But while Clough's conflict was fresh, raw and would end in defeat after only 44 days, Boycott had been engaged in a drawn-out war of attrition since the day he needed a split decision by the committee to earn the captaincy. Results had been disappointing and there was no shortage of players who by their words, planted in the right ears, and deeds, in leaving the county, made clear their dissatisfaction with the new regime.

On top of that, Boycott had his own form and his benefit season to worry about.[4] After struggling, distractedly yet inexplicably, against the gentle left-arm medium pace of India's Eknath Solkar in the first Test he chose to excuse himself from international cricket. 'When I took stock of my situation I realised to my horror that the drive and desire to play for England had gone,' he explained years later. 'Yorkshire's lack of success on the field and the infighting off it, benefit problems, lack of form, lack of motivation to play for England; they all mounted up until I couldn't take it any longer. It made sense from everybody's point of view to tell Alec Bedser that I was in no mental or emotional condition to play well for England.' Amid such turmoil he still managed to finish the season with 1,783 first-class runs at an average of more than 59 and now, so it seemed, was ready to resume international duties. Not everybody in the sport liked him but, even as he approached the age of 34, few could claim there was anyone better in England with a bat in his hand.

The rest of the batting line-up, to the dismay of some observers, was easily predicted, comprising those who had played throughout the summer. Lancashire's David Lloyd had cemented his place as

---

4 Boycott's benefit season ended up earning him £20,639, beating the previous Yorkshire record set by veteran seam bowler Tony Nicholson a year earlier.

Boycott's replacement by scoring a double century against India; Amiss was in the form of his life and threatening the record for most Test runs in a calendar year; Edrich was re-established and was another with runs in Australia on his resumé; and Fletcher was now a fixture in the middle order. All-rounder Tony Greig and wicketkeeper Alan Knott were as good a number six-seven combination as any country could boast.

The flamboyant Greig, however, would be offered a diminished role on this tour. The vice-captaincy that he bore in the West Indies was being transferred to Edrich, who, according to journalist and broadcaster Henry Blofeld, 'thinks about cricket as sensibly and uncompromisingly as any Australian'. The 37-year-old Surrey captain, veteran of 65 Tests, was a safe option, more aligned to the personality of Bedser than a man who had almost caused a riot in the West Indies when he ran out Alvin Kallicharran as he departed the crease after the final ball of the day. Denness, who made it home to Canterbury at 3.30 a.m. after the selection meeting and had to excuse himself from Kent's game the next day because he was 'completely shattered', remembered, 'The selectors were not happy with Greigy's incidents. Their view was, "We don't want someone like Tony Greig getting up to mischief if he is there representing the country." That was their decision rather than mine.'

The selectors were seemingly offered instant justification for their decision when a story appeared in the *Melbourne Herald* under the headline 'Greig Blasts Nice Guys' Team'. He was quoted as suggesting that the selectors' nervousness around forceful characters had cost him the vice-captaincy and accused them of picking 'unassuming guys'. The Australian Associated Press said it had conducted the interview via telephone and its content had not been submitted for official approval. Strangely, the *Herald* was the only publication to run the story, despite its broad distribution via AAP. Greig's employers at Sussex were asked to investigate and report to the TCCB's disciplinary sub-committee, which would be allowed to take 'whatever action it may think fit'. A few days before departure, Greig met with TCCB officials, who accepted his explanation that he knew nothing of the article and cleared him of intentional wrong-doing,

He maintained his place on an on-tour selection party that also included Bedser, Smith, Denness and Edrich, but there was no doubt that the latter's appointment as second-in-charge characterised the make-up of a squad that was, Swanton noted, a clear reflection of its manager. The restriction of the party to 16 players had allowed for only one spare batsman and no room to look beyond the obvious candidates. The only way to add depth and/or take a punt on an untried talent would have been to leave behind one of the seamers or take a batsman who could also keep wicket instead of selecting the best pure gloveman in the country, Derbyshire's Bob Taylor, as Knott's deputy. Nottinghamshire's Mike Harris had been the most likely candidate if the selectors had chosen the second of those options, but Bedser admitted, damningly for English cricket, that there had been no young batsmen making them think seriously about depleting the bowling.

'The cupboard is bare,' Bedser declared in naming a squad with an average age of 31, causing *The Guardian* to place the heading 'Damning of rising generation' above its report. 'As for the touring side,' Arlott wrote, 'those of the past usually carried at least a couple of young players as an investment against the future. This one does not. Every man in it has earned the passage – but it offers a depressing prospect for the future.'

Having filed his on-the-day piece for the *Telegraph*, Swanton had time to give the selection further thought for his opinion column in *The Cricketer*. 'One can only hope that the two members of the committee who did know Australian touring conditions were outvoted by the four who did not – which is among other things a condemnation of the composition of the selectors,' he wrote. 'It was never going to be easy to find a party with the right balance – the nucleus of the 1974 side needed a couple of star fielders and men who could do two things well, and the third at least usefully. In my view the chance has been bungled.'

The touring party showed only four changes from that which had gone to the West Indies a few months earlier. In three cases the replacements were older than those who had been omitted. It was a situation Arlott had feared when the MCC party to face West Indies was named a year earlier. 'This is a poor period for England. There are plenty of capable county players to be seen, but winning Test teams are composed largely of great players,' he had warned.

'Some of the younger men should increase their stature under the pressures of the tour. If they do not, England have few remotely acceptable alternatives available.'

While supportive of Edrich's selection, Martin-Jenkins conceded that his inclusion ahead of Lancashire's Frank Hayes, a failure in the Caribbean, was 'dull dependency replacing potential flair'.

Bedser and his colleagues, though, were soon to get another opportunity to speculate.

The day after the squad announcement, newspaper headlines dropping through letterboxes reflected the latest shots being fired as Britain prepared for its second general election of the year. Harold Wilson's minority Labour government featured on the front page of the *Daily Mirror* accusing Edward Heath's Conservatives of producing an 'irresponsible and half-baked' policy aimed at helping home buyers. The plan to use state subsidies to reduce mortgage rates from 11 to 9.5 per cent were outlined by the Tories' environment spokesperson, a certain Margaret Thatcher, and instantly described as 'midsummer madness' by Environment Secretary Anthony Crosland.

For the 16 players earmarked to be flying off for the winter shortly after the country went to the polls, there was a more important arrival on the doorstep. Lloyd, who had yet to travel outside of Britain, remembered receiving 'the correspondence I had been waiting for. It was in the form of an official letter from the Test and County Cricket Board, penned by [secretary] Donald Carr. It was a bit like receiving a letter from the Queen: You have been selected to represent England on the MCC tour, blah, blah, blah.'

Boycott's letter arrived at the Fitzwilliam home he shared with his mother. Unlike Lloyd, he was in no rush to fire off the required acceptance to Lord's. Kent batsman Brian Luckhurst was among the first to be given a hint of the doubts occupying the mind of his former England opening partner when their paths crossed at Scarborough a week after the MCC tourists had been identified. As the men chatted before their two counties met in the semi-final of the Fenner Trophy, Boycott, in what Luckhurst described as 'a sarcastic but knowing tone', concluded the conversation by saying, 'Well good luck today and send me a postcard from Sydney, won't you?'

Luckhurst recalled, 'I thought he was joking at first, but then I realised that it was his way of telling me he wouldn't be going to Australia.' The next day, Luckhurst suggested to Denness that he check with Lord's whether Boycott had accepted his invitation to tour.[5]

Two weeks later, Boycott had still not done so, causing Carr to send a telegram to his home seeking an urgent response. In the meantime, Boycott's days had been full of 'soul searching', resulting in a previously unimaginable conclusion. 'I knew I could not go to Australia and do a good job for England.'

Speculation about the overriding motivation for that decision would continue over the next half-century, with the starting point being Boycott's disaffection with the appointment of Denness as England skipper, a role he coveted for himself. 'He wanted to be captain,' said Amiss unequivocally. Lloyd added, 'Geoffrey seemed to have a difference of opinion with Alec Bedser. I think Bedser might have said that he would never be considered as captain and I think that tipped Geoffrey over the edge.'

Yorkshire teammate Old remembered, 'I had toured the West Indies with him the previous winter and it hadn't been one of the happiest tours. I don't think he got on well with Mike Denness. It started with Geoffrey feeling that he should have been captain, but was passed over, and there was one situation where he batted at four in one of the Tests. He didn't seem to like Denness as a Test captain and I don't think he even thought of him as a Test match player. He felt a captain should pull his own weight.'

Boycott would admit that he had 'no confidence in Denness's professional ability and no respect for him as a man'. How had Denness inherited the captaincy from Illingworth ahead of him – without even having proven his worth as a Test batsman? Why had his own reward for a decade of productivity at the top of the England order, including 13 hundreds, been getting dropped for slow scoring after a double century against India; or being summoned to Lord's by the MCC to account for his behaviour after a triumphant Ashes tour in which he scored a bucketful of runs? Boycott had hated touring under Denness in the West Indies, where he felt that

---

5   Luckhurst's autobiography recalls this exchange being at a John Player League game at Headingley, but the relevant dates suggest it was the Scarborough contest later in the year.

organisation and discipline left much to be desired, and he was choking on the irony that his innings of 99 and 112 – along with Greig's 13 wickets – had kept Denness in his job by securing the series-levelling victory in Trinidad.

In fairness to Boycott, there had been plenty of surprise around English cricket when Denness was made captain after nine underwhelming Test appearances. But, recalling the West Indies tour, Fletcher said that 'Boycott was the only one who turned it into a personal issue', adding, 'For much of the tour I felt he gave Mike little cooperation at times when his experience and knowledge might have been of great benefit.' Fletcher dismissed Boycott's suggestion that the senior players should push for change in mid-tour but acknowledged that 'it says much for Boycott' that his runs helped rescue the series.

Meanwhile, Boycott was harbouring concerns over the security of his Yorkshire captaincy and the time-consuming business of maximising his benefit year. 'It is being involved in all the organisational things,' explained Old. 'You are making sure you have got people who can do articles for your brochure, or getting sponsors for various things, and fixing up dates for events and everything else. There is a lot that you have to do personally. Even if you find somebody willing to take on the role of benefit organiser you still have a lot of matters to deal with.'

By way of example, Underwood had just announced the timetable for his upcoming benefit year. A 'welcome home from Australia' dinner in late March would be the first of 41 events, including 14 dinners or dances, six golf days, ten celebrity cricket matches, three darts matches and assorted quizzes, treasure hunts, fashion shows and racing nights.

Out of the public domain but prominent in Boycott's state of mind, was the health of his widowed mother, Jane, a long-time sufferer from rheumatoid arthritis. Many were the evenings when Boycott returned home to find her 'sitting in the dark, hunched over like a woman twice her age, moaning to herself with pain'.

On 23 September, almost a full month since his invitation to tour, Boycott travelled to London to tell Bedser and Carr that he would be staying at home. Feeling that 'it didn't seem fair' to use his mother's affliction as an excuse – however big a factor it had actually become

– he described the pressure he was feeling at Yorkshire and its impact on his mental wellbeing.

In a follow-up letter to Bedser he said he had only participated in the West Indies tour after persuasion from friends and had ended up considering retirement in the early summer. Highlighting the apparent benefit Edrich had gained from a spell out of the England team, he suggested that a period away from the highest level of cricket would help him recapture his form. He could also not resist pointing out the pressure the press placed on him every time he walked to the wicket and the higher expectations they had of him than any other player – although few held their own performance to higher standards than Boycott himself. Urging Bedser not to see him as 'selfish' and noting the Test match appearance fees he had already foregone and the loss of his tour payment, he also opened up in writing about his concerns for his mother and the anxiety of leaving her for a long period. He concluded with his hope 'for some measure of understanding' from 'cricket administrators, press and public alike'.

Bedser did respond positively, offering the hope that Boycott's rest would 'bring you back refreshed'. He recalled that the player's letter contained 'unjustified self-doubt' but left the impression that it was a 'passing phase and, disappointing as it was, I expected his early return'. Yet when Boycott's withdrawal became public, with Bedser explaining that the batsman did not 'feel up to the pressures of a four-month tour', it quickly became evident that his wishes for an easy ride from the media were naïve in the extreme.

Quite apart from the fact that most could not understand why Boycott had not assisted the selectors by turning down his invitation much earlier, 'mental health' was not a phrase much heard in the mid-1970s. Therefore, the notion of wanting to protect it, in the manner that Ben Stokes, for example, would find generally accepted in the next century, was given no consideration by those passing judgement on Boycott's choice. In the *Sunday Telegraph*, Michael Melford said he had spoken to commercial travellers who would have liked to pull out of a trip for 'personal reasons' and an actor who said he toured when he was ill and even though it badly affected family life. 'Such a withdrawal from an important obligation, so soon after a benefit, seemed notably unprofessional,' he concluded.

Former teammate Fred Trueman, a *News of the World* columnist, called Boycott's decision 'unforgiveable' and said, 'There are dozens of players in the game who would pay their own fare and play for nothing – except the honour of wearing an England sweater.'

In Australia, Jack Fingleton, the former Test player who was now one of the country's leading cricket writers, suggested that Boycott needed 'an old resolute Yorkshireman' to 'administer a verbal kick in the pants and tell him to get on out there and stop his ruddy nonsense'.

Martin-Jenkins at least displayed uncommon empathy when he wrote, 'If great batsmen like Peter May and Ken Barrington can be forgiven for retiring whilst still in their cricketing prime, largely because of the strains to their nerves, their bodies and their family lives imposed by the constant pressures of international cricket, one should not condemn Boycott for seeking temporary respite himself.'

Physiotherapist Thomas did his best to offer an explanation to which the cricketing public might relate. 'Unfortunately you cannot put Geoffrey's condition into a pigeon-hole and treat it with pill number nine or powder number ten. There are mental plateaux in sport that, after a prolonged period, can cause inner problems which, in turn, can lead to a fixation. Once that happens there is no simple solution. If it happened on tour I should try to assist by quietly helping him to battle it out and making certain that the rest of the blokes recognised the problem. But under normal circumstances you cannot help unless you are asked.

'Let us assume the extreme view that first-class cricket today is a nasty professional world in which everyone is jockeying for position. Dennis Amiss in India was a failure because he feared being a failure. It was not until halfway through the Pakistan tour he realised he had what was required – and produced it. From that point he increased immeasurably both in performance and in stature. But one man's success puts another under pressure. Maybe it creates jealously. And that, in turn, causes anxiety.'

Thomas explained how such a situation could be recognised during a tour. 'The man under anxiety will start sitting in a corner and not communicating. Not eating, perhaps. Or the reverse may be true. A normally quiet type will suddenly become flamboyant and boisterous in an attempt to cover up his anxiety. I think it would have been a mistake in Geoff's case to persuade him to change his mind.' He feared that if Boycott had not hit form right away 'it could ruin him permanently' and suggested, 'There's little one can offer Geoff Boycott right now but sympathy and understanding.'

Yet most observers were happy to assume Boycott was simply pissed off at the thought of playing for Denness once more. Frank McGhee, chief sports writer of the *Daily Mirror*, compared him to 'the kid who takes his bat, ball and stumps home in a huff, refusing to play when the others won't let him have his own way the whole time.' And former Sussex captain Robin Marlar, the strident cricket correspondent for the *Sunday Times*, called Boycott's decision 'so bad that there appears no gain for anyone in it, least of all the man himself'. Referring to the England captaincy, he suggested, 'On this issue Boycott seems to find it impossible to compromise within himself.'

Decades later, in 2022, Boycott himself said on social media, 'What a muppet I was for staying out for three years, But I wasn't good at playing with people who treated me badly.'

At the time he was offered support by his former county teammate and England captain, Illingworth, interviewed by *The Sun*. 'In the West Indies [Denness] handled the England side very badly,' he said. 'It was more like Fred Karno's Army[6] and Denness was at fault. I don't blame Geoff for not fancying being part of a repeat performance this winter. The Aussies will be laughing their heads off. First they were let off when John Snow wasn't picked and now Geoff isn't going. Decisions like those add up to cricket suicide.'

Boycott's ability to divide opinion was underscored when Swanton pounced upon Illingworth's comments. 'It is apposite to remark here that if England had not looked like Fred Karno's Army when they were being beaten by an innings and 226 runs by the West Indies at Lord's at the end of the 1973 season the captain would not have been deposed at the last minute in favour of Denness.'

The bottom line was that England's players would now be

---

6 Fred Karno was a renowned slapstick comedian of the late 1890s. The term 'Fred Karno's Army' became attached to the disorganised volunteer soldiers of the First World War and was still in use in the 1970s to describe any chaotic group situation.

travelling without two of their most valued teammates. 'No Boycott, no Snow, no controversy,' was the headline that *Cricketer* magazine would use in its series preview to summarise what was now viewed as a rather bland touring party. The publication originally greeted news of the Yorkshireman's withdrawal by putting him on the cover of its November issue with the headline 'The Boycott Shambles'. Within the nine pages devoted to the subject, Beecher argued, 'Australians have found Boycott's defection inexplicable, frustrating, bordering on the cowardly and, after all those feelings, a little sad.' It also called it 'a tragedy of weak-kneed officialdom', implying that he should have been told that if he wasn't willing to play for England now he should forever be disregarded. 'Boycott will always regret this decision,' he concluded, not entirely inaccurately.

The scrubbing of Boycott – who had again led all Englishmen in the first-class batting averages in the latest season – from the flight manifest offered the selectors an opportunity to think creatively and look into the darker corners of Bedser's bare cupboard for a replacement. Those mentioned most prominently in the newspapers included Harris, Luckhurst and the latter's Kent colleague Graham Johnson, whose fresh features seemed to make him a perennial promising youngster even though he would be almost 28 by the time the tour began.

Among opening batsmen, there was no more compelling argument made in the summer of 1974 than that of Warwickshire's John Jameson, who scored close to 2,000 first-class runs, including an unbeaten 240 in a world record second-wicket partnership of 465 with Rohan Kanhai. Yet Jameson had been given chances already, most recently on the West Indian tour the previous winter, and his carefree style of hard-hitting batting was considered to come with technical frailties and a preference for the front foot that might not serve him well on Australia's bouncy pitches. Not to mention that he had become the first player in Test history to be run out in three consecutive innings against India in 1971. 'John was probably a bit unlucky, wasn't he?' suggested Warwickshire colleague Amiss. 'I think other people got more opportunities than John, but in the West Indies they got the impression that he probably wasn't going to be a Test player.'

Another who had previously batted at the top of England's order was Lancashire's Barry Wood. Even though he had averaged only 26.26 in 1974 – less than Old – and scored only one century, Lloyd was hoping to see his county partner get the call. 'Barry should have been nailed on,' he argued, 'He was a bloody fabulous player of quick bowling.'

To support Bedser's argument, there were no young openers making a strong case for selection. Northamptonshire's Roy Virgin had been the fifth-ranked player in the national batting averages, but he had first played for Somerset as far back as 1957 and was now 35. He had only ever played for 'unfashionable' teams and had no county colleagues in the England set-up to argue for his inclusion. Middlesex's Mike Smith had played in the two limited-overs Prudential Trophy games against Pakistan shortly after the original squad announcement, but had a highest score of only 31 in five one-day internationals.

There was no reason, of course, why Boycott's replacement had to be an opener. Of the five remaining specialist batsmen, three were ostensibly openers – although Edrich had played his share of Tests at number three and had scored three centuries in that position on previous Australian tours. Perhaps another middle-order player to support Denness and Fletcher might have been desirable. But who? Lancashire's Hayes, having scored a debut century against the West Indies in 1973, had been discarded after a poor tour of the West Indies. Surrey's Graham Roope had averaged only 23 in a run of eight Test matches. Perhaps there was a case for Basil D'Oliveira. The Worcestershire veteran had not played a Test since the summer of 1972 but had just averaged more than 44 in the County Championship. Yet he would be 43, and surely the selectors were not desperate enough to pick a batsman in his fifth decade of life, were they?

As Boycott had hinted, his place ended up going to Luckhurst, who was enjoying a family holiday in Spain when a news bulletin on Radio Luxembourg made him aware of his selection. 'The letter that Lord's had sent out to me had ended up at another place in Spain called Callela and not the Callela where myself, my wife and the boys were staying,' he remembered.

Luckhurst had been overlooked by England since the previous year's home series against West Indies or, as Frank Tyson put it, had 'dwindled to disappear over the horizon of disfavour that draws ever closer with the mid-30s'. He averaged an unspectacular 32 in the season just completed, although he added more than 1,000 runs in one-day matches. There was no attempt at justifying his selection on the basis of anything other than his two centuries and batting average of 56 in the 1970-71 series against Australia, against whom he had then struggled at home a year later. 'If Lillee or some other top class fast bowler were to appear in the opposition, he might be in trouble again,' warned Melford.

Tyson said of the MCC's final squad, 'Their batting was shallow in specialists and their fast bowling smacked of insurance policies and endeavour rather than hostility' – both accusations that might not have applied had Boycott and Snow been present.

Bedser explained the latest selection by saying, 'We had to choose between a young player and a seasoned player. We decided it would be better to take Luckhurst because of his experience in Australia.' Swanton responded with an air of resignation, writing, 'No one who knows [the selectors'] thinking will be surprised.' Clearly they endorsed the sentiment of the theme tune of *Whatever Happened to the Likely Lads?*, which had been telling BBC viewers for the past two years, 'It's the only thing to look forward to, the past.'

MCC touring party, 1974/75 (ages/appearances at start of First Test)

Mike Denness	RH Bat (Kent) (captain)	Age 33, Tests 20
John Edrich	LH Bat (Surrey) (vice-captain)	Age 37, Tests 66
Dennis Amiss	RH Bat (Warwickshire)	Age 31, Tests 32
Geoff Arnold	RH Fast-Medium (Surrey)	Age 30, Tests 27
Keith Fletcher	RH Bat (Essex)	Age 30, Tests 39
Tony Greig	RH Bat, RH Medium/Off-spin (Sussex)	Age 28, Tests 30
Mike Hendrick	RH Fast-Medium (Derbyshire)	Age 26, Tests 5
Alan Knott	RH Bat, Wicketkeeper (Kent)	Age 28, Tests 61
Peter Lever	RH Fast (Lancashire)	Age 34, Tests 12
David Lloyd	LH Bat (Lancashire)	Age 27, Tests 5
Brian Luckhurst	RH Bat (Kent)	Age 35, Tests 19
Chris Old	RH Fast-Medium (Yorkshire)	Age 25, Tests 18

Bob Taylor	RH Bat, Wicketkeeper (Derbyshire)	Age 33, Tests 1
Fred Titmus	RH Off-spin (Middlesex)	Age 41, Tests 49
Derek Underwood	Slow Left Arm (Kent)	Age 29, Tests 47
Bob Willis	RH Fast (Warwickshire)	Age 25, Tests 11

Alec Bedser (manager), AC Smith (assistant manager), Bernard Thomas (physiotherapist) *NOTE: Does not include the England v Rest of the World series of 1970, which subsequently lost Test status.*

The players, who would earn a basic £3,500 per man, spent the seven or so weeks between hearing of their selection and gathering in front of Eagar's camera lens doing … well, not a lot actually. Certainly very little that could be described as preparation for the tour that was, and remains, the pinnacle of an England cricketer's Test career.

Amiss was in the minority in recalling that 'Bob Willis and I probably had a few nets and a practice session or two' at their Warwickshire base, where they were also able to call upon the services of Smith. One of the last men to play for England as an amateur, Smith had just retired after seven seasons as captain of the county and his appointment as assistant manager was to mark the start of a long career in cricket administration.

The 31-year-old Amiss, something of a theorist – especially in contrast to his off-the-cuff county opening partner Jameson – had scored five Test centuries already in 1974, but he remained acutely aware of having bagged a pair in his only Ashes Test at Old Trafford in 1968. 'I had met Arthur Milton, who went to Australia [in 1958-59] and he was talking about staying leg side of the ball because in Australia they bowled the top of off stump. He said, "Get yourself in and get the pace and the bounce of the wicket." I was playing about with that and I had a few net sessions with Bob and [former England seamer] David Brown. But it really didn't suit me. I couldn't get back into the ball again, so I think I discounted it a little bit. I had got all my runs playing a certain way as an opener, letting the ball go as much as you can until the newness has gone off the ball and it has lost its hardness. I ended up saying to myself, "You have got runs, so carry on as you are."'

Old, who had already had two operations on his knees, got

himself fit for the tour by training with Otley rugby club, although stepping out when they went into full-contact practice. 'It was up to you to look after your own fitness and prepare yourself,' he said. 'I had exercises I did to work on my knees and Bernard Thomas knew what my situation was. I would get myself as fit as I possibly could and hope that things worked out.

'You were told what injections you needed and you had to arrange them with your doctor. The only one they did for us was the last one, which was yellow fever, because it didn't last for too long. So we had to have it the night before we flew out. I think we had the injection before we had our meal because it was in the backside and some of us had difficulty sitting down after that. We all thought it was highly amusing.'

The most important task facing the majority of the players was ensuring that their correct measurements were recorded so that Simpson's of Piccadilly[7] could prepare the tour uniform. This included the navy-blue travelling blazer with the white MCC St George and Dragon emblem on the breast pocket above the lettering 'Australia and New Zealand 1974-75' on a scroll.

The goodies were distributed when the players reported to Lord's on the afternoon of Sunday 20 October, the eve of their departure. 'In those days you were given all your paraphernalia in one leather cricket bag,' Lloyd explained, 'Your tour blazer, your MCC cap and sweater, and your shirts and trousers all tucked inside.' As was traditional for overseas tours, the cap bore the MCC badge rather than the coronet and three lions of the England crest worn at home, while sweaters, made by Jaeger of London, were trimmed in MCC's scarlet and yellow, free of other markings.

The London rain added to the off-season other-worldliness of the sport's headquarters, making cricket feel remote and the players impatient to reach the sun-baked reality of their next four months. Without any of the maintenance or administrative staff who might have been around during the week, the only voices echoing through

---

7 The central London department store provided the basis of the BBC sitcom *Are You Being Served?*, which had launched two years earlier and was co-written by former employee Jeremy Lloyd.

the empty pavilion were those of the chosen few.

'See the football last night?' was a typical conversation point for any group who followed sport, and the previous evening's *Match of the Day* had been of particular interest to these men. The star of the BBC's main game had been one of their own, Aston Villa goalkeeper Jim Cumbes, whose outstanding performance helped his team gain a valuable 0-0 draw at fellow-Second Division promotion hopefuls Sunderland. A former teammate of Edrich at Surrey and Lloyd and Lever at Lancashire, Cumbes's fast-medium bowling had played a role in Worcestershire winning that summer's County Championship, even though he'd had to return to Villa Park before the title was secured.

No one was more delighted at Cumbes's heroics than assistant tour manager Smith, who was serving as a Villa director at the time and would be the celebrity Villa fan interviewed by BBC Radio from New Zealand when they previewed the League Cup final against Norwich City in the spring.

Less happy with his footballing lot was Titmus. An Arsenal fan who had only taken up cricket when he found out it was how his Highbury hero, winger Denis Compton, spent his summers, he had arrived at Lord's after *The Big Match* had shown the Gunners' 2-0 defeat at local rivals Tottenham Hotspur, which left them bottom of the First Division.

Once fitness, football and family had been discussed, it was time for the first team meeting of the expedition. Bedser spoke briefly, focusing on the arrangements that had been made for the party's arrival in Australia and mentioning some of the social functions they would be expected to attend. Denness, too, kept it simple, expressing his hope that the players would find the tour happy and enjoyable and inviting them to bring any problems to him or the management team.

Once in Australia, the team would meet up with the scorer, John Eldridge Sandes. Usually referred to by his initials, 'JE', Sandes was the first person to be inked into the touring party, having been appointed in July. The son of a doctor, Sandes was born in London but was only three weeks old when his family moved to New South Wales, north of Sydney. Working in banks, first as a clerk and then as chief receiving teller, Sandes – who said that 'figures attract me'

– became a scorer in grade and state cricket and spent five seasons as scorer for the Australian Broadcasting Corporation. Having worked with the England team in the Sydney Test match during the 1965-66 Ashes series and in a couple of tour matches at the Sydney Cricket Ground, he applied for the MCC tour job early in 1974 and was quickly confirmed in the role, reportedly to the annoyance of the Australian Cricket Board, who had not been consulted about having one of their own working for the old enemy.

'My work has always been immaculate,' he said. 'In the bank I always tried to be neat and tidy and my scoring is a carry-over from that profession.' He knew that gruelling days lay ahead, no rest or rotation for the scorer. 'You need patience and concentration and good nerves in cricket scoring, especially during the six hours of a Test match. You can't afford to make a single mistake. After a day in a Test, I'm ready for the cot, I can tell you.' Not that Sandes would have the opportunity to switch off entirely away from the scorebox. His duties would also include those of an additional baggage coordinator once the team arrived in Australia.

For now, Smith, Thomas and the players made their own final checks on kit and equipment and set about signing the miniature bats and 1,500 autograph sheets that would travel with them for future dispersal.

Bedser took the time to speak to reporters, whose memory of England's assault on Australia's batsmen four years earlier and knowledge of recently published comments by Dennis Lillee meant that the potential of a 'bouncer war' was on the tip of their pencils. The last thing the manager needed was for any inflammatory comments to precede his party to Australia. Choosing his words carefully, he insisted, 'I shall make sure we have nothing to do with this sort of thing. Bumpers are a genuine armament for any quick bowler, but there are bumpers and bumpers. And their true value is as a surprise weapon.'

The manager, of course, could call upon the credibility of his own successful career as a Test seamer in continuing, 'The thing is that if you overdo it – and I reckon four or five of our seam bowlers are quick enough to give as good as they get – you are vulnerable on two counts. First, you waste the enormous amount of energy required to drop the ball short. Secondly, you eliminate two ways of getting the batsman out – bowled and lbw.'

With the knowledge of what lay ahead, it is interesting to observe that the line of questioning was built on an assumption that England were the more likely aggressors, forcing Denness to reiterate, 'We are no way interested in this sort of intimidation.' Denness left the journalists with the observation that 'from the viewpoint of our record over the past 12 months, the next five months look very rosy.'

The day concluded with a cocktail party for MCC officials and guests of the TCCB, and a team dinner. Then it was off to the Excelsior Hotel – or back home for the London-based players – before a morning rendezvous with Eagar's camera.

The final shot before departure was taken on the steps of their British Airways[8] 747, where those sponsored by equipment maker Duncan Fearnley unashamedly held up bats in logo-emblazoned covers in the hope of some free publicity. The fact that Amiss was one of the Worcester-based company's ambassadors was a coup, but if the blades of Hendrick, Lever and Willis were to the fore in Australia it would not bode well for the tourists' chances.

---

8 British Airways had been created only a few month earlier, in March 1974, after a merger of the two nationalised airlines, British Overseas Airways Corporation (BOAC) and British European Airways (BEA).

2
IN SICKNESS AND IN HEALTH

Lillee broke down in the Caribbean. We had heard about Thommo, but we didn't know what he was going to be like. Were either of them going to be playing? Were both going to be playing? It was wait and see.
Mike Denness

Mike Denness was determined to make good use of the long hours of travel that lay ahead. The players who had enjoyed a buffet lunch at Heathrow Airport before boarding their plane were mostly familiar to him, ten having toured under his captaincy in the West Indies and two others having played for England throughout the summer. With Brian Luckhurst being a Kent teammate, it meant Fred Titmus and Peter Lever were the only tourists with whom he'd not had extended interaction. But he wanted to know everyone's state of mind, their thoughts on the coming weeks and how their past experiences could be best capitalised upon. He also wanted to store away titbits of personal trivia that could be used to make more interesting introductions at the various functions around Australia.

'On top of the world,' was the feeling of Dennis Amiss, fulfilling the ambition of an Ashes tour at a time when he was in the most prolific form of his career. 'The mood of the party was good and we were looking forward to what lay ahead.'

After a short first leg of the journey and a brief stop in Frankfurt, where the players were able to exchange blazer and slacks for more comfortable attire, Denness made his way round the cabin – economy class, of course – and was pleased to note that additional leg room had been procured for the likes of Bob Willis, Tony Greig, Chris Old and Mike Hendrick. While Derek Underwood checked the proofs of his forthcoming autobiography, Lever and Luckhurst – who had made this trip together four years before but experienced no England tours since – engaged in a game of chess.

Players were free to visit the bar for a drink or check out the flight deck. They could even chat and share jokes with the members of the media making the trip. EW Swanton and Michael Melford (*Daily Telegraph*), John Woodcock (*The Times*), Henry Blofeld (*Guardian*), Peter Laker (*Daily Mirror*), Alex Bannister (*Daily Mail*), Pat Gibson (*Daily Express*) and Clive Taylor (*The Sun*) would be able to mix freely with the players over the next few months in an atmosphere of mutual trust and confidentiality, something that within a decade would become increasingly rare thanks to the impact of the searing heat of the tabloid wars on player/press relationships.[9]

MCC committee members had been told at their October meeting of the TCCB's appointment of Peter Lush 'as secretary to administer public relations and promotion on behalf of the Cricket Council and its constituent bodies'. But there was never any suggestion that the man who would go on to serve as PR and marketing chief for the TCCB and act as a tour manager in Australia and Pakistan would require a seat on the plane on this occasion.[10] 'There were no press conferences with the players back then,' said David Lloyd. 'And there was no press knocking on your door, asking what you think of this and that. You just had a drink in the bar with a bloke from the *Daily Express*.' Australia's players, meanwhile, had been told that they were allowed to speak with the press during the series as long as they were not critical of teammates or selection.

Willis, Hendrick and Lloyd, noted Denness, were busy entertaining their fellow travellers with jokes, anecdotes and opinions. Titmus's cheerful manner reflected his joy at his unexpected presence, the nerves he had felt at the start of previous tours completely absent. That did not mean he saw his role as team jester, even if he and fellow-spinner and roommate Underwood would soon be christened 'Steptoe and Son'.

---

9   According to a story in *The Cricketer*, former England captain Ray Illingworth had been asked to join the press corps, reporting on the series with the aid of a ghost writer, but the National Union of Journalists objected on the grounds that it would 'damage the journalistic profession'.

10 A further MCC committee meeting in January 1975 discussed the 'possible needs in respect of the PR requirements of the club' and approved the setting up of a working party to explore further.

Meanwhile, Lloyd was facing an in-flight hazard as serious as the risk of boredom. 'These days it is easy to forget what it was like back then whenever you travelled on a plane,' he recalled. 'People would be lighting up their cigarettes all around you, so that when you sat down it was reminiscent of when the lights get switched on for the first time down the front at Blackpool. They would spark up the minute they had parked their backsides and chain smoke for the entire journey. You couldn't see a bloody thing. It was like being sat in a thick fog for a day. We were shoved at the back to join in the economy chorus of coughing and wheezing. By the end, it would have made Adele sound like Shane MacGowan.'

Discarded newspapers littered the cabin. The front pages speculated about a challenge to former Prime Minister Ted Heath's leadership of the Conservative Party, while the sport sections focused attention on the likelihood of Arsenal being able to buy their way out of trouble and concerns over the state of First Division football after Chelsea had seven men booked and one sent off in their most recent match.

As the journey to Sydney continued, Denness's preoccupation with 'wondering what was in store on and off the field' gave way to the realisation of how unwell he was feeling. He became increasingly tired and feverish during a stopover in Beirut, extended to five hours because of engine trouble. Even an invitation to the cockpit as they completed another interlude in Hong Kong failed to revive him, instead creating panic that the plane would not clear the mountains and skyscrapers that confronted it on take-off. 'I wish I'd been at the back,' he said. He had little energy for the required press conference when the squad disembarked at Sydney.

Fast bowlers were again the topic of conversation among waiting reporters, but this time it was the speed at which they bowled their overs rather than the trajectory of their deliveries that was of interest. Asked about fears that the series would be dogged by slow over rates, Bedser was forced to concede that four fast bowlers would obviously not get through their overs as quickly as four slow bowlers, but also pointed out that India, with three spinners, had bowled more slowly than England during the summer. Asked about the absence of Geoff Boycott, he sidestepped by stating, 'All I know is that we are going to have a happy side here' – the kind of diplomacy for which he had been appointed.

Denness found himself having to defend the age of his team in the face of the same 'Dad's Army' comments that had dogged his predecessor, Ray Illingworth. 'We were called that last time,' he reminded his audience, 'and we won the series. I don't agree our age is a handicap.' It was his own state of health rather than anyone's birthdate that was his immediate concern. 'I do not remember much about them,' he recorded of those initial media engagements, 'except that I felt really miserable.' The travelling was not yet done. The players climbed aboard another flight to Adelaide, arriving 36 hours after their original departure from Heathrow. Having made it to their hotel, they unpacked in rooms assigned to them by Bernard Thomas.

Finding the most suitable pairings was an underappreciated part of Thomas's remit to ensure the physical and mental well-being of the players. Willis, who called Thomas 'a confidant and shoulder to cry on for a lot of players', remembered, 'He always did the rooming list, keeping apart people who were likely to collide. It was vital to get the right mix.'

Thomas explained, 'In the past, I have had to juggle with players on tour to ensure their individual peace of mind. For instance it would never be a good idea to have Geoff Boycott and Dennis Amiss sharing the same room if either of them were having a bad patch.' And, referring to the England wicketkeeper's preference for rising early, he added, 'You were careful who you asked to share a room with Knotty.'

As captain, Denness had his own room. And he was desperate to see the inside of it. Having tried to sleep on the final flight but getting weaker all the time, he could have done without having to travel from the airport in a car with Bedser and Sir Donald Bradman, Australia's greatest Test cricketer and now the driving force at the South Australian Cricket Association. 'I slumped in the back seat, taking very little part in the conversation,' he remembered. Relieved to arrive at last in his room, he was visited by Thomas, who made a note of the captain's temperature of 103. There was much trauma ahead before Denness would register another century.

On their first Friday in Australia, four days after departure from Heathrow, the MCC party faced an interesting day. Not only would they be in the nets at the Adelaide Oval, but a certain Dennis Lillee was making his comeback in first-class cricket on the same ground after an 18-month absence because of a back injury. His promising three-wicket performance in a recent one-day game suggested that the England batsmen might be facing him during the Ashes series, and several of the tourists intended to take the opportunity for a first-hand view of his progress when Western Australia began their Sheffield Shield game against South Australia.

Lillee's own comments the day before the match might well have been designed deliberately to mislead. If so, they did their job well enough for the *Daily Mirror* to run with a headline declaring, 'Lillee's back – but only at half pace.' In fairness to the publication, Lillee had said, 'I am bowling a lot differently now. It is mainly medium pace. But I throw in a fast one now and then. I get a lot of wickets now with a slower ball I have perfected.' It was hard to believe that the man speaking to the approximately 40 reporters and numerous camera crews who had been crammed into an Adelaide hotel meeting room was the same demon who had made comments about hitting batsmen in the ribcage in a recently published autobiography. Western Australia and Test wicketkeeper Rodney Marsh confirmed that he was standing three paces closer to the stumps than he had before Lillee's injury.

Born in the Perth suburb of Subiaco, Lillee had first faced England as a 21-year-old in the sixth Test of the 1970-71 Ashes series, only one year after making his first-class debut for Western Australia. He took five wickets in his first innings as an international bowler. A career-best return of 8 for 29 on his home ground in the following season's unofficial Test against the World XI[11] was described by opposing skipper Garry Sobers as the fastest spell of bowling he'd seen, and it served England with notice of what to expect when he arrived for an Ashes series in which he subsequently took 31 wickets at an average of 17.67.

'I always ran in for a long, long run-up trying to look fearsome and trying to send the ball down as fast as I could, right from the first time I played cricket in the back yard when I was five or six years of age,' he said of his approach to his craft,

---

11 As in England in 1970, the cancelled South African tour was replaced by a series against a World team.

Lillee credited the English summer he spent playing for Haslingden in the Lancashire League in 1971 for having helped him to increase his control; both because the pitches in the north of England were almost a world away from those of Perth, but also due to the enforced modification of his approach to the crease. 'Quite often footholds would be too slippery to bowl really fast,' he said.

Unleashed upon relatively manicured Test pitches a year later he was able to let himself go. None of the top-order England batsmen found a consistent solution to the problems he posed, with Luckhurst, Edrich and Boycott averaging 24, 21 and 18 respectively in the series. 'He walks back 44 paces to his bowling mark, which looks, and probably is, too far,' began John Arlott's description in his book *The Ashes 72*. 'His run-up is in effect a sprint in which he positively races as fast as he can; so fast that his coordinated, flowing delivery action comes almost as a surprise. To use public reaction as a yardstick, like [Frank] Tyson and Wesley Hall, he makes crowds gasp when they first see him bowl; that is the measure of real speed in a bowler.'

All was not well, however. Lillee had been suffering discomfort in his back before the Ashes series and was only able to participate fully after a session of manipulation under general anaesthetic. Back in Australia, the pain intensified during the 1972-73 series against Pakistan. Eventually he broke down completely during the subsequent West Indies tour. It was former Warwickshire seamer Rudi Webster, a radiologist Lillee had met in Perth, who suggested that he might be suffering from stress fractures, as Webster himself had done during his career. Webster accompanied Lillee to hospital in Barbados, where X-rays confirmed the diagnosis: three fractures on the third and fourth lumbar vertebrae. The marks they left on the x-ray were so tiny that only the most trained of eyes could discern them.

The first part of the solution was a choice between fusion of the bones, which would likely have ended Lillee as a fast bowler, or to treat the injury like a fracture in any other part of the body and allow himself to be placed for around six weeks in a plaster cast that prevented movement of his torso. He chose the latter, despite his orthopaedic surgeon, Bill Gilmour, never having attempted such a procedure before. In order to continue his day job in a bank, Lillee had to cut his trousers to make them big enough to go over the cast.

Beyond that, after a similar period in a special restrictive harness, his rehabilitation revolved around mile upon mile of lonely road-running, hours in the gym and the development of a new, kinder bowling action. Any of those factors might have been a barrier to the continuation of a fast-bowling career for someone with a less stubborn, determined outlook.

'It was very mundane, repetitive stuff,' remembered Lillee. 'We had to look at my action and see what might have been causing the problem. I was hyper-extending. I was also pushing the ball in a bit so my back was twisting one way then the other way and then going over the top, plus landing heavily all the time when I jumped too high and landed. I think it is up to 11 times your body weight every time you land on your leg. All those things we had to reassess and come up with a smoother action that put less pressure on my back and my body.'

Frank Pyke was the man Lillee called on to aid his recovery. A notable Australian rules footballer and opening bowler for Lillee's Perth Cricket Club, Pyke had returned home to a position as lecturer in physical education and recreation at the University of Western Australia after completing a PhD in physiology and human performance in the United States. 'I knew that he had the stress fracture problem in his back and I knew he had been given a period of time to recover,' Pyke recalled. 'He said, "I am going to take a crack at this, I am going to see if I can make it back."'

Pyke mapped out a three-pronged programme to improve Lillee's fitness: isometric exercises designed to aid flexibility and complement the redesigned action; running, with an increasing number of sprints being introduced; and strength and power training in the gym, with a focus on technique before increasing the weights being used.

Meanwhile, Lillee made the decision to write off the 1973-74 first class season, a moment of clarity that came to him 'in a flash' during one of numerous phone calls with an anxious Western Australian captain, John Inverarity and after weeks of considering Dr Pyke's advice to take a complete break from bowling.

'It's no good,' Lillee replied to the latest enquiry about his back. 'I'm not going to bowl this summer.' Instead, he played as captain, batsman and occasional medium pacer for Perth. His 'pot of gold' as he worked in the gymnasium – up to three hours every other day – and pounded the streets was the thought of bowling out more English batsmen in the next Ashes series.

With the first Test now only a matter of weeks away, it was still anyone's guess whether that was a realistic ambition. Those who managed to get a glimpse of Lillee in action on the first day of the Sheffield Shield game in Adelaide saw nothing in the 44 wicketless deliveries he bowled at the cost of 36 runs before rain halted play to contradict his own remarks the previous day. There was little evidence of the man whose high-kicking delivery stride seemed designed to intimidate.

According to Western Australia batsman Ross Edwards, 'Lillee was working on his run-up and making sure he got his balance right and that sort of thing. He wasn't bowling as an opening bowler. On the western side of the old Adelaide Oval there was a grandstand and down the back of that were these nets. We are in the field and Lillee is bowling and you saw the Poms come up and stand in front of the pavilion watching him. You could almost see the delight in their faces as Lillee, who had given them a going over in '72, was bowling this medium pace. They watched for about five minutes and then went back to practice.'

Amiss attempted to study Lillee from as many angles as possible and could see nothing to suggest the speed of 1972 would return. 'I thought he would pick up occasional wickets, no more,' he admitted.

The bad weather curtailed an MCC training session that saw Luckhurst and Keith Fletcher as the first batsmen into the nets and Edrich taking command while Denness, who could not remember how he had got himself into bed on arrival in Adelaide, nursed his high temperature. Fast bowlers were reduced to bowling off two or three paces because of slippery conditions and the whole thing was given up as a bad job after 20 minutes.

The following day offered conditions for a proper practice session, the most notable elements of which were the appearance of Denness, who wisely didn't face the fast bowlers, and a painful blow on the hand for Luckhurst, who did; struck by Willis.

Opportunity for extensive practice as an England squad in the mid-1970s was exclusive to those on tour. For home Test matches, which all began on Thursdays, players would drive to rendezvous with their teammates after finishing County Championship matches on Tuesdays, often arriving bleary-eyed in the early hours of the morning.

Even when travelling, though, players were limited in their options and absent of any expectation that extended preparation time should generate any original thinking in the way they went about their work. 'A big difference to now is that we didn't have local players bowling at us,' Lloyd explained. 'It was just you and the rest of the team and you had a bat and a bowl and that was it. It was like club cricket. It was just day after day of netting. And when we weren't in the nets we would be playing one of our many warm-up matches.

'There were no drills as such for fielding, although there was a lot of catching practice, particularly spiralling high catches because in the thinner air the ball travels further and quicker. To lads like me who had not been Down Under before, looking into a clear blue sky for a ball was quite a new experience and took some adjustment. As a Lancashire lad I was more used to fielding in light drizzle. Despite the glare, nobody wore shades like your average 21st-century cricketer. We just squinted and got on with it.'

As for the bowlers, Chris Old remembered, 'A typical net session before the series started would be a matter of us trying to get rhythm, bowling off full run-ups at the batsmen and getting used to the pace and the bounce of the pitches. You've got to know where you're trying to pitch the ball to be able to hit the stumps and the lines and lengths you've got to bowl. There was a difference in the ball as well. Two or three of us hadn't played with those balls before and some adapted to them more quickly than others.'

Tour observer Christopher Martin-Jenkins was struck by the 'cool unflappable way' in which Edrich supervised early proceedings and the obvious relish with which Titmus approached his work. Noting that he 'kept everyone amused', Martin-Jenkins recorded, 'Titmus admits that towards the end of his original Test career he was no longer enjoying the game: now he was revelling in his return to the top and his open *joie de vivre* was happily contagious.'

It certainly infected first-time tourist Lloyd. 'It was really good fun. It was such an adventure for me. I thought it was marvellous. You might have net sessions morning and afternoon but then you were left to your own devices. It was very relaxed. You certainly weren't cocooned, and there was definitely no security.'

While the rain cleared in Adelaide and the tourists hit, bowled and caught, Lillee took the opportunity to take seven wickets across the two innings of his Western Australia team's two-wicket victory, including the double dismissal of Australian captain Ian Chappell, who had treated his bowling harshly on the rain-restricted first morning. Elsewhere, Jeff Thomson was also on the winning side, taking six wickets in Queensland's ten-wicket win against New South Wales. The MCC party read that with interest, knowing they would have opportunity enough to assess him for themselves before the first Test.

For now, a gentler engagement lay ahead; a one-day contest against a South Australian Country side in the coastal town of Port Lincoln. Government workers and schoolchildren were given the day off and local cricket association secretary Brian Arnold confirmed, 'All the shearing has stopped, the kids have a holiday. We're expecting to have fun. We are expecting 4,000 adults and a million children.'

What would be a throwaway game at any other point in the tour assumed great significance as MCC faced their first real cricket of the trip. As Blofeld observed, 'In the middle of Test matches continual journeys upcountry to play one-day matches against inferior opposition can become an irritant for they increase the already considerable demands on the players and can easily cause injuries.' Just as well, then, that the MCC party had five seam bowlers to share the burden, one might have expected someone to point out. Blofeld went on, 'At the start of the tour, however, an upcountry match or two can be very useful.' Whatever happened in the game, it was likely to be buried deep in the sports pages back home as later in the day England's football team would be starting a new era under the management of Don Revie with a game against Czechoslovakia – which they ended up winning 3-0.

If nothing else, such matches gave the MCC players a break from city surroundings as the itinerary took them into fishing towns, agricultural communities and the like. On this occasion, only the 11 players selected for the match took the one-hour flight west from Adelaide. The others – Amiss, Knott, Willis and Hendrick – stayed behind for more nets or, in the case of Denness, further recuperation.

Bedser also travelled, his influence on the tour already evident in comments such as this by Melford. 'When they turned up,' he wrote in the *Telegraph*, 'smartly and uniformly clad in blazers, ties and grey trousers, any resemblance between them and the last MCC side here was purely coincidental.'

Those who stayed behind missed a visit to an area that suffered well above the state average annual rainfall – as much as 18 inches per year – which was fine for the growing of barley and wheat and the grazing of sheep, but not so conducive to games of cricket. Only 23 minutes of play was possible, all in the morning, with Arnold capturing a wicket bowled with the second ball of the tour[12] and the home team reaching 7 for 1 after winning the toss. Instead, the players spent their time enjoying a hearty seafood lunch and taking the opportunity to watch Muhammad Ali's eighth-round knockout of George Foreman to regain the world heavyweight boxing title in Zaire.

The 'Rumble in the Jungle' turned out to be the extent of the afternoon's competitive action. Even though the rain eased, the covers were found to have leaked and the match was abandoned. The locals who stuck around at least got to see Edrich, Luckhurst and Lloyd getting 45 minutes of batting practice in the middle between showers. Their teammates back at base fared even worse, with rain confining them to barracks, 24 hours after a full-scale practice match on Adelaide Oval's second field had been scrapped because of the sodden ground.

Adelaide's wettest October for 25 years meant the tourists were short of meaningful preparation before their opening first-class match, reduced to more fielding and fitness sessions than they would have desired. It did give *The Australian* the chance to observe of the MCC squad, 'Their harmony and enthusiasm are tributes to far-sighted selection and team leadership.' It would, of course, have been a pretty poor state of affairs if team spirit had not survived the first few days of a five-month journey, but any compliments being thrown out by Australian media outlets were gratefully received. Recently retired Australian opener Keith Stackpole, for example, had used his newspaper column to stir things up by asking, 'Who

---

12 On the previous tour to the West Indies, he had taken a wicket with the first ball in St Lucia.

is England's captain, Mike Denness or manager Alec Bedser? It's time Bedser took his nose out of his captain's affairs.' Stackpole apparently took offence at Bedser's prominent role in the early-tour press conferences, prompting Edrich to respond, 'What a pity that players seem to feel they have to say something critical once they leave the game.'

The rain had made it more difficult than usual for the groundsmen at the Adelaide Oval to get ready for the cricket season after a winter of Australian rules football. The strip on which Lillee had performed a week earlier had been selected at the last moment because of the ill-prepared state of others. Woodcock told *The Times* readers that 'the actual square is as rough as the roughest of village grounds'.

The opposition was considered weaker than that encountered by Illingworth's team four years earlier, when the great South African Barry Richards had scored a double century in a total of 600-plus. Chappell and the two spinners, Ashley Mallett and Terry Jenner, were the only men that England were likely to encounter in the Ashes series. It meant that the most intriguing part of a first morning that ended with the home team five wickets down was seeing Chappell unable to resist hooking against the MCC seamers' pre-meditated plan to bowl short at him. Willis, whose second ball lifted to remove discarded Australian opener Ashley Woodcock, had Chappell caught by Underwood at long leg, ensuring that such an approach would be a feature of the Test matches. 'Sure, it's a risky shot,' Chappell conceded, 'but it gets me plenty of runs.'

South Australia rallied from 82 for 5 to 247 all out behind a half-century by John Nash, who had been playing for Hampshire seconds earlier in the year. There was concern over Old's lack of rhythm and the acquisition of his first injury of the tour – a sore knee ligament – and about Hendrick's 11 no-balls, even though he found a probing full length. 'On his first tour of the West Indies Hendrick had repeatedly shown up the other more experienced fast bowlers by keeping to the basic virtues of a good line and good length and in the South Australian match it was the same story,' noted Martin-Jenkins.

Underwood took a wicket with his first ball on his way to a four-wicket haul, but Greig generally bowled his off-spinners too short. Some decent fielding around the square could not hide the deficiencies of weak arms and slow feet in the deep. But, overall, a promising enough first full day of work, especially when Amiss and Luckhurst survived the final five overs.

Several of the MCC batsmen managed a couple of valuable hours in the middle in their first innings, Edrich and Greig making fifties and Amiss and Fletcher just missing out. Denness's rustiness showed when he scored his first run of the tour via an attempted off-drive that squirted between his legs off the inside edge, but he stuck around to score 27. With a first-innings lead of 102 and Hendrick having picked up two quick wickets when he took the new ball in place of the absent Old, the tourists had visions of opening their first-class programme with a victory, but South Australia went on to bat for seven and a half hours against a depleted attack. The 219 runs in 106 minutes that the MCC required to win was merely a scorebook detail, although Lloyd took the chance to demonstrate neat footwork against the opposition spinners. Amiss sat things out after a pain-killing injection in the arm he'd jarred when throwing the ball in the field.

Little more than 36 hours later, in which time they had travelled to a new state and seen rain ruin another practice session, MCC's selected 11 were on the coast again to play a Victorian Country XI at Warrnambool. It was the first time an English team had made the journey 165 miles west from Melbourne since WG Grace was there a full century earlier. Luckhurst might not have been an obvious heir to Grace's crown of popularity but he entertained the locals with 94 runs scored at a steadily increasing pace – like many of his finest Sunday League knocks – before the game petered out into a draw.

As well as playing Luckhurst into form, the trip earned the MCC some public relations points, as Woodcock recorded. 'As MCC's aircraft took off from Warrnambool, with the locals waving farewell, I had the same kind of feeling as when, on the way to Australia in the fifties, our ship sailed away from the Cocos Islands[13] after dropping the provisions.'

Having returned to the big city for a day of preparation ahead of the four-day game against Victoria at the Melbourne Cricket Ground,

---

13   A group of coral islands in the Indian Ocean, with a few hundred inhabitants. It passed from British to Australian administration in the mid-1950s.

Denness had more than his lack of runs to worry about. His sore head and throat had been gradually replaced by backache, which increased with greater activity. 'While I was just sitting and chatting I could still feel an ache but it was not that painful,' he explained. By the end of his innings against the Victorian Country side he felt as though his spine had locked completely.

Instead of playing at the MCG, he was taken for X-rays and blood and urine tests to determine if he was suffering from gallstones. A high blood count in his urine indicated possible kidney problems, leading to more X-rays, the results of which Thomas received while the team were at a cocktail reception given by the Victorian Cricket Association. Doctors feared Denness could possess a third kidney.

'You might need surgery,' Thomas informed the patient, news that the captain admitted 'scared me to death', not only because it would mean the end of his tour. Denness would end up remaining in Melbourne while his colleagues moved on to their next destination, Canberra. His wife, Molly, prepared to fly to Australia. Newspaper reports speculated that there were now serious doubts about whether he would lead England into the first Test at the end of November. John Jameson, Barry Wood, Colin Cowdrey and Frank Hayes received mentions as possible reinforcements. Bedser admitted, 'If all goes well he will only have a couple of innings behind him before the first Test and this will make it damn difficult for him. We are all concerned about Mike and just want this thing cleared up.' Happily, it was.

When Denness's consultant called upon other experts for their opinion and further tests were conducted, the presence of an additional organ was ruled out. Another course of antibiotics produced a positive response, and the conclusion was reached that Denness's kidneys were inflamed rather than seriously infected. On 13 November, he was able to fly to Sydney. His public insistence that 'I feel as well as I ever have; I have been keeping in trim playing squash' might have been designed to deflect any lingering concerns, but even privately he had 'free peace of mind' for the first time since landing in Australia.

Apart, that is, from resolving the issue of who was paying for the additional medical expenses he'd incurred. When, understandably, he suggested to Bedser that these would be covered for him, he was told, 'Oh no. MCC won't allow these, Mike, you'll have to pay for them yourself.' It was such frugality that led Woodcock to observe, 'Alec would be up at six o'clock in the morning, going through the books and working out how many oysters the team had consumed the night before.'

On-field, meanwhile, the four-day game against Victoria had thrown up the kind of encouragement and anxiety one expected of such occasions. With Australia's most obvious apparent concern being the make-up and constitution of their opening batting, Arnold struck a blow by removing the redoubtable Ian Redpath in the second over. But a series of missed chances allowed the home team to declare at 293 for 8 on the second day.

Amiss had been passed fit to play as long as he was spared throwing duties and he proceeded to construct an innings of 152, based largely on off-side strokes that had Martin-Jenkins purring. 'For Australians it was a first sight of the serene and commanding batsman that Amiss had developed into over the last 20 months, and those who had seen him before could not recognise him as the man who had made a wretched pair in his only Test against the Australians in 1968,' he wrote. 'His driving through the covers evoked memories of Walter Hammond.'

Luckhurst continued his good form by contributing to a partnership of 268 with a century of his own; 'less fluent' but 'equally significant' according to Martin-Jenkins. With Lloyd given the number three berth it appeared as though the preferred openers for the first Test had been identified. Yet on a pitch rendered benign by recent rain and becoming slower and slower, England struggled to build on that foundation and led by less than 100 on first innings. Only Knott's impish shots to the leg side had any real effect.

The worry when Victoria batted again late on the third day was the absence of Willis because of sore knees. It was an issue that, according to Denness, 'was to have an important bearing on the series ... he was sadly never completely fit'. Describing him as 'the type of bowler who has to have a rhythmic run-up', Denness continued, 'Although he bowled very quickly at times he was always restrained and probably handicapped by the trouble he was having from his knees. I remember how concerned he was in Melbourne when he accompanied me on one of my medical sorties. He needed injections, which did help but did not, unfortunately, cure.'

Having shared a hospital waiting room with his captain, Willis ended up offering an interesting perspective, believing that Denness had 'improved dramatically as a communicator'. Willis explained, 'Guys were forever popping in to ask how he was and the shyness which had been such a barrier in the West Indies a year earlier was now broken down. We looked forward to a happier tour, feeling we had every chance of retaining the Ashes.' That it took a medical emergency for Denness's players to find him more approachable is not exactly a ringing endorsement. Safe to assume that, had he been on tour, Geoff Boycott would not have been the first one turning up at his bedside with a bunch of grapes.

Without their spearhead leading the attack and with rain and bad light curtailing the final day, MCC were unable to exact revenge on the only team to beat them on their previous tour. At least Old was fit enough to reappear on the field as a substitute. Greig showed noticeably more control with his slower style of bowling than in Adelaide, but he was also the next man in the doctor's waiting room after suffering the severe effects of hay fever. Tests revealed an allergy to grass, not a helpful condition for a cricketer, but the prescribed drugs proved capable of keeping the symptoms at bay.

The build-up to Ashes series in the 1970s might have lacked the flashy television montages that these days begin the sign-posting for viewers several weeks in advance and the in-depth personality interviews demanded by modern media, but a month of warm-up matches did allow plenty of time for examination of all news angles. Unusually, it was umpire Jack Collins – considered a candidate to stand during the Test series – who served up a storyline at the completion of the drawn game against Victoria.

With journalists regularly discussing declining over rates, Collins fed them a line by complaining about the way Lever had loitered close to the stumps after delivering the ball at the MCG. 'He stands there and waits for the ball to be handed back to him instead of going back to his bowling mark,' he said. 'It is simply not good enough.' He chose to give those remarks exclusively to reporters rather than include them in any official report to the MCC management, prompting Melford to tell *Daily Telegraph* readers, 'It was unfortunate that these comments should have been made in a match in which the umpiring was far from flawless.'

Lever, it was noted, walked back 36 paces before turning to begin his run-up, taking around five and a half minutes to bowl an eight-ball over. Challenged over Collins's statement, Bedser was forced to say, 'We are doing all we can. We began talking to the team about it before we left Lord's and have been putting it to the bowlers that they might shorten their runs and walk back more quickly, and to the wicketkeeper that he should change ends quickly.' Even a manager as keen as Bedser to create a good public impression was unlikely to suggest seriously that any bowler risked compromising his potency in the heat of battle by rolling up to the crease off a truncated run. As it turned out, there would be more pressing fast-bowling issues to occupy attention once the real action began.

Rain once again affected the MCC's minor one-day game in Canberra against an Australian Capital Territory and Southern New South Wales Country side. After an agreement that the tourists would bat first to provide them with more practice, Lloyd and Edrich both made half-centuries.

Preparations for the four-day match against New South Wales at the Sydney Cricket Ground included Old and Hendrick seeking inspiration for future endeavours by paying a 70th-birthday visit to Harold Larwood, who had settled in Australia since terrorising the home batsmen in in the Bodyline series four decades earlier. More importantly, Denness proved his fitness by batting in the nets for 45 minutes, stating, 'It has taken very little out of me and I am very pleased with the way I feel.'

Willis was left out in order to protect his knees, while Amiss was rested, allowing Luckhurst and Lloyd to continue their fight for the right to partner him in the Test. Underwood was selected ahead of Titmus, even though early signs on the tour suggested that what the slow bowlers could do in flight might be more important than potential productivity off the deck, which favoured the Middlesex off-spinner.

Denness put NSW in to bat. After an early Lever wicket, MCC's bowlers pitched too short on a wicket that had a green hue and the home team progressed to 150 for 2 before being pegged back in the final session of the first day. The fact that three wickets fell to the hook shot – including that of Test batsman Doug Walters – seemed to justify what appeared to be the only tactical option. Meanwhile, Lever's overs took slightly less time than in the previous match, but there were still cries of 'Get a cab, Lever' from fans on the Hill as he walked back to his mark.

After the home side declared on the second day, MCC had to bat without Edrich, whose strained back muscle, which had forced him to retire in Canberra, prevented him from heading to the crease. The highlight of the innings was a partnership of 138 in 110 minutes between Fletcher and Greig, before Denness closed the MCC reply a few runs in arrears. On the remainder of the third day, Lever produced the fastest bowling spell of the tour – hitting Marshall Rosen on the head with one of three bouncers he gave him just before lunch – and Greig profited from directing his off-breaks into the fast bowler's foot marks. Martin-Jenkins would record that Greig 'had one of those games where he changes from a competitive workaday all-rounder into an incredible world-beater'.

Taking four wickets before the close, he completed a five-wicket haul on the final day and, with Underwood claiming three victims, MCC were left needing 181 to win in 274 minutes. According to Melford, the tourists' bowling performance 'startled an Australia cricket public prepared to believe they were not much good'. Lloyd's 80 runs helped to see MCC home with 45 minutes to spare and, coupled with Luckhurst's double failure in the game, now looked to have secured his Test place. Fletcher scored his second half-century of the match, yet it was the form of Denness that continued to preoccupy the tabloids. 'DENNESS FLOPS' was how the *Daily Mirror* began its headline after he had been dismissed for 3 in MCC's first win against a Sheffield Shield team since the 1965-66 tour.

'The picture was looking quite rosy,' Denness remembered. 'Some people, including myself, had not got runs, but we were bowling sides out. It was not the cricket but the injury situation which was causing concern as our dressing room began to resemble an emergency ward.'

Back home, cricket fans were given confirmation of how they would be able to follow the action. Commentary would begin each day on BBC Radio Three at 6.30 a.m. UK time, meaning listeners would be restricted to the final few overs of each day, except when the different time zone for the second Test in Perth would mean an extended passage of play. On television, BBC 2 would offer nightly highlights, the first time an away Ashes series could be seen in colour.

3
STORM WARNING

Don't show the bastards anything.
Greg Chappell to Jeff Thomson

As the MCC party travelled to Brisbane, site of the first Test match, the main topic of discussion was the rain that preceded them rather than the fast bowler who awaited them. Jeff Thomson was still just a name that loitered on the edge of conversations about the forthcoming series; it was the city's Lord Mayor, Alderman Clem Jones, who loomed as the more immediately consequential figure.

The tourists' first sight of Jones was of him dressed in shorts, wellington boots and a pith helmet, scrabbling around on his knees in what looked like a solid pack of mud in the middle of The Gabba, as the city's cricket stadium, situated in the suburb of Woolloongabba, was known. 'During the day we had seen this chap in a pair of shorts and a singlet preparing the pitch,' David Lloyd laughed, 'and then we go to a civic ceremony and there he is all dressed up in the mayor's regalia.'

MCC were pitching camp in Brisbane for two weeks, first facing Thomson's Queensland and then beginning England's defence of the Ashes. But after storms had devoured the ground's covers it seemed inconceivable that decent pitches could be prepared in time, even with Jones having dispensed with the services of groundsman George Cawthray and taken responsibility himself, returning from an official lunch to roll grass into an area that he tried to make look like a cricket pitch. Jones had made a late decision not to use the track that had staged the most recent Sheffield Shield match, preferring to conjure up a new strip.

Mike Denness, wearing a light blue golf jumper to ward off the chilly air, strolled across the outfield. This should have been a time of high excitement for a visiting Ashes captain; his first sight of the place where it would all begin. A moment to look up from strands of green to the banks of seats and imagine them bursting with humanity; to anticipate the clench of tension as he walked out for the toss; to hear the hum of the crowd, the crack of the ball off bat, the applause from beyond the distant boundary rope.

But instead of enjoying visions of a fantastic future, Denness was forced to direct quizzical looks in the direction of a patch of grey earth where a pitch was supposed to be. When he asked Jones about the available rollers he was surprised to be told there were six options; before discovering that this was the mayor's idea of humour and he meant that he could offer light, medium or heavy at a choice of slow or fast speeds.

John Woodcock took one look at the scene and told readers of *The Times*, 'The most sensible thing to do would be to decide here and now to play the first Test match somewhere other than Brisbane. To anyone who knows Mr Clem Jones, or the ground's astonishing powers of recovery, such a move is unthinkable.'[14]

Denness ended up grudgingly admiring the hard work Jones put in, but not 'his interference in many matters outside the groundsman's jurisdiction'. The skipper came close to leading his players out of a mayoral reception, having arrived ten minutes early and been held in a small, sweltering anteroom with other guests while awaiting the arrival of their host. After 20 minutes, Denness confronted Alec Bedser, who offered to write a letter of complaint. Wanting more immediate action, Denness warned that he would wait five more minutes, only for Jones to swing open the door to the function room as the deadline approached.

As great a concern as the mayor's timekeeping was John Edrich's speed of recuperation. He had seen a back specialist before leaving Sydney and been excused the 70-mile trip to Nambour for the obligatory goodwill game against Queensland Country. In the end, that match was abandoned in advance because of more torrential rain, although a handful of MCC ambassadors made the journey to play some squash and attend the planned civic reception.

Those who stayed behind managed to get in some fielding practice, with disastrous consequences when Lloyd suffered a fracture to the

---

[14] Mayor of Brisbane since 1961, Jones had led the drive to have new stands built at the Gabba, to be unveiled during the first Test by Prime Minister Gough Whitlam, and would play a major role in securing his city's status as host of the 1982 Commonwealth Games.

little finger on his left hand. 'Of course, people have played in Test matches with this sort of injury,' Bedser reminded reporters, 'but he must be regarded as doubtful.' Expecting both Lloyd and Edrich to be fit soon enough, Bedser said there was no thought of sending for a replacement, while some observers tutted once more about the insistence on bringing five seam bowlers on tour instead of including another batting all-rounder.

On the day before the Queensland contest began, Bob Willis was given a long workout in the hope of being able to play and claim a place in the first Test, while much attention focused on the trio of seamers MCC were likely to face on a helpful wicket: the swing of Max Walker, the left-arm variety of former Test man Alan Dell and the unknown element of Thomson. The latter had apparently been working with former Aussie great Ray Lindwall, but the combination of his performance in his only Test match and modest returns for his new state team meant he was viewed with mild interest rather than mass panic.

Yet the warning signs had been there for those who cared to look, many of them emanating from a club game on the final day of 1973 that was already taking on the status of myth.

Phil Wilkins had written about the match between Bankstown and visiting team Mosman in the *Sydney Morning Herald* back in January, reporting, 'There is another speedster in Australia who has batsmen running for cover when he takes the new ball – but he cannot even gain a place in the NSW Sheffield Shield team. He is Bankstown-Canterbury's Jeff Thomson.'

Former England and Essex all-rounder Barry Knight, Mosman's skipper, said the then 23-year-old's slinging action made him as hard to pick up as West Indian Charlie Griffith, who was adept at hiding the ball until the point of delivery. 'Thomson's bowling was the fastest I have encountered since Frank Tyson played in a game in Peterborough for Northamptonshire,' he raved. 'I have never seen stumps flying so far out of the ground. Thommo just went berserk, He yorked four batsmen and hit three in the head. Greg Bush was taken to hospital with a blood clot behind the eye and Robert Jeffrey was knocked into his stumps.'

Jeffrey had been the first victim of a man fired by the fury of being overlooked by New South Wales even though he had already made a Test debut. The old stories about the state selectors refusing to cross Sydney Harbour Bridge to watch Bankstown players were clearly true, an annoyed Thomson believed. The men from Mosman, a relatively well-to-do suburb on the acceptable side of the water, were the ones to suffer for it. David Lord, who had preceded Knight as Mosman captain and would soon be acting as Thomson's agent, remembered him bowling at bespectacled tail-ender Johnny McKenzie. 'Thommo bowled him a bouncer and McKenzie just stood there, he didn't see it,' he told the paceman's biographer and Australian teammate Ashley Mallett. 'Fortunately it whistled past his nose and Knight yelled out, "Declaring, declaring!" He waited at the gate for Thommo and he said threateningly to him, "Wait until you bat."'

According to Lord, Knight grabbed the ball when Thomson came to the crease and deliberately delivered it from 'about 15 yards from Thommo' and 'threw it straight at his head'. The story ends with Thomson chasing Knight around the field, which suggests it has been subject to embellishment down the years. But it is indicative of the impact of this particular match, which would also become the subject of an essay by Christian Ryan for the 2013 *Wisden Cricketers' Almanack*, under the title, 'The Fastest Spell Ever?'

Sharp-eyed cricket fans in England had the chance to learn about it in July 1974 through the *Lancashire Evening Telegraph* column of former Australian Test bowler Neil Hawke, who was playing for East Lancashire Cricket Club. Under the headline 'New Australian Terror Bowler', Hawke explained how he had come across another article by Wilkins about the match in the latest edition of Australia's *Cricketer* magazine and had left it, pointedly, in the Yorkshire dressing room at Hull when he went there for a match as part of Geoffrey Boycott's benefit year.[15] It was the magazine in which Thomson made his infamous comment about deliberately trying to hit batsmen.[16] Reporting many of the writer's observations, Hawke

---

15 Hawke described such matches as 'a chore which will inflict the Yorkshire players increasingly in the coming weeks'.

16 In future years, Thomson would claim, 'A lot of it was blown up out of proportion ... It wasn't true to say I enjoyed seeing batsmen twitching on the ground and bleeding all over the place after I'd hit them but it probably didn't do my image any harm.'

described Wilkins as 'someone not prone to over-dramatising the truth'.

The original newspaper article by Wilkins had also quoted Sydney University captain Ian Fisher as saying, 'These days we give batsmen who haven't faced Thomson the warning to take a black arm band, wish them luck and tell them to get out quick.' It was why Thomson ended up describing that period of his career as 'five years of getting wickets and breaking bones and upsetting captains and scaring Christ out of everyone that ever walked onto our particular cricket field in Sydney'.

Yet English opinion about a man no one had seen bowl had evidently been determined by figures of 0 for 110 in his one Test match against Pakistan in 1973, a debut earned after only five first-class matches for New South Wales. Even Lillee admitted, 'Everybody thought that was going to be the end of him.'

Lithe and explosive enough for Greg Chappell to end up likening him to Olympic decathlon champion Daley Thompson as an all-round athlete, Thomson had grown up in Greenacre, an area of Bankstown, adopting a style of bowling delivery akin to a javelin thrower. It could have been described as unique had it not been that his dad Don had bowled the same way. 'I just run in and go "wang",' was how Thomson described an action that saw him trot to the crease, cross his feet with the light touch of a ballroom dancer and slingshot his arm in a perfect, frightening arc that started all the way down at his right heel, hidden from the view of the batsman. Maintaining his full height of 6ft 1in throughout his action, it felt, according to Chappell, as though he was delivering from 6ft 9in. 'He was the quickest bowler I've seen by quite a margin,' he said. 'Only Michael Holding approached him. On the SCG one day he fired a return in from eight yards out and nearly knocked Rod Marsh off his feet.'

At age 16, Thomson had agreed to remain in education to study for his high school certificate, but only so that he could continue to play sport. 'I just had one exercise book for all my lessons,' he said. 'I didn't write in it.' Yet as he moved out of his teens, his interests had progressed to drinking, surfing and chasing girls; all of which held greater importance than adhering to match-day timetables and maximising his potential as a cricketer. Along with friend and fellow paceman Len Pascoe, he was told by the Bankstown hierarchy to apply himself more diligently. As a warning, he was dropped to the third team and proceeded to take 10 for 31 in a two-innings game.

While he would never shed his image as an easy-going larrikin who lived life to the full and never took cricket too seriously – his idea of fitness training was to go chasing wild pigs[17] – he earned a whole other reputation among the batsmen in New South Wales grade cricket. Former Australian Test player John Benaud remembered waiting for Thomson to race in at Bankstown Oval while the latest tale of terror played in his mind: ex-NSW opener Warren Saunders, an expert hooker, being sent to hospital by a Thomson bouncer and then calling state selector Neil Harvey to tell him, 'He's the fastest I've ever faced.' Benaud continued, 'On that day in Bankstown, "wang" meant a ball landing just short of a good length outside off, steepling past my unhelmeted head, up and over the wicketkeeper and one or two bounces into the fence for four byes.'

Future Australia teammate Rick McCosker, another grade cricket opponent, remembered, 'It was a bit terrifying, particularly as the grade wickets weren't quite up to the standard of first-class. His bowling mate was his best mate, Len Pascoe, so when you came up against his club it made things interesting. He was so strong and he got so much pace and bounce. In the first part of his career he wasn't 100 per cent sure where his deliveries were going to go, so that made it difficult for the batsmen. You might find there were four or five balls in the over you didn't have to do anything about, the others were wicket takers or you were going to get hit. It was very different to anything the England batsmen had been used to.'

Thomson revelled in the reputation he and Pascoe developed in grade cricket, where hitting a batsman became a greater ambition than taking his wicket. 'This is no bullshit; most weekends we put somebody on a stretcher or in hospital,' he said. 'It was just carnage. They were pretty scared shitless to play us. I know some blokes didn't turn up in club games.'

A first-class debut for New South Wales in the 1972-73 season led to rapid selection for Australia after only 17 wickets. But a wayward

---

17 Something that made for an obvious television sequence when his subsequent success generated a frenzy of media interest.

and wicketless Test display, hindered by what was later revealed as a broken bone in his foot, took him out of contention for the subsequent tour of the West Indies. He then spent 1973-74 out of the first-class game until performances such as that against Mosman earned him a recall for NSW's final match against Queensland. Opposing captain Greg Chappell was intrigued to open his newspaper on the morning of that game to read Thomson saying, 'This is my last game for NSW. I'm not going to stick around waiting to be picked. I'm off.'

After Thomson had taken nine wickets to help prevent Queensland landing the Sheffield Shield, including 7 for 85 in the first innings, Chappell made sure to have a beer with him and asked how serious he was about finding a new cricketing home. He knew exactly the kind of character he would be taking on if he could entice him to Queensland. 'The real problem was that he didn't care much for cricket,' said Chappell. 'He'd turn up late for club games at Bankstown or, if the surf was up, not at all.' Nor did he spend much time thinking about the mechanics of his craft. Lillee, who recalled him asking which side of the ball he should shine for an outswinger, called him 'a natural', while an oft-repeated tale has Thomson asking his captain where he should begin his run-up because the tree outside the boundary that he had previously used as a guide had been cut down. 'I just walked back, threw down a marker and thought, "Shit, this looks all right,"' he explained. 'I didn't go out there with string and measure it; all this bullshit.'

But, boy, he could bowl fast. Never mind that he required a job, a new cricket club, somewhere to live and a car, Chappell told his state bosses to do all they could to get him to Queensland. 'I don't ever want to bat against him again,' he said. With a deal done and the 1974-75 season approaching, Queensland staged a trial game in which Chappell ensured Thomson was on his side and saw him spray the ball all over the place. One newspaper report noted that he was 'very erratic and will need to lift his game against NSW next week if he is to live up to the reputation that preceded him to Brisbane'.

That was if he played, of course, Queensland selector Peter Burge told Chappell it would be 'a disgrace to send him out in Queensland colours when he's going to bowl like that'.

Chappell, secure in his status as captain and his conviction of Thomson's potential, argued back, 'Don't worry about it. We'll get ten wickets in run-outs with blokes trying to get up the other end. He'll frighten them out.'

Making his Queensland debut against his former team, he took four first-innings wickets before having to go to hospital with heat stroke, an episode that persuaded him to wear a floppy hat in the field in future. Having spent a night at Chappell's home he returned to the field to take two more wickets.

When Western Australia travelled to Sydney to play New South Wales, tales of Thomson were on everybody's lips. Ross Edwards remembered, 'I vividly recall sitting with the New South Wales players and talking to Alan Turner, who was a swarthy guy. Someone asked how quick this bloke Thomson was and Fitter-an[18] went absolutely white and said, "He is fucking quick." Cricketers don't say things like that, they say things like "Oh, he is a bit slippery", but Fitter-an said that with awe in his voice. We should have taken a lot of notice of that because when we got up to Brisbane we found out why. No one had ever seen anyone as quick as this before.'

Edwards recalled those first encounters. 'I remember sitting in the change room watching the first couple of overs and everyone was going, "Oh, deary me, this is fast." In the first innings I can vaguely remember I was at the bowler's end when I first went out to bat and John Inverarity was facing. My recollection is that he didn't even get the bat out of the block hole and the ball was taken by the wicketkeeper. I thought, "Jeez, how quick is this?" I got on strike and I got about ten off one over. I think it was a ten-ball over and the one thing I really didn't need was to face two extra balls from him. There were two yorkers and I was fortunate to get an inside edge to both of them and they went for four down to fine leg. There were two bouncers, which were the easiest balls to deal with because he didn't bowl a good bouncer; you could get underneath them easily. I think the two best shots I ever played in my life were when the ball pitched on leg stump and went to off and I managed to get an outside edge to both. I'd forgotten this, but the boys tell me that I was bowled off one of the no-balls and I started off to the boundary.

---

18 Turner's nickname, as in "fitter and turner", an occupation within metal manufacturing.

When I heard it was a no-ball I walked back to the crease very reluctantly. The last ball, I remember thinking if he bowled it off the stumps I would let it hit the pads. I put my leg out and it hit the outside of my thigh and went straight through and hit the stumps. I remember thinking. "That's gonna hurt in a couple of hours."

'That was the first innings, and it was a shocking experience. In the second innings, it starts to rain while I am on strike and I'm thinking, "If his front foot slips, that is when the ball comes out head high – and that is scary." He's just marking out his run again when Greg Chappell shouts, "Thommo, you're off." I've never been so relieved in my life.

'If there was a way to play him, none of us had any experience of it. I think you just played dead; made yourself very small. Because the pace was outside our experience. You've got to start a lot earlier until you get the hang of things. No one was used to anything like that because he was not only quick, he was unorthodox.'

Aussie opener Ian Redpath recalled, 'I'd probably faced Thomson twice; once was on a very flat wicket in Melbourne and once in Brisbane, where he was playable but very sharp, very dangerous. He didn't run in very far and he bowled like an absolute rocket. He was very difficult to score off and you really had to rely on deflections; he was too quick to look to drive and cut. He never bowled flat out all the time, but when he slipped himself he was very quick. He bowled with a very straight front leg and he bowled over the top of that. He didn't give you a look at the ball, so you didn't have much time to work out what you were going to do.'

By the time Queensland's match against MCC came around, Australian captain Ian Chappell had seen Thomson in action against Western Australia, saying that he 'bowled as fast as any speedster I have seen in my career'. Yet the English batsmen, aware of Thomson's recent remarks about leaving 'blood on the pitch', took more notice of figures of 2 for 96 in that game than the hyperbole coming from Chappell, who had been trying to talk up the same bowler when he'd visited England earlier in the year.

The Chappells were quite happy with that state of affairs. While modern selection policy would undoubtedly prevent a key weapon being exposed to opposition batsmen prior to a Test series, Greg Chappell sent Thomson into action against the MCC with an order that was the equivalent tactic of the time: 'Don't show the bastards anything.'

Burge, his earlier doubts about Thomson eradicated, could not resist telling Edrich, 'We have got somebody special down here. We have got a chap called Jeff Thomson. It is going to be different to last time; you wait and see.'

Even the desire to protect the secrecy of Australia's new weapon could not prevent Chappell inserting MCC when he won the toss, an act that was not a ringing endorsement of the work of Alderman Jones but did allow Thomson to bowl the opening over of the match. The very first ball, a little short of a good length, rose sharply and struck Amiss above the waistline. Another warning had been delivered.

'He bowled quite sharply,' Denness recalled. 'He was, however, somewhat wayward in his direction. Most of us found it a little difficult to pick up the ball because when his arm goes back the ball was hidden behind his body. The first ball he bowled me, the first of my innings, pitched outside off stump and flew over the middle stump.'

Yet in the course of MCC's innings of 258, Thomson bowled only 11 overs, compared to workhorse Dell's 26. Amiss, who never achieved an impression of comfort, gave him his only wicket when he chased a wide delivery on 35. In his report of the first day, the *Daily Mirror*'s Peter Laker dismissively referred to Thomson as 'the "alleged" fast-bowling fiend' after watching him send down 12 no-balls in 'an indifferent performance in ideal seam bowling conditions'. It could not deter Australia's selectors from naming him during the second day's play in their 12 for the first Test.

According to Denness, 'At that time we were open-minded about the threat he posed,' although Edrich was unconcerned. Having taken Burge's warning as 'all part of the build-up', he recalled, 'Thomson was all over the place. We thought there is no need to worry about him. He can't bowl, this chap.'

Meanwhile, one man taking the threat of what Thomson might serve up in the series seriously was Frank Tyson, whose pace had been a defining feature of the contest two decades previously. His concerns centred on that much-publicised interview in *Cricketer*, prompting him to write an open letter to Thomson. 'The knowledge that you have physical superiority in terms of fast bowling speed is an exhilarating experience,' he began. 'Sadly, however, only time brings the awareness that unless this inborn advantage is harnessed to intelligence and not to brutality and intimidation it will not yield any harvest.'

He warned that 'physical assault on Test match batsmen, whilst it may be frightening to behold, is not a rewarding long-term exercise', and was likely to be blunted by stubborn and skilled opponents. 'Intelligence, dear Jeff, is the necessary additive to pace,' he continued. 'You are not a butcher, but a wicket-taker – at least such should be your aspirations.'

Another old-schooler, Jack Fingleton, voiced his distaste for Thomson's bluster. 'It is a thousand pities that our officials have not got him publicly to recant or say he was immature and that he was taking nonsense through the top of his crepe sun hat,' he wrote.

Against Thomson and his fellow Queensland seamers, Edrich batted doggedly before enjoying himself with three sixes against the leg-spin of Malcolm Francke in a knock of 48 off 52 balls. It was an untypical innings by a man known at this stage of his career for getting his head down behind dark, bushy eyebrows and grafting for his runs, but with one MCC batsman said to have complained that the wicket was no better than his front lawn it felt like a day when one might as well attempt to score quickly before receiving an unplayable ball. Chris Old also thumped the Sri Lankan-born slow bowler for three maximums, but Denness continued to cause concern by managing only 14.

Greg Chappell dominated Queensland's innings by scoring 122 out of 226, the one batsman to get on top of Underwood. Only Hendrick, whose four wickets secured his Test place, troubled him consistently with his late movement. On the third day, Thomson celebrated his Australia call-up with a brief burst that left Fletcher bruised. 'I had not been there long when he pitched only just short of the length and made the ball rear up, smashing me on the left elbow,' the Essex man remembered. 'It was one of the more painful blows I have taken while batting.' His response was to slash him for four boundaries in an over.

Thomson's overs were again rationed, ten this time. 'I bowled only a couple of overs flat out and got a couple of wickets,' was his memory of the match. 'I was just having a look and I was real happy at what I saw.' Again, Amiss was his only victim. He fell lbw, as did Denness to Dymock after getting a start and reaching 21. The skipper's six first-class innings on tour had now produced only 104 runs.

A winning target of 208 proved too many for the home team, who were bowled out for 161, although not before Willis had stirred things up by bowling bouncers at last pair Dymock and Dell when they threatened to stick around for a draw. 'Something faster will be coming back at Willis this summer,' snorted Dymock, who had brandished his bat at the MCC paceman.

Hendrick's third sharp slip catch of the innings clinched victory with less than six overs remaining, MCC's first win against Queensland since 1932-33. 'ASHES HOPES ARE SOARING,' trumpeted the *Daily Mirror*, whose correspondent Laker felt that 'for the moment the war of nerves is drifting England's way'. Old's four wickets, including a spell of 3 for 5 in 16 balls, were backed up by a couple each from Hendrick and Willis, leaving Denness to announce, 'We couldn't be happier. We can and we will get better.'

Australia, too, were in confident mood. 'Invariably,' said Redpath, 'we were winning games that we should have lost because blokes would play the innings of their life or bowl beautifully. I can remember three or four games that we won when we should have lost; times when we were in awful trouble. There was self-belief in the players when they went out there. It was a happy side – and the blokes still keep in touch with each other.'

Since winning the fifth Test to draw the 1972 Ashes series 2-2, Australia had beaten Pakistan in all three home Tests before going on to win a five-match series in the West Indies 2-0. The following summer had seen them play two three-Test contests against New Zealand, winning 2-0 at home and drawing 1-1 away. Defeat in the second Test in Christchurch had been their first loss since Derek Underwood caught them on a diseased wicket at Headingley 14 Tests previously. It was also the first time they had been beaten by their near neighbours – although the two series had been the teams' first meetings since the inaugural game between the countries as far back as 1946.

Victory at The Oval, giving them a share of the 1972 series, was a triumph for the Chappell brothers, who both scored centuries, and for the tearaway Lillee, who took five wickets in each innings. It was also confirmation that Australian cricket was entering a new era.

'The winning of the last Test of 1972 at The Oval gave me one of the biggest thrills of my life,' Ian Chappell said before the start of the 1974-75 series. 'It was a Test we were terribly keen to win and we really had to battle for victory over every one of the six days we played. When it was finally won I think we realised that once again Australia was as it should be, a power to be reckoned with in world cricket.'

Chappell had warned Edrich as they spoke at the post-series dinner in 1971, 'When you come back next time it will be very different.' Edrich added, 'I think they learned a lot from John Snow and Ray Illingworth's hard-nosed approach. They didn't give an inch. When we went back in '74-75 they had the same sort of attitude.'

Under Chappell, who had taken over as captain from Bill Lawry before the final match of the 1970-71 Ashes, Australia went about ridding themselves of the reputation for dour cricket they had borne for much of the 1960s. West Indian journalist and broadcaster Tony Cozier, having observed the Aussies on his patch, said, 'Chappell led his team positively, almost arrogantly. He emphasised that he would be satisfied with nothing less than a victory in every match and his men responded by playing attractive, aggressive cricket. It was not long before they were oozing confidence from every pore.'

Australia had also been forced to demonstrate their depth of talent. Not only had Lillee's back failed him in the Caribbean, but Bob Massie, whose prodigious swing had earned him an astonishing 16 wickets on his Test debut at Lord's, had apparently forgotten how he'd worked such magic and was no longer a threat. Jeff Hammond had provided the pace to help beat West Indies but suffered his own back problems. Max Walker might not have had the same amount of swing as Massie at Lord's but he delivered at a greater pace and was a consistent performer rather than a flash in the pan. He had become the mainstay of Australia's seam attack.

But now, rather than carrying the attack with the support of steady left-armers Dymock and Gary Gilmour, Walker could look forward to reverting to a support role behind Lillee and Thomson – if the former could find his fitness and the latter his accuracy.

Having consulted by telephone between Perth and Sydney, it had been no surprise when Australian selectors Neil Harvey, Philip Ridings and Sam Loxton named their trio of pacemen for the first Test. More unexpected was the selection of two leg-spinners in Terry Jenner and Kerry O'Keeffe, rather than finger spinner Ashley Mallett. 'I've been kicked in the guts before, so what's new?' said Mallett. In a clear dig at O'Keeffe, he questioned whether he might do better if he died his hair blond and bowled 'straight breaks'.

The selection also angered Ian Chappell, who took the opportunity to confront Loxton, a batsman on Don Bradman's 'Invincibles' tour of 1948. 'What's the theory behind no Mallett in the Test team?' he demanded in support of his South Australia teammate.

'He's bowling a load of rubbish,' Loxton replied. 'Too much variation in his length.'

'Hang on, Sam,' Chappell continued. 'I'm playing in the same state side as him and that's not what I am seeing. The one thing I know about Rowdy, even if he's not getting blokes out he's going to be hard to score off and he's going to help us get wickets down the other end. The other thing I know about him is that when the fucking heat's on he'll be there. I can't say that about any other spinner in Australia.'

Knowing he could do nothing about the selectors' decision for Brisbane, the captain was determined to plant a flag in the sand for the second Test in Perth. 'Spin's not going to decide the Perth result, but the problem is if you play one of the leg-spinners in Perth and they happen to get a couple of wickets and we win the game then you won't be able to get rid of them,' he argued. 'Then we've got Adelaide and Sydney coming up, which is when we do need some spin bowling so for fuck's sake pick Mallett in the Perth Test, then we've got him for Adelaide and Sydney, Melbourne as well, places where it is going to count.'

Unlike the English system of involving the team captain in selection issues, Chappell explained, 'I always heard the team at the same time as everyone else. I only ever asked for one player and I never got him. When we went to New Zealand [in 1973-74] I asked for Alan Hurst because we didn't have Lillee and we didn't have Thomson yet so we didn't have any speed. I felt Glenn Turner was the only bloke who could beat us but he was not that comfortable against pace. Graham McKenzie had troubled him quite a bit. If you look at the Test we lost in New Zealand, Turner got a hundred in each innings. Greg [Chappell] ended up bouncing him, but Greg is not going to bother anyone at his pace.

'I didn't have a say in selection and Sam Loxton was more likely to take the opposite tack with me if I wanted someone. I didn't think much of him and I don't think he thought much of me. The only selector I got on with in regard to talking cricket was Neil Harvey.'

Meanwhile, Wally Edwards, the left-handed Western Australian was named to fill the vacancy at the top of the order created by the retirement of Keith Stackpole. Both he and namesake Ross could justifiably have been omitted for bank employee Rick McCosker, whose ledger in his last five innings for New South Wales read: 138, 136, 52 not out, 58, 140. His opportunity was not too far away, however.

With a tough match against Queensland behind them and the first Test beginning in three days, you might have expected MCC's players to be given a break. Not in the 1970s. Barely 12 hours after Willis took the final wicket against Queensland, the majority of the squad were setting off along Brisbane's wide suburban roads for Southport, 50 miles south of the bustle and white skyscrapers of the city centre.

Their opposition, a South East Queensland XI, offered little resistance, folding for 52 as Greig took five wickets for a single run in his 3.6 overs of medium pace. In front of a largely swimwear-clad crowd in heat approaching 100 degrees Fahrenheit, Amiss and Luckhurst knocked off the runs with ease before MCC were allowed to give various other batsmen some time in the middle. Lever's appearance at number four, from where he made 33, was an indication that he was likely to have a place in the Test team. Wisely, or misguidedly, depending on which observer one paid attention to, Denness declined the opportunity to feel the ball coming onto his bat.

Back in in Brisbane, the England team had two days to finalise Ashes preparations on the manicured grounds at Brisbane Church of England Grammar School. Selection issues were crystalised by Lloyd's confirmation that his finger was not sufficiently healed for him to be considered and Old straining his groin while bowling in the nets. Arnold, meanwhile, was continuing to struggle for form, with Henry Blofeld saying that in his latest outing he 'bowled without the control or enthusiasm he finds when the conditions are right for him in England'. It meant that Lever, Hendrick and Willis, who might have lost out to Old, would be the three seamers for the Test.

All that remained before the series began was for the final predictions to be made. Keith Miller noted that 'Australia has a good team' and urged his readers, 'Get your rent for the year and back them if you can.' Observing from afar, Cozier warned that 'England's batsmen are still to prove their worth in the face of hostile quick bowling'. But some of those same concerns expressed by English journalists at the start of the tour had been placed in the shadows by the glow of a couple of first-class victories. 'What is worrying the Australians is the streak of steel that has consistently shone through in the performances,' said the *Mirror*'s Laker. 'On paper, Australia's batting looks infinitely more suspect under fire than that of England.'

One Englishman apparently unconcerned about the absence of Geoff Boycott and John Snow in the touring team was the winning captain of 20 years earlier, Sir Leonard Hutton, visiting Australia in his capacity as director of Fenner International, makers of conveyor belts for mines. Asked for his thoughts on the absentees he said, 'Boycott is not seeing the ball as well as he did four years ago. Luckhurst is probably a better batsman than Boycott,' and added that 'Snow is not the bowler he used to be'.

Michael Melford argued in the *Sunday Telegraph* that England would 'go into battle feeling like they have something of an even chance', saying that there was '[no] certainty that England are going to have to cope with the blend of extreme pace and accuracy which can upset the best'.

Cricketer produced a Kookaburra-sponsored 44-page broadsheet preview of the series that was more interested in hyping the contest than making firm predictions. Yet it had succinctly identified a difference in personality between the teams that the home team's inclusion of Lillee and Thomson had further crystalised. 'England – old, traditional, tried, proven performers. No frills about them,' was its summary, followed by, 'Australia – younger, aggressive, with more than a dash of flamboyance about them.'

In *The Times*, Woodcock was eager to remind readers that Thomson 'has little idea of direction' and was selected purely 'to put the fear of God into the opposition', which was not far off Greg Chappell's original justification for persuading the Queensland hierarchy to sign him. While he avoided offering an outright prediction, Swanton recalled that the MCC party had travelled as underdogs and argued that 'the picture has changed in their favour'. He noted that most of the Australian team were either out of form or 'have done nothing startling' during the season and concluded, 'England, I believe, are the proper favourites. They have a rather better chance than any of their seven predecessors since 1946-47.'

But any English forecast about the outcome of the series was born of an ignorance of the storm about to break around the touring team. 'They had no concept of what was going to happen,' Ross Edwards recalled with undisguised relish. 'It was a well-kept secret.'

Meanwhile, former Australian Test bowler and survivor of the Bodyline series Bill O'Reilly had seen and heard enough over the last few months to warn, 'All the sickening signs of a nauseating rubber are flying high.'

4
WE DIDN'T START THE FIRE

Shut up, Greigy. Don't wind him up any more.
Dennis Amiss

England had been forced to rule out two unfit players for the first Test, while Australia had survived late injury concerns over leg-spinners Terry Jenner and Kerry O'Keeffe and been relieved when the threat of a domestic air strike receded, allowing their squad to gather in Brisbane on schedule. Yet any pre-series concerns afflicting the two competing teams appeared miniscule next to the problems that had mounted for mayor-cum-groundsman Clem Jones, who'd had to race to The Gabba at 1.30am three nights before the Test when a thunderstorm broke over his uncovered square. 'In the end we just sat down and cried and drank beer,' he reported.

It meant that while the MCC tourists were practising on a pristine and dry school ground nearby, Jones was driving a heavy roller over his sodden surface and then getting on his hands and knees to remove clumps of mud with a wire brush. Observers wondered where on earth the Test wicket actually was. In the end, Jones was forced to move the pitch from its intended location to avoid a damp patch that had developed where the short leg fielders had been standing in the MCC-Queensland game just completed. Not until hours before the scheduled start did he settle on re-using the strip of grass that had staged a Sheffield Shield game two weeks earlier.

An exasperated John Woodcock wrote, 'The Lord Mayor of Brisbane trying to combine his official duties with preparing a Test pitch is becoming really rather a poor joke. This is too big a sporting occasion to be jeopardised by the whims of one man.'[19] According

---

19 One year later, Jones would find himself in an almost identical battle to locate and prepare a pitch in time for the first Test against the West Indies. It prompted John Herbert, Queensland's Minister for Sport, to urge the Trust that owned and ran the Gabba to 'wake up to itself and get rid of this megalomaniac'.

to Greg Chappell, Jones was 'one of the few people who could not grow grass in Queensland. He buried the pitch in grass clippings and a strong breeze would blow them away.'

On the morning of the match, *The Australian* was a little more forgiving, saying, 'Alderman Jones has done a tremendous amount of work since Wednesday morning's storm flooded the ground. Where there was a drying quagmire is now a reasonably hard … strip of unevenly-textured turf from which he will cut the Test strip. Strong winds and bright sunshine have brought a remarkable transformation.'

It would not prevent a stony-faced Richie Benaud intoning to his TV audience, 'There has been no more controversial pitch preparation in the history of Anglo-Australian Test matches than the one for this opening Test of the series.'

Even Jones was forced to admit that the wicket was 'a bit crook at one end', referring to the Stanley Street End. There was an obvious risk that the ball would misbehave off the surface, but Jones suggested, 'Because the wicket is so soft underneath it will only rear up slowly.' He was not reckoning on the performance of Jeff Thomson.

Australia's new secret weapon spent the evening before the match completing his final preparations. Dennis Lillee, who scarcely knew Thomson at this point but took to him immediately because he was 'the easiest going guy all of the time', found his new bowling partner sitting at the bar of their hotel shortly after the team dinner. Seeing his tumbler brimming with ice, Lillee observed that a drink of water before bed was a good idea and said he would join him.

'Water?' scoffed Thomson. 'That's straight scotch. I'm going to have a few of them.'

'What if you have to bowl tomorrow?'

'When I go out to bowl I want a hangover from hell. I bowl real well when I have a headache. It makes me want to get in there and get them.'

Lillee's first encounter with Thomson, in a Sheffield Shield game two years earlier, had given him some insight into his new teammate's personality. After Lillee had edged for four, Thomson came back at him with a fearsome delivery that lifted and struck him on the gloves. Holding his hand while he ran a single, Lillee arrived at Thomson's end and snarled, 'I hope you can hold a fucking blade, pal.' A grinning Thomson replied, 'Listen, pal, you've got the bat at the moment, just get up the other end and see how fucking good you are.'

Now Lillee was in no doubt that he would be sharing the new ball with 'an unusual character'; someone whose line to reporters that he was 'training on whisky' was perhaps not such an exaggeration after all.

The fast bowlers awoke to see the front pages of Australia's papers regarding the Ashes as important enough to share space with the deferment of a government vote on a new Family Law Bill, aimed at reforming divorce legislation, and Prime Minister Gough Whitlam's defence of spending A$280,000 on a Qantas charter plane for a trip to Europe on security grounds. 'If we can play our best, we can win,' said Ian Chappell on page one of the *Sydney Morning Telegraph*. 'But it will need to be our best.'

As well as the right to consider themselves owners of the Ashes urn – which, of course, always remained at Lord's regardless of results – the teams were competing for a modest A$18,000 in prize money provided by a low-key sponsorship of the series by Benson and Hedges. The winning team in each Test would receive A$2,000 and the losers $1,000, with any money from a drawn game going forward into a pot for division at the end of the series, including A$1,000 each for the team achieving the better over rate and higher scoring rate.

Such loose change was in no one's mind at The Gabba as English journalists settled into their workplaces and, averting their eyes from the controversial pitch, enjoyed the sight of 15,303 spectators making the most of a bright Friday morning by filling up a ground that had been modernised since they had last attended a Test match there. EW Swanton called the facilities 'trim and sophisticated', saying, 'What a far cry it is from the crude and ill-equipped country field of earlier days wherein the press, in the midst of one sizeable stand, were segregated from outside contact by a barbed wire surround and the heavy roller was pulled by an aged horse.'

Frank Tyson described the moments immediately before and after the start of the series in his chronicle of the tour, *Test of Nerve*. 'There is a tension in the air, which is only softened by the pleasure of meeting people from the four corners of Australia and from the other side of the world. The press pundits such as Fingleton and Swanton meet in a commonality of interest tinged with a rivalry, which the game accentuates rather than softens. Millers meet Lindwalls and Bedsers and it is as if the years between now and their playing days never existed. In Brisbane there is always the traditional parade of young cricketers before the game. They foregather, club pennants flying, on an arena which one day they hope to tread on such an occasion as this.'

In the middle, Ian Chappell, Mike Denness and the match officials gathered to conduct the first toss of the series. The most nervous member of the party was umpire Robin Bailhache, who, at 37, had gone into the season with only six first-class games behind him. 'I was in a sheer state of fright,' he remembered. 'It was so unexpected. No way at the start of the season did I think I was in contention for the Test matches.'

Bailhache, state marketing manager for an insurance company who had stood in MCC's earlier four-day match against South Australia, had not long arrived home in Adelaide the previous Sunday evening when he received phone calls from local cricket writer Mike Coward and Richie Benaud congratulating him on his appointment. 'I knew nothing about it until then,' he explained. 'I had to be in Brisbane on Thursday and I was in Adelaide, which is like the distance of Europe away. I had a busy week lined up and that all went by the board.It was bedlam for the next four days. I had a very understanding manager, who was a cricket fanatic and he said, "Go for it, Robin." I arrived in Brisbane on the Thursday after a hell of a rush.'

Meeting up with his fellow umpire, policeman Tom Brooks – almost two decades his senior and four years into his own Test career – Bailhache went to check out conditions at The Gabba. 'I had no pass for the ground, they didn't have time to give me one,' he explained. 'They wouldn't let me in at first. The doorman said, "You are too young to be the umpire. He can go in, but not you."

'I was very raw, I hadn't seen some of the Australian players; I had never met Tom Brooks in my life; never been to the Brisbane cricket ground, I had no umpire's badge on my coat. I had to get the girl at the hotel to sew it on overnight so I could walk out with a badge on the next day.'

Properly attired, Bailhache and the others reached the middle to find that things were not as bad as had been feared. Chappell was happy to bat after winning the toss, a decision that would also allow time for the pitch to dry and harden before Thomson and Lillee were unleashed upon it. 'Good game, mate,' the Australian captain offered as he and Denness exchanged a final hand-shake.

'I never said "good luck" because I didn't particularly want my opponent to have good luck,' Chappell revealed. 'But I was looking for a good game.'

While the Australian openers padded up, Chappell made for the bathroom. 'Mike must have used a lot of aftershave and always smelt of Old Spice,' he explained. 'So I would get back in the dressing room and have to wash my hands because I didn't want to smell like bloody Old Spice.'

Viewers watching the Australian Broadcasting Corporation's first-ever colour cricket coverage settled into their seats. According to reports, the ABC was paying A$110,000 for a year's worth of international and domestic matches, including the sum of A$26,000 for Australia's overseas games. Various commercial stations had opted into paying additional amounts for non-exclusive coverage, with the Channel Seven network of major-city stations said to have paid A$10,00 for each of three Tests. For the Second Test in Perth, all three local channels would show the final session of each day.

Denness led out his men to begin the 47th Ashes series in the kind of temperature absent for most of the previous month, causing him to fret that they'd not had the chance to acclimatise to such conditions. Locating jumpers had taken precedent over becoming used to the heat and the brighter light of Australia and he feared that 'the temperature of up to 100 would sap our energy as well as our concentration'.

Bob Willis was thrown the new Kookaburra Turf ball as he made his way out to a wicket he felt the groundsman had made 'a dangerous mess of'. He strode south towards the Stanley Street End to bowl the first over to Ian Redpath, a man he knew would not give away his wicket cheaply. The seventh ball reared up from a good length and hit the batsman in the ribs.

Peter Lever was given the task of opening from the Vulture Street End, marching 40 paces back from the crease before turning to charge in at the left-handed Wally Edwards. As someone whose run-up created a greater air of urgency than control, it was no great surprise when he overstepped on his second delivery. Denness withdrew him after a single over and introduced Mike Hendrick, whose lithe, measured approach was in such contrast to Lever's that one might have been delivering fine dining on a silver platter and the other chucking quick-fried burgers out the side of a van.

The new bowler picked up the first wicket of the series with his sixth ball, delivered only slightly short of a length on a line just outside off stump. Hurriedly and ill-advisedly, Edwards attempted a hook that ended up as an ungainly swipe, sending the ball flying off the edge to fine leg, where Dennis Amiss made ground to his left, took the catch and flopped involuntarily onto his backside. On the third ball of the next over, Redpath was beaten by Willis's near-yorker, his stumps flattened and his bat ending up shaping to play through midwicket. Australia were 10 for 2 in the fifth over and England could see the next few weeks unfolding joyously ahead of them.

Yet the tourists quickly discovered that they would have to work hard for further wickets on a track that offered little movement and no great pace. Bowling steadily, but sometimes a little too short, they were unable to ruffle the Chappell brothers as they set about rebuilding the innings with a three-figure partnership. Skipper Ian, determined to justify the decision to bat, was taking no risks. He took 21 minutes to get off the mark and faced 42 balls before scoring anything more than a single.

In a hotel close to the ground, one man was relieved to hear on the radio that Chappell was not trying to hit the cover off the ball. John Newbery, bat-maker for Gray-Nicolls, had shown up at the nets the day before with a product the Sussex-born company was still developing, the GN100, soon to be known around the world as the 'Scoop' and to occupy a prominent place in the cricketing culture of the 1970s. As the name suggests, the unique feature of the bat was the hollowing out of the back of the blade, enabling weight to be more evenly distributed and edges to be made slightly thicker, without losing the impact of the bat's sweet spot. That, at least, was the theory behind the prototype designed by Newbery and crafted by his colleague, Robert Richards, in Melbourne.

The Scoop had been in the works since 1972, when South African golf club engineer Arthur Garner and course designer Barrie Wheeler developed a concept based on the science of golf club design. Various manufacturers dismissed their innovation before the forward-thinking Gray-Nicolls, the first company to put distinctive stickers on their products, agreed to develop the idea, granting royalties to Garner and Wheeler over the 18-year lifetime of their patent.

Richards, who had learned his craft at Gray-Nicolls's legendary workroom in Robertsbridge in the south of England countryside, recalled, 'Just after I left they started playing around with these perimeter weighted bats and they came here and we really set it alight.' There were some false starts along the way, with many of the early models splitting down the middle because there was simply not enough wood there – 'no guts' as Richards called it. 'John Newbery kept working on it and kept refining it. As soon as we played around with it and got it right we never changed it. The only thing we changed was the colour of the Scoop. The Chappell one was red.'

The Chappell brothers had used Gray-Nicolls bats for some time and were, according to Richards, 'the easiest players to deal with'. But Newbery's intention on arrival in Brisbane had been merely to tell the Australian captain what was in the works and show him the prototype. Impressed, Chappell asked Newbery if he could try the bat in the nets, where he felt so comfortable with it that he announced his intention to use it in the Test match. Newbery protested, emphasising its experimental status and his desire to offer it to other players for trial and feedback. Chappell refused to let him have the bat back. Fearful of the consequences if the bat was seen to shatter into pieces, Newbery could not bear to attend the match. In his hotel room, he was spared having to watch every ball from behind bed cushions by broadcasting regulations that meant only the final session of the day could be shown in the host city. By the time those in Brisbane became part of the viewing audience, Chappell was still at the crease and his Scoop was fully intact.[20]

---

20 By 1976, a survey revealed that 34 per cent of English county professionals were using the Scoop, with the figure closer to 50 per cent in Australian first-class cricket.

Using the traditional blade, Greg Chappell, who survived an lbw appeal against Tony Greig, was a tad busier than his brother, but lunch was little more than two overs away before he finally scored the first boundary of Australia's innings, driving back past Hendrick with an exaggerated lift of the left elbow. Welcoming the opportunity to drive the Derbyshire man, he was among many who felt Hendrick could have been more potent had he risked that outcome more often. 'If he'd pitched it a metre fuller he'd have been one of the great Test seamers,' he said of a man who finished his career with 87 wickets in 30 Tests and an economy rate of 2.17 runs per over. 'His pitching it a little short made him hard to score off, but it reduced his chances of taking wickets.'

Ian Chappell at last hit his first four in the next over, getting into position across his stumps so early that he had to do little more than guide Greig's attempted bouncer fine to the rope. For the most part, both batsmen had resisted the hook, and even when they did succumb their execution was precise and directed towards the safety of the outfield grass. There was little risk involved when, seven balls after lunch had been taken at 56 for 2 from 23 overs, Ian Chappell again jumped across the crease to get enough bat underneath Greig's harmless bouncer to see his shot carry over the fence for six. Lever might have been quicker than his colleague, but the short ball he directed at Greg Chappell proved no more threatening and was pulled for four.

Back at the southern batting crease, the junior Chappell drove Greig wide of mid-off. Derek Underwood gamely gave the kind of chase that in the modern day would have ended with a sliding stop by the foam of the boundary marker, but in the mid-1970s saw the fielder having to pull up short and put out his hands to stop him smacking dangerously into the white picket fence surrounding the playing area. Greig responded by bowling fuller and wider, although it was hard to tell with him if it was a deliberate attempt to draw the batsman into a false shot or a simple loss of line and length. The result was a perfectly-middled drive that sent the ball through extra cover.

An object of desire for club and school cricketers, the Scoop was relaunched with modern ultra-thick edges in 2017. Meanwhile, original 1970s models change hands on eBay for prices well in excess of the original price of around £50.

Greig decided it was time to revert to the off-spin that had proved such an unexpected asset on England's previous tour when he'd attempted to find an antidote to West Indian conditions that offered no help to his medium-paced swing and seam. 'I loved the opportunity to make a difference with bat or ball,' he explained. 'It happened when I started bowling off-spinners in the Caribbean. It was partially a way out of bowling seamers on pitches that weren't helpful, partly because they had a lot of left-handers. I just loved that; I revelled in that type of situation.'

The 13 wickets he took in the fifth and final Test of that series, including eight in the first innings, made a believer of his great friend Knott, whose claim that, for a while at least, Greig was among the best off-break bowlers in the world was a genuinely held conviction. 'He started fiddling about with it in Jamaica and then he bowled a big spell in Barbados and by the time he got to Trinidad he was ready,' Knott said. 'In Jamaica he was bowling cutters then it became spin as he went on. He had the loop and he had enough spin. Of course, with his height and with all that bounce, you didn't want it to spin too much. If he could have done that as a young lad it would have been a fantastic bonus, but to start that late was difficult. He always looked as though he was going to bowl the ball full toss to me, but it would suddenly dip and make it very difficult for the batsmen. It was amazing that for a short spell in his career he was such a great off-spin bowler.'

This had the potential to be a big moment of the tour. Not always potent enough to be considered a specialist third seamer, nor a genuine second spinner, if Greig could be effective as a multi-style bowler in Australia it would add enormously to Denness's armoury. Yet, according to Willis, 'Knotty was a great disciple of the gospel according to Tony Greig' and of his claims that Greig's off-breaks would win a Test in Australia, he remembered, 'I thought that a little fanciful at the time, and Greig never made real advances as a spinner.' In fact, there would be valid arguments that his quest to rediscover the stardust that had touched him in Trinidad made him a less effective bowler in the long run.

Brisbane was certainly no Port-of-Spain and Greig, it was about to be proved, was no Lance Gibbs. He dropped his first slow delivery too short and Greg Chappell, whose wearing of a sleeveless sweater added to the impression that he had ice in his veins, thrashed it through the off side to reach a half-century.

Driving Lever off the back foot and cutting Greig for a pair of boundaries. Ian Chappell doubled his score from 19 to 38 in the space of 19 balls, raising the century partnership in the process. Underwood had been used sparingly to that point – only two overs before lunch – but his third ball from the Vulture Street End bit and turned enough to catch the edge of Greg Chappell's tentative push and offer a straightforward slip catch to Keith Fletcher under his white flowerpot hat.

The elder Chappell exacted some fraternal revenge in the left-armer's next over. Down on one knee, he aimed an angry-looking sweep shot behind square leg, just wide of the flower beds that added purple and pink splashes to the area between boundary rope and the perimeter fencing on one side of the ground. Three balls later he advanced to hit a classically driven four. After passing 50 in the next over, he hooked Willis for four and set about Underwood again. By tea, taken at 157 for 3, Chappell had reached 70, the last 51 of those runs representing a marked change of gear in taking only 68 deliveries. In his newly-acquired haste, however, he did endanger batting partner Ross Edwards when taking a quick single off Lever, the throw of Denness from wide mid-on just missing the target.

The innings of Edwards was following a similar pattern, underlining the difficulty of finding instant fluency on the sluggish surface, especially with Underwood bowling tightly and Greig in his face at silly point.

As the final drinks of the day were removed from the field, Chappell had a personal milestone in sight. Fours off successive balls against Underwood had helped move him to within ten runs of a 13th Test century when Willis, in the fourth over of his spell from the Stanley Street End, pitched short. Chappell took the bait. Unable to get above and outside the ball, his pull shot sailed high off the top edge and a delighted Greig clutched the ball at backward square leg. Australia were 197 for 4 and England had found a method of dismissal that would serve them again before stumps. Doug Walters had already survived a wild hook off Greig – now back to medium pace – before he hacked at another Willis bouncer that was outside off stump and lobbed it to Lever, moving to his right from mid-on and managing to avoid the low evening sun shining in his eyes.

The final wicket of the day fell to Underwood, turning one just enough for Ross Edwards to give Knott his first catch of the series. After three wickets in 20 minutes, Rodney Marsh and Terry Jenner survived a final half-hour in which the new ball was taken and the erratic Lever was warned for bowling three bouncers at the leg-spinner. But England could be well pleased with their first serious day of work in Australia; six hours that EW Swanton felt had 'drama and variety, if no great overall quality'.

The only performance review the tourists were interested in was the verdict of the scoreboard, which at 219 for 6 from 68 overs was undoubtedly balanced towards them. 'That suited us,' Amiss recalled. 'Several batsman got out trying to hook but I would not say we overindulged in bouncers on that opening day.'

Day two began under clear skies with a cooling breeze that ended up being welcomed by an England team kept in the field far longer than they had anticipated. Willis removed Jenner in the second over, another victim of the hook shot, and Marsh offered up his wicket in the next over, a skier off Hendrick. This one fell to Denness at extra cover after the Aussie wicketkeeper had got too far under an attempted heave down the ground. Marsh's indiscretion might have been excused as a sign that he had little confidence in new partner Lillee and the remaining pair of Walker and Thomson. But it meant that of the eight wickets to fall, five had been gifts to the outfield. Of those, four had been the result of short-pitched deliveries, but now Willis and Hendrick became more amiable, keeping the ball pitched up to their opposition counterparts.

Hendrick put a third slip in place and floated up a half-volley in the hope of inducing an edge from Lillee, who drove him through mid-off. After being cut to the boundary by Walker, Willis did get Lillee to snick behind the stumps, only for it to evade the reach of Knott, who diverted it past Fletcher at first slip. Lillee waited for more half-volleys, whipping Hendrick through square leg and driving him for another four, the surprised excitement growing all the time in the crowd of 15,597. 'Listen to that roar, it's like a football crowd,' was the observation from the commentary box.

Lever slowed the scoring with a maiden over at Walker, but it was during these unthreatening eight deliveries that Greig became increasingly agitated. The Aussie seamers had added 28 runs without the kind of danger to welfare that would make them less comfortable planting themselves on the front foot. Greig would just have to do it himself. Eagerly grabbing the ball at the Vulture Street End, it took precisely two deliveries to create the ill-tempered departure of Lillee described in this book's introduction.

'Greig's shortened his run and looks as though he might bowl cutters,' said Tyson in the commentary box as the bowler approached the crease for the decisive delivery. Lillee almost toppled over as he tried to respond to Greig's bouncer, succeeding only in diverting the ball to the wicketkeeper. 'I would hazard a guess that when Tony Greig came to the batting crease that he might be the recipient of one or two shorter pitched deliveries from Dennis Lillee,' ventured Tyson.

Battle lines had been drawn. 'Shut up, Greigy. Don't wind him up any more,' Amiss urged when Lillee and Greig came almost nose to nose as the Australian left the scene. 'Tony told him where to go and that was the start,' Amiss remembered.

Similar concerns were going through Edrich's mind. 'Wait a minute, Greigy. They have got those two, what have we got? We haven't got that pace and I have got to go out there against this lot.'

If there was a single candidate in the England team to rile the Aussies without any thought of consequences then it was Greig, whose 28 years had been a series of challenges. Even his privileged white middle-class upbringing in South Africa's Cape Province had not been straightforward, with his Scottish-born father Sandy battling alcoholism, generally considered a legacy of the multiple Lancaster bombing missions he had flown over Germany in World War II. Then Greig had been diagnosed at age 14 with epilepsy, having suffered his first attack during a game of tennis. Although a few of those close to him in cricket knew of his ailment, which he kept under control with drugs, he would not reveal it publicly until publishing his autobiography in 1980. 'I knew him for years and never gave his epilepsy a thought,' said Knott. 'I never noticed any sign of it. He used to have a nap instead of sitting on the balcony.'[21]

---

21 When Greig finally returned to England after this tour, following a family holiday

Even his professional cricket career in England had been born out of challenge and ultimatum. Accepting an invitation to join Sussex in 1966, he promised his father that if he did not make the grade in three years he would return home. A centurion in his first County Championship match, he was representing England by 1970 – even though his first games against the Rest of the World were later downgraded from full Test status – and had been an automatic selection since winning back his place for the 1972 Ashes series.

A man who never denied his South African heritage while playing for England, he embraced it, loving the extra edge of competitiveness he felt it gave him, especially when Australians were the opponents. Yet Greig never accepted the idea that it was his actions, his streak of venom, that prompted the storm of short-pitched bowling that would soon be breaking over the England team in Australia. 'I reject the theory totally and refuse to accept that it made the slightest bit of difference,' he said. And it was rather self-serving of Lillee to say, 'Those bouncers from Greigy really fired us up. That's where the so-called bumper war started' – especially when one notes his pre-Ashes comments about hitting batsmen.

Ian Chappell explained, 'Greigy always said to me over the years that he was urging the England quickies to bowl bouncers at Lillee and Thomson, but they just wouldn't do it. He said, "Well I am going to get them anyhow, so I might as well bowl a few myself." That was his rationale.'

It was a view that Robin Marlar expressed when he wrote his report of the day's play for the *Sunday Times*. 'England became slaves to one of cricket's most inane conventions – that fast bowlers do not bowl bouncers at one another,' he said. 'Thus did they surrender the initiative to Lillee, Thomson and Walker.' And his matter-of-fact view of Greig's actions was, 'Lillee got the needle. He would. But our batsmen were bound to be tested so what was there to lose by unleashing the full treatment at Walker and Thomson?'

---

and participation in a Derrick Robins XI tour of South Africa, it was reported that he had collapsed at Heathrow Airport. It was put down to fatigue, whereas he had actually experienced an epileptic fit after storing his medication in the hold rather than having it available during the long flight.

There had been so much talk before the series of how frequently the bouncer would be employed that it was inevitable that accusations would be directed towards the first team to have the ball. 'If you are fielding first and if you bowl a bouncer, then everyone says, "Well you started it,"' Denness pointed out, although he added, 'Greigy bowling a bouncer or Bob Willis bowling a bouncer didn't matter; it wasn't going to be quite as ferocious as Lillee and Thomson.'

Ross Edwards remembered, 'The Poms had picked five fast bowlers, but most of them were fast-medium, not outright fast. They couldn't compare with Lillee. The papers built things up, saying the Poms are going to start a bouncer war, so when they bowled a bouncer Dennis said, "Well, they started it and they are gonna get this back." But there was never any doubt they were going to get it anyway.'

According to Knott, 'There was no doubt that they were going to bowl aggressively, and we fired the first shots.'

Despite Lillee's flurry of runs, England could still consider themselves on top if they took the final wicket quickly. But for an hour and a quarter up to lunch Walker showed decent technique and a good enough eye to punish any bad balls, while Thomson enjoyed the fortune of the bold as Denness adopted more defensive field settings. The innings eventually closed at 309 when Thomson played Willis towards Denness at mid-off and was beaten by the England captain's direct hit. Walker was left unbeaten on 41, his highest Test score, after a partnership that had added 52 valuable runs.

It had been a fascinating day or so of Test cricket. But with Lillee and Thomson pulling on fresh shirts and bowling boots, the 1974-75 Ashes series was about to begin in earnest.

The MCC touring party strike an unusual pose outside their Heathrow hotel before departing for Australia. Front to back: captain Mike Denness, vice-captain John Edrich, Alan Knott, Bob Taylor, Fred Titmus, physiotherapist Bernard Thomas, Keith Fletcher, Dennis Amiss, Peter Lever, David Lloyd, Brian Luckhurst, Derek Underwood, Geoff Arnold, Chris Old, Mike Hendrick, Tony Greig, Bob Willis, assistant manager AC Smith, manager Alec Bedser.

(Patrick Eagar/Popperfoto via Getty Images)

Australian captain Ian Chappell with his revolutionary Gray-Nicolls Scoop bat, which he insisted on using in the first Test despite its experimental status.
(Patrick Eagar/Popperfoto via Getty Images)

Jeff Thomson in full flight, a sight that shocked England's batsmen and blew them away in the first Test.
(Patrick Eagar/Popperfoto via Getty Images)

Tony Greig's counter-attack and baiting of Dennis Lillee made his innings in Brisbane one of the Ashes' most memorable centuries.
(Patrick Eagar/Popperfoto via Getty Images)

Colin Cowdrey prepares to depart Heathrow Airport after his surprise call to join the injury-hit MCC team in Perth a few weeks short of his 42nd birthday.
(Wesley Keystone/Getty Images)

Rival captains Ian Chappell and Mike Denness shake hands before the second Test in Perth. Chappell would head to the bathroom after the toss to wash the scent of Denness's after-shave from his hands.
(Patrick Eagar/Popperfoto via Getty Images)

Colin Cowdrey is welcomed back to Test cricket by a Dennis Lillee bouncer. David Lloyd is the non-striker.
(Patrick Eagar/Popperfoto via Getty Images)

David Lloyd is felled by a Jeff Thomson delivery that has struck him in the box, giving birth to one of cricket's most popular after-dinner anecdotes.
(Patrick Eagar/Popperfoto via Getty Images)

Chris Old and Mike Denness are joined by Santa Claus as the England team and their families celebrate Christmas in Melbourne. The arrival of wives and children was a controversial element of the tour.
(Patrick Eagar/Popperfoto via Getty Images)

A packed Melbourne Cricket Ground on the first day of the third Test on Boxing Day. The record-breaking crowds that watched the home team regain the Ashes reflected a growing mood of national pride and made the Australian players realise how poorly they were being financially rewarded.

(Patrick Eagar/Popperfoto via Getty Images)

More pain for England as Fred Titmus is struck on the knee by Jeff Thomson in Melbourne. Greg Chappell and Rodney Marsh go to his aid.
(Paul Popper/Popperfoto via Getty Images)

'I just couldn't believe what was happening on the Hill during a cricket match . . . every known bodily function.' The scene at the close of play at the Sydney Cricket Ground, where ground staff had to clear away 864,000 empty beer cans over the course of five days.

(Patrick Eagar/Popperfoto via Getty Images)

Surrounded by the usual ring of close fielders, Keith Fletcher takes evasive action against Jeff Thomson during an ill-tempered fourth Test that intensified the debate about intimidatory bowling.
(Patrick Eagar/Popperfoto via Getty Images)

The elegant Greg Chappell, on his way to a century in Sydney, was the pick of the Australia batsmen throughout the series.
(Patrick Eagar/Popperfoto via Getty Images)

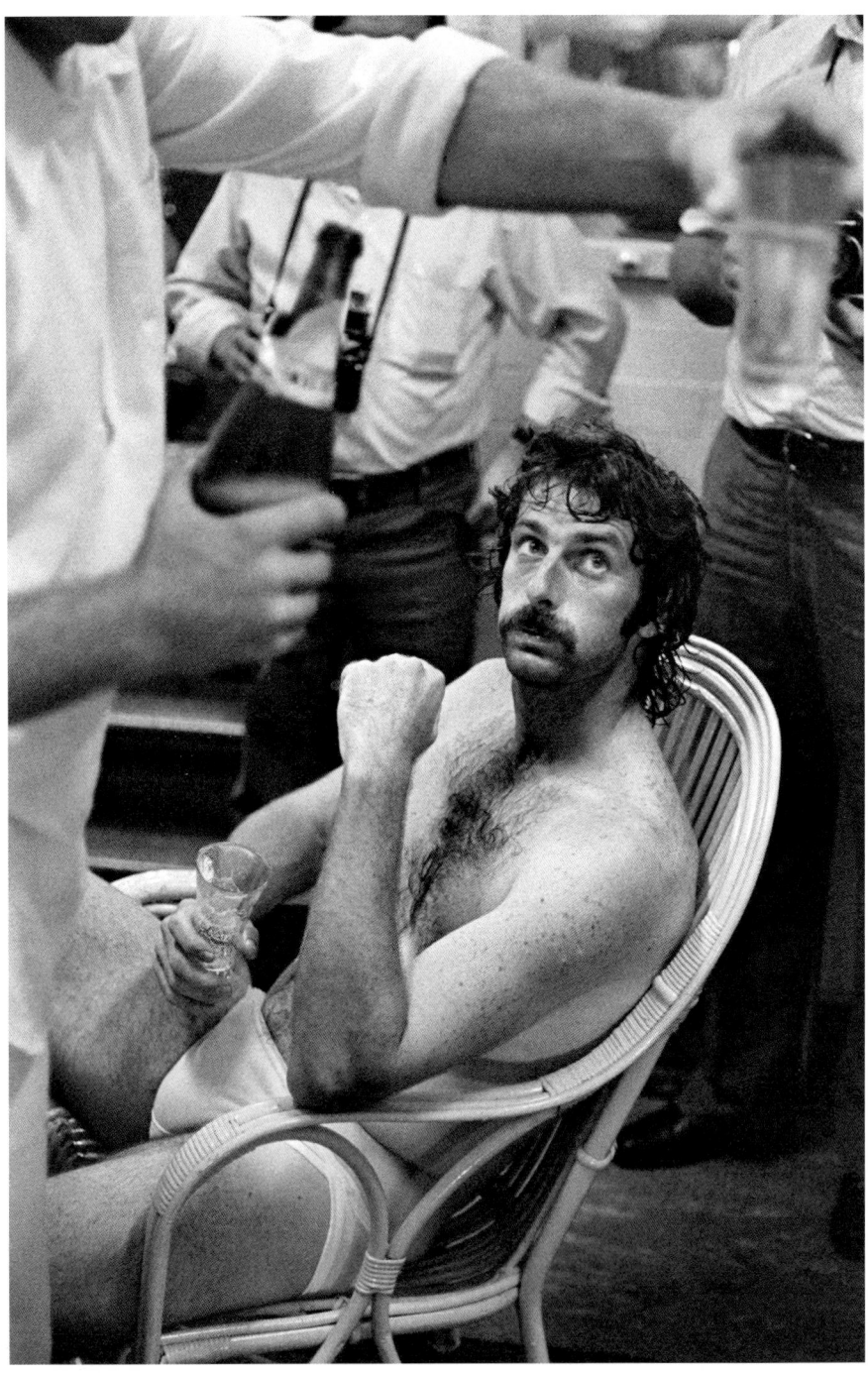

Dennis Lillee relaxes in the Sydney dressing room after helping his team regain the Ashes with two matches still to play. By the fourth Test, he was back to his brilliant best after a long recovery from a back injury.
(Patrick Eagar/Popperfoto via Getty Images)

Mike Denness on his way to a redemption century in the sixth Test in Melbourne, two matches after dropping himself in the midst of a torrid tour.
(Keystone/Hulton Archive/Getty Images)

New Zealand tailender Ewen Chatfield ducks into a Peter Lever
bouncer, resulting in England physiotherapist Bernard Thomas
having to administer the kiss of life on the field in Auckland.
(Press Association/Alamy)

When Dennis Lillee and Jeff Thomson arrived in England for the 1975
World Cup and subsequent Ashes series it turned out to be the last
time the duo would line up together against the old enemy.
(Patrick Eagar/Popperfoto via Getty Images)

5
FAST AND FURIOUS

Looking back at the England dressing room,
you could almost see the eyes opening.
Oh yes. it was a complete shock.
Ross Edwards

Strapping on his pads, Dennis Amiss reckoned Australia's total was 'rather more than they should have made but only just adequate'. Meanwhile, Mike Denness had refused the roller, worried it would bring moisture to the surface of a pitch that so far appeared to have fewer demons than its appearance had suggested, but whose true nature was likely to be revealed under interrogation by the host's faster bowlers.

Amiss was still quietly optimistic about what lay ahead, with good reason. Since establishing himself at the top of England's order during the winter of 1972-73, having converted to opener for Warwickshire only the previous summer, he had scored his first eight Test centuries. A pipe-smoker and bridge player, Amiss was the man expected to carry the weight of Geoffrey Boycott's absence, although he insisted before the series, 'I know I have to make runs, but there are five other batsmen with the same responsibility.'

'We had a really experienced and top player in Edrich,' he recalled. And – although injured for this particular game – 'David Lloyd was a good fighter, and off the pitch he was a really good character and really good for team spirit. And we thought Lillee had got a bad back and Thommo was all over the place.' It was not a lot to build Ashes hopes upon, but there really was no expectation from anyone about what Australia were about to unleash.

Opening partner Brian Luckhurst had taken exception to the doubts voiced by so-called experts about his vulnerability against the pacemen. He felt his achievements in 1970-71 had earned him a greater level of respect. 'They said I was weak against fast bowling before that tour but I worked out the extra pace and bounce of

Australian wickets and aggregated 455 runs in the series. While there's never any guarantee you will succeed on tour, surely if you have proved yourself once there is no reason why it can't be repeated?'

He dismissed the relevance of his failures against Lillee in 1972 because they had occurred in English conditions. 'He was a very fine performer although I doubt that Lillee or any other seam bowler who has done so well in England would have the same ability to make the ball move about in the air and off the pitch out there,' he said before departing for Australia. 'In any case, after two years Lillee has to prove himself again, the same as I have.'

The misplaced English expectation that Lillee would be a shadow of his former fearsome self was why Amiss, making his way to the middle, was surprised to see the length of the run-up being measured out at the Stanley Street End by Australia's opening bowler. 'How much further is he going back?' he asked Luckhurst, adding, 'You can take the first ball if you fancy it.'

Chris Old remembered, 'I was on the edge of the ground as the Aussies went out to field and the way Lillee and Thomson ran past us onto the field, there was something different here. Normally people had a leisurely stroll, but these two sprinted out. I thought, "This is going to be interesting."'

As for Lillee, this was 'like starting my career all over again'. The excruciating physical pain from his back, coupled with the mental anguish of not knowing the cause for so long; the weeks stuck in plaster and then a harness; the long months of rebuilding strength and relearning how to bowl; all were behind him. Any doubts he retained over whether his body would be up to the task ahead were secondary to the sheer joy of standing at the end of his run-up. the crowd chanting his name, a new ball in his hand, and an English batsman in the cross-hairs.

Amiss faced up to the first ball, a bouncer that he was able to duck under comfortably but which swung enough after passing overhead to force Rodney Marsh to scurry to his left. 'The first ball whistled past Dennis's nose,' said Old, 'and you could actually see him blink and think, "Right, it is going to be like this, is it?" It was a shock to everybody's system.'

What was also a new experience for many was the sight of Lillee's new action. Gone was the sprint towards the wicket with arms and legs going in all directions. His approach was controlled, balanced and more sustainable. The result, though, was still lethal. Later in the first over was a delivery so quick that all Amiss could do was get the edge of his bat to the ball, his head snapping in panic towards the four-man slip cordon in time to see it pass through on the way to the boundary. 'It was quite frightening at Brisbane,' admitted Amiss, who was left reconsidering the wisdom of trying to get on the front foot as he would at home. 'The ball just flew around.'

At the mid-point of Lillee's first over, Ian Chappell had an epiphany. 'Ian, you're an idiot,' he told himself. He had planned to give Max Walker the new ball, leaving Jeff Thomson to bowl downwind after Lillee's opening burst. 'I began to think how I might feel facing two genuine quick bowlers first up,' he said. He wouldn't have fancied it, so he signalled to Thomson to warm up. 'He didn't do a thing,' Chappell recalled. Instead of stretching and loosening up, Thomson simply waited until the end of the over, wandered up to the bowling crease and took the ball from his captain, who offered a 'good luck, mate'.

It was Luckhurst who needed fortune on his side. Amiss recalled him going 'as pale as ash' after narrowly evading the first ball from Thomson, who quickly signalled his intentions by discarding his sleeveless sweater and positioning two short legs. Chappell reckoned he was witnessing 'the fastest into-the-wind bowler I had ever seen'.

Watching from the dressing room, Alan Knott was given a jarring reminder of the first time the England team had witnessed Lillee in full flight in Perth four years earlier. 'Everybody soon knew Thomson would be a force to be reckoned with,' he said. The rebuilt Lillee, meanwhile, was 'obviously as great a threat as ever'.

It was after one particularly venomous Thomson delivery that Marsh uttered his oft-repeated line as the ball slammed into his gloves. 'Jeez, that hurt. But I love it.'[22] Luckhurst less so. He looked just as uncomfortable as he had in 1972.

Luckhurst walked down the pitch to meet his partner. 'What do you think?'

---

22 Before long Marsh was getting the team physiotherapist to cut strips of tape every morning and stick them on the wall next to his changing space. He would then put the strips across and between his fingers in an intricate pattern designed to protect his hands against bruising.

'Don't play at anything you don't have to,' was Amiss's reply. 'They'll tire in time. See them off.'

Bu when Thomson directed a ball at Luckhurst's hip, it was a sign of its speed that by the time the batsman had caught up with it all he could do was direct it down the leg side to wicketkeeper Marsh. 'With most bowlers Luckhurst would have been aiming a stroke through midwicket to that delivery,' Amiss observed. 'With Thomson's pace he found it impossible to take evasive action.'

The ball with which Thomson dismissed Amiss in his next over was equally unplayable, rising off a full length and leaving the opener to depart with a look of resignation after the ball looped off his glove to Terry Jenner in the gully. At least Amiss, whose only previous Test match against Australia had resulted in a pair, had been relieved to score a handful of runs this time. Criticism from some observers that he had failed to drop his gloves to avoid dismissal seemed harsh when delivered from the safety of the press box rather than from a potentially lethal distance of 20 yards. 'He frightened me,' wrote Keith Miller in the *Daily Express*, 'and I was sitting 200 yards away.'

Ashley Mallett would reflect upon Thomson 'sending the nation wild with excitement'. He said, 'His figures were almost inconsequential for it was the devastation of his attack which had the Poms in desperate survival mode, ducking and diving, and the nation's pulse racing.'

Ross Edwards recalled, 'Lillee bowled downwind and Thomson bowled upwind at twice the speed. Dennis didn't want to let himself go, but it was always going to happen. He was gonna bowl as fast as he could. We didn't know whether he would get back to his original speed because it was a completely different action. We knew he was going to be at least fast-medium but it was clear he was going to let himself off the shackles.'

Just as Australia had, England found themselves 10 for 2. But greater long-term damage had been done. Lillee was clearly no medium-pacer and Thomson's opening spell of the series – two wickets for four runs in five overs – had forged psychological scars in England's batting deep enough that they would remain visible for the next few weeks. 'Undoubtedly in Brisbane,' was Denness's answer when asked when he knew that England were going to be up against it. 'Except for Perth, all the wickets were unevenly grassed and quick and they had two great bowlers who were able to get the ball up from just short of a length. It was coming up somewhere through your chest and your head. It was very difficult to combat it. Lillee would bowl four or five bouncers at you per over and you would get a few just short of a good length.'

According to Frank Tyson, 'Within the space of half a dozen overs after the commencement of the tourists' innings it was brutally clear that, in Thomson and Lillee, Australia had acquired their speediest opening attack since the salad days of 1958-59.' He said it was 'a long time since I had seen batsman such as Amiss and Luckhurst approach their admittedly unenviable task with such physical distaste'.

An Australian-published review of the series and the Ashes contest in England that followed, *The 10 Test Matches*, would say of this day, 'England's batsmen had been subjected to a pace barrage, the likes of which had not been seen in this country since the post-war days of Lindwall and Miller. They had been visibly shaken.'

Into such an intimidating environment, Denness trod a tentative path. 'After seeing Thomson dismiss our openers quickly and cheaply I was concerned about his hostility,' he said, although he was not totally immersed in his own dark thoughts. 'I still sensed the reaction of the crowd as I walked to the wicket for my first Test innings in Australia. There are noisy crowds throughout the world, but the Australian crowds are generally very biased. They all tried to elevate their own bowlers the whole time. I sensed that the entire crowd were behind Thomson, which made me even more determined that he wasn't going to get me out.'

The England captain had just cut the relatively benign Walker for his first and only boundary when a horrible misjudgement did for him; given out lbw as he padded upto a big inswinger from the man whose wrong-foot delivery and windmilling arm action earned him the nickname 'Tangles'.[23] Denness returned to the dressing room to

---

23 Like South African Mike Procter, his contemporary, Walker did not actually deliver off the wrong foot. What gave that impression was that instead of his left (front) foot hitting the bowling crease and then the right arm being pulled through to deliver the ball a fraction of a second later, the placement of the foot and the bowling of the ball occurred simultaneously.

find that one of the short balls he'd been struck by had embedded his St Christopher medallion into his shoulder.

Keith Fletcher was next to perish after adopting a somewhat frenetic approach against Thomson, stepping away and slashing him unconvincingly for one boundary and sending an airy drive to the long-on rope. They were shots that spoke more of anxiety than confidence, a state of mind underscored when he played on trying to steer Lillee through the off side when the ball was too full for such an endeavour: 57 for 4.

John Edrich was the one left-hander in England's top order for this Test, and Marsh, who batted left-handed, knew exactly the challenge that Thomson offered him. Before the match, the wicketkeeper had told his captain that Thomson was 'unbelievably quick', but often bowled at him too wide of off stump. 'Then he got smart,' he reported. 'He started to bowl across my body, angling from a line of outside leg stump. Most deliveries came at my body and lifted off a very good length. Then came the death ball. The ball was heading straight for my head and it would have hit me between the eyes had it not struck the handle of my bat.'

Similarly, Edrich recalled that suddenly 'he got it straight'. He continued, 'He didn't know where it was going. You certainly didn't know where it was going, but he got this great bounce. He bowled a lot of rib balls; he didn't have to bowl bouncers. The most difficult ball to play is the one in front of your chest. Then, of course, you had Dennis at the other end.'

Lillee had been giving Edrich a torrid time, beating his outside edge and getting him to parry the ball dangerously close to Ian Redpath at short leg before the left-hander wafted one through the slips. It was the kind of sequence that had Robin Marlar noting in the *Sunday Times* that Edrich was 'tough and brave, if no longer as sure of the ball's line'. A force wide of gully gave evidence that there was still some sharpness in those 37-year-old eyes. The addition of only six runs in 80 minutes after tea, including a sequence of three consecutive maidens against Lillee, supported Marlar's observation of doggedness. Significantly, Edrich also took a blow on his left hand that would threaten his participation in the second innings. 'It was short pitched and straight and I tried to fend it off,' he explained. 'It hit my bottom hand and it cracked. It is a very difficult ball to play at that pace. You can't get out of the way if it is chest high.'

Of greater concern to Lillee, however, was the duel with Tony Greig that the dismissal of Fletcher had heralded. 'The storm signals are up,' Frank Tyson told viewers as Greig strode to the crease. 'Lillee has intimated to Greig what his intentions are; he did that when he was batting. And I think he is a man of his word.' Lillee waited impatiently while Greig dug out a leg-stump guard. The crowd's roars accompanied each step of the bowler's approach. An anti-climactic delivery passed down the leg side, followed by a harmlessly high bouncer. The nature of Greig's attack was quickly revealed. When Walker pitched short he sliced at the ball, confident that any edge would fly clear of danger, and anything full was met with a flamboyant drive. Such methods, Greig reasoned, would be even more effective against the greater speed of Lillee and Thomson, although he initially found himself struggling to locate the right line when the latter returned to the attack.

Having bowled eight previous overs at top speed, Thomson proved he was more than a mere intimidator by taking a little pace off the ball and finding movement in the air and off the wicket. One particular delivery was like a 90mph leg break, pitching on leg and middle and fizzing over the top of off stump. 'Far from being a tearaway,' noted Marlar, '[Thomson] offered away swing and movement off the pitch as no other had done, and with considerable control.'

Greig met Edrich with the suggestion that the left-hander should handle Thomson for a while. Edrich agreed on the surprising condition that Greig took responsibility when the leg-spin of Jenner was introduced. 'His request seemed comparable with asking a man if he would eat steak when he had been starved for a week,' recalled Greig, who duly took all 16 balls that Jenner bowled before England reached stumps at 114 for 4, with Edrich on 40 and his partner 34.

The third day enticed the highest attendance of the Test – 17,127 – away from other Sunday diversions. Most arrived in the hope of seeing Thomson inflict more pain upon the English batsmen. This time, Denness asked for the heaviest of rollers in the hope of flattening any remaining life out of a pitch that had lost most of its green hue.

Having stood tall, planted his feet and driven Thomson to the cover boundary in the second over of the day, Greig could have fallen in the third, guiding Lillee into the gully, where Jenner spilled the chance. The bowler scratched his boots in the ground in frustration, unaware that future Australian team selection would shore up that fielding position. The home team had to wait only until the next over to achieve their first success of the day, Edrich falling two short of his fifty when he guided Thomson to Ian Chappell at first slip. It was a timid ending after the doughty performance of the day before.

Greig flashed Lillee wide of gully for four and steered Thomson more sedately into the same region of the outfield for the single that give him his fifty, before the introduction of Jenner offered a couple of cheap boundaries each for Greig and Alan Knott. England were learning quickly that any respite from Australia's frontline bowlers had to be fully capitalised upon, which made it more disappointing when Knott and Peter Lever fell in quick succession to Walker, both offering straightforward catches to the cordon.

The scoreboard read 168 for 7 and the new ball loomed not far in the distance as Derek Underwood arrived in the middle. 'What's the story?' he asked.

'It's a straightforward question of fighting for your life,' Greig replied in the knowledge that Jenner was being replaced at the Stanley Street End by one of the fast men. 'Just get in there behind it and do your best.'

Underwood drove Walker for a boundary, splaying his feet in the manner that gave him his distinctive walk, before settling at the other end to await the approach of Lillee. Greig remembered, 'Underwood went to school in Kent where his coach taught him, "Keep your elbow up and you will be OK." He was a brave guy as well. He got a bouncer and the ball actually disappeared into here [indicating the area under his raised elbow]. He had his elbow up all right, and how it didn't kill him I will never know.'

Such incidents made Greig relish the challenge even more. He forced Lillee off the front foot to the green boundary mesh behind deep point and, once the new ball had been taken shortly after lunch, he leant back and lifted Thomson to third man for his 11th boundary. 'He started this thing,' Lever recalled, 'of putting the right hand underneath the handle with the blade of the bat facing straight up the air, pointing back towards the keeper. Thommo's the quickest

I have ever seen and when he let it go, Greigy would just retreat slightly and flick his bat underneath the ball.'

Lillee replaced Thomson and delivered his first ball a foot outside off stump. Without moving his feet, Greig hammered it for four through the covers. Still in the crease, he signalled four with a big sweep of his arm and, to be sure Lillee had not missed his gesture, walked down the wicket waggling his wrist as though listening to a marching band in his head.

'I will never forget that innings,' Underwood recalled. 'I batted a long time with Tony and he was driving Lillee on the up and then giving him the signal for four. I said to him, "For Christ's sake, don't do that. Think of the poor bugger who is batting at the other end." Lillee just charged in and bowled too short.' Ironically, Underwood's innings ended when, having driven and ducked bravely against the pacemen, he presented the first ball of a new spell by the medium-paced Doug Walters to Redpath in the covers.

Greig had goaded Lillee further by pretending to head a bouncer – the implication being that even his fiercest weapon could not scare him; much like Muhammad Ali had told George Foreman how little he was hurting him during the fight they'd all watched on TV a month earlier. And when he wandered casually down the wicket and started poking at the ground not far from Lillee's point of delivery, Amiss knew exactly what was going on out in the middle. 'Greigy had this little laugh that baited people,' he said. 'Dennis has come down breathing fire. "I am going to kill you, Greig. I am going to knock your head off" and Greigy is just giving it the "hee, hee, hee, hee", just baiting him.'

When Lillee presented a fuller length instead, Greig shuffled his back foot towards leg to give him the necessary shape to drive the ball to the off-side boundary. Greig waited on the next ball just enough so that his shot went squarer to the fence, completing a breathtaking century – the last 29 of which had arrived in a flurry of 22 deliveries.

'Greigy certainly had confidence,' said Knott. 'He was exceptionally talented. How anybody could be that tall and that athletic was ridiculous. When he batted he was flexible and quick. He had a terrific advantage against the quick bowlers because of his height. When they pitched it short to him it rose, and he just stood there.

When I first started playing, when they bowled short you ducked. But wickets changed and it became more awkward, and I had to change my game. That was Tony's skill. He stood up, and if they got it up outside the off stump, he hit it. And when he upset the fast bowlers they were not bowling the deliveries that would get you out. Although he was concentrating, he could be relaxed out there and enjoying it and loving every moment.'

Greig's manic methods had been fully vindicated. 'The Aussies went after me,' he said. 'I didn't take any backward steps and if you could find a way to stoke them up a little bit, getting them to bowl a bad length as opposed to what they would like to be doing, I was up for that.'

Geoff Arnold, a spectator for this game, explained, 'Greigy riled Lillee up so the batsmen coming in after him got the bloody backlash. He got away with it by giving it his all and, anyway, if you had stopped him doing that sort of thing he wouldn't have been half the cricketer he was.' On this occasion it was Willis upon whom Lillee exacted some revenge, doubling him up with a ball that thudded into his mid-section.

After a final pair of big hits against Walters, and a Lillee bouncer delivered with such venom that it flew over Marsh for four byes, Greig finally fell to Lillee when his firm-footed swipe went off a thin edge to the keeper. But there was no doubt that Greig's five-hour innings of 110 – including 81 scored between slip and extra cover – had won this first battle. 'It was one of the most magnificent hundreds I have ever seen,' said Amiss, while Willis placed it 'among the most audaciously brilliant innings I have ever seen'.

Greg Chappell called it 'the best innings I ever saw Greigy play', adding, 'He made the most of a pretty modest talent . . . He was a great competitor, not a great bowler or batsman but a most stubborn and willing fighter.'

Greig, who entered at 57, had scored the first century by a visiting number six from such a desperate situation. Writing in *The Sun*, Clive Taylor suggested the innings had made the South African 'a folk hero in his own time' and claimed, 'It will have the legend makers speaking of him in the same awesome company as Hammond, Compton and the golden men of the game.' Time might have proved that statement to have been a product of hyperbole, but even the more considered

EW Swanton said, 'I can't think of an innings calculated to do more for English morale since Ted Dexter took Hall and Griffith apart on that memorable day at Lord's.' *The Guardian*'s Henry Blofeld also referred to the former England captain's famous 70-run assault against the West Indies in 1963 and described Greig's effort as an innings that 'only he of contemporary batsmen could have played'. He added, with characteristic quirkiness, 'It was a strange innings in that it did not have a beginning, middle or end but was a jumbled collection of isolated incidents based upon consuming desire to come out on top.' As teammate Lever said, 'Tony had no thoughts about losing, although I think a lot of it was bravado. He wouldn't let anybody see he could possibly be on the losing end of a battle with some quick bowler.'

Willis was struck twice more by deliveries from Lillee before Walker's fourth success accounted for Hendrick and concluded England's innings at 265, a deficit of 44 that put England at a definite disadvantage but by no means out of the match. An hour into what would be an extended final session after an early tea between innings, the match appeared evenly poised with Australia 39 for 2.

The discomfort, and good fortune, of Wally Edwards had been clear when he turned his back on a short delivery by Willis and was struck on the right ear. England's fielders showed their concern as they inspected their opponent for injury and Willis responded with another bouncer that hit Edwards on the torso and fell dangerously close to his stumps. It was a reminder that Willis, if he could remain healthy, might offer England a vehicle for retaliation against the assault of Lillee and Thomson. It was hardly a surprise when the discomfited left-hander failed to get into line to a ball moving across his body and edged to Knott.

Ian Chappell could only divert a forward prod to a diving Fletcher at slip in the first over of a spell in which Underwood turned the ball so much that Blofeld suggested in his close-of-play report that he 'could still be the match-winner'. Redpath played out four of the five maidens that Underwood bowled in his seven overs and he and Greg Chappell went 25 minutes without a run. By the time stumps were drawn their partnership had accrued only 12 runs in 58 minutes. The body language of the imposing Greig at silly point and Luckhurst at short leg suggested a team that felt they had the upper hand, while the threat of Underwood made it a surprise that Denness had not called upon Greig's off-spin.

Monday's rest day brought media speculation that Brisbane might be seeing more of Greig the following summer, with Queensland keen to capitalise on England's blank calendar by securing his services. It also returned England's bowlers to The Gabba refreshed, Willis needing only 15 minutes to cut one back through Redpath's normally reliable defence. With Australia's lead only just into three figures and their top three dismissed, Chappell and Ross Edwards made consolidation the priority for the morning, taking the score to 125 at lunch as the temperature rose to 90 degrees. Edwards did not hit his first boundary until facing his 80th delivery in the over before the interval.

His timing sometimes awry, Chappell was the first to reach his fifty, but Edwards was not far behind after dispatching two Greig long hops through square leg. Greig became an easy target as Chappell injected some urgency into the innings before playing around Underwood and being bowled for 71 just prior to the new ball, ending the 114-run partnership. On a potentially helpful wicket, Greig's performance with the ball, described by Christopher Martin-Jenkins as 'a policy of bowl and hope', was concerning for England's prospects in the series. Even Swanton, Greig's great champion, was forced to observe that he had bowled 'without the control that must always be the off-spinner's prerequisite'.

At 190 for 5, after Edwards edged Willis, England might still have been in the game if they could have broken, or even contained, the new partnership of Walters and Marsh. Instead they conceded 98 at more than a run a minute. Walters accelerated to 32 not out at tea – including 20 off two Willis overs – and Marsh launched into Underwood after the break. He compensated for failing by one bounce to swing a six over midwicket by making no doubt with the next ball. Some more thumps down the ground by the Aussie wicketkeeper allowed Ian Chappell to declare just before quarter past five at 288 for 5, a lead of 332.

Perhaps there was some hope for England's survival in the bouncer that Lever had bowled towards the troublesome Stanley Street End just before the closure. It had sat up so benignly that Walters had the time to pull it through mid-on. And then a few minutes were taken out of the fourth innings when the roller broke down and the groundsmen were able only to administer four minutes of attention, causing the umpires to delay the restart by recalling them to complete the required seven-minute roll.

Amiss eventually took guard at 5.30pm and was relieved to be gifted four runs from Lillee's gentle full toss on leg stump; like the guest of honour being given a first run in a benefit game. It was a rather different story against Thomson, bowling from the Stanley Street End in fading light. 'I faced the most frightening fast bowling I have ever seen,' declared Amiss, who twice had to jerk back as balls passed in front of his eyes before another beat the involuntary stab of his bat. That caused the umpires to meet and Robin Bailhache to approach Thomson.

'When Thommo was bowling from my end, Tom and I were looking at each other and making signals,' the umpire explained. 'We weren't happy with the light so when Thommo let go a bouncer. I said to him, "Look, Thommo, if you want to stay out here and have the chance of taking wickets you had better not bowl any more of those."'

Thomson indicated that his skipper should be the one hearing this. Chappell's agitated run from slip betrayed his annoyance at the intervention and he was even more angry when told what had been said. 'They're not bouncers, Robin,' Chappell pleaded. 'They're just short of a length.' He recalled later, 'He virtually told us to keep the ball up to the batsman. It was pointless being out there.'

Greg Chappell described Thomson's most dangerous delivery as being one that 'just attacked your throat'. He said, 'It would come straight up like a snake out of the grass at your feet or off a good length. It would pitch and cut back in, following your face as you withdrew. So it was very hard to duck but it wasn't the sort of length you'd be looking to hook.'

Amiss, despite the threat to his safety, agreed with his opponents' assessment. 'I did not blame Thomson,' he said. 'He was not bowling deliberately short of a length, merely making the most of his own pace and the uneven pitch.' However, when the next ball passed through to Marsh to end the second over of the innings, the look Amiss sent in the umpire's direction made clear his thoughts about continuing. And when he received the formal offer of an early finish he loosened his gloves and headed towards the pavilion.

The MCC tour hierarchy had more to do on the evening following the fourth day's play than get their heads straight for the next day's fight for survival. Edrich's injured hand and the uncertainty about how long David Lloyd would remain sidelined by his broken finger meant that Alec Bedser had been on the telephone to Lord's. The 16-man restriction on the original party had always threatened to leave them susceptible to injuries, particularly among the batsmen, and Bedser asked the permission of TCCB cricket committee chairman Doug Insole to add another player to the squad. Such a request from the chairman of selectors was never likely to be refused, but who would that man be?

Inevitably, half a century of recollections offers a somewhat varied narrative, but what is clear is that it boiled down to a choice between former England captain Colin Cowdrey, a 41-year-old veteran of four previous MCC tours of Australia who had not played Test cricket since 1971, and Basil D'Oliveira, a 43-year-old who had last played for England in the 1972 Ashes.

Denness, who remembered that discussions about a potential replacement had begun among the selection committee several days earlier, said, 'Right from the start the player I had in mind was Colin Cowdrey. We were looking for somebody who was a good player of quick bowling, who could open if necessary, who had Test match experience, and who was willing and keen enough to come out and work hard for us. These qualifications completely ruled out any youngsters.'

The senior players, who you could argue would have been happier to see a stop-gap old stager recruited ahead of a younger player who might offer a long-term threat to someone's place, were asked for their opinion. According to Amiss, 'They talked to us and then we told Greigy, who was one of the tour selectors, who we wanted and he spoke to the management on our behalf. I think the Kent contingent knew that Kipper [Cowdrey] wasn't playing quite as well as he had been earlier in his career, and we felt the best person would be Basil D'Oliveira because he took the fast bowlers on. He was a good hooker and puller. I don't know what happened, but we didn't get our way.'

According to vice-captain Edrich, 'There weren't many options. There was David Steele, but I couldn't see him playing forward out there and by that time we were a little bit shell-shocked. You didn't expect what happened. We hadn't seen two fast bowlers like that before. We talked about one or two players and then Mike said, "Well, I think we should go for Colin." We decided he had the class and he was a great player of fast bowling, had plenty of time.'

Fred Titmus recalled, 'I was happy with the decision. After all, Colin was almost as old as me.' Meanwhile, some players were left to await the outcome of conversations from which they were excluded. 'I was only a junior member of the whole shebang,' said Lloyd, 'so I wouldn't have had a call on that. But Mike Denness was captain and when they needed a first replacement player they got Brian Luckhurst and when they needed another replacement player they got Colin Cowdrey. It was all Kent.'

Denness, who acknowledged that the lack of realistic candidates was 'a sad reflection of the state of English cricket' explained, 'Cowdrey's name came up because he had gone through Wes Hall and Charlie Griffith [West Indies], Peter Heine and Neil Adcock [South Africa], Ray Lindwall and Keith Miller [Australia]. He had played all of them.'

Once again, the claims of the likes of Barry Wood, John Jameson and Frank Hayes had been disregarded. Wood, who had begun his on-off Test career with a second-innings 90 in his only match of the 1972 series against Australia and had now been overlooked for the tour for a third time, remembered, 'I did think I had a chance of going and I think I was equipped to go.' Of his reputation for being able to handle fast bowling, he added, 'People reckoned it was my thing, although I can't say I loved it. I don't think anyone relishes it when the ball is flying around your head all the time. I do remember being disappointed when they took Cowdrey out instead of me. He was a great player but towards the end of his career.'

Telling reporters only that Lord's had approved the addition of a reinforcement, allowing them to speculate about the identity, Denness headed for the telephone. Cowdrey was at home in the Surrey village of Limpsfield, preparing for a typical winter's morning, when the phone rang and a familiar voice greeted him.

'I don't know if you have been watching what's been happening out here?' Denness began, receiving an answer in the affirmative. 'I have a request. Would you like to come out, because we have a few injuries and we need somebody to bat up the order? How would you feel about it?'

'I would love to,' Cowdrey replied, as nonchalantly as if accepting an invitation to a dinner party.

Telling Cowdrey to expect Lord's to be in touch with details, Denness hung up, thinking, 'If you were out here, you'd know no one is loving it.'

Perfect weather greeted the final day, with Benaud telling viewers that there was a 'tinge of green' in the wicket. Woodcock was more concerned about the whiff of cordite in the air. 'The day began to the echo of some unedifying remarks made by Lillee on television,' he wrote. 'The idea of the bouncer, as he uses it, is to hit the batsman "somewhere between the rib cage and the stomach". That is what he said and he had written in previously in a book. Thomson is already on record as saying that he enjoys felling a batsman with a bouncer. This is the talk of the underworld, not of Test cricketers.'

Amiss sliced a drive between second slip and gully for the day's first boundary, although the ball might have gone to Redpath had he not just been moved to short leg. The first dismissal arrived quickly, when Luckhurst's limp prod at a Lillee outswinger went to Ian Chappell. The muted Australian celebrations suggested there had been no great expectation of much else for a batsman whose selection for the tour was looking ever more questionable. Although intended as a one-liner, there was an underlying truth when Luckhurst, in later years, recalled that conversation with Geoffrey Boycott by saying, 'I soon began to say to myself, "Why aren't you here, Geoffrey, because this should be your job, not mine?"'

The Kent man, a nervy character who rarely ate on a day when he was expecting to bat, was honest enough to call the tour 'a trip too far for me', admitting, 'By the time it ended I don't think in all seriousness I should have been there. Sure, replacing Boycott with myself was a like-for-like selection in the eyes of the management, but I had not really been in the front of the England selectors' minds since the summer of 1972. The England team needed Boycott, to be honest, but now needed a pair of eyes – and reflexes – that were younger than mine.'

Even older than Luckhurst, Edrich managed to squirt four off the edge against Thomson, but when play halted for drinks he left the field for another pain-killing injection in his hand. So hampered was he that when Thomson switched ends Chappell felt able to set a field that left the area between cover and the more forward of two short legs unguarded. All fielders were rendered superfluous, however, when Thomson cut one back to beat Edrich's late stab and clip his off stump. Amiss, who 'felt the game could be saved' at the start of play, fought his way to 24 before he fended another sharp lifter via his bat handle to Walters at third slip, his fourth dismissal to Thomson in four innings on tour. Denness was greeted by a delivery that smacked into his forearm. 'We knew what was going to happen,' he said. 'And if you looked at the field placings they had, they were never going to pitch the ball up to the stumps. They were going to hit you if they could. It was just a matter of: could you get yourself out of the way?'

Denness veered between the comfort of driving and cutting against the lesser pace of Walker to the confusion of an inside edge that dropped perilously close to the stumps when facing Thomson. The faster man also left Fletcher gazing down the track in disbelief after the ball reared past his outside edge and was still on the up when taken by Marsh.

England made it to lunch at 80 for 3, hope of survival not yet fully extinguished. But in fewer than 25 minutes of the afternoon an Australian victory had become just a matter of time. Denness's desire to keep playing his shots saw him dismissed by a diving Walters in the slip cordon after he waved at Thomson, and Fletcher made what, in the circumstances, was the unforgiveable error of gifting Jenner his wicket via second slip when he pushed at a delivery wide enough to be of no danger. 'They were both gone in a flash of madness,' was how the *Daily Mirror*'s Peter Laker described the sudden double dismissal.

'There was no Churchillian resolution in their defence,' Tyson observed. He suggested that Denness, Luckhurst and Fletcher could not have been selected as the 'backbone' of the English order because 'to qualify for such a role it was imperative to show some rigidity of the spine'. He continued, 'It was not a rewarding experience to step into line with the express deliveries of Thomson and Lillee on the up-and-down wicket. It was more of an unpleasant duty, and some English batsmen were found to be derelict in that duty. The Brisbane Test established a psychological superiority for [Australia's] fast bowlers over the English batting.'

Thomson now had his sights on Greig and the words of the Chappells in his ears. Ian Chappell remembered, 'Greigy really got under Dennis's skin in the first innings, which wasn't a very difficult thing to do. Before Greigy came out to bat in the second innings I remember saying to the team, with Dennis and Jeff in mind, "Is there any danger we can try and actually knock his stumps over instead of trying to knock his fucking block off?"'

Brother Greg had already pointed out the lightweight, rubber-soled footwear that their opponent wore for batting and now he reminded Thomson. 'Hit him in the sandshoes; that'll slow his footwork down.'

It was a perfectly executed plan. Greig, forced by his height to stand with his bat well above ground level, almost fell over as Thomson's yorker homed in on his leg stump. The delight among the fielders and the roar of the crowd as the wicket broke was in marked contrast to the nonchalance with which some of the earlier dismissals had been received.

Three wickets for two runs had left England 94 for 6 and Lever could soon have been the seventh man out as, in quick succession, he played and missed, survived an lbw appeal and saw the ball fall safe after he left his bat flailing in the air when ducking a bouncer. All before the end of that same Thomson over. Lever happily swished Jenner for a couple of boundaries before being tested by more short stuff by Lillee, evading one bouncer and then falling to short leg.

The pattern continued, Knott and Underwood fortifying their tallies against Jenner before facing the high-tempo music coming from the Vulture Street End, where Chappell rotated Lillee and Thomson in short, brutal bursts. Underwood recoiled in pain and threw down his glove after being hit on the right hand by Thomson immediately after tea but enjoyed some revenge by stepping away towards leg and swiping three fours in the same over. His score had reached 30, the best of England's innings, and the partnership with Knott was worth 47 when he tried to hoist Jenner over the leg side and top-edged an easy chance to Walker at mid-on. Underwood had not only scored the second-most runs of any England player in the match but was the one man who neither Thomson nor Lillee managed to dislodge.

The end was administered quickly by Thomson, who beat Knott with a full ball that clipped the inside of his bat on the way to off stump and then shot one through Hendrick's inadequate defence, having just struck him on the hand. England were all out for 166, halfway to their target, with 20 minutes plus the final hour remaining. Australia's 166-run victory was only their third in 17 home Ashes Test matches since 1959. Denness was the first England player to emerge at the boundary fence to congratulate Thomson, prompting Adrian McGregor to ponder in *The Bulletin*, 'Perhaps in shaking Thomson's hand he was wondering what demonic powers this Australian possesses in his right arm that are not included in his own battery of 6ft-plus fast bowlers.'

Thomson finished with second-innings figures of 6 for 46, the majority of dismissals achieved via full deliveries against batsmen bracing themselves for balls homing in on their throats. Woodcock observed, 'Within a fortnight he became a face, then a threat and finally a destroyer,' while McGregor reckoned, 'He has assumed the proportions that Lillee, Snow, Tyson and Hall reached in past years.'

The bowler's own succinct summary of his match-turning performance was, 'I managed to bowl a few quick ones.'

No one had been happier with Thomson's heroics than new-ball partner Lillee, who had only made up his mind the night before the match to attempt to bowl as fast as his back would allow. 'I did bowl fairly fast in patches, but I didn't feel all that comfortable,' he would write. 'I thought I bowled fairly well, though mainly because Jeff Thomson was really sending them down at the other end. This was a blessing really because if Thommo had struggled I'm sure I'd have been battling too.'

There were more words still to be spoken about the state of the pitch, of which Denness was critical without attempting to offer an excuse for defeat. Had he done so he would have had little support from the likes of Swanton, who observed that 'too many imprudent strokes were offered by seasoned cricketers'. Wearing the iconic symbol of 1970s leisurewear cool – an adidas T-shirt, this one in light blue – Chappell told the TV cameras, 'I thought it was a pretty good cricket wicket … there was just the odd one keeping low and the odd one taking off from a good length. It probably had a lot to do with the pace of the bloke who was bowling, Thomson. He bowled tremendously quickly and he seemed to be able get the ball up off a good length.'

In summing up the match for his viewers, Benaud offered his thoughts on the wicket. 'This one here I thought was a little bit untrustworthy,' he said. 'In the end, not quite up to Test match standard. At one end the ball came at varying heights and I don't believe any Test match batsman should be faced with the problem of batting against bowlers of that pace and not being quite sure at what height the ball will come.'

Blofeld would give *Guardian* readers his view that 'it was the manner of losing which was so depressing', while Swanton suggested that 'only Amiss got a ball against which there was scarcely a defence'.

It was true that no England batsmen had suffered more at the hands of Thomson and the pitch than Amiss, who was now suffering an injury on top of the insult of twice falling to sharply rising balls he could not avoid. 'I got hit on the end of the thumb two balls running, he explained. 'One from Thommo that lobbed over gully's head, which was the last ball of the over, and the next ball Dennis hit me on the thumb again.' An X-ray would reveal a break and put his right hand into a cast.

For now, though, nothing was said to the media, who had also yet to be informed of the decision to add Cowdrey to the touring party. Benaud had signed off his report by suggesting that England should go for an experienced player with knowledge of Australian conditions rather than a younger player such as Hayes, and when he suggested the former England captain it sounded as though he had been tipped off.

Other reporters were kept waiting until post-game formalities had been concluded before being told that Cowdrey would be flying to Perth to join the tour. 'We considered everyone and we felt that experience was necessary,' Bedser explained. 'The fact that Cowdrey had been here before was a major consideration. It is a gamble, but we are not thinking of the future, we are thinking of now.'

The man who would be 42 on Christmas Eve and whose 7,700 Test match runs ranked behind only Garry Sobers was not expected to see first-class action until after the second Test, but his summons was one of the defining storylines of the series.

Perhaps it also acted as a comfort blanket for the England selectors. Writing to the author and scorer Irving Rosenwater four days after the match in Brisbane, Brian Taylor concluded, 'The news from Australia is not bad even allowing for the unfortunate outcome of the first Test.' In hindsight, he was not far wrong. Things were about to get a lot worse.

6
FLIGHT OF FANCY

*At Brisbane both Thomson and Lillee had a little bit
to bowl to and they had a good match. Let's hope
it's the last good match they have in the series.*
Colin Cowdrey on Australian TV

Before Colin Cowdrey faced a ball from Jeff Thomson or Dennis Lillee, he had a barrage of questions to negotiate from reporters who'd beaten a path to his door upon hearing of his call-up to the MCC party. Here was a feel-good story of sporting heroism to lighten news bulletins focusing on the hunt for those responsible for a spate of IRA-suspected bombings in Britain, most notably one in a Guildford pub eight weeks earlier, and a national bread shortage caused by striking bakery workers.

'Obviously I am delighted to be going,' Cowdrey told the assembled media, who had him pose for various photographs outside his home. 'It's a challenge to which I'm looking forward. Since the end of the season I have kept fairly fit playing squash and I hope to have a net tomorrow.'

He would recall later, 'I was as fit as I have ever been, batting and catching with a sharpness that surprised myself.' He had been felled during the previous season by a bouncer from Hampshire's West Indies paceman Andy Roberts on an uneven surface at Basingstoke but had gone on to top 1,000 first-class runs and score five centuries, which was enough for speculation that he could be a candidate for a place on tour. 'I felt in good enough form to justify that, and I have to admit I was a disappointed man not to be selected in the original party.'

He had marked the end of the English season by announcing his intention to return for a 26th year with Kent and promising, 'I shall set out to be the best batsman in England.' Yet he was realistic enough to acknowledge that the best days of his career were a distant memory. 'Some people have advised me I should go out at the top,' he said. 'That's a proud and arrogant attitude to adopt. I would have retired 15 years ago if I had given up at my peak.'

According to youngest son Jeremy there was no question of him having to ask for his family's blessing to accept his mission, even though Cowdrey said he 'did discuss it' with his wife, Penny. 'He lived for cricket and had to answer the call,' Jeremy told author Ian Brayshaw. 'And he wasn't remotely worried that he'd get his head knocked off, whereas the rest of us were.'

Penny – given the obligatory 'pretty blonde' description by most newspapers – was also sought out for her views, revealing that she'd thought the days of waving her husband off on tour were behind her. 'Whenever he used to go away on a winter tour we always used to say the same thing as we kissed goodbye. "This really will be the last time, darling." Three years ago I was sure it really was, but I was wrong.'

Her biggest concern, she said, was that 17-year-old son Christopher had already claimed all of his dad's cricket socks to take with him on a trip to South Africa. She added, 'My first thought was to celebrate Christmas before Colin leaves, but we'll save all our presents until he comes home in February.' And with 1974 still being the relative stone age of long-distance communication, she was resigning herself to not even hearing from her husband on Christmas Day because 'the lines will all be booked now'.

Much like a condemned man, Cowdrey was given a few days to get his affairs in order. He sat through a board meeting of the Whitbread Fremlin brewery and, the night before departure, fulfilled an obligation to attend Limpsfield Cricket Club's dinner. Throughout his speech, he ducked and swayed, telling his audience to roars of laughter, 'Sorry, but I'm just getting in the mood.' As well as being an illustration of Cowdrey's gift for self-deprecation, it also demonstrated how quickly – two innings, to be precise – the new reality of what the English batsmen faced in Australia had been established in the national consciousness.

Awaiting Cowdrey in Australia would be a division of opinion, largely along lines of nationality, over the wisdom of his summons from the English winter. Former opponent Keith Stackpole, calling it an 'amazing' selection, asked sardonically if Alec Bedser would be called into action should one of England's fast bowlers be injured.

Greg Chappell saw the invitation to Cowdrey as 'an act that betrayed desperation, if not outright panic' and thought it was 'crazy for him to accept'.

Among the English writers on tour, John Arlott pointed out that the whole situation had been created by the selectors' mistaken assumption that the tourists would not be confronted by genuine pace. It had left Edrich and Luckhurst – previously successful in Australia but both undone by Lillee in 1972 – in the firing line, alongside men such as Denness and Fletcher who were unproven against the quickest bowlers. 'The replacement batsman had to be one of unquestionable capacity against genuinely fast bowling,' he wrote, concluding that Cowdrey 'still possesses the natural gifts to justify himself on this level'.

Frank Tyson, a man who could be said to have a foot in both camps and who was a teammate on Cowdrey's first tour 20 years earlier, observed, 'The most important ingredient Cowdrey will bring to the English tourists is guts and determination. There is no doubting that Cowdrey possesses physical courage in proportion to his girth.'

But Ian Chappell saw it as a typically backward-looking English move. 'If there was any trouble they'd always go for an experienced player,' he noted correctly. 'At that time Australia would be more likely to go looking for a good young player.'

Bob Willis broke national lines in later years by supporting Chappell's point, while EW Swanton, who had been on every Ashes tour since the Second World War, highlighted 'a basic difference in attitude – perhaps no more significant than that of an old country and a younger one'. He pointed out, 'The Aussies almost never bring a man back. They quickly get bored with the old hand, eagerly hail the new boy.'

Cowdrey left England with the debate simmering and MCC engaged in their first-class match against Western Australia at the WACA ground. He acknowledged that his recall was 'as dramatic as any in the history of the game' but was expecting a friendly welcome from his new teammates. 'It is warming to know that the players themselves sat down around their hotel room one evening and chose the man to help them out,' he would write. 'It was a superb compliment. At least that is how I felt it.'

Cowdrey had been identified as the man for the job as early as age 17, when picked for his Kent debut. Runs for his county and Oxford University earned him a surprise selection for his first Ashes tour in 1954-55, making his Test debut in the first contest of the series. Over the next 16 years he became an elegant presence in the England middle order, with bravery to match his strokeplay, even taking the field with one arm in plaster to save the Test match against the West Indies at Lord's in 1963. Such a symbol of sportsmanship and fair play would he become that in 2001, the year after his death, the MCC renamed its annual invitational address around the 'spirit of cricket' as the Cowdrey Lecture.

Despite his achievements and stature, Cowdrey had been an intermittent captain of England. His last stint, which began in the West Indies in 1967-68, lasted until he ruptured an Achilles tendon early in the summer of 1969. It meant that, even at his advanced cricketing age, Cowdrey felt he had unfinished business.

He had been denied the opportunity to lead the team on his fifth Ashes tour – vice-captain for the fourth time after Ray Illingworth kept the job that Cowdrey's injury bestowed upon him – and he described the trip as 'something of an anti-climax'. He averaged 20.5 in four innings and played in only three Tests, watching the decisive matches from the boundary. It was the first time he'd finished a series in Australia without a Test century. 'I tried too hard,' he concluded. 'I just could not get going with the bat.' He took little joy in being part of a victorious Ashes tour for the second time. He was honest enough to admit, 'It was most disappointing.'

Despite championing his recall, Bedser's summation of Cowdrey's career revealed some reservations about whether he had truly achieved everything of which he was capable. He said there were 'times I felt he ought to be the greatest batsman in the world', but they were balanced by days when 'he could be comparatively easy to contain'. Even by the end of his career, Bedser remained unsure how to judge him. 'One always had the feeling that he could have been better had he been a bit tougher, less modest, or found it less easy in his days at Tonbridge as a cricket prodigy.' Perhaps a desire to offer Cowdrey one final chance to determine his legacy played a part in Bedser's preference for him over a younger English batsman.

Cowdrey's unexpected journey to the other side of the world offered him plenty of time to ponder redemption for his failures of four years earlier, especially when engine trouble forced a day's delay in Bombay. He arrived in Perth on the Monday prior to the beginning of the Test match on Friday and headed to bed with the news that he might well be playing.

Before long he was contacting John Woodcock, who was staying at the Weld Club in Perth. The man from *The Times* had travelled the globe with Cowdrey and it was he who took a late-night call asking if he fancied a game of snooker because the jet-lagged new arrival couldn't sleep. They were joined by Henry Blofeld. Woodcock warned Cowdrey that, having only seen brief highlights of the first Test, he could not possibly fully appreciate what he had let himself in for. Not the kind of message likely to aid restful sleep. Charmingly, Woodcock observed, 'If he plays it will be as though he dreamt of batting against Australia at Perth and woke up to find that he was.'

Cowdrey's possible inclusion in the Test team stemmed partly from the events of Sunday, the second day of the Western Australia match. It began with Keith Fletcher facing assistant manager AC Smith in the nets, as recalled by Dennis Amiss. 'AC loved bowling with a new ball and he got the Kookaburra and wanted to show pace and bounce. He was bowling off about 18 yards.' Fletcher ended up being struck on the elbow, suffering minor nerve damage that forced him to forego his innings later in the day. His place at number four was taken by Tony Greig, who – seven days after his Test century in Brisbane – proved his liking for Aussie Sundays by launching into a career-best 167. While Fletcher missed out, David Lloyd returned to action for the first time since his broken finger. He was clearly hampered during his innings of 42 by a ricked neck, a legacy of a previous car accident and something that would be a burden to him throughout the rest of his tour and his career.

The MCC declared with a first-innings lead of 49 and set about trying to achieve a third successive victory over state opposition over the final two days. It was not to be. After the home team, who would be that season's Sheffield Shield winners, piled up 346 for 5, MCC fell woefully short of their target. They were bowled out for 177 in the face of a seven-wicket haul for Bob Paulsen, generally reckoned to be only the fourth-best leg-spinner in Australia.

It was what was happening in and around the treatment room, though, that led the *Daily Mirror*'s Peter Laker – never shy of offering the typical tabloid take on events – to state that 'a tour plagued by injury problems and technical errors reached the point of absurdity'. What angered the writer was that Bedser had announced during the morning that John Edrich was ruled out of the second Test because X-rays had belatedly revealed a hairline fracture in his right hand, only for Mike Denness to say at the end of the day, 'I have not ruled out Edrich by any means. If he can hold a bat on Friday morning then he is in.' Fletcher, meanwhile, had missed another innings to protect the elbow injury caused by friendly fire.

While MCC's batting was crumbling from 126 for 2 – after another Greig half-century and an innings of 45 by Denness that looked better on paper than it did to the eye – focus inevitably intensified on the pale, portly figure in the nets.

Privately, Cowdrey's opinion was, 'One needs three weeks to acclimatise to Australian conditions. It was infuriating to have to try to do this in three days.' Publicly, he smiled and insisted, 'I'm not afraid of the situation. I've got to work to the one end of getting stuck in out there on Friday.' Explaining that he had slept well, he was disappointed with his first half-hour net, which he had begun at 9.30 a.m., admitting that the bright light had the ball arriving earlier than in England. His second knock, in the cooler late afternoon, 'went better than expected'. The man who had held 117 Test catches, mostly at slip, also had some fielding practice, but took the precaution of wearing batting gloves to protect his hands.

MCC had one final duty before the Test match, squeezing in a match in Geraldton against a Western Australia Country XI. Selection was easy at least, with the unprepared Cowdrey the only fit player not to travel. Yet, as if to prove the futility of such an engagement, fate conspired to strike down Mike Hendrick with a throat infection during the short flight and he spent the day in hospital having tests. An Australian Colts bowler, Peter Bronsdon, was recruited to play for MCC in the manner of a Sunday village side turning up a man short and persuading the son of an opposition player to field at fine leg and bat number eleven.

The one positive outcome was Luckhurst's 76, one more than he had scored in his last eight innings. It offered no indication, of course, of whether he would be able to force himself into line against Lillee and Thomson and rid himself of the habit of being caught in the slips. The game ended in a draw with the home team nine wickets down, while Bronsdon had a wicket in his three overs to tell his grandchildren about.

Again, the greater interest focused on Cowdrey, who ventured out at 1 p.m. in order to experience the height of the sun before showering and returning for a second net four hours later. Bowling at him were former Australian Test quickie Graham McKenzie and ex-England spinner Tony Lock, who was now living in Australia. McKenzie kept the ball pitched up to begin with before testing Cowdrey's reflexes with some short stuff. 'I had to settle for being hit the odd time in the net,' Cowdrey remembered. 'It is all part of the sharpening up process.'

Lock, a former Test teammate, saw enough to hope that England could avoid selecting Cowdrey for immediate action, believing 'it could kill him for the rest of the series'. His verdict on what he had witnessed was, 'I suppose he did pretty well today, but his bat wasn't always as straight as I remember.'

Woodcock observed, 'Whether or not he makes runs, Cowdrey's presence is reassuring,' adding, 'Simply by watching Cowdrey, MCC's other batsmen should be able to learn something about getting into line.'

Having been on his first Ashes tour in 1950-51, Woodcock had been regularly voicing his concern about the amount of short-pitched bowling he was now seeing, describing the first Test as 'a bad start to the rubber' and expressing a hope that things would improve in the second. 'For the match to be as enjoyable as it should be to watch, there will need to be much less short-pitch bowling than in Brisbane,' he said. 'Willis and Lever have a lot to answer for in that respect. It was they who started it before Thomson made their efforts look like child's play.'

Yet, bolstered by Cowdrey, he concluded that 'it is not unreasonable to hope that [England] will get enough runs to avoid defeat', although his conviction was not given much support by the first-class figures of the leading batsmen. Luckhurst had scored six runs in his last four innings; Lloyd had made one fifty in his last 19 first-class innings; and Denness had now played 50 innings on

MCC tours without ever scoring a century. It was numbers like that that prompted Blofeld to warn, 'It needs no great stretch of the imagination to see England losing three wickets for 10 runs at the start of their innings.'

Jeff Thomson, meanwhile, had continued to fire the imagination in the days between Test matches. Before arriving in Perth he was pictured with leather-clad singer Suzi Quatro, who squeezed his right bicep while gazing admiringly at his smiling face. Thomson, now a rock star in his own right, was sought out for his opinion on England's latest recruit. 'Cowdrey is going to cop it as quick as anyone,' he offered, warning that he would be 'around their ears again' at the WACA.

The English press happily perpetuated the image of Thomson the tearaway, to the extent that when the bowler encountered the immaculate EW Swanton at a function he challenged him with, 'You're one of those Pommy bastards who've been writing all that shit about me.'

Bob Willis, however, had already witnessed enough to see through Thomson's façade. Even though the Aussie fans had latched onto his 'vindictive streak', Willis argued, 'I never thought he bowled with the intention of maiming. I liked the guy and even came to find his rough anti-Pom manner engaging.'

Besides, Willis was more concerned with his own fitness than his opponent's 'false image'. MCC's solitary day of dedicated preparation for the Test, unencumbered by a match, might not have offered much hope of fixing the faults of the batsmen, but it did provide Willis's knees and Lever's back a chance to be tested by bowling off shortened run-ups against Cowdrey and Fletcher. In the end, Willis was passed fit, with Chris Old and Geoff Arnold replacing Lever and Hendrick from the Brisbane line-up. Titmus was preferred to Underwood.

The bowling line-up was decided only on the morning of the match, taking Old by surprise after he had been told that England would play both spinners, which would have left him watching on the sidelines once more. 'I think I was actually fit enough to play in the first Test. When I didn't play I was always the fielding 12th man, so I can't have been that unfit. But I didn't feel I had bowled particularly well. I had bowled a fair few no-balls, which was a slight issue, and also it was the first time I had used the Kookaburra ball. It took me a long while to get used to it because the seam is different to ours and it feels a different shape. It didn't feel round. Mike Hendrick had bowled a little bit better than me and they thought he might get a bit more out of the pitch in Brisbane.

'Originally I wasn't playing in Perth either. I was supposed to be 12th man with Derek Underwood playing. We turned up on the morning and if I had been playing I would have just put on a light pair of shoes and bowled for ten minutes off half a run-up and got everything warm and loose. But that morning I had spent half an hour or more bowling almost off my full run in the nets at some of the batsmen. As we were about to toss up, I walked into the dressing room absolutely wet through, to be met at the doorway by Mike Denness to say, "Oh, by the way you are playing." It was a relief we ended up batting because I had to send someone back to get all my stuff from the hotel. I only had a shirt or two and one pair of trousers.'

Denness admitted that the 'last-minute change of plan' had been based largely on the hope of winning the toss and inviting Australia to bat first, which was not how things transpired. That Underwood was the spinner excluded was down to the belief that Titmus, on the evidence of the state game, was more likely to take advantage of Perth's afternoon wind, the 'Fremantle Doctor'. As excited as he was about his return to Test cricket, Titmus recalled the mood of the team after their heavy defeat in Brisbane as 'pretty sombre'.

The inclusion of Lloyd and Cowdrey for the injured Amiss and Edrich made it five changes in all, leaving the loyal understudy wicketkeeper, Bob Taylor, as the only member of an already expanded MCC tour party not yet picked for a Test in a series that had barely begun.

7
THE WILD WEST

> *There is no doubt in my mind that fear was a factor in the series, batsmen emerging shaken and bewildered as if they had just come out of the trenches after some particularly violent crossfire.*
> **Bob Willis**

The Perth pitch had appeared soft on the day before the start of the Second Test. Now, on the morning of the match, observers were looking at the quickest surface in the world and saying they would bowl first if they won the toss. The fact that former Test pacemen Graham McKenzie and Frank Tyson were among those experts was neither here nor there to most England players or fans. But to have John Snow sitting in the press box passing judgement on the wicket instead of lacing his boots ready to bowl on it was an irony made even more unpalatable by events in Brisbane.

Bob Willis, who had to bear the burden of enforcer in the England attack in Snow's absence, recalled that he and Peter Lever had picked up a couple of wickets with short deliveries in the first Test. 'But when Lillee and Thommo got stuck in, it was obvious our efforts were not in the same league.'

Ian Chappell knew that his bowlers had 'struck fear' into the opposition. 'I sent them into bat after winning the toss purely on the basis that they were so hammered mentally from the Brisbane Test that I thought we had the psychological advantage – let's bang it home,' he explained. 'The other reason was it was a rare overcast day in Perth.'

Colin Cowdrey had spent the night before his first encounter with the new Australian attack believing the newspapers' assumption that he would be 'tucked away down the order at number six'. It was not until after England had lost the toss that Mike Denness interrupted Cowdrey's conversation with a couple of teammates by asking him, 'How do you feel about batting at number three?'

'It is like a dream now,' was how Cowdrey recalled those moments.

Brian Luckhurst looked uncomfortable from the moment Thomson got his fifth delivery to spit off the pitch and rap his left glove as he fended the ball away from his chest. From the pavilion, the injured Dennis Amiss recognised that Luckhurst was so out of touch that 'it would have been kinder to leave him out'.

Luckhurst flexed his hand to relieve the pain. 'Thomson had struck me a nasty blow on the back of my hand and to make things worse he had hit me again in the same spot from the very next ball,' he remembered. 'It hurt a lot, I can tell you, and it took me a while before I could carry on.'

Too long for the liking of Chappell. 'Are we going to get on with this fucking game or not?' he growled from the slips.

'That was Chappell, I'm afraid, and that was how Test cricket – led largely by his team, it must be said – was then going,' wrote Luckhurst, one of the game's gentler souls. 'The Australians were now the best team in the world, and they were about to claim back the Ashes as further proof of it. But they never behaved in the way that world champions, in my view, should behave. Sledging doesn't make you a tough guy.'

Those remarks perhaps say more about Luckhurst's nature than accurately reflecting the intensity of the war of words during the series. According to Dennis Lillee, 'there was not much personal abuse' amid the verbal back-and-forth. And certainly none from Thomson. 'I have hardly ever seen him blow up against a batsman,' Lillee would confirm. 'He seems to possess an extraordinary inner confidence in his own ability and takes the attitude, "Oh well, he got away with it that time but I'll get him soon enough." Thommo is a really relaxed fellow, both on and off the field.'

Umpire Robin Bailhache, who along with colleague Tom Brooks was on the field for every ball of the series, insisted, 'Tom and I hardly witnessed a damn thing that was nasty or over the top. There were maybe a couple of little ones we didn't hear. Any sledging, if you want to call it that, was taken to an art form, but was mainly humorous. Things were only said by blokes who had reputations and could back up their little bit of humour with actions. We didn't find that a problem at all.'

Willis, a cricketing traditionalist despite his bohemian off-field persona, felt differently. He disliked the manner in which Lillee played up to his 'macho image' with 'histrionics, gestures and verbal performances which to my mind did nothing for the game at all' and recalled, 'Sledging was a prominent and unsavoury feature of the tour and Ian Chappell was the orchestrator. Dennis Lillee was a willing player.'

Chappell was indeed unafraid to chirp up on occasions but has always maintained that his team's reputation has been exaggerated over the years. 'It's a joke to hear what is supposed to have happened when I was captain,' he once told *Wisden Cricket Monthly*. 'First, if people thought I had to abuse batsmen to get them out they are fooling themselves. I had plenty of faith in my bowlers to get the batsmen out without sledging them. Second, if I was doing all of that the critics don't know much about captaincy. You've got too much to think about.'

That didn't mean that Chappell was unhappy to have his team thought of as a 'bunch of bastards', preferring that description to 'a nice bunch of blokes'. Even with Tony Greig in the line-up, the England team undoubtedly fitted the second description much better than the first. 'Between 11 a.m. and 6 p.m. there was no time to be a nice guy,' was Chappell's view.

What really wound up Chappell was an opposition batsman looking aggrieved if he was the subject of an appeal or trying to do the umpire's job by indicating he had edged the ball after an lbw shout. 'I would tell him where to get off and, knowing me, there would be an expletive or two thrown in. Some opponents thought I was trying to put them off and trying to unsettle them, but it just annoyed me.'

Yet Chappell was of the school of player who felt that everything should be set aside over a beer with the opposition at the end of play. 'It's so important to sit down and have a laugh about it,' was his approach, recalling occasions when he and Greig would have been at each other on the field and chuckling about it in the dressing room, causing Doug Walters to comment, 'How could you two be so stupid?'

For those on the receiving end of the physical and mental assault, which on this tour usually meant the England batsmen, there was a mixed response to socialising after stumps. Amiss enjoyed the 'opportunity to get to know Thomson and Lillee and explore their personalities rather more than I cared to out in the middle' and gregarious new tourist David Lloyd saw it as part of the rich experience of playing Test cricket to 'have a good laugh, a couple of beers' and say, 'I'll see you tomorrow'. Yet quieter characters such as Luckhurst and Keith Fletcher found less attraction in sharing a can and a craic with people who had been bowling at their heads at 90 miles per hour.

Lillee admitted, 'The atmosphere against England in that 1974-75 series was not the best. They were not happy with the aggressive way in which we approached the games and not many of them stayed around for a drink after play or came to our dressing room. They didn't want to mix.'

Nursing his aching hand, Luckhurst, who took half an hour to score his first run, was soon having to withdraw his head from another rising delivery. He looked understandably unsettled. Sensing blood, or a wicket at any rate, Chappell gave Thomson four slips, a gully, leg slip and forward and backward short legs. Only Ross Edwards at cover was posted in front of the wicket. His tail up, Thomson had Marsh diving in front of Lillee at leg slip to gather a wild bouncer.

Even on a wicket that looked less unpredictable than Brisbane, Lloyd had it no easier against Lillee, who had dismissed a sore foot before the match by telling everyone, 'I have been through some pain before, I can stand a little more.' Lloyd's unconvincing flap at a rising delivery dropped in front of the two short legs and another looped just over the fielders' heads. Luckhurst managed to steer Lillee into the gap between fourth slip and gully and when the slip moved wider he edged it to the space that had been vacated. The only answer was for Lillee to create an arc of six catchers, only for Luckhurst to squeeze the ball off the inside edge between the two short legs for the third four of Lillee's fifth over. By the time Luckhurst had scored two fours to third man off Max Walker all six of his boundaries had been behind the wicket. His methods only ever seemed to be stealing time from the inevitable and it was painfully predictable when Walker had him caught by a diving Ashley Mallett in the gully with the score on 44.

Luckhurst's exit brought the moment that had intrigued fans of both nations; the entrance of Cowdrey, who gave his Kent colleague some gentle applause on the blade of his bat as they passed a few yards inside the boundary. Luckhurst paused, passed on some information, and offered a good luck pat as the rotund, exaggeratedly padded figure of the former England captain headed to the middle.

Greig recalled, 'It was the first time I ever saw proper padding. When he opened his bag in the dressing room, there was a hissing noise as the top of the bag lifted and there were orange bits of stuff he could stick on to his chest.' Cowdrey's wife had even sewn some of them on to an undershirt for him to wear beneath his kit.

To a cruel eye it looked as though England had sent Humpty Dumpty out to bat. 'I thought, he's had a good Christmas eat,' said Thomson. 'I didn't realise he had all these towels and shit round him. He looked like a pear.' Whatever his appearance, Cowdrey was accompanied to the middle by applause so generous that he felt compelled to lift his bat in acknowledgement.

It was the start of a wave of benevolence that accompanied Cowdrey across the country over the ensuing weeks. Along with the captivating and instantly recognisable Greig, it was the old-timer who attracted the greatest number of autograph hunters and hand-shakers, although Lloyd observed one occasion when a young lad greeted him with, 'Oi, Cowdrey, you pudgy fucker. Sign us this.' Ever the gentleman, Cowdrey muttered, 'Absolutely charming,' and politely wrote his name.

Cowdrey had never batted with his partner, Lloyd, whom he barely knew other than as a county cricket opponent. 'I had to play Walker, who was bowling into the breeze,' Cowdrey recorded in his autobiography. 'David Lloyd then did something which I will never tire of recording for all to know. He walked down to me and said that he would take Lillee, who was really running, bursting himself downwind, producing tremendous pace and bounce. And David did exactly that for three consecutive overs. What a generous thing to do.'

Watching the highlights at home, before any thoughts of his own participation, Cowdrey had been urging England's batsmen to stay still, restrict the ducking to a minimum, and play with virtually no backlift for the first few overs. Keeping the head still and defending the stumps was all that mattered; forget trying to score runs in the early stages. He might even have thought of taking with him to Australia a copy of his *Tackle Cricket* book, originally written in 1964 but re-published a few months earlier. In it, he stressed, 'In every stroke, the head should maintain one solid position, never falling to one side… this is one of the most forgotten and least emphasised tenets of good batsmanship.'

Confronted with putting his theories to the test, Cowdrey took guard on middle rather than his favoured leg stump, something he often did when facing the fastest of bowling. He lunged forward nervously at his first delivery, prompting a half-appeal by Walker for leg before. He also played and missed before Walker offered him the chance to score his first runs with a pulled four off a gentle long hop. Having faced 22 balls exclusively from Walker, Cowdrey was sent to Lillee's end by Lloyd's push for three. He soon had a bruised chest to show for it, rubbing away the sting.

Ross Edwards, who'd thought the Cowdrey selection was 'old-time thinking', could not help but admire what he was seeing from his side-on position in the covers. 'Batting him in that situation was suicidal,' he said. 'Just silly. But, I tell you what, he raised a lot of people's respect. He walked into that cauldron and he played well. Had a few more of the batsmen shown a bit more of the guts he showed, they might have done better.'

As much as Cowdrey was an unexpected adversary in this series, some Australians found his cheery demeanour in the middle equally incongruous. He made a point of seeking out Thomson, approaching him with a handshake and an introduction, an act the Australian found 'a bit bizarre'. 'Dennis Lillee and I had just dismantled his team in Brisbane,' Thomson remembered, 'and we were about to do the same here, and Cowdrey arrives at the crease all smiles and looking for a nice chat in the middle.'

Nor could the Aussies believe their ears when they overheard Cowdrey remarking to Lloyd what fun it all was. 'I've been in funnier situations than this,' was Lloyd's response.

Cowdrey recalled it as 'challenging and stimulating cricket; very much the way I learned to bat with Peter May, the game so much more fulfilling'. A score of 63 for 1 from 23 overs gave England more reasons for cheer as lunch arrived.

Cowdrey was grateful for Mallett dropping short, allowing him to force the ball square for his second boundary. Less comfortable was the blow he took on the left hip, almost the buttock in fact, as he looked to skip out of the path of a Thomson delivery spearing on a line just outside leg stump. Later he took one on the chest trying to hook, prompting Ian Chappell to approach from slip.

'You okay, Kipper?'

'Ian,' Cowdrey answered, 'I am a bloody old fool trying to hook this man.'

Walters urged his captain to take Thomson off 'before he kills him', while at one point a voice in the crowd yelled, 'Thommo, I've searched everywhere for a vet but can't find one. You can put the old boy to sleep!'

Meanwhile, Lloyd, who had fought his way to 25 at lunch before opening the afternoon session by taking ten off the first over from Mallett, moved to 44 by slashing Thomson square for his sixth boundary. The lesser pace of Walters almost did for both batsmen, Lloyd playing early and nearly clipping the ball back to the bowler, and Cowdrey dropped by Marsh down the leg side. But neither lasted much longer. Lloyd, one short of a half-century, steered Thomson to Greg Chappell's left hand at second slip, and Cowdrey's 125-minute vigil ended when he shuffled across too far to Thomson and was bowled behind his legs for 22. 'In context this will rank as one of the bravest performances in the history of the Ashes series,' said the *Daily Mirror*'s Peter Laker, indicative of the goodwill directed towards the old warrior. The ever-supportive John Woodcock felt that 'technically Cowdrey looked in a different class to anyone else, which of course he is'.

Elevated to number four on the strength of his century in Brisbane, Greig was clearly intent on reprising that performance. He guided his first ball, bowled short by Thomson, over the cordon to the boundary, and scored three fours in his first 13 deliveries. Fletcher managed one four, jabbing Thomson behind square, before prodding at Lillee to give Ian Redpath another gully catch.

Denness, having moved himself down to number six, was immediately off the mark by nudging two off his legs. But in the first over after tea he played the shot of a man bereft of ideas of how to tackle the task ahead of him, wafting at Lillee as his feet argued over where to plant themselves. Inevitably, the ball ended up in the hands of Greg Chappell at second slip. Six balls later, Greig found Mallett at gully as he tried to force Walker off the back foot. 'Greig's arrogance, while admirable in one way, was hazardous in another,' wrote Woodcock.

England had slipped from 99 for 1 to 132 for 6, prompting Peter Laker to blame 'a mass of timid self-destruction against the short ball outside the off stump, a flurry of glassy-eyed head-back dabs.'

Accompanied by number eight batsman Fred Titmus, who had often batted two places lower during Middlesex's latest season, Alan Knott batted busily and gathered runs quickly. At one point almost having to jump in the air to snick a Thomson bouncer to the rope, he reached his fifty by hitting the 66th ball he faced for his fifth four. But he became the latest victim of Australia's remarkable catching when Redpath pulled off another diving effort.

Chris Old took a long stride down the wicket to lift the leg-spin of Ian Chappell over extra cover for four, but when he clipped the next ball into the leg side brother Greg took a sharp left-handed catch at short midwicket. Geoff Arnold was run out by the throw of Walters as he tried to get back for a second run on the first ball he faced and yet another catch, Redpath's third grab at gully, saw Walters remove Titmus after an hour and a half of doggedness, ending the innings at 208.

Australia had held five fantastic catches in the gully – three by Redpath and two by Mallett – and two at second slip by Greg Chappell. 'Our fielding probably hit its peak,' said Redpath, 'and this resulted in some of the best catching I have ever seen from an Australian side. From the point of view of someone who stood in the slips for most of the series, our chaps were expecting catches, possibly because the English were playing at balls that they shouldn't. We were almost always in a state of anticipation.'

In the book he wrote about Thomson, Mallett would explain, 'With Thommo and Lillee bowling in tandem, fielding in the gully was something else. I had to very smartly develop a method to see the edges and slashed shots which were bound to come my way. With all the other fast bowlers – even Lillee – you could watch their delivery all the way from the time they let go to the time it was about half way down the track, then quickly focus your attention on the edge of the bat. With Thommo there was no time for that strategy. I found that I watched him until his load-up at delivery and a split second before he was about to release the ball I directed all my attention to the edge of the bat. It gave me a split second more time to see the ball. I decided to get as close to the bat as possible and worked out that seven paces was the way to go. The closer you get to the bat, the tighter the angle and there are lots more catching opportunities.'

Marsh described Mallett as 'the best gully fieldsman we may ever see', calling some of his catches 'unbelievable. Even more so when you consider his poor vision… Ashley made it look so easy. He'd merely thrust out a hand and the ball would stick as if glued.'

According to Greg Chappell, Thomson's speed made it easier to take catches off his bowling. 'You didn't have any problems with the ball dropping short off Thomson,' he explained. 'Your problem was it flying over your head. We were five yards further back than for Dennis . . . we were so far back you couldn't drop them if you tried.'

The one over that Australia were able to bat before the close of play merely emphasised the importance of their performance in the field. Redpath pushed at the sixth ball from Willis and found it leaving him enough to take the edge, sending it at a low but catchable height to first slip. It slipped through Fletcher's hands. Willis was left punching the air and a moment that Richie Benaud said 'could have changed the whole course of the day' had eluded England.

The fact that Lillee and Thomson had taken only two wickets each was seen as evidence that the Perth wicket had been easier-paced than expected. Woodcock went as far as saying, 'It was possible to watch Thomson bowling without fearing that at any moment he would knock someone's block off.' Try telling that to Luckhurst.

It did not dissuade Willis, on the second morning, from attempting again to expose the vulnerability of Wally Edwards against the short ball. Both Edwards and Redpath moved into the 20s as the end of the first hour approached, and Redpath had just stood straight to drive Greig for four when Edwards could only direct a widish ball from the all-rounder into the hands of Lloyd just in front of square on the off side.

Ian Chappell arrived with a flourish, three boundaries in a single Greig over, although he was more watchful against the accurate

Old. Australia breezed into three figures in little more than half the time England had taken to get there. Denness turned to Titmus, the first England captain to do so in almost seven years. Delivering the ball with his gentle rocking action, like a man balancing across the centre of a see-saw, Titmus enjoyed assistance from the south-westerly wind. The ball dipped in as Redpath advanced and even a deflection off the batsman's boot could not prevent Knott executing the stumping.

After lunch, Denness posted Greig at leg slip to Chappell in the belief that he might guide the ball in his direction. The move was justified when the Australian skipper fell by flicking at a leg stump delivery by Arnold, even though it went fine into the gloves of Knott.

Greg Chappell, who survived a bat-pad appeal against Titmus, hit the first boundary of the afternoon with an elegant drive off Arnold and he found the same piece of rope when sweeping a wayward Titmus. Respectful when the ball was in the right location, he was quick to punish anything off line, clipping Willis through mid-on for his fifth boundary to reach his half-century. Brother Ian recalled that while it had needed a stint in county cricket with Somerset in 1968 to improve the younger Chappell's off-side game, 'His on-side shots were always strong and Dad tells me that even as a young kid he always had that incredible shot he whips away off his left hip.'

At the other end, Ross Edwards had been in for almost 90 minutes before cutting Titmus for his first four and too often was allowed to sit on his favoured back foot rather than being tempted forward. It was all too comfortable for Australia until, with tea approaching, Chappell cut Willis to the area where Denness had posted two gully fielders. Cowdrey could not hold the catch, but the ball fell into the hands of Greig. The veteran hammed it up with wobbly legs to show his relief. 'Nine times out of ten I'd smash that ball on that score (62), but I had no energy,' said Chappell, who never felt in full health throughout the summer and booked in for a tonsilitis operation at the end of the series.

Later events have turned the exchange between Chappell and the incoming Walters into legend. 'Sorry, Doug, but I wanted to get out so you could get your eye in now and get 100 in the session after tea,' Chappell told his teammate, to which Walters's unspoken reaction amounted to, 'Yeh, good joke,' adding later, 'He wouldn't have got out to give his mum a knock.' Walters, who had achieved such a feat in Trinidad the previous year,[24] had enough time to face five balls and score three runs before the break arrived at 201 for 4, an Australian deficit of only seven runs.

Scorer of a century in his first Test innings against England in Brisbane in 1965, a few days before his 20th birthday, Walters proved too inconsistent to live up to those who hailed him as a new Bradman. Instead, his batting reflected the vibrancy with which he approached life. He was someone who boasted, 'We played cricket hard on the ground, but we enjoyed life off the ground. I'd be there until the last bottle was drunk.'

Ian Chappell remarked, 'Never has Walters's technique been one of conforming, more one of distinct flair and good old country style – "just be yourself, son." I think this is one of the reasons for his success. He is just plain Doug Walters and no one else.'

Walters was a representative of the Rothmans tobacco company, which allowed him to indulge his love of the product and offered David Lloyd a chance for fun later in the series. 'You could go to joke shops and buy fake packets of Rothmans with fire crackers underneath. When they were out in the field, I would go in their room with about ten of these things and I would spread them around the room. He was paranoid by the end of it. He was picking these things up and "Boom!" He'd not a clue who were doing it.'

According to Willis, 'Dougie was a bit of an enigma. You wouldn't find a less athletic guy.' He certainly had that status in the eyes of English cricket fans, who would never see him at his best on their own pitches. He had already performed disappointingly on the 1968 and 1972 tours and would do so again in 1975 and 1977, playing a total of 18 Tests in England without scoring a century. Typically, he used humour to disguise his disappointment, commenting after he was dropped in 1972, 'Beauty. I won't have to be up early for nets.'

A square cut for four and a glance for three in Greig's first over after the break showed his intent. Denness continued with his ploy

---

24 The feat of 100 runs in a session was performed only three times in Test cricket in the 1970s and three times in the 1980s. In the first two decades of the 21st century it was achieved on 36 occasions.

of two gully fielders, but that was rendered redundant when Old dropped short. Greig, now bowling spin, was equally errant in his length and when Walters swatted away another long hop by Old, he had taken only 32 balls to overtake Edwards's score of 34, which had taken 128 balls.

Greig was withdrawn after conceding 33 runs in four post-tea overs, but Titmus was equally generous, allowing Walters another free hit to leg to bring up his half-century at better than a run a ball. When the bowler repositioned his fielder on the leg-side boundary two balls later Walters swept him beyond his reach. 'After tea, the Poms bowled badly and fielded badly and went to pieces, and Dougie played his shots,' Edwards recalled.

While Edwards went past 50 with classical cuts and drives, Walters made no pretence of finesse, dealing mostly in cross-batted thrashes. The Australian dressing room could tell that the thought of scoring 100 runs in a session for the second time was guiding his bat. As 12th man Terry Jenner prepared to take out the mid-sessions drinks skipper Chappell told him, 'Check with the little bastard and ask him how he is going.'

When Jenner made his enquiry he received the reply, 'All right. It's a bit warm out here.'

'No, no, Doug, that's not what I'm talking about,' said Jenner. 'You know what I'm talking about. How are you going?'

'I think I've got a chance.'

Chappell had issued his instructions to Jenner in the knowledge of how much Walters loved a challenge. 'I don't know when the thought went in his mind about getting the hundred in the session. I don't know whether he was thinking about it beforehand or whether once Greg said what he said that put the thought in his mind.' But he recognised the ambition in Walters's batting.

Even when denied boundaries, Walters continued to accumulate brisk runs, moving through the 70s and 80s with ones and twos. When Willis began the final over of the day, he was at the non-striker's end on 93, making it down to the face the bowling when Edwards scored three off the second ball. Edwards explained, 'Willis is bowling down the hill from the southern end and the sea breeze is coming over his shoulder. Dougie had that habit in those days of getting out with what we called the parachute shot, when he holds the bat out and gets caught in the gully. That comes about from bowlers bowling bouncers at him.'

Edwards met Walters in mid-track and reminded him, 'Come on, we've got these blokes on the run. Whatever you do, don't chuck your wicket away today. We can get you a hundred tomorrow. We'll start all over again, and we can take them apart.'

'Yeah, yeah, yeah,' came the distracted reply.

Willis pitched short and a swish above his head brought Walters four runs off a top edge. Now needing only three to complete his century and six to record 100 runs in the session, Walters failed to make contact as another bouncer passed over his left shoulder. 'In the end I gave up talking to him,' Edwards admitted. 'I just did it at the other end. I said, "He's a bloody idiot. Cut it out and let's get back here tomorrow."'

Walters patted down the wicket and adjusted his box and sweater. Willis shared a smile with a teammate as he turned to run in again. When he pitched the ball up it appeared that Walters had heeded his partner's warning and lost interest in taking a risk in search of a personal milestone. His score had not advanced further by the time Willis delivered the last ball, short and on the line of off stump. Walters made no attempt to get behind the line, trusting his eye to make proper contact as he fell away to the leg side. The ball flew from the middle of his bat over the deep square leg boundary, although Edwards recalled, 'I'm not sure it was a six because the crowd was running on.'

Umpire Bailhache admitted, 'We had no idea where the ball landed because they knocked the boundary over and we never found the ball. An English fielder on the boundary stuck his hands up in the air to signal six and that was good enough for me.' As young fans raced towards the square, commentator Norman May described events as 'one of the greatest finishes we've ever seen to a day's play in Australian Test cricket'.

Edwards laughed, 'Mate, I was about 80 not out[25] at stumps and nobody noticed. Another thing, in that session there were times when the bowling was quite good and I deliberately took the strike to keep Dougie away from it because I figured if he's playing

---

2579, to be exact

shots this is not the best time to be playing them. Subsequently he blames me for not getting his hundred earlier because he reckoned I hogged the strike. My recollection is quite different. I was quite happy to give him the strike, but it was wise to keep him away from it at times.'

The scene in the Australian dressing room has also entered the country's cricketing folklore. 'I ran off the ground because I knew that was the last ball of the day, expecting that the boys might have the top off a bottle by the time I got in there,' Walters explained. 'I run up the stairs into the dressing room and there is no one there.'

The Aussies had decided it would be good sport to hide in the showers, denying Walters the hero's welcome he deserved. They reckoned without the batsman's equanimity. He made no effort to seek out his teammates' attention. 'Nothing happens for about five minutes,' remembered Ian Chappell. 'Eventually I said, "Well, this is a waste of time." So we walk out and there he is, just sitting there taking his pads and gloves off and having a smoke. Terry Jenner hands Doug a beer and I ask Ross Edwards, "What did he do when he came in the dressing room and there was no one there?" He said he did what he always does – took his clothes off and lit up a cigarette. It just made no difference to him. One of the great things I'd say about Doug Walters was that if you didn't see his innings and you were just sitting in the dressing room when he came back in you would never know whether he got nought or 100.'

Walters made a rapid return to the dressing room on the third morning, having edged his second delivery from Willis to Fletcher, the solitary slip. 'Dougie had a drink or two that night,' Edwards remembered. 'The next morning I'm on strike and he had to run five twos off the first five balls. He was so buggered by the time the bowling was at his end that he hung his bat out and got caught behind.' According to Greg Chappell, his instant dismissal 'only added to the mythology of his performance'.

Entering at 362 for 5, Rodney Marsh enjoyed the freedom offered by a lead of 154, playing several false shots before driving Old cleanly down the ground and pulling him through midwicket. Almost unobtrusively by comparison, Edwards continued to steer the ball into gaps, although it was a firmly struck back-foot drive at a fielder that allowed him to scramble the single that made him the first Western Australian to score a Test century at Perth.[26] 'The one I am most proud of is being the first Western Australian to score a Test century in 1972,' Edwards explained. 'Being the first at Perth was just luck.' Eventually, he fell for 115 when he dragged Arnold on to his stumps.

Marsh continued to ride his luck, dropped by Arnold at mid-on and Fletcher at slip, before holing out off Titmus for 41. As Australia's lead extended beyond 200, wickets were interspersed with lusty hits and dropped catches. Fletcher was unable to hold another difficult slip chance off Walker and Knott seemed to have made a diving grab off the same batsman before the ball fell to the ground. Eventually Walker feathered to the keeper to end Australia's innings on 481, Old having accounted for the final three wickets.

Shortly after half past two, and with a deficit of 273, England sent out their opening batsmen, Lloyd and – to the astonishment of every observer – Cowdrey. An X-ray had revealed a fracture in Luckhurst's hand, making it impossible for him to take his place at the top of the order in the second innings. 'By a process of elimination it fell to me,' said Cowdrey, who'd discovered his fate during lunch. 'The Perth wicket is one of the fastest in the world and this was a torrid experience.'

Denness, a former opener, might have taken on the role had he been in better form, while Titmus had been Geoff Boycott's first opening partner for England more than a decade earlier. Neither was a better option than the unlikely figure of Cowdrey, which demonstrated the straits in which England found themselves.

Lloyd fended a brutish delivery in Lillee's first over perilously close to the short leg trap and Cowdrey could have been out without scoring when he prodded at Thomson and the ball was spilled by gully fielder Redpath, diving to his left. Cowdrey was also fortunate to survive when he tried to withdraw his bat to a ball from Walker that bounced alarmingly, his edge clearing the slip fielders.

Against the odds, England reached tea without losing a wicket, 26 scored off 13 overs. Cowdrey had reached 19, while Lloyd had managed only three scoring shots from 60 balls, a pull off Walker giving him his solitary boundary.

---

26 Perth had only staged one Test previously, in 1970-71.

Cowdrey's chest protection was put to the test when he missed an attempted hook against Thomson, bowling with the wind at his back. He was not too proud to rub his right breast. Dennis Amiss, watching Cowdrey take the blows that should have been his, said, 'My God, you have to take your hat off to him in that first match for the way he just left it alone and occasionally let it hit him.'

Fletcher, to whom it appeared that the ball was in Marsh's hands before Cowdrey came close to completing some shots, could barely believe he was surviving. 'His defensive technique was as sound as ever, though,' he said. 'He got into line and played the ball on its merit, often being struck on the body but never flinching from the job.'

Cowdrey's most productive shots were behind the wicket, a mixture of the deliberate and involuntary moving him into the 30s. His colleague pushed a couple of runs off Walters to complete a half-century stand, but the partnership was about to come to a painful end.

Thomson let go another rocket, this one pitching around leg stump, too quick for Lloyd's defensive stroke and moving a little off the seam. The ball smacked sickeningly into the batsmen's groin, and he dropped to his knees, head bowed to the ground as if praying for relief. 'Somebody told me he'd said he could play me with his dick,' Thomson recalled.[27] 'He obviously couldn't do that. I said, "He can't bat an eyelid," because he was shit scared of me.'

One of cricket's great after-dinner stories was in the making. 'I am very square on, and you have that moment, that glimpse, when you hope this hits the bat,' goes one of Lloyd's versions. 'It missed and everybody knows where it hit me. It is 1974 and all cricketers would remember what I was wearing for protection. It was a pink Litesome [box] and it had holes in it. Completely useless for the job it was supposed to do. Everything that should have been inside it had found its way through these holes and was trapped now on the outside. No wonder I have somersaulted into the floor. I swear that particular day we didn't need a doctor, we needed a welder to get this box and all its contents pulled apart. I had to sit with everything I hold dear in a pint pot of iced water.'

---

[27] Richie Benaud recalled being told that Lloyd had said at a team meeting 'he could play Thomson with what was laughingly known as his appendage'.

Thomson has heard the story recounted by his adversary so many times over the years that he could not help growling at the camera in Peter Dickson's 2017 documentary *Forged in Fire: Cricket's Greatest Rivalry*, 'That prick owes me so much money because if I hadn't hit him in the balls no one would know who the fuck he was. All anyone ever remembers is me hitting him in the nuts and he has got all these fucking jobs out of it, and I haven't received one cent.' Or maybe that is just Thomson reciting his lines in the ongoing pantomime that has grown up around the incident.

The disappearance of Lloyd into the pavilion meant that, in the space of barely one and a half Test matches, the four men selected to contest places in England's top three – Amiss, Edrich, Lloyd and Luckhurst – had been struck blows by the Australian bowlers that had forced them to miss matches, retire hurt or drop down the order. Even the 1932-33 Australians in the Bodyline series had not suffered that extent of physical damage. Greig, who had begun the series at number six, would soon find himself batting with one wicket down; skipper Denness, who had spent days in hospital because of illness and had sought refuge at six, had now been forced back into the firing line at three; and the batting was being opened by a man of almost 42 years who had been on his sofa in his slippers less than two weeks earlier.

It was the sheer speed of the descent into disarray that was so shocking.

The situation almost became even worse. Cowdrey had no way of playing another Thomson ball that rose towards his chest, nor the reflexes to avoid being hit on the left forearm. As he paced around his crease trying to get his arm into a comfortable position, Lillee offered a consoling hand on the shoulder. As if to prove that bravery could compensate for the cruel passage of time, he was fully in line to push forward defensively at the next ball. Relieved to find a ball arriving close to his toes, Cowdrey clipped Thomson square for four.

'I think we have just about seen Thomson off,' Cowdrey told new partner Denness between overs. 'He can surely bowl only one more over in this spell.' Yet Cowdrey's admirable 131-minute battle ended in Thomson's next over, one ball after he had moved his score to 41 with another four. The bowler won an lbw decision from Brooks as Cowdrey shuffled across his stumps. The English newspapers would be effusive in their praise for the old-stager, the romance of the storyline permeating some of the reporting. 'Cowdrey's well-proved technique stood him comfortably in stead,' wrote EW Swanton in the *Telegraph*, while Laker in the *Mirror* argued that he had 'won the most daunting battle of his distinguished career'. Writing for the *Express*, Keith Miller said, 'Cowdrey has more cricketing ability in his little finger than most of England's batsmen. He's a genius and the crowd loved him. I admit I advised him not to come out here, but the crispness of his strokes, especially his cutting, turned the clock back 20 years. Had England 11 men of his courage they would win the series.'

Tour observer Martin-Jenkins summed up the affection that followed Cowdrey onto the field. 'Everyone wanted this player to succeed, for his courage in volunteering to open the innings in place of his injured colleague was magnificent,' he said, adding that some teammates 'ought to have been shamed by the way he was withstanding two of the fastest bowlers in the world after only five days' practice'. The prevailing hope was that if this was what Cowdrey could do right off the plane, there must be even better to come once he was used to being back on tour. Yet the second innings at Perth was to be the highlight of his adventure, even though he headed back into the nets the following day, the rest day – 'for a little more acclimatisation,' he explained.

Before that, however, there was enough time left in the third day for Greig to show his usual aggression, driving and slashing his way to 28 in 41 deliveries, and for Denness's feet and bat to continue to operate independently as he struggled to deal with the speed of the bowling. He survived to be 13 not out when England reached the close at 102, still 171 in arrears.

It was going to need something remarkable by England on the fourth day to get themselves back into the game. At least conditions were in their favour, nothing in the atmosphere to help the bowlers and intense heat to hinder the fielders. As Woodcock pointed out, 'The only clouds in the sky were from the bushfires burning in the hinterland.' But the only thing remarkable about England's batting was the rapidity of its collapse.

Greig cut the first ball of the day, bowled by Thomson, behind square for four, but could only squeeze the over-pitched and wide fifth delivery to Greg Chappell at second slip. Greig's success in Brisbane appeared to have convinced him he had no need of playing himself in. Martin-Jenkins would end up advancing the theory that his century might have been detrimental to teammates, too, making them believe that their best chance of runs against Lillee and Thomson was to take similar liberties.

It took Lillee only two balls to find the edge of Denness's bat, the ball falling in front of third slip, but the escape could not prevent the England captain driving again with bat away from body, this time getting it through extra cover for three runs. It was of no surprise to anyone, least of all bowler Thomson, when Denness was out in the fifth over of the day, feet again in a different postcode to his bat as he fended to Redpath at fourth slip.

Thomson's first ball to Fletcher was, according to the batsman, 'one of the most lethal deliveries I have ever faced'. It was just outside off stump, climbing as usual from a good length. Almost involuntarily, Fletcher jabbed at it, getting a thin edge that barely altered the ball's trajectory on its way to Marsh's gloves. 'I had time only to get my glove in front of my face, and the deflection was travelling so fast that it actually thumped the chest of [Marsh] before he got his gloves to it.' Fletcher was immediately on his way, turning his head briefly as an afterthought to check that umpire Brooks had not offered him a reprieve. England had lost four wickets in less than five overs to slump to 124 for 4 and the day's play had quickly acquired a last-rites feel.

Knott survived the hat-trick ball and lasted unconvincingly for a further half an hour. Playing and missing in defence, he slashed hard in attack and took Thomson for three fours in the third man region before flashing at Lillee and sending the ball chest high to Greg Chappell.

Lloyd, who had resumed his innings with the fall of the day's first wicket, had advanced to 35 with a couple of off-side boundaries and survived several more blows from Thomson, but now he chased a wide delivery from Walker and gifted Greg Chappell his sixth catch of the match. The wounded Luckhurst and Titmus took the score from 156 to 184 at lunch. Titmus, in particular, enjoyed the respite offered by Mallett, clubbing him over long-on and extra cover either side of a steer to third man.

Lillee and Thomson returned with the second new ball early in the afternoon, but when Walker replaced the latter after two overs he was close to removing Luckhurst when Mallett almost held a difficult diving chance at gully. Lillee tried bowling round the wicket to Titmus, who tucked him square for three, but returned to over the wicket next ball, instantly having Luckhurst caught at gully for 23. Six of England's top seven had now been dismissed by catches behind the wicket in both innings. Cowdrey was the exception, avoiding such an ending each time he'd batted.

Former Australian captain Bill Lawry remarked that 'except for Colin they have forgotten where their off stump is,' while Woodcock concluded, 'This is what happens to a side that gets softened up by bowling which is much faster than they are accustomed to.'

The injured Luckhurst had batted with heart, but his dismissal was to prove to be his last in a 21-Test career that had begun at the advanced age of 31 during the previous Ashes tour. He became a peripheral figure over the next few months. 'It's not that I didn't give it my best,' he said, insisting that he appreciated 'the chance to witness the Lillee and Thomson phenomenon at close quarters'. He would recall, 'To look back at us walking out there in those pre-helmet days to face two of the fastest and most dangerous bowlers the world has seen – on lightning quick and bouncy surfaces – still provides almost a ghoulish fascination. And, given everything, my two last Test scores of 27 and 23, made in the second Test at Perth, one of the quickest and bounciest pitches in the world, represent not the worst way to bow out of international cricket. I did not enjoy that tour, though, especially after I was left out of the Test side.'

There was not much left in the match now other than for Titmus and Old to bat with the freedom of lower-order batsmen with no responsibility for saving what had long since been a lost cause. 'I concentrated hard and tried to get right behind the line and even began to deal with the pace,' Titmus recalled. He drove Walker's full toss for three to reach his half-century, and the remainder of that over belonged to Old, who had already muscled Walker down the ground and pushed Thomson square on his way to 13. He now blasted a further 17 runs, stepping back in his crease and unleashing flat-footed drives that sped back past the bowler for two fours and a six.

Taking tea at 264 for 7, nine runs behind, England managed a few more hefty thumps, notably Old's six off Mallett to cow corner. But when Old top-edged the next ball to midwicket on 43 it began a run of three wickets for eight runs that concluded the innings with a lead of only 20 runs. The second of those dismissals, more Mallett acrobatics to remove Arnold, gave Thomson his second five-wicket haul in consecutive matches. Titmus was the last to fall for a gutsy 61, Greg Chappell setting a new Test record for a non-wicketkeeper with his seventh catch, this one away from the wicket at mid-off.

Australia completed victory with the best part of an hour of the fourth day remaining, but not before Wally Edwards had put his Test place under greater threat by walking across his stumps against Arnold. The lbw decision was the first gained by England in Australia since the third Test of the 1965-66 Ashes series – they'd won in 1970-71 without gaining a single lbw judgement in six matches.

Bookmakers Ladbrokes stated after the match, 'It doesn't seem that we can offer a bet on the series anymore,' while Australian Prime Minister Gough Whitlam could not resist a dig at the England team during his visit to London. 'I am perfectly willing to make my plane available for MCC to fly their first eleven to Australia,' he quipped.

Meanwhile, Denness could do nothing but make the right noises about players having to work even harder in the nets to find their own technique against the Aussie fast bowlers – no suggestion of anyone receiving any kind of help, of course. The early finish allowed the MCC party to leave Perth a day ahead of schedule, the scathing words of Benaud sending them on their way. 'I haven't seen a more pathetic batting display by an England side for many years,' he'd said at the game's conclusion. 'Some of those batsmen won't sleep too well tonight.'

No one was being scrutinised more closely than Denness himself. Even when he stood 13 not out on the rest day, Laker was writing in the *Mirror* that 'his advance as a field captain and his affable dealing with both Australian and English press are hardly the qualities that influence the dramatic change in batting performance he so desperately wants now.' There was little pretence at hope that Denness might play a major hand in the second innings; merely an acceptance that he was out of his depth and that the time might not be far away when Edrich took over as captain.

8
FAMILY FORTUNES

It'll be lonely this Christmas, without you to hold.
It'll be lonely this Christmas, lonely and cold.
Mud, 'Lonely This Christmas' (Nicky Chinn, Mike Chapman, 1974)

The highlights of England's fourth-day submission in the Second Test had not long aired on BBC Two when London shook to the sound of three bombs, detonated in quick succession after 9.15pm in Chelsea, Soho and close to Tottenham Court Road. One man was killed and five people were injured in the blasts, which were reported to have been preceded by a warning telephone call to the *Daily Mirror* by a woman with an Irish accent. The incidents happened, it was noted, while Scotland Yard inspectors and senior members of the Bomb Squad were enjoying their Christmas party.

Earlier in the day, a 16 per cent increase in the price of petrol had been announced, taking it to 72 pence for a gallon of four-star. Meanwhile, car manufacturer Chrysler told 4,300 workers in its Midlands plants that they would have to take a further three days of unpaid leave – on top of a five-day Christmas hiatus – because of falling sales. An independent arbitration was outlined as a way to end the dispute involving print workers on Fleet Street, which had disrupted production of London's national and evening newspapers.

Terrorist bombs, inflation, hardship for the workforce, and industrial unrest. Welcome to Britain in late 1974.

For a lucky few, however, there was escape. While Fred Titmus said the players were 'blissfully unaware of most day-to-day news,' it was the turn of the wives and children of some members of the MCC touring party to leave behind the depressing front-page headlines. The husbands they were to join in Melbourne might have been battling through events that were the subject of equally distressing back-page news, but at least their loved ones could enjoy the southern hemisphere sun from the safety of the swimming pool or the family seating area. Early arrivals Stephanie Titmus and Dawn Underwood had already been pictured in their bikinis in Perth.

It did not, however, mean there would be unadulterated familial peace and goodwill around the squad as they prepared to spend Christmas at Melbourne's Windsor Hotel. If tour manager Alec Bedser and the MCC committee had their way, the wives would be sitting at home on the end of long-distance phone calls, singing the song that glam-rockers Mud were taking towards the festive number one position in the UK pop charts. Bachelor Bedser had been lonely at Christmas often enough in the cause of English cricket and only begrudgingly were family members allowed their trips to Australia on this occasion.

Even less welcome, of course, were females in the dressing room, which was why the manager was left spluttering in outrage when Tony Greig wandered in one morning with singer Shirley Bassey in tow. Titmus tried to explain to Bedser that this was not just any old woman, but the manager 'mumbled something unrepeatable and shuffled off'.

Two down after two matches, any change of environment and tour dynamics was likely to lift spirits, but it was not all mistletoe and wine. For those unable to bring nearest and dearest out to join them, the presence of others' wives and children was a reminder of the people they were missing after two months on the road. And even those who now had company were faced with the frustration of having to work with, or around, the limitations imposed by the tour hierarchy.

Before the trip, TCCB secretary Donald Carr announced, 'For the sake of cohesion within the team, getting the best results and because wives want to be with their husbands we feel they should be allowed to stay with the team for a reasonable period.'

That statement disguised the truth that Bedser and his Lord's paymasters viewed a cricket tour as no place for guests, which was why players had to use their own money to fly wives to Australia and were allowed to spend no more than 21 nights in the conjugal bed. Bernard Thomas was charged with keeping a chart tracking how often a player had cashed in his chips, so to speak.

Dennis Amiss remembered, 'After 21 nights, Bernie would come and tell you; in my case that my wife, Jill, couldn't be in the hotel anymore. She would have to go and find somewhere else. In those days you had to pay for everything yourself, and you could only get a decent airfare if you spent so long in the country – it made the flights a little bit cheaper if you stayed for a certain time, longer than 21 nights.'

In the early weeks of the tour, the social highlight had been the 'Saturday Night Club', staged in the team room in whatever hotel the players found themselves. It was the scene of games, jokes, sessions of charades and the imposing of fines for all sorts of obscure reasons. David Lloyd remembered, 'We had a team room where we had a beer and we all got on well. They were all really nice blokes. I can't think of any nasty pieces of work. Geoff Arnold could get a bit miserable, but he's always been miserable and that is part of his charm.

'I had a wonderful time and it was very relaxing. We got beat, but the press out there were fantastic and we all got on together. There were no investigative journalists following us around. You had a roommate, which was always good fun, and we got on really well.'

There was also the round of official functions to break up the routine and distract from the on-field travails. As a bonus, Famous Grouse offered bottles of its product in return for attendance at some events. Titmus, Derek Underwood and Denness – described by Titmus as 'a Scot with a serious enthusiasm for whisky' – proved eager collectors.

There was less excitement over the contribution to those engagements of Bedser, with Amiss referring to him as 'not a leader to inspire' and arguing that he 'lacked the common touch and any sense of spontaneity'. As evidence he recalled that he told the same story about a racehorse owner at every gathering, 'without ever changing a single word or adjusting the speed of delivery and intonation'.

Chris Old explained, 'Everybody gets a bit homesick or is missing English beer or missing various things, but in general I always went out with the idea of trying to enjoy it. I think on that tour we were probably the most popular side ever to tour Australia because we were being heavily beaten, so we got invited out and wined and dined quite a lot. When we were winning in 1978-79 the only people pleased to see us were the Brits that were out there. The family thing was a bone of contention. Most of the wives and families were out for longer than 21 days but stayed in other areas. So they're out there but not really part of us.'

Denness had been summoned to a pre-tour meeting at Lord's where Gubby Allen and MCC secretary Billy Griffith voiced concerns about the number of wives planning to make the trip and explained the 21-night restriction. Denness attempted to argue that if the players were paying then the wives should be able to stay wherever they chose. 'Don't be so ridiculous,' was the response he received. Denness's subsequent suggestion to Thomas was that as long as wives were not disrupting team meetings, he should not go round doing bed checks.

Old continued, 'I had my wife and daughter out there with me and Bernard had his big chart of when everyone was in the same hotel. I felt sorry for Alec because he was supposed to keep in charge of it, but I think he looked at the chart once and said as long as the press don't pick up on it then he didn't mind.'

The *Daily Mirror*'s Peter Laker, never slow to find fault with the tourists, would end up offering Bedser some sympathy for having to spend most of his time dealing with logistics and social affairs. 'Not to mention the pressures of having 13 players' wives and six children at various points of the tour,' he added.

Bedser had another unlikely ally in the shape of Bob Willis, not exactly known as an establishment supporter. After the first two Tests were lost – and, he sensed, the series as well – he decided that he might as well 'enjoy the rest of the tour, come what may'. That entailed getting away from the MCC camp, seeing as much of Australia as possible and meeting new people.

He would admit, 'One aspect of the tour which did stir me into my outspoken vein was the appearance of a multitude of wives and children. They came for Christmas and many stayed up to a month, with some players forced to economise to the extent that a whole family was sharing a room, which can hardly have helped mental preparation for a Test match.'

Willis spent much of the tour rooming with Bob Taylor, who had left wife Catherine and his two children at home in the belief that their presence did not help his game and that there were better uses for his money. The passing of years and the maturity it brought led

Willis to soften his stance, but at the time he remained 'against the distracting company of children and was not prepared to make any secret of my feelings that winter because it divided the party just when we needed to stick together'.

Amiss continued, 'As the tour progressed we had a bit of a split because certain people like Bob Taylor and Bob Willis didn't have their wives coming out and were in the team room, whereas Denness, Fletcher, Greig, Underwood and I were having a nice time with our wives. Obviously during Test matches we had to be careful, but we were going out to decent restaurants. I think we all got together and we were quite lucky that we found a lovely family in Sydney for the wives to stay with. But we had this 21-day thing hanging over us and that wasn't good.'

Amiss called the rule 'a source of considerable tension between players and administrators'. He had recently become a father for the second time, to son Paul, and was keen to avoid a repeat of the previous tour of the West Indies, when he had missed four months of daughter Rebecca's development while separated from family. Yet he felt that a relaxed domestic atmosphere was almost impossible to attain with Thomas constantly counting down how much of his permitted three weeks he had left. 'It was like having a sword of Damocles hanging over our heads,' he said. 'It also put marriages and relationships under unnecessary stresses and strains.'

All of this had been foreseen before the MCC party left England. From the other side of the globe, *Cricketer* magazine had taken apparent delight in declaring, 'The issue of the MCC players' wives in Australia is far from dead. *Cricketer* predicts it could become a hot potato during the forthcoming months, and if the England side fares badly in the Tests could be a reason levelled for any poor performances.'

Even Bedser wasn't naïve enough to believe that the absence of wives on tour would promote celibacy among the players, but his theory was that denying his men access to families and forcing them to spend time in each other's company would enhance team spirit. Amiss called it 'counter-productive', while Greig described the 21-day rule as 'an entirely arbitrary regulation' and 'an appalling encroachment on the privileges of every married man'. Not only was Bedser restricting family time, the intrusive way in which some felt he had it policed could not help but undermine the quality and efficacy of those periods.

As a father in his 40s, Titmus did not feel he should be subjected to supervised visits with Stephanie, daughter Tandy and his in-laws. 'There were lots of jokes about whether 21 nights were quite enough to sustain normal appetites over a tour of five months,' he recalled. 'I'm glad there was no one monitoring how many nights this player sneaked off to spend the night in his wife's hotel. It was an international cricket tour, not a holiday, and I suppose the powers that be were just trying to do the right things. I feel, though, that at my age nobody should be telling me whether to sleep with my wife or not.'

Alan Knott was becoming more disaffected every time he went away with England. 'I had a bit of a fight about wives on tour and it just wasn't getting any easier,' he said. 'They had to come out at certain times, sometimes at the end of the tour, and we had to pay for them ourselves. If you went against it, you worried that they would leave you out.' He would choose after his next England trip – to India and Australia in 1976-77 – to give up touring. The fact that Kerry Packer would pay for wives to travel with players for the entirety of his World Series Cricket programme was a large element of Knott's decision to sign up for the rebel circuit in 1977.

Mind you, no one welcomed the sight of Knott's wife, Janet, on tour more than those players spared the ordeal of having to share a room with the man whose idiosyncrasies and routine became the stuff of legend. Amiss remembered him, at 10 p.m., meticulously unfolding and straightening the back warmer, vest and shirt he would wear on-field the next day, before hanging them carefully. The process would be 'conducted in an almost ceremonial manner' and would keep him busy until midnight. At 7 a.m. Knott would be in the bathroom beginning a series of stretches that lasted more than an hour, frequently ending with a dash to avoid being late for the departure of the team bus.

On his eighth Ashes tour, *The Times*' correspondent John Woodcock made clear that he was an opponent of the family environment suddenly surrounding the MCC party. When the arrival of Denness's wife brought the total of wives on tour to 12, he noted, 'Along with the wives are enough children to start a nursery school. It cannot possibly be the best preparation for playing in a Test match to have a fractious child in one's room.'

Asked for a comment on the subject, Bedser responded, 'Don't talk to me about the wives. I'm having enough trouble with the flaming husbands.'

The players felt that their form was, at worst, unaffected and, in fact, enhanced by having families present. According to Amiss, 'There were a number of players, including Mike Denness, Keith Fletcher and Geoff Arnold, whose form improved noticeably after their wives had joined them.' That might be stretching the argument, given that those batsmen needed other factors – such as injury to Lillee and Thomson – to improve their returns, but even the old traditionalist EW Swanton was prepared to speak up for domesticity.

'There is another scapegoat which in time of defeat has been trotted out before and this is the presence of wives and, even in the case of two or three, young children,' he wrote. 'True, tours in the past were celibate affairs apart from the presence of some wives of amateurs. In these more affluent times players can afford to bring their wives in many cases and some no doubt acquit themselves better in consequence. I would say that on recent tours these ladies in all outward appearance have got on well together and have been conscientious in not intruding on the business and purpose of the tour. If England lose this rubber and surrender the Ashes it will be because they are up against a better side and not because they are accompanied by these agreeable camp-followers.'

9
PROTECT AND SURVIVE

> *The Australian government should deport the English geriatrics now posing as cricketers and MCC should be charged with fraud under the Trade Practices Act.*
> **Barry Cohen, Australian MP**

The MCC party's route from Perth to Melbourne had been via a three-day game in Adelaide and through the inevitable storm of press criticism and speculation, much of the latter having centred on the form and future of the captain. 'SACK DENNESS' was the headline in one of the Perth newspapers as the tourists headed east once more. 'He's taken a fair old battering in the last 18 months,' Alec Bedser observed. 'I think he's pretty used to it by now.'

It was suggested by Christopher Martin-Jenkins that some condemnation of Mike Denness was motivated by critics wanting to be proved right after arguing that his batting was not up to the test it faced in Australia. But he added, 'It certainly looked as though all those of us who had questioned Denness's ability to play top-class fast bowling on the evidence of his tour of the West Indies seemed to have been correct. He simply did not look as though he would ever conquer his inability to get right behind the line of rising balls on the off stump.' Damningly, he concluded, 'He did not look like a good batsman out of form.'

Ian Chappell revealed, 'I think I can speak for a lot of our team in that we thought Mike was a pretty good player, I thought he was a better player than Luckhurst. But he had an unfortunate habit that his first step with his back foot was towards the leg side. I don't think it was anything to do with courage, it was just part of his method. But that was the worst thing you could do against Thommo, because Thommo angled it in at the right handers and when the ball is following you that is bad news. To make a movement like I did, back and across, means at least if the ball is going towards leg you are going towards the off side. Therefore I always thought that was a huge advantage to us.'

Scorer of 206 runs in 12 tour innings, Denness insisted he had not considered leaving himself out of the Test team, a stance that received support from EW Swanton, who called it 'a time when perspective is to be striven for and panic avoided'. He added, 'No self-respecting body of selectors would start elbowing out their captain at the first opportunity, especially when he happens to be about the best fielder in the side and has carried out all his duties both on and off the field in an exemplary way.'

Such had been the weight of issues ahead of the MCC party since arrival in Australia, Denness had spent little time worrying about his own game. While out-of-form colleagues were sitting in their hotel rooms, sipping a beer and trying to make sense of their failures, the responsibilities of captaincy meant a greater part of Denness's thinking time centred on the problems of those men. What could he do to bolster confidence among those struggling? How could he best manage fitness issues? Was team morale as high as it could be? Not to mention the logistics of nets and official functions that had to be managed.

Meanwhile, the captain was not the only batsman under scrutiny, especially if Dennis Amiss and John Edrich were fit to return in the third Test on Boxing Day. Keith Fletcher had yet to reach 20 in the Test series and had never made a first-class century in Australia. Bedser admitted that the form of the Essex man and Edrich were of equal concern to that of Denness. Even Tony Greig was testing the patience of some, with John Woodcock complaining, 'He seems to think he can launch into an attack without needing to play himself in.'

Denness promised increased net practice, stating, 'Every batsman must work at improving his own technique.' Not that there was a lot of thought, planning or discussion going into England's work in the nets, even with the tour having descended into near crisis.

Perhaps that was, as Chris Old remembered, because there was still a blind faith that things would turn around. 'Perth was the quickest of the tracks, so it was one that was going to suit them more than us. I won't say we expected to lose but it wasn't as big an upset to lose it. To be 2-0 down does hit you a little hard, but we knew we had two Tests in Melbourne coming up and felt we had a chance there, and then Sydney was a pitch that varied in what it did, and Adelaide was usually fairly flat anyway in those days.'

Also it was because this was the 1970s, where merely having someone to distribute practice balls in the nets was considered an extravagance. Even so, Amiss, unable to remember much sharing of ideas, admitted, 'You would think you would talk about it a bit more, or have a coach who says, "Right, let's try this."'

Bedser said, 'England's batting was short on technique. Too many were guilty of not getting behind the line of the ball.' He, of course, was not about to exchange his managerial jacket and tie for training gear.

According to Denness, 'In England we tend to play the square cut a great deal but in Australia we were trying to play it to balls that were rising unexpectedly to a great height. This explained how five of us were out to catches in the gully [in Perth].' He was mired too deeply in his own technical problems to be of much use as a coach to others, while assistant manager AC Smith's bowling on a shortened wicket was little preparation for Lillee and Thomson in full swing.

Denness required teammate Amiss and others to point out to him that he was taking an initial step backwards with his right foot when facing the fast bowlers, so eager was he to get himself into position to cut the ball. But such was the state of confusion into which England's batsmen had been plunged Amiss could not be sure that Denness's involuntary approach was incorrect. 'The circumstances of that series were unusual for most of us,' Amiss remarked. 'For the first time in our cricketing careers we were faced with searing pace at both ends. We had to try to work out a way to combat it.'

Alan Knott was clever enough to have quickly developed a method that took advantage of his 5ft 8in stature, allowing him to ape more easily Greig's method of cutting under the ball when it was pitched short. 'My technique was to be ready to play the ball in front of my chest or head and leave as many deliveries as possible,' he remembered. 'I would wait for them to bowl slightly wide of off stump so I could play the uppercut over slips and gully. Greig was the first batsman I had seen do that consistently in a Test match. If you didn't attempt to do something like this, Thomson and Lillee would simply run in on wickets which were not very good and gain the upper hand. Playing those shots outside the off stump was a necessity otherwise you were going to stand there all day and not get any runs because there were very few deliveries which you could drive.'

Already the scorer of one half-century in the series, he would achieve one in each of the next two matches and follow up with a century in the fifth Test. 'I was extremely fortunate to be at the top of my batting form,' he said. 'When you are in good form you don't worry because you are seeing the ball so clearly. But when you are out of touch and not seeing the ball it is a completely different game. Thomson's deliveries would take off even when pitched up. Out of form, you would have had a nightmare of a time.'

Amiss continued, 'The two players who got runs were the long and the short of it, Greig and Knott, and they stayed leg side of the ball, which nobody else did as successfully. I hadn't noticed this in practice, I didn't see them doing it quite as much. It looked like they had got something going there, but that was never talked about or shared between us. Obviously we saw them doing it and one or two of us started trying to do it in the nets, but I came back to what I had done pre-tour. I can't remember Knotty mentioning to us that this was the way to play and maybe we should think about it. We just thought that is the way he does it and we play the way we play and hopefully we do it well enough to be successful.'

Instead, the conversation among the batsmen tended to be one of resignation rather than an attempt at solutions that evidently did not exist. Brian Luckhurst remembered the Kent contingent dining together and having 'a fascinating discussion about the difficulty of competing against fast bowling of the ferocity and quality of Lillee and Thomson'. Challenged to name the six batsmen he'd played alongside who were best equipped to take them on, Colin Cowdrey 'could not pick any top order capable of taking the attack back to [them] in those conditions'.

Cowdrey was pragmatic enough not to attempt it himself, employing what Denness recognised as a 'wearing down process; hour after hour playing nothing except the ball bowled straight to him'. Yet the captain felt, 'That way we were never going to get enough runs to win a Test match. The only way to score runs was by playing shots.' But he conceded, 'Everyone had to use his own technique and play to his limitations and strengths.'

Fletcher, who admitted he never got to grips with being able to leave the ball that was rising harmlessly above or outside off stump, ended up wishing he had tried a different approach during the series, adopting a trigger movement that took him forward rather than back. Yet some unpredictable wickets and the nature of the bowling made it impossible for even the most courageous of batsmen to follow a course of action that their sub-conscious instinct for self-preservation simply wouldn't allow.

Which prompts the question of how big a part the basic fear of injury played in the downfall of the English batting. No batsman, even in the days before helmets, likes to admit to being scared, and while Thomson might delight in the memory of the opposition 'shitting themselves', the truth probably lies somewhere in the middle. A batsman's first thought might not be 'I hope I don't get killed', but the preoccupation with safety can't help but undermine technique, stifle the scoring of runs and make dismissal more likely.

'I never thought about [being hit],' said Edrich. ' I think you have to back your own ability. I used to think. "There is Dennis Lillee and me. I don't want him to get me out." Being injured didn't come into my thinking.' But he conceded, 'When you play at Test level you don't actually enjoy a lot of what you are doing on the field, but you enjoy the results and I scored quite a lot of runs against Australia.'[28]

'None of us enjoyed going out to bat,' Fletcher recorded. 'The knowledge that one needed to move very fast to keep one's body intact was not a pleasant way to spend a day in the sunshine.'

Denness insisted, 'I was never frightened about getting hit. I was always prepared to take something on the body from the chest downwards. I never thought about getting hit on the head, I always thought that one way or another I would have quick enough reactions that I wasn't going to duck into the ball; that I would get my head out of the way.'

Yet Amiss confessed, 'When I went on *Test Match Special* and was talking about my book, Jonathan Agnew asked me if you really fear for your life. You did a bit, with the ball flying around out there. In

---

[28] 2,644 runs against Australia at an average of 48.96, including seven centuries, in 32 Test matches

the middle of having to deal with it you just think, "Get out the way, get out the way," as much as you can.'

It meant that methods of protection were frequently discussed. Taking a lead from Cowdrey, Denness recalled, 'Many of us tried some form of body protector. I remember trying one put on me that was polystyrene The problem with that is it doesn't give, so if you tried to go down under the ball the polystyrene was going to stick in no man's land, so you just hoped it didn't hit your rib cage.' Even so, he insisted that such experimentation was not down to fear, saying that if the batsmen had been scared they would have looked at helmets and face masks. 'It was just a logical approach,' he said.

Amiss explained, 'We were all a bit concerned about being hit and we put on a little bit more protection, like body guards we had made for us with foam that would stop you getting anything broken. It was like an inner jacket that you could put the shirt over and didn't restrict us too much.'

Edrich remembered the discussion of protective headwear. 'That was when we first started taking about helmets,' he said. 'We were sitting in the dressing room at the close of play and we said, "This is ridiculous, we should be wearing helmets." That was the first time in my career there had been that much short-pitched bowling. I was brought up playing against Fred Trueman and Brian Statham and they bowled you the odd bouncer. Suddenly you were probably getting two or three an over. It made sense then.'

Greig, who would be an early adopter of the helmet in World Series Cricket, commented publicly, 'When I get home I'm going to see if I can't design something to protect my skull.'

Fletcher, who would recall that 'we must all have been mad' to be facing such hostility without protecting their heads, said in his honest autobiographical account, 'Batsman do get shell-shocked in series like this one.' He added that 'there is no point in pretending an immunity because no one is safe from the psychological problems which inevitably result. The problems begin as soon as you start to wonder if you're quick enough to keep getting out of the way of the short ball. Tailenders get frightened, which is fair enough under the circumstances, but even the leading batsman are apprehensive.'

And such apprehension could not remain completely hidden from the opposition. 'There were times when I felt a little bit sorry for the Englishmen,' said Ian Redpath, 'because a lot of them had their families out there and they thought they might never see their families again when they went out to bat.'

Ross Edwards added, 'They were shell-shocked. They were rabbits in the headlights. I think any other team in the world would have been. It was such a change from the norm. This was cricket beyond your experience. You don't learn that during a season, that is when you go away and change your whole attitude and your confidence and spend a lot of time in the nets with the bowling machine at full speed. You learn to play it. These blokes didn't have a chance to do that. I was fearful for them. I was fielding in the covers, and I was scared for them.'

Meanwhile, the England bowlers, as well as trying to block out thoughts of decapitation when batting, were charged with dismissing the Australians for fewer than their batsmen could muster. And they had no option other than figuring out themselves how they did that, looking to each other for whatever support they needed.

'The players were very much left to work out their own way,' said Old. 'As bowlers as we used to talk a lot about the batsmen we were coming up against and then looking at how they played and where their strengths and weaknesses were. A few of us would work together and try and help each other and see what was happening, what we could improve upon, where people are having difficulties. The major problem for me was the no-balls because I'm used to pulling my feet out of the ground in Yorkshire, whereas over there you're tending to bounce off the top of it. Your stride becomes a little bit longer and you try to adjust to it.

'Bob Willis had problems for a long time and the worst thing in Australia, one of the hardest parts for me, was playing eight-ball overs. Suddenly having to bowl a third more balls in an over you have to be that much more aware of pacing yourself. In England you could go flat out for the first four or five and then by the sixth you've got through it, but over there you've got two more to bowl. It was a difficult thing to come to terms with.'

The English newspapers were by now reporting on Denness's performances in practice with the kind of attention normally reserved for matches. The *Daily Mirror* noted that he 'struggled in the nets against a battery of fast bowlers aiming short at his off stump'.

Denness's wife, Molly, would not be flying to Australia until 2 January. Instead of waiting for her arrival, the newspapers sought her out at her mother's home in Ayrshire to get her response to the furore they were generating about her husband. 'I cannot stand it,' she said. 'I have turned into a complete ostrich. I daren't look at the papers any more. And the moment anyone comes on TV discussing the tour I dive for the off switch.'

It is important to remember that of all this was happening only two Tests into a six-match series. Already, it felt like it had been a long tour.

The day before MCC played South Australia for the second time was the first time all 17 players had been able to practise. Denness had two nets, Edrich and Amiss each batted for half an hour and Peter Lever tested his back. The game itself answered a few questions, although the perfect batting conditions and friendly spin-based attack MCC faced on the second day offered a poor imitation of what they could expect in the Melbourne Test beginning on Boxing Day. David Lloyd's Lancashire colleague, Barry Wood, explained, 'I remember Bumble telling me that when they played the state and up-country games the pitches were white and flat and when it came to the Test matches they were green and hard.'

Amiss fought through the pain in his thumb to score 73 in just under two hours and Cowdrey, finding his rhythm and the gaps in the field, batted with effortless control against Ashley Mallett and Terry Jenner to make 78. He hit only four boundaries and complained that the number of cold drinks he consumed while batting gave him stomach cramps. Most significantly, Denness helped himself to 88, including eight fours, denying himself a century when be declared at 277 for 2, seven runs ahead, in the interest of achieving a result. One report said he showed an arrogance previously absent on tour, although he did miss out on dispatching some full tosses that could have taken him to three figures, Cynically, one could point out that the closure of the innings also denied Fletcher, his probable rival for a Test place, a chance to bat, but no one seriously considered that the amiable Denness would stoop to such tricks. Fletcher, an automatic selection since 1972 and having gone only two Tests without a century, would now be able to indulge himself on Christmas Day.

After Underwood had claimed seven of the 11 wickets taken in the match by MCC's bowlers – Cowdrey also picked up a couple – the tourists were left to chase 216 in 167 minutes. Amiss scored another half-century, but Denness's decision to mix up the order to give more people the chance to bat – with Old, Taylor and Titmus at four, five and six – undermined a proper push for victory. Denness and Cowdrey could not get the ten runs required from the final over.

MCC set off immediately for Melbourne, a journey that quickly turned into an ordeal for Old. 'Late in the afternoon I started off with a migraine and all my medication had gone off to Melbourne ahead of us,' he explained. 'I had to fly to Melbourne without any medication and consequently I got up the next morning to go to the nets and I've gone into the dressing room and bent down to take my shoes off and ended up on the floor. Bernard Thomas got me in a taxi back to the hotel and I spent the rest of the day in bed. I got a phone call that night from the captain saying I could enjoy Christmas because I wasn't selected for the Boxing Day match. Thanks very much for that good news.'

Christmas Day – lonely for some, tense with anticipation for others – was spent in the team hotel. Many friends and family back home had been sent good wishes from across the globe by way of the tourists' official Christmas card, with the St George and Dragon crest on the front and a team picture on the inside.

As Santa Claus handed out presents, the MCC group were insulated somewhat from the horrifying news of one of Australia's greatest natural disasters after the Northern Territory city of Darwin had been struck by Cyclone Tracy in the early hours of the morning. Winds estimated to have reached 150 mph – after recording equipment broke down at 130 mph – devastated the city, eventually leaving 71 dead, destroying more than three-quarters of all homes, and leaving around 30,000 of the 47,000 population homeless. More than 500 people, injured by debris, required hospital treatment on Christmas Day itself and with all water, electricity and sewerage out of action an immediate drive began to provide 25,000 anti-cholera vaccinations. Queen Elizabeth was said to be 'much distressed' by the news, while Australian Prime Minister Gough Whitlam made plans for an urgent return from his European tour.

Cowdrey left the team bubble to make a speech to 150 guests over lunch at a local golf club, but the rest remained in surroundings described by Martin-Jenkins as 'a city and a hotel which seemed in some ways to have gone to sleep with Queen Victoria.' He added, 'The solid old imposing buildings, the parks and the rocking trams with their dark wood interiors that resemble old railway carriages take you back to the old country in the days of Empire.'

There were few, however, who found they could succumb to the environment and give themselves up to the kind of post-dinner slumber their countrymen back home would be enjoying a few hours later after watching Rolf Harris presenting BBC1's morning show from the National Children's Home in Hertfordshire and Jimmy Savile hosting *Top of the Pops*.[29]

'For the players,' observed CMJ, 'the cheer of Christmas was all too soon replaced by that nagging feeling in the pit of the stomach which comes not from indigestion but from anxiety.'

---

[29] 1974 was the only year of the decade in which *Morecambe and Wise* was not the centrepiece of BBC's Christmas Day schedule. With Eric Morecambe suffering from ill-health, fans had to be content with a late-night compilation on BBC2.

10
SIGNS OF LIFE

Apart from those who had a genuine vindictiveness behind their battle cry of 'Kill the Poms' there had developed since England's crushing defeats at Brisbane and Perth an almost patronising air of sympathy for the struggling touring team.
Christopher Martin-Jenkins

Melbourne Cricket Ground on Boxing Day. Tier upon tier of imposing concrete, steep enough to give the sprawling green playing surface an air of claustrophobia, especially once the first-day crowd of 77,165 – the second-highest to have watched an Ashes contest – were all in place. Even the umpires, supposedly detached and dispassionate, could not remain unaffected.

'Look, when I walked out on the ground on Boxing Day, jeepers, it was really something,' recalled Robin Bailhache. 'They opened the bowling from my end. I can remember saying, "You okay, batsman?", then I pointed to the scorers and got the signal that they were ready, and as I turned around and said, "Play," I could feel the electricity in the air. There was no place on earth I would rather be.'

There had been rain showers on Christmas Day, leaving a little moisture in the MCG wicket. But when Ian Chappell won the toss and asked England to bat it was more to do with putting their batsmen back in the firing line than the conditions. It was the fourth time he had inserted the opposition in Test matches, one short of the record set by another great gambler, Garry Sobers. England left out Brian Luckhurst, Keith Fletcher, Chris Old and Geoff Arnold and brought back Dennis Amiss, John Edrich, Derek Underwood and Mike Hendrick. Australia saw no need to change their line-up.

Dennis Lillee opened from the Pavilion End, bowling to Amiss. 'It's like the amphitheatre,' the batsman remembered. 'It must have been how the gladiators felt.' Lillee shaped the seventh ball towards the slips and Amiss edged to a diving Doug Walters.

At least England's early loss produced stodgy resistance rather than a procession of wickets. There was no boundary until David Lloyd's inside edge evaded leg slip in the 13th over. Colin Cowdrey's first four was rather more classical, a pull off Max Walker, but other than that he was strokeless – 'almost motionless' according to Christopher Martin-Jenkins, although John Woodcock felt he looked better than at Perth.

Switching ends after a wayward first spell, Jeff Thomson brought loud cheers from the crowd and frantic rubbing by Lloyd after hitting the batsman on the left hip, a painful reminder of their previous encounter. He then had Lloyd dropped by Walters and, after dealing with a troublesome bootlace, sent a fearsome delivery climbing towards the batsman's face. All Lloyd could do was protect himself with his gloves, giving Ashley Mallett the easy task of stepping forward from gully to take the catch. He had batted 109 minutes for his 14 runs.

'Thomson was certainly the quickest I had faced,' said Lloyd, 'and the pitches had good bounce and good pace. Eight-ball overs were significant because you would get four or five bouncers an over, so your scoring opportunities were very limited. Playing a hook shot with no helmet was out of the question for me. You tried to work out a method of survival and scoring, but the scoring was a problem because your opportunities are only about three deliveries per over. I batted a long time for not much reward. That was a frustration.'

Walker allowed only 12 runs in his first 13 overs, prompting Martin-Jenkins to lament, 'The situation cried out for a May or a Dexter, a player with the class and natural aggression to take the bowlers on and steal the initiative.' Instead, it was the stoic figure of John Edrich who was greeted by two short legs, with Lillee barely off the cut strip as the more forward of the pair. He dived forward to grasp the ball off Edrich's thigh pad.

Cowdrey cut Walker's first ball of the afternoon for four. He nodded his head as if in casual introduction to evade a Thomson bouncer, and then saw Wally Edwards spill a straightforward chance at short leg off Walker.

Settling into his work, Edrich cut both Thomson and Lillee to the boundary, but a partnership of 76 in 125 minutes ended when Thomson's pace beat Cowdrey on the back foot. Tom Brooks raised his finger for lbw, despite suspicions that it might have been missing leg stump. Having been cheered to the middle in Perth, a more demanding and boisterous holiday gathering at the MCG booed him off after he had taken the best part of four hours for his 35 runs.

The atmosphere inside the ground slapped Denness around the face as he walked out to replace his county colleague. 'In the dressing room there is the comfort of air conditioning so you notice the change very abruptly as you leave the pavilion,' he recounted in his autobiography. 'When the wicket fell I opened the dressing room door to leave and for the first time became aware of the noise of the 80,000 crowd. You get a chance to attune yourself, both to the crowd and the humid atmosphere, as you take your 30-yard walk through the members' pavilion and begin the very long walk to the wicket.' Later in the match he was struck by how breathless Geoff Arnold became after bowling his first over in such stifling, chest-tightening conditions.

Denness quickly bore witness to a decision even more contentious than Cowdrey's lbw – the judgement by Bailhache in the next over that Edrich had been caught down the leg side as Rodney Marsh reacted sharply to the bowling of Mallett. Marsh's original appeal had been to Brooks at square leg for a stumping and Mallett had not even claimed the wicket. Edrich was clearly aghast to be given out, slapping his pad in disapproval. It sent England to tea 110 for 4, only seven boundaries having been struck in two sessions.

Typically, Tony Greig set about amending that, scoring his first 12 runs with three fours in a single Thomson over, jabbing two balls over the slips and digging out an attempted yorker with such force and timing that it shot to long-off. Whatever happened in Melbourne, Greig would be occupying a prominent place in the Boxing Day television schedules back home, one of the seven sportsmen shown competing for the 1974 *Superstars* crown on BBC1 at 4.50 p.m. – either side of the film *Chitty Chitty Bang Bang* and the *Cilla Black Special*, featuring David Essex and The Wombles.

Greig, who came fourth in the second staging of the multi-sport competition,[30] would rather have had a prominent role on BBC2's

---

30 Filmed at the Crystal Palace National Sports Centre in July, with the result kept under wraps until broadcast, *Superstars* saw Greig take maximum points in the

late-night highlights of the Test, while Denness's appearance on that programme would be fleeting after he attempted to cut Mallett against the spin and edged to Marsh. He had already been dropped by Ian Chappell low to his left. It was the kind of performance that rekindled debate about his tenure in the team and prompted Chappell to recall years later, 'We looked to the gate and Mike Denness was walking through and Dougie said, "Not this bastard for another 20 seconds."'

Greig was a far greater obstacle to Australian ambition, but the home side were gifted his wicket. He might have thought better of taking on Ian Chappell's throw for a third run after Alan Knott cut Mallett to third man, but he clearly believed his long legs had reached safety before Marsh removed the bails. Television pictures from the end of the ground – no side-on camera in those days – were inconclusive but tended to support the batsman. Always happy to play the pantomime villain, a trait that made him fantastically popular in the Indian sub-continent, he made no attempt to hide his disapproval, exchanging words with Chappell as he departed.

The umpiring gave England's newspapers something other than their team's inept batting to get their teeth into. 'ROBBED – THREE TIMES', was the *Daily Mirror*'s back-page splash, with Peter Laker describing the disputed decisions as 'one doubtful, one bizarre, the other absurd', saying of the catch behind, 'This was officialdom gone stark, staring bonkers.'

Denness, happy not to be interrogated about his own failure, argued, 'All three players indicated that they weren't satisfied with their decisions.' Greig, always outspoken, added, 'It's fair to say that in an issue as close as this the batsman should receive the benefit of the doubt,' and said of Edrich's dismissal, 'John wasn't satisfied with it and, from my end, I wasn't satisfied with it either.'

It wasn't quite a return to 1970-71, when England felt every decision went against them, but the tourists were having trouble enough building meaningful scores without having the umpires to

---

swimming and football competitions to finish behind winner John Conteh, the world light-heavyweight boxing champion, Olympic gold medal hurdler David Hemery and England and Manchester City footballer Colin Bell. He beat John H Stracey (boxing), Chay Blyth (sailing) and Mick Channon (football) in the final standings to win the £1,000 fourth prize.

contend with as well. According to David Lloyd, 'It was inevitable that the standard of umpiring would get a mention. Some rules applied to them that didn't apply to us. That had always been the case in Australia. You are playing the umpires as well.

'I recall we noticed that Thommo was pushing the front line. Tactically, we would try to draw attention to it, like drawing the line where his foot should be with your bat. I remember saying to Tom Brooks, who was a lovely chap, "It's very tight." So Tom said, "Yeh, we don't worry too much about that over here." When I said they did when we were bowling, he said, "Yes, but you are used to it."'

Martin-Jenkins reflected, 'As for the unfortunate umpires, it was perhaps as well that both, rather than just one, were involved in incidents. Everyone makes mistakes, especially if they are under intense pressure, and there can be nothing more demanding than making hair's breadth judgments before 77,000 people in a vital Test match. Both men were doing their best to be strictly impartial, but neither seemed blessed with the effortless authority of a Frank Chester or a Syd Buller. Their actions always appeared to be self-conscious.'

In London's *Evening Standard*, John Thicknesse was more forthright, declaring, 'It must be said that their umpiring fell short of required standards.'

'We did cop heaps from the press and a lot of it came from the UK of course,' Bailhache remembered. Yet it had largely been down to the MCC tour management that the former club cricketer had received his surprise Test call-up only five years after he'd taken up umpiring 'for all the wrong reasons'.

He explained, 'I was umpiring Aussie rules football in the winter, doing first-class games, and someone said that if you want to improve your concentration why don't you umpire cricket because there's no sport that demands so much continuous concentration. With six hours at a time, I thought that wasn't a bad idea. They used to say that umpiring was for the ranks of the old, the bold and the buggered but I was none of them, and found I quite enjoyed it.'

Within two years, Bailhache had taken charge of his first Sheffield Shield match, but appointments were still spread sparsely until he was named to partner Test umpire Max O'Connell for South Australia's game against the latest MCC tourists. 'The touring side had a match against each of the state sides, so they got to see the umpires and apparently they weren't impressed. One umpire tried to change the ball without telling the bowlers, another guy they thought was too officious, and Max didn't have a good game. He gave a couple of decisions I thought were iffy. I had a good game, including giving Ian Chappell run out after a direct hit from Tony Greig. I found out later that MCC said I reminded them of an English umpire, although I don't know what the parameter was. I think I was probably one of the best of a bad lot, so Tommy Brooks and I got the gig.'

And the next gig. And the next. They would end up standing in all six matches, although Bailhache explained, 'They only ever appointed us one game at a time, although we heard unofficially that nobody else was in the van. But we never got told officially. I was so surprised that when I got my first Test match I said to my wife and also to the secretary of the South Australia Cricket Association that if I got another Test I would take my whole family. He called me two weeks later and said, "I have already booked you and your family in for Perth." I didn't expect to get all six. It had never been done before. There was a bit of resentment among other umpires. Every time the phone rang for these poor fellas around Test match time, they must have thought that someone was ringing to say they have the next Test match.'

There was a danger, too, that familiarity bred resentment and contempt among the teams and press, with any dissatisfaction about actions and decisions being allowed to roll over into subsequent matches, especially with the series now in its decisive stages. 'It wasn't right to give us all six,' Bailhache admitted. 'We must have had some ability and we got through without starting World War III, but at times it was too much. More by good luck, perhaps, we got through.'

Bedser queried the persistent reappointing of the same men. 'The Australian board argued they were the best available and there was no advantage in having a panel system,' he reported. 'I had a large measure of sympathy for the pair. They took on probably more than was right to expect.'

'I don't recall having much sympathy for any umpires,' said Ian Chappell. 'Brooks I would have thought was the best umpire in

Australia at that stage, but Bailhache? No way. If Tom Brooks is your best umpire I don't think the standard is that high and as long as Bailhache is there they are not the best two umpires in Australia.

'I remember a game at the start of 1975-76, South Australia versus New South Wales, and it was a pretty aggressive match. We knew each other pretty well and both a had a few players in the Australian side. I remember out on the field Bailhache said to me, "I wish your teams got on better," and I said, "Robin, we don't get on with any other team on the field, but you look at us after six o'clock we will all be together having a pint." That night there were 24 players in the South Australian dressing room and Robin, who was a non-drinker, came in to get his Fanta or Coke or whatever the hell he was drinking, and I said, "Hey, Robin, look at how many are here. There are 24 here, but at 11 o'clock tomorrow we will be arguing again." I thought Robin had no sense of humour, which is not a good start for an umpire.'

Whether that is a harsh comment or not, the umpires' good nature would be stretched to breaking point in the next Test.

For now, England were spared the presence of Thomson for the final 90 minutes of play while he nursed a tight hamstring. They got to what ended up being the final ball of the day before losing Titmus, who Fletcher recalled 'showed a good deal of fortitude against the quicks'. Bowling round the wicket towards a cordon of five catchers – which would have intimidated many a batsman – Lillee pitched short and Titmus might have been able to let the ball go had he not already committed himself to moving outside the off stump, a method that had served him well at Perth. He was forced to fend off the ball at head height and it looped off the bat handle to Mallett, leaving England 176 for 7 at stumps.

Underwood began the second day by swinging his bat at Thomson because, well, what else could he do? Lillee knew that England's tail-ender was equipped with nothing but courage in such a situation and, ruthlessly, took the decision to continue bowling short from round the wicket. Underwood was left wringing his right hand when unable to avoid such a delivery and found Ian Chappell at his side joking, 'Shame. We were aiming for the left hand.'

Knott had the skill to play Lillee through the covers off the front foot and take Thomson to the square boundary with a controlled cut, but he was soon jerking his head back to avoid a sharp lifter from Thomson. He recovered his composure to guide Lillee for another four. 'Few have been blessed with Knott's unique combination of verve and nerve, of steely concentration mixed with almost mischievous enterprise,' remarked Martin-Jenkins.

Underwood offered a routine edge to Marsh off a Walker outswinger, and Bob Willis thrust his considerable front leg own the wicket to drive for four before Knott turned Thomson to leg for the single that completed his fifty. Willis edged a leg glance to the rope but then slogged into the air and saw Walters take a neat catch as the ball dropped over his shoulder. Mike Hendrick threw the bat a couple of times before Knott surprisingly missed an ordinary-looking Thomson delivery. England were all out for 242, leaving Australia a little over half an hour's batting before lunch.

The only casualty in that period was Hendrick, whose languorous approach had Keith Miller quipping in the press box, 'This bloke looks like I feel.' He pulled his left hamstring, bringing the session to a close and ruling him out of the remainder of the series. 'There was no warning at all,' he explained. 'When I reached the delivery stride I heard the damn thing go.'

'If this luck continues,' dead-panned Edrich over lunch, 'I'm going home by boat.'

Underwood found himself bowling the eighth over of the innings, Ian Redpath moving his feet pleasantly to drive him down the ground and looking more fluent than in previous innings. Surprisingly, Titmus was held back until the 33rd over and not used in tandem with his left-arm colleague. He quickly posed a threat and Redpath survived a confident lbw appeal as he tried to sweep a ball that floated from leg to off and hit him on the back foot.

Wally Edwards was less pleasing on the eye, reaching 27 mostly in singles. He could have edged any number of deliveries. His apprehension showed itself in an over-eagerness to back up, for which Titmus gave him a warning. Greig bowled with control but, against a depleted attack, it was a surprise when the Aussie batsmen accepted the offer of bad light half an hour before tea with the score on 62.

The crowd were entertained during the interruption by two fake umpires striding convincingly to the middle to inspect conditions before they were escorted away, shaking hands with the real officials as they passed. It was the final noteworthy event of the day as darkening skies and eventual rain ended the last session after only ten minutes.

Australia lost Edwards on the fourth ball of the third day, slashing a short ball from Willis to Denness in the covers in the manner of a village cricketer. Dropping his gloves in his embarrassed rush to depart the scene, he would learn of his exclusion from the fourth Test before he had the chance to bat again.

Greg Chappell would never hand over his wicket so lightly, but a rearing, angled delivery did for him in Willis's next over, the ball falling to Greig as he moved to his right from second slip. Titmus continued to vary his flight and position of release on the crease, and it was his quicker ball that removed Ross Edwards, who nicked to Cowdrey – the third wicket to fall for three runs in 14 minutes.

Without the usual dominance of their team to get caught up in, the Aussie fans made do with aiming chants, jeers and abuse at the English fielders. Amiss, a favourite target, felt there were times when it moved beyond the 'good humoured' to the 'personal and abusive'. One fan, in particular, delighted in tracking Amiss around the boundary, reminding him in piercing tones that he was the 'worst bloody player' he had seen and that his three-year-old could do better. 'Had I been scoring runs it would have been water off a duck's back,' Amiss conceded, 'but with a run of disappointing scores behind me it wasn't so easy just to shrug it off.'

As Australia looked to rebuild their innings Walters set off as though he had thoughts of another three-figure session, laying back to pull Titmus through midwicket and driving him through the covers as he moved briskly into the 20s. Redpath brought up 100 with a single and placed a straight drive out of bowler Greig's reach to record his first fifty of a series in which he became more and more productive. 'Redpath was a real sticker, a top player,' observed opposite number Lloyd. 'He knew his game and he knew how to survive. He was a good foil for the Chappells and Dougie Walters.'

'You are never happy as a batsman,' Redpath recalled, 'but I was playing fairly solidly. I was occupying the crease a fair while which I was happy with. You always like to make hundreds but as an opener sometimes it's just as valuable early in the innings to survive when the ball is shiny. I got lots of starts, which I suppose means you are doing three-quarters of your job. Then we had players after me with the ability to play shots.'

Redpath's productivity made skipper Chappell even more grateful that the selectors had managed to see past the blind spot he felt they had for the opener. 'Neil Harvey didn't think Redder was a good player. They tended to pick him when it was tough. Harvey's reasoning was a bit silly. He didn't think he was a great player because he came down the track a lot and defended. Because Harvey was such a great player of spin bowling and could belt the crap out of it when he came down the track he thought everyone should do that. It's not that easy. We were all huge Redder fans and thought he was a good player. He toured South Africa twice when I did and they thought that technically he was our best player.

'We obviously wanted Redder in all the time and his selection is probably an indication of two things. Deep down they thought Redder was more likely to get runs when the going was tough and also I think Sam Loxton, being a Victorian, would have been a Redpath fan and maybe held sway there.'

On this occasion, Redpath's removal was not far away. Walters, one ball after he moved back and across to force Greig for another leg-side boundary, perished tamely when he clipped to Lloyd at square leg. Then England rounded off their best session of the series when Redpath was caught by Knott off an attempted cut, leaving Greig pounding the air in delight and pointing the batsman's way to the pavilion. Australia went to lunch at 126 for 5.

Ian Chappell had missed much of the mayhem, a dislocated right index finger suffered in the field dropping him to number six in the order. Several times immediately after lunch he looked troubled by Underwood, surviving a fierce appeal for a bat-pad catch by Greig at silly point. As always, he showed willingness to hook Willis, almost being caught by substitute fielder Old at deep square leg before middling one more cleanly in front of the wicket. He swept Titmus fine and clipped Underwood square to move into the 30s. It was the arrival of the new ball that halted his progress, given out lbw as he aimed a leg-side drive against Willis, who then greeted Walker with a bouncer that had the batsman looking like he was swatting at a fly.

Marsh thumped a straight drive against Underwood and a mistimed hook fell into a gap in the leg-side field. But with the first innings advantage in the balance, he favoured circumspection. It was a rare show of aggression when he swung Underwood towards the deep midwicket boundary for two runs.

After tea was taken at 207 for 6, both batsmen appeared more willing to take chances, Underwood conceding 20 runs in three overs. With Australia only five runs in arrears with four wickets remaining, Titmus replaced his colleague at the Southern End and quickly got Marsh in a tangle. He missed one sweep completely and top edged the next ball into the air for Knott to catch, ending his innings on 44 after a partnership of 64. Walker went immediately, marching off after edging Willis.

Brooks had seemed reluctant to give that decision and now Bailhache upset Titmus by rejecting an appeal against a sweeping Mallett. It was not long since the same official had reprieved Walker when hit on the back leg. The bowler turned slowly, hands on hips to show his displeasure, and was booed by the crowd. 'I don't know what I'm doing out here,' he said to his captain. 'They're killing me.'

Denness, who could see the Australian batsmen struggling to combat Titmus's drift and dip, explained, 'Batsmen picking up the right line and length for the off-break normally go to sweep the ball but once committed suddenly find that it straightens out, pitching in line of wicket to wicket so giving them little chance of survival when hit on the pads. The vast majority should be given out … There was much ill-feeling about it in our dressing room.'

On this latest occasion, England had to wait only until the next ball to celebrate, when Mallett pushed behind square on the off side and failed to beat Old's underarm throw after being sent back. Thomson was cleaned up by a Willis yorker, the bowler's fifth wicket, and Australia's innings ended on 241, one run short of England's total. Willis, bowling with a strained thigh muscle strapped, had now taken 14 wickets in the series and had put the tourists in a position where, at last, they felt like they were in the contest.

'This is the first time we have been in a very good position,' Denness told reporters. But it was not exactly a rallying cry when he added, 'With all that grass about and our bowling strength down to four it's still going to be difficult for us. We've just got to get stuck in.'

He was rather more assertive when asked about the match officials. 'It seems there is no way the umpires will give an lbw on the lap. It's very hard on Fred and they're just killing his art because this is what he is bowling for all the time. The difference is the 30 runs that could decide the match.'

Having survived one over before bad light halted play on the third evening, England had the rest day to ponder their approach, the challenge being not merely survival but scoring quickly enough to give themselves an opportunity for victory. For the best part of the fourth morning, they appeared to have solved that conundrum. After scoring only 176 runs during the whole of the first day, they saw Amiss and Lloyd post the team's first – and only – century opening partnership of the series in fewer than 18 overs.[31]

Amiss used Thomson's pace and width to steer himself briskly into the 20s, although he looked less at ease when Lillee got a straighter one to lift, forcing him to sway out of the way. Lloyd also looked to score when Thomson strayed, but the bowler's pace still meant he could meet an attempted cut with nothing but edge, only for Ian Chappell, injured finger and all, to spill the chance at first slip.

Deciding to play some shots against Lillee, Amiss got lucky with a back-foot drive that ended up at the third-man boundary, but the clips off his legs came off the middle of the bat and fizzed to the boundary behind square. Finally, on the slowest and lowest batting surface of the series – which forced the fast bowlers to bowl a fuller length than in previous innings – here was a glimpse of the man the Australians had heard about throughout his prolific 1974. Lloyd, meanwhile, had remained in single figures until slashing Thomson square of the wicket.

Having put some unexpected pressure on the Australian bowlers, Amiss and Lloyd had been the subject of such a level of language by Lillee that umpire Brooks, after being alerted by his colleague, spoke to Australia's captain. Questioned about it later by one journalist, Chappell snapped, 'Ask the fucking umpire,' but later he said that Brooks had repeated Bailhache's instruction to Lillee: 'Calm down. You're getting a bit too excited.'

---

31 In the 1970-71 series, England's openers shared five century partnerships.

Amiss, who had provoked the outburst by intentionally steering Lillee wide of third slip, had put enough runs against his name to be unconcerned about such melodrama, while Denness explained, 'I knew the swearing had been going on out there and I asked Dennis and David about it at lunch. Amiss told me Lillee had called him something pretty uncomplimentary in the middle of the pitch. I later asked Lillee to repeat what he had said and he wouldn't. I can assure you it wasn't very clever.'

Bailhache recalled, 'Lillee's language was an issue at times and in the third Test I had to ask Ian Chappell to try to calm him down after a verbal sound bite unleashed on Dennis Amiss, who said he thought the umpires handled the situation very well. As for Thommo, he was no problem at all. He virtually didn't say boo for two bob.

'I gained a lot more respect from players as I went along. I didn't chit chat and got this reputation for being a dour, staid sort of character. That was me. I was polite and got in no arguments. If you read reports they said I was fair but strong, whatever that means. I didn't consciously work on that but as I matured during the series I wasn't frightened to tell the players to pull their heads in.'

Amiss ran well to get a third after forcing Thomson through midwicket and, at 67 without loss after little more than an hour, the game suddenly seemed to be the fun that Cowdrey kept insisting it was. Thomson, giving up 46 runs in seven overs in his opening spell, had misplaced his air of menace. Amiss directed him through point to reach 50 off 58 balls and then dispatched a Walker full toss. Only the size of the MCG outfield denied him additional boundaries.

Lloyd on-drove Mallett for two to post the three-figure partnership and his sweep took the total to 115 and his own score to 44. But he drove the next ball straight back at the sure-handed spinner. 'Having done all the work, I got out caught and bowled to Ashley Mallett,' he remembered with obvious pain. 'That is pretty poor, it shouldn't happen. I went down the pitch and hit him back low, and he was a good catcher. I am not getting much against the fast bowlers so once Mallett comes on I am thinking I've got to try to score. There is an impatience. If I had been coaching I would have said, "What the fuck are you doing?"'

When Lloyd returned to the dressing room, Denness saw startling evidence of the duress under which England's openers were operating against Australia's fast bowlers. 'The whole of Lloyd's body was quivering,' he remembered. 'His neck and the top half of his body in particular were shaking. He was shell-shocked, suffering from the effects of never having to move around so quickly in all his life. It was the reaction from his continual ducking and weaving to get out of the firing line.'

Mallett, however, continued to bowl throughout the afternoon and England's batsmen, perhaps wary after seeing Lloyd's demise, were guilty of not trying to knock him off his line and length. Fletcher, noting the off-spinner's effectiveness in Australia, felt he would 'get slogged' in England.

When Lillee had begun the session by finding Amiss's edge it appeared to be a sign of the pitch's benevolence that the ball dropped short of the cordon. But Cowdrey got a lifter and was out caught for the first time in the series, Greg Chappell reaching up left-handed to grab the ball. Edrich then edged a wide one from Thomson to Marsh. Suddenly, after it had appeared that the under-pressure Denness might be coming out to bat in a healthy position, he now had to arrest a tumble of three wickets for 37 runs. It was a task beyond him. Thomson pitched full, the ball moved away fractionally, and the wretched England captain could only throw back his head in despair once more as Ian Chappell took a catch off the edge.

Amiss was soon gone, too, clipping Mallett to the Australian captain at midwicket when he was ten runs short of his first century against Australia, and two runs behind Bobby Simpson's record of 1,381 Test runs in a calendar year, set in 1964. He departed to generous applause from the MCG spectators and opponents who'd had a close-up view of his earlier struggles. In a series dominated by the perils of facing Thomson and Lillee, the men who had built England's most solid platform of the tour had both given their wickets away to the spinner. Amiss, who regretted having allowed himself to be tied down by Mallet after lunch, said, 'I was very disappointed when I got out for 90. The new ball was coming up and I thought, "Just keep chipping away for once," and I checked Mallett to short midwicket. I think I was trying to get the hundred before the new ball came on. I should have waited. I threw it away when I shouldn't have done.'

Next to go was Knott, momentum rushing inexorably towards the Australians. He'd scored only four when he jabbed at Thomson. At least he would have appreciated Marsh's diving take.

Tea halted the collapse for a while, although Titmus lasted only two balls beyond it. He had already suffered injury when a ball from Thomson that he shaped to leave outside off stump moved back in to smack him painfully on the inside of the right knee. Now the off-spinner had the insult of falling to his Australian counterpart, bowled by a full Mallett delivery that he initially looked as though he intended to leave. Underwood, who swiped a four on the leg side, was out before the end of the same over, pushing forward and edging to Ian Chappell. England had plunged from 115 without loss to 182 for 8 in little more than a session. 'The capitulation of England's middle order was beyond comprehension,' wrote Laker in the *Mirror*, 'for at 12.45 Australia were a rabble.'

Only Greig and his swashbuckling Gray-Nicolls bat[32] stood between Australia and a 3-0 lead in the series and, with Willis at the other end, he had the perfect excuse for adopting the adventurous tactics he'd employed throughout the series. Yet this time he took an uncharacteristically conservative approach. The six he hit over extra cover after dancing down the track to Mallett was the only boundary in his first 100 balls faced.

He couldn't resist some more slapstick with Lillee, though, against whom he played and missed several times. After one drive, Lillee stopped the ball smartly and shaped to hurl it back at the stumps. Greig, in his crease, stood with his knees knocking together, whereupon Lillee, not to be upstaged, pretended to run up and bowl from only five yards before turning back to his full run with a broad grin.

Willis justified his partner's patience, and it was his scythe over the slips off Lillee that seemed to empower Greig, who progressed beyond another half-century with a flurry of boundaries. One hit off Walker bounced only a couple of times before reaching the distant long-on boundary and it was a sweetly timed glance off Thomson's yorker that took him to his fifty. The drive with which

---

32 Greig had not yet begun using the flat-backed St Peter bat that he endorsed later in his career.

he sent Lillee to the long-off boundary was indicative of the greater control he was displaying in this knock. Even the shot that brought his downfall was an intentional steer behind square, rather than one of his slashes, and it needed a brilliant diving catch in the gully by Greg Chappell to end his innings on 60.

Willis, partnered now by Hendrick and his runner, Lloyd, thrashed one more ball through the off side before Thomson took his revenge by sending back his middle stump, ending an hour and a half's resistance by the big-hearted bowler. It left Australia needing 246 to win and one over to negotiate before stumps.

It was an equation that tested Chappell, who changed his mind about Australia's approach multiple times. As much as he wanted to grind down the Poms, he knew that, win or draw, success in the fourth Test would secure the Ashes. It was England who were desperate for victory right now, which made some of Denness's tactics on the final day a little difficult to interpret.

More than 42,000 were at the MCG to see England make a perfect start when Greig, forced to take the new ball, had Wally Edwards falling over towards off stump and trapped lbw by his cutter. Edwards departed in the knowledge that the Australian selectors had already announced Rick McCosker to open in the fourth Test.

Ian Chappell followed in the next over, another straightforward decision after he was beaten for pace and low bounce by Willis and felt the ball thud into his pads as he played on the back foot. Two wickets had come at the cost of a solitary leg bye. Yet it was almost three hours before England struck again.

Underwood bowled only three overs before lunch as Greig followed his opening spell of four overs by switching ends to bowl another seven. Greig believed he had Redpath leg before on 12, but as well as he bowled it was surprising once again not to see Underwood and Titmus operating together. Lunch was reached at 67 for 2, Redpath having ground out 22 from 94 balls and Greg Chappell scoring 37 with his usual precision, coupled with a willingness to hit over the top on the leg side against Underwood.

Denness had been content to set defensive fields and wait for batsman error, which made it all the more ironic when, early in the afternoon, it was he who dropped an easy chance at mid-on after Redpath finally came down the wicket to Titmus.

Chappell continued to drive elegantly on both sides of the wicket, although it was an edge off Willis past the only slip fielder, Cowdrey, that completed his half-century. Denness belatedly posted Greig at second slip. Having driven Titmus majestically over mid-off and helped the partnership into three figures, Chappell was beaten by a ball that the off-spinner got to hurry through, hitting him low on the pads as he looked to the on side. Leg before for 61, and the game now in the balance. Yet neither team was prepared to go all out for victory.

Ross Edwards cover-drove Titmus for four, but later in the over Redpath turned the ball to long leg and called unwisely for a second run, Underwood's throw beating him back to the striker's end. Knott still had work to do to take off the bails, but the batsman was well short of safety.

Eight minutes later Edwards pushed forward at Titmus and Lloyd took a diving bat-pad catch. Australia had lost half their wickets for 121 and were not quite halfway to the target. 'It was England who held the aces,' Martin-Jenkins noted. 'The situation called less for bowlers of tight control such as Underwood and Titmus, more for sharp spinners and bold captaincy, but English county cricket has so brainwashed players into safety-first tactics at all times that the opening was not seized.'

The destructive potential of Walters and Marsh was what guided Denness's field setting rather than any scent of glory and the Australian pair were able to add 50 runs either side of tea. An injection by Walters of 20 runs in the first four overs after the break threatened to defeat England, but he was removed for 32 when he drove Greig into the covers, where Denness stooped and this time held the catch.

When the last 15 overs began, Australia needed 55 to win with four wickets left. 'Our policy had to be one of containment,' Denness admitted later, somewhat damningly. 'To stop them winning, rather than attack to win the match ourselves.' Marsh was 30 not out, with Walker offering solid support, and in one sequence – overlapping the start of the final hour – Australia played out 11 maidens in the space of 17 overs, rarely even showing interest in pushing the singles that would have kept the scoreboard moving.

Denness, content that Titmus was bowling well and aware that the veteran would stiffen up after his spell and be unable to return late in the day, delayed taking the new ball, available after 65 overs, until the 73rd when Australia were 199 for 6. Woodcock wrote of the spinner's marathon, 'For Titmus, at 42, to bowl 29 consecutive[33] overs for 64 runs and two important wickets, with one knee twice the size of the other and four toes at the bottom of a distant ocean, was heroic.'

Slow handclaps made their way down from the stands and Marsh responded by casting pointed looks at the six leg-side fielders. 'I understand there was some unwritten rule in Australia that you could only have five men on the leg side,' said Denness. 'Underwood requested, and I readily agreed to, his normal John Player League field, with six men on the leg side.'

'It was baffling to watch,' said Martin-Jenkins, referring to the tactics of both teams, while EW Swanton was no less confused. 'It was one of the more bizarre situations,' he wrote, 'with both sides for the best part of an hour groping in a tactical vacuum.'

Amiss's observation was that 'Australia lost their nerve in the final session, which was strange for a team two up in the series'. He was surprised by Marsh's reluctance to take the initiative 'when two or three singles an over were all that Australia needed to win'.

England's fielders had been divided on whether the new ball should have been taken earlier, but Denness was fearful that the Australian batsmen would be able to score more quickly against a hard, shiny Kookaburra. Cowdrey had urged him, 'You must take the new ball, don't delay. What will you tell the press?'

'It's not about the press, for goodness' sake,' Denness snapped. 'I want to win this Test.'

When he eventually made the change it was 'a final gamble to try and win the game'. Marsh instantly dispatched the new ball to the leg-side boundary off Willis, but was out for 40 in the next over, strangled down the leg side against Greig, whose bowling in this innings had been his best of the series. Australia needed 38 to win with three wickets and 51 balls remaining. Lillee clipped Willis through midwicket for four and when Walker turned Greig behind square and ran three it meant the target was down to 21 in four overs. The flurry of runs convinced Denness he had made the right

---

33 Titmus, in fact, bowled only 24 of those overs consecutively.

decision in delaying the new ball. Another five came off Willis's next over, three of them slashed by Walker through the covers. According to Ian Chappell, the mood in the Australian dressing room was now 'frantic', except for Walters, busy playing cards as usual.

A couple of sharp singles were all the batsmen could manage off Greig. Two overs left, 14 to win. Denness beckoned to Underwood. 'I had a quick talk with him, hoping to keep the situation calm, and gave him a moment or two to prepare himself for the task of saving the match,' he explained. 'It was a situation in which no bowler in the world would have revelled. But Underwood did the job perfectly as he has so often, particularly in the one-day game.'

Without pace on the ball Australia were determined not to take the chances that might hand the game to England. Lillee patted back a maiden, every ball delivered to the perfect line and length. 'In this one over, the tightest slow bowler who ever wore an England cap earned most of his tour money,' said Martin-Jenkins.

Enough tension remained for Bailhache to fail to notice – until calling a no-ball on the fourth delivery – that Greig had three men posted behind square on the leg side. But even after Lillee spooned the next ball to Denness in the covers there was no time left for anything other than the draw. Australia ended eight runs short, England two wickets. A greater dose of courage on either side might have made a difference. For the tourists, the hope was that this would become a platform for recovery rather than an unexpected high point of the series. 'It was the best that could reasonably be hoped for,' Swanton said of securing a draw with an injury-hit attack, 'and in achieving it they have revived their own self confidence and at the same time disclosed certain cracks in the Australian machine.'

According to Titmus, the view in the England dressing room was, 'Perhaps the Australians were not really as wonderful as we thought they were.' As well as relief, Amiss remembered a feeling that England's spinners might be in a position to get them back in the series in future matches.

Denness, meanwhile, enjoyed being in a position to have a dig at the opposition for the first time. 'I was amazed when Marsh and Walker blocked out the first seven of the last 15 overs,' he said. 'They had always been in the driver's seat and if I had been two up in the series I am sure I wouldn't have allowed that to happen.'

Only 24 hours later, England were able to celebrate a real, rather than moral, victory over Australia when Melbourne hosted the only one-day-international of the tour. A washed-out Test at the same venue had resulted in the hastily-arranged inaugural ODI four years earlier, and Australia had played a three-game one-day series in England at the end of their 1972 tour. But even with the first World Cup looming in England the following summer, the only nod to the growing phenomenon of limited-overs cricket was to stick on an extra day of play after the Test match.

Lloyd described the occasion as 'nothing like the limited-overs game as we now know it: there was barely a soul in attendance' and as 'a bit of a knockabout'. The public, wrapped up in an Ashes series that would continue with a potentially decisive contest in Sydney in three days' time, shrugged their shoulders. Only 18,977 bothered to show up to the cavernous MCG, which had ushered a quarter of a million through the turnstiles over the previous five days.

Denness put Australia in to bat and was relieved to see them dismissed for 190 with 5.3 of their 40 overs unused after the Chappells were both out in the 40s. Old picked up both of them, bowling Ross Edwards and Walters to complete a four-wicket return.

Amiss and Lloyd, no doubt relieved to see Lillee rested, batted well again to compile a partnership of 70 at the start of England's reply. Both of them, too, were dismissed in the 40s; Amiss for 47 off 54 balls and Lloyd run out by partner Brian Luckhurst one short of a half-century. Luckhurst received his payback when, having been warned by bowler Greg Chappell for backing up too far, strayed down the track again later in the same over and was the victim of a 'Mankad'. Ian Chappell, unsurprisingly, turned down umpire Brooks's invitation to withdraw the appeal and supported his brother's actions. The incident ruffled some feathers and was taken by English observers as further proof of the uncompromising, even unsporting, manner in which the Aussies had chosen to contest the summer.

Having fallen behind the rate with Luckhurst struggling at the crease, England accelerated towards a three-wicket triumph, Fletcher playing some nice on-drives and Old thumping Greg Chappell for a straight six. Perhaps the most intriguing element of the day, however, was the decision of Denness to hide himself at number seven in the batting order, where he made 12. Did it mean he was seriously considering dropping himself for the Test match that might determine his team's fate?

11
CAPTAINS AT WAR

Part One

The most momentous decision I have ever made in my cricket career was to drop myself from the fourth Test match at Sydney.
Mike Denness

Sydney in the first week of 1975 found Mike Denness and Ian Chappell at war. Not with each other, even though the fourth Test had the potential to be an Ashes decider. Denness's battle raged within himself, his feeling of responsibility as captain and his pride as a batsman being bombarded by the inescapable truth that he had become an imposter in England's batting order. Chappell was in a fight with his sport, at least the men running it in Australia, those enjoying the spoils of his team's victories. Before the fourth Test was over, the lines of that particular conflict would be drawn more visibly than ever.

The two men could scarcely have been more different: Denness, the neat, softy-spoken Scot, diffident perhaps to a fault; Chappell, the grandson of former Australia captain Vic Richardson, blunt, confrontational, competitive from the curve of his archetypal '70s moustache to the tips of toes that would frequently be seen around the ground in flip-flops. 'Throughout the tour we never got very close to each other,' said Denness, 'but a bad word was never exchanged between us. We got on perfectly well.' Their personalities were as contrasting as the roots of their respective struggles: Denness's being born of failure, Chappell's of triumph.

'DROP OUT, DENNESS,' was the order blaring from the back page of the *Daily Mirror* two days before the Test match started. 'It is the only decent thing Denness can do after his systematic destruction as a Test match batsman,' wrote Peter Laker. Even the less sensational articles in the English broadsheets could not avoid the truth that, having celebrated his 34th birthday earlier on tour, Denness was unlikely to find miraculously a new level of batsmanship. Under the *Guardian*'s headline, 'High time the captain stood down', Henry Blofeld highlighted Keith Fletcher's superior Test record and argued that 'in terms of sheer technique and determination he is streets ahead of Denness'.

By the time readers in England were digesting those articles, Denness had determined his course of action. His choice to bat down the order in the one-day international was indeed because he had resolved to step out of the Test team, admitting, 'Ever since the end of the second Test in Perth there had been the possibility at the back of my mind that I might have to drop myself.'

The decision was made on his own, in his hotel room, without consultation with anyone on the selection committee. He wanted to have his position determined before they met to pick the team for Sydney. The unavoidable conclusion he reached was that the seriousness of the team's predicament meant there was no room for a passenger, even if it might mean there was no way back in subsequent matches. His mind made up and his conscience clear, he slept soundly.

When Bedser knocked on Denness's hotel room door for their usual 7.45 a.m. meeting two days before the Test, Denness shared his thoughts. 'Stick it out,' the manager told him. As unselfish as Denness was being, Bedser thought it was wrong for the captain to stand down because of his own form. 'I did not believe he was all that much out of touch,' recalled Bedser, feeling there were other struggling batsmen who could make way. Yet, recognising that Denness was a 'man of high principles', he accepted that it was his own choice to make.

When the pair joined AC Smith, John Edrich and Tony Greig for their selection meeting in the team room later in the day, Bedser opened by sharing Denness's decision, explaining that he disagreed with it but it was not a matter for further debate. Individuals expressed their reactions, but the meeting quickly moved on to determining who would play in a match that England dare not lose. 'I had not looked forward to this meeting,' Denness recalled. 'The only consolation I had was that my colleagues accepted my decision.' Edrich was duly confirmed as captain, with Greig his deputy. Denness was keen not to interfere with the new captain's planning but as the meeting broke up he promised him any assistance he required. Edrich offered a 'thanks very much' and resolved to 'just get on with it'.

Denness's next task was to inform those other players who would not be playing. Word of his abdication quickly spread throughout the party before the next team meeting. 'They were probably a little surprised,' he remembered.

'You could see the pressure on him,' said Dennis Amiss, 'To see your leader under so much pressure wasn't easy and we appreciated that. I think it was a bold decision by Mike. But Fletch was coming in, so he was being replaced by a quality bat.' Similarly, Alan Knott called it 'an immensely difficult decision', but acknowledged Denness's pragmatism. 'If you are not playing well and there are players of high calibre around then you should not play.'

Fletcher's views are interesting, coloured by his status as beneficiary of Denness's withdrawal and the fact that, dating back to the West Indies tour, he was no fan of his captaincy. He would record in his autobiography that even though 'team spirit had stood up remarkably well' the captain's batting problems made things more difficult. He also suggested that had Denness's captaincy taken greater advantage of those around him, he might have had greater ability to focus on his batting.

'I cannot rate Denness as a great captain, either tactically or inspirationally,' he wrote. 'I could not help feeling that he contributed to his own unhappy position on the tour by failing to listen to well-intentioned advice. I admit it was not always offered – and if I am to make criticism of Edrich it would be for his reluctance to fully support his skipper – but when it was, Denness gave the impression that he was already in command and beyond interference.'

Fletcher, a future England captain who said he would not have chosen Denness's course of action, went as far as saying, 'Certain players did resent his attitude, and I believe one even got to the stage of considering a refusal to play under Denness, such was his difficulty in communicating with him. No tour is ever entirely free from personality clashes, particularly a losing tour, but I will say this one was probably a more contented party than the winning squad of four years earlier.'

David Lloyd offered a different picture. 'I found Denness brilliant, absolutely brilliant. A lovely fellow and a good friend, a very caring chap.' A happy-go-lucky rookie tourist, Lloyd also remembered Denness's decision having little impact on him. 'We just shrugged our shoulders and didn't really give it much of a mention. "Right, he's not in the team, am I in it?" It was very relaxed.'

Yet Chris Old said, 'I think we were stunned by Mike leaving himself out. OK, he wasn't having the best of times, but whoever played as the replacement wasn't in any sort of form anyway. Why do that? It was all a matter of trying to react to what was going on and seeing if they can find a way out of it, rather than having a plan.'

On a personal level, Old, having been led to believe he was playing the next day, was not sorry to see a change of captaincy. 'We didn't get on very well at Test match times. I never knew where I stood with Mike because sometimes I would be taking the new ball and sometimes I didn't come on until third or fourth change, and it's difficult to know what your role really is. In the West Indies, Bob Willis and I opened the bowling and in the third Test they played Geoff Arnold as well. When I asked who was going to take the new ball Mike said we were keeping it the same. But then my county colleague Geoffrey [Boycott] turned round and said, "But Geoff is the best new ball bowler in England," so Mike said he would open. I said, "Hang on, we're not playing in England, we are playing in Barbados." At a function I was met at the door by Garry Sobers, who said they were delighted when I didn't get the new ball.'

Bedser announced the Test team to the media members on the afternoon before the game, after which Denness and Edrich attended a press conference. 'It was a straightforward choice,' Denness told the reporters. 'If England are to keep the Ashes, and if they will benefit from my absence because of lack of form, then I have to relinquish the leadership.'

The English reports focused on the precedent-setting nature of Denness's self-demotion. In 1928-29, an out-of-form Percy Chapman had handed over the team to Jack White at 4-0 up in the Ashes series, but influenza was cited as the reason. Similarly, when Norman Yardley took charge of Wally Hammond's 1946-47 tourists it was lumbago rather than poor form that was offered as explanation. This was the first time an MCC captain had owned up to dropping himself in the midst of an Australian series. 'A sad piece of cricket history has been made,' Henry Blofeld told his readers. EW Swanton noted of Denness, 'He has stepped down with the dignity that has characterised all his actions and behaviour in Australia,' although he also felt that the media frenzy around the decision was an 'over-dramatisation of a perfectly straightforward situation'.

John Woodcock was hardly enamoured with Denness's replacement, saying, 'Edrich never gives the impression in the field of being born to inspire, but then few do.' Observing that Denness had matured as a captain and 'made a better job of it both on and off the field than he did in the West Indies', he said there was no disgrace in failing against 'an attack as fierce as I have seen on seven tours to Australia'.

In Australian outlets it was a big enough story to dominate the front page of the *Melbourne Age*, along with a picture of Denness meeting wife Molly at the airport. In the home team camp, eyebrows were raised. A state of such disarray in the opposition could only be good for their own chances of success in Sydney. Ian Redpath suggested, 'I suspect it probably had as much to do with his mental attitude as his form. I think that the tremendous pressure exerted on him had taken its toll and he had lost his confidence.'

Opposite number Chappell had sympathy with his counterpart. 'I thought that showed a fair bit of courage, not that it ever entered my head to drop myself as captain,' he recalled. 'It is a pretty tough thing to do, and to me it showed he thought that maybe there is someone out there who is a better player.' Chappell's compassion extended to describing the England captaincy as 'the last job in the world I would want'. He felt there were 'too many people who think they can do the job as well', explaining a few months later, 'You only have to listen to them on the field. I felt sorry for Mike Denness for this. Sometimes he had six blokes trying to place the field.'

So that was it, Denness's choice made and announced. Yet now he felt no great lifting of weight. 'I was more annoyed that I had been forced to make the decision,' he said. Unaware at the time of whispered accusations of him running scared, he admitted years later, 'I can see where people were coming from.'

Various messages from the cricketing public reached him in Australia, one of the more positive coming from a well-wisher who sent a copy of Rudyard Kipling's poem, *If.* Someone in Oxfordshire wrote with the advice that he should return to Scotland to become a haggis maker, while another envelope, addressed merely to 'Mike Denness, Cricketer' arrived with a note that read, 'If this letter reaches you, the post office think more of you than I do.'

Part Two

I would be a fool if I said I didn't enjoy having a fight occasionally with the board because I did think they were a bunch of pillocks a lot of the time.
Ian Chappell

No one would ever accuse Ian Chappell, publicly or privately, of being afraid of any kind of challenge. Three years junior to opposite number Denness, he was four years into his captaincy of the Australian side during the Ashes series. He was a productive number three bat in any circumstance or condition: unequivocally the team leader.

'If you don't evolve as a captain you are pretty stupid,' he suggested. 'Because you are doing the job all the time. It was like Rodney Marsh used to say about wicketkeeping: if you are the incumbent and you don't get better you are pretty stupid. The only way you learn about captaincy is by doing the job and when you make mistakes, which you will do, you learn from them. I never tried to be this or that as a captain. I just tried to do the job the best way I saw.'

By 1974, Chappell was as secure in his position as he knew any Australian skipper could ever be. But he had not forgotten the circumstances that led to him being given the job, Bill Lawry having heard on the radio that he been replaced towards the end of the 1970-71 Ashes series. 'The thing that pissed me off with Bill is that they didn't have the guts to tell him face to face. He had earned that right as a very, very good player for Australia. I remember saying to my first wife, Kay, "The bastards will never get me that way." That was a great incentive, I wanted to do the job well enough so that I would go when I wanted to go and not when they pushed me.

'When I took over I thought, "Shit, this is a really tough job," but then I thought about it a bit and thought that Bill wasn't winning as a captain, so if I don't win they won't think that badly of me, and if I happen to win they will think I am a genius. It was a pretty stupid statement because anyone who thinks you are a genius is a bloody pillock themselves. I promptly lost the first two I captained and won the third one.'

Chappell interpreted the appointment of John Inverarity as his vice-captain during the 1971-72 series against a World XI as a warning from the ACB. 'That was a good motivating factor,' he explained. 'As much as Invers was a decent bloke, he wasn't a good enough batsman to play for Australia and therefore I don't think he should have been considered as a captain. When they made him vice-captain that made it pretty clear to me that if I bugger up the job he will get it. I always felt if they sacked me the captaincy should go to someone like Stacky [Keith Stackpole] or Greg, who were definitely good enough to play for Australia.'

It was in England in 1972 when Chappell began to feel like a worthy custodian of the role. 'Being captain for the tour meant I knew I had five Tests, and if you can't win one in five you probably shouldn't have the job anyhow. The Lord's win [in the second Test] was a really important one for me. As it turned out, the fifth Test at The Oval was a real watershed moment, but Lord's is the win that gave me a bit of time in the job.'

Chappell calculatedly ensured that the name he had made for himself on the field could sustain him off it, allowing him to retain control of his destiny however sharp the selectors' knives might become. He had left his employment with WD & HO Wills in 1973, nine years after elevation from South Australia to the Test team, and through his own company, Ian Chappell Enterprises Pty, was making a living through endorsements, promotional work and media engagements, both written and broadcast.

Such street smarts mirrored his manoeuvring in the middle, which could not help but elicit admiration from the opposition. 'Ian did have a great command of the game of cricket and he could read a situation very quickly,' said Denness. 'And he led from the front. He was a great players' man.'

Amiss concurred, saying, 'He was a fine captain, someone you would much rather have on your team. He handled his bowlers so well. He knew when to bring on someone like Ashley Mallet, a fine bowler who could keep it tight, and Max Walker, who was line and length, hitting the wicket hard occasionally. Any time we looked like putting together a good partnership, something seemed to happen and they got one of us out.'

Inasmuch as Australian males of the 1970s were not known for outward displays or acknowledgements of affection, Chappell inspired a loyalty and respect from his own teammates that could be said to have bordered on love. 'I've always believed the most important thing in captaincy was to have the players' respect. And I think this can make up for a lot of deficiencies as captain,' he said. When Kerry Packer was hatching his plans for World Series Cricket two years later it would be Ian – not brother Greg, who was by then the Test captain – that he wanted to lead the Australian side; Ian who commanded the level of devotion needed to convince players to follow him down a new and unknown path that might threaten their establishment careers and reputations.

Dennis Lillee, for example, would never forget the debt he owed his captain for believing him when he'd attempted to explain how much distress he was in when his back was at its worst, even though 'no one knew much about stress fractures at the time' and some people felt Lillee's problems were as much psychological as physical.

Ross Edwards, meanwhile, acknowledged that not only did Chappell have a great knowledge of the game but he was also willing to trust that of his players. 'The reason we had a good side was largely down to the captain, because he was a great captain of good players,' Edwards said. 'He didn't instruct players, he expected you to be good and he simply set the parameters in which you could perform. In the four years I played I would think I saw him speak to Dennis Lillee on the field no more than two or three times. At drinks and certainly at lunchtime he would sit and talk to him, but on the field he wouldn't tell Dennis what to do. There were lots of times when Dennis, like anybody else who is learning, would stuff it up but you learn from experience and that's how he became a great bowler. He was given permission and encouragement to go and learn, which we all did.

'In 1972 I'm the new kid on the block. I was a relatively good fielder and we were playing at Lord's against MCC and I am in the covers and someone came in and was square driving, something I had never seen before because it was never common in those days. You didn't drive through point with an open face. The ball keeps going down the hill at Lord's and Ian's walking up to me and he says, "You are the cover specialist in this team. I've got a few more things to think about than what you are doing. If he's hitting the bloody thing square, you go square. I'll tell you if you're wrong." He was giving me licence to do what I thought was the right thing, and he had confidence in my fielding. That was the first time I ever started thinking on a cricket field.'

According to Redpath, 'Ian was very popular and a good captain. He had an aggressive side to him, but he was a very positive captain. Whoever was going out to bat or to bowl, he always gave the impression to that player that he believed in him and that they would do the job that was required.'

Rick McCosker, about to make his Test debut at Sydney, explained, 'Ian was the best captain I played under. He was a great reader of the game and always appeared to be one step ahead of everyone else, He was never afraid to do the tough work himself, and the long partnerships I had with him were the most satisfying and enjoyable I had. You were very happy that he was on your side. He had the respect of everybody in the team, because of his own ability and because he treated everybody as individuals.'

Umpire Robin Bailhache argued, 'Of all the skippers I saw over the years, Ian Chappell was by far the best. He was a real leader of men. He was almost anti-umpire because he thought we were there to do a job and should be seen and not heard. I would have spoken about ten words to him over the whole six Test matches. But under him players showed no dissent with umpiring decisions – although they dare not walk, my goodness.'

Edwards explained Chappell's method of guiding the team's pre-match preparation. 'We would have played the previous weekend and would fly early in the week to the Test venue. You would practise each day with decreasing pressure, so that you were only polishing yourself up the day before. Ian was never a great one for team meetings. He was a captain; this was not a democracy.

He would spend time with individual players, particularly bowlers, but he didn't have to worry about the batsmen because they were being picked for their performance anyway. The only thing we had team meetings for, on a very cursory basis, was to go through the opposition batsmen and bowlers, but not in any great detail. You were expected to know that yourself. The team meeting the night before was a social gathering as much as anything else.'

Offering his own assessment of his performance as skipper, Chappell explained, 'I didn't think about captaincy a hell of a lot and I was not expecting to get it, but it fell in my lap. I just felt you did the job. Captaincy is a very subjective thing and I have always said that you make a decision as captain because you think it is the right decision at the time. If down the track – and this is a big part of the art of captaincy – you find the decision you made is not going according to plan, it is important how quickly you correct and start going in a different direction. To me, the best captains correct pretty quickly and the bad captains let poor decisions go on for too long.'

Which perhaps explains Chappell's empathy with Denness and his decision to go in a different direction by dropping himself in Sydney. And while previews, reports and reviews of the series frequently highlighted the greater experience and leadership qualities of Australia's captain over England's, it was not something that Chappell dwelt upon. 'I always liked Mike as a person,' he said. 'I am not sure I ever felt superior to any other captain, but you have always got to feel like you have got an advantage and the great advantage I had in my opinion was the team. To have Lillee and Thomson on your side, and the great faith I had in our batting side, I thought the big advantages were with us. I thought we were a better team. I never thought about how many Ashes Tests I had played or Mike had played.

'It is not true to say I didn't watch what the other captain was doing because I learned a lot from playing against Ray Illingworth, for instance, and from Bill Lawry when he was captain of Victoria. So I was taking note of the opposing captain, but I wasn't thinking he should have been doing this or he should have been doing that.'

As much as Chappell was revered by the men playing under him, so his side was winning the hearts of the Australian public. According to *Cricketer* editor Eric Beecher, 'Chappell typifies the 'new look" that has made Australian cricket the young mod of the sporting world.' With their extravagant moustaches – many of them grown as part of a dressing-room contest in England in 1972 – unruly, shoulder-length hair and unbuttoned shirts they looked as though they would have been just as at home sitting in Bay 13 at the MCG or on the Hill at Sydney, sharing a beer with those chanting, 'kill, kill, kill' as their fast bowlers approached the crease.

Chappell suggested, 'The crowd seemed to align themselves with our team and my feeling was that it was pretty well around Doug Walters, Rod Marsh and Dennis Lillee. I always felt the guys sitting up on the Hill thought, "Well Doug is just like me, he likes a beer, he likes a cigarette, it is just that he can bat a hell of a lot better than me."[34] With Rodney they seemed to like his personality, the fact that he loved to have a go as a batsman. They liked Lillee in '72 because of his pace and his attitude, he was always wanting to win games and take wickets. But then when he overcame the back injury and came back in '74-75 they were all on his side.

'We were just being ourselves. That was the main thing with the crowd. We wore jeans and T-shirts because that was what we liked wearing, but also anybody who has seen a cricket dressing room will realise that it is a bloody shit fight in there and you don't want to be wearing good clothes too often because some silly bastard will spill beer or there will be clothes lying around getting dirty. If we had to go to an official function we wore a tie and a suit, but our dress of preference was jeans, which was the dress of the day.'

Future Australia captain Allan Border, destined to make his Test debut in the next Ashes series, recalled, 'The long hair, the moustaches, shirts open down to the navel; it was a bit rebellious. That was a sign of the times but what a fantastic cricket team. That group were an inspiration to all of us.'

Brett Gosper, who was a teenage fan at the Melbourne Test and went on to become one of global sport's most powerful figures as chief executive of World Rugby, said, 'That team was exactly what

---

[34] While Australian greats such as Bradman, Trumper and O'Reilly have stands named after them at the 21st-century Sydney Cricket Ground, it seems entirely appropriate that 'The Doug Walters Bar' can be found on the concourse behind where the Hill used to be.

the Australian public liked. They were coming of age and they had huge attitude, the ugly Australian element – brash, bold and good at what they did. They were such a contrast to an England side which was a bit of Dad's Army, typified by Cowdrey being flown out. And they had a Scottish captain, which to us implied even more of a weakness in English cricket. Our team was exactly how Australia likes to see itself as a country: young, vigorous and aggressive, not dithery and older. It embodied Australia's desire as a nation.'

The sheer size of Australia's biggest Test grounds, notably the MCG and SCG, meant that the crowds for the Test matches were less elitist than, for example, Lord's. Which meant they were rowdier and more partisan. 'They would hit the beer pretty hard,' said Gosper, 'so they were more aggressive than an English crowd, which was a little older and a little more up-market because there were fewer places in the ground. If you are going to fill 90,000 at the MCG you are going to get a real cross-section of the community.

'Someone like Doug Walters was a national icon to the fans. The public like to see the average Aussie succeed and Doug was the guy you might have a beer with. Being a big drinker worked in his favour with the male population.'

From his seat in the press box, Martin-Jenkins observed the fans' connection with Lillee and Thomson and noted, 'There is no doubt that their fury, fanned by the sensationalist press, helped to attract the ghouls as well as the cricket purists. These two spectacular bowlers had as much to do with the financial success of the series as they did with Australia's success on the field.'

Whether or not those fans wanted to witness actual injury is open to debate. Denness acknowledged that the words and antics of Lillee and Thomson encouraged fans to attend matches 'just to see a bit of blood and thunder', but he could not believe they really craved the sight of serious injury. 'They want to see a quick bowler, operating with hostility, but without deliberately trying to hit and maim the batsman,' he suggested.

Even if it was merely pantomime rather than a declaration of war, Edwards acknowledged that 'the Lillee factor was a focus of crowd expectation'. But he had sensed the nation rekindling its passion for its team since the drawn Ashes series in 1972. 'It was broadcast here and people saw the way we played. Ian Chappell said the way to play cricket is very simple. As a batsman your job is to get runs quick enough to allow the bowlers to have enough time to take 20 wickets. So you went out there to look good. I didn't have the strokes, but I wasn't that far behind the stroke players. That was the way we played the game.'

According to Chappell, 'I was never one to worry about the crowd because I always felt that if we played good cricket we would be entertaining the public, so that was always my aim. There were huge crowds during that series and I think they came out because they enjoyed watching the cricket that we played. One big facet of my captaincy was I always felt that we had to be trying to win the game from ball one, whereas Bill [Lawry] had been more conscious of the draw. It was important that my team knew it and the opposing team knew it. The crowd weren't stupid and they quickly caught onto that. The Australian public thought, "Shit, we are in this game to win it."'

As the end of the third Test had proved, there were times for pragmatism as well, but Chappell's generally positive approach was a welcome characteristic of the new era of Australian cricket.

'I got a hell of a shock when we came back in '72 and they organised a charity game at the Drummoyne Oval in Sydney,' Chappell continued. 'I thought it was a great opportunity to get together with the guys again have a few beers and a laugh, which we did on the Saturday night. On Sunday we went by bus to the Drummoyne Oval and we got reasonably close to the ground and the driver said, "Sorry, I can't take you any further. It is too crowded, there are cars in the way and I can't get through." When we walked into the ground it was packed to whatever the capacity was.

'Obviously we heard in England that people were buying the record "Bowl a Ball, Swing a Bat".[35] It took off in Australia so we knew there was interest, but we just thought, "Silly bastards, they will buy any record." But then suddenly to see this huge crowd come along; to me that was the first time I really thought, "Shit, this mob have really taken to us. We've captured their imagination."'

---

35 Written by Daniel Boone and Rod McQueen and sung by members of the Australian 1972 touring party, the record made it into the Australian top 40. On the B-side of the single was 'Here Come The Aussies,' in which Boone and McQueen reworked the lyrics to 'Blue is the Colour', the UK top-five hit they had written earlier in the year for Chelsea's appearance in the League Cup final against Stoke City.

An interviewee in the book *Living in the 70s* recalled, 'If I think back to what was really significant in Australia in the 70s, it was cricket. We had such a fantastic team. We stuffed the Pommies, stuffed the West Indies. Thomson and Lillee were pretty well unplayable. And experiencing all this – sitting on the Hill … watching Thomson bowl when you couldn't even see the ball going, he was so fast, and Rod Marsh right down by the screen almost – was just great.'

The Australian Broadcasting Corporation had on this occasion paid almost double what they had forked out to screen the Ashes in 1970-71. Perth had been connected that year by permanent carriage systems, completing the east-west broadcast chain and making it the first series since televised broadcasts of Test cricket began in 1958-59 to be fully aired in every state.

Now, for the first time, an Australian television audience no longer had to rely on monochrome pictures from the cricket. Officially, colour broadcasts in the country were not due to begin until March, but in preparation for that a restricted amount of TV hours were designated for trials of the new technology. The senses of the viewing public were at last allowed to be assaulted by the full colourful spectacle of an Ashes contest and a reported average of around 1.5 million per day tuned in.

For the Australian Cricket Board and the sport's various state authorities, the response to the team represented money in the bank, even if the ABC was considered by many to be filling its air time on the cheap. Richie Benaud recalled that he had 'never seen so many people coming through the turnstiles'. Yet of the gate generated by the 900,000 who attended Test matches in the 1974-75 series – the highest average daily attendance since 1946-47 and almost 40 per cent up on 1970-71 – only two per cent found its way to the players. They had to be content with their A$200 per game (at the time around £115), plus $50 match expenses and a share of the A$2,000 winning prize money. The cleaners who piled up and disposed of the beer cans at the end of each day's play earned several times the players' basic pay. As Gideon Haigh put it in *The Cricket War*, 'Cricketers remained voyeurs to their own popularity.'

Marsh recalled a few years later, 'During the 1974-75 season a good deal of discussion took place in the press and elsewhere about the financial rewards of cricketers, and I for one am glad that the subject was widely discussed. The fact is that playing for cricket for Australia involves a considerable financial sacrifice for most players and, whilst I have no doubt that they would all rather go broke than not play, it is understandable if they begin to ask if that should be necessary. It is not that we are insensitive to the honour of playing cricket for Australia, but you can feel a little disgruntled when you see what other top-class sportsmen can earn.'

Edwards complained, 'The grounds were full and we were getting nothing. We couldn't understand where the money was going. I mean, you've got a situation where on a public holiday the bloke who moved the sight screen at the Sydney Cricket Ground was getting more money for the match than the Australian captain. There is something wrong with that.'

The Queensland Cricket Association's (QCA) annual financial report would note an operating profit of A$65,000 on the 1974-75 season, a third of which was represented by its surplus on the first Test, while the South Australia Cricket Association would record a profit of A$44,000 on the fifth Test.

'The crowds were quite enormous,' recalled Greg Chappell. 'All of a sudden you could see there was a multi-million gate at the Melbourne Test match and a $750,000 gate at the Sydney Test … With huge gates like that there just seemed to be something wrong.'

Instead of being offered any level of security, the Aussie players clung to the hope that good individual performances and collective success would keep them in the team. 'There were no contracts,' said Redpath. 'If you got dropped from the side you just went back to work and it was part of the system. A lot of the officials had come up in the traditional way and didn't realise what kind of a product they had. There were tens of thousands of people out there and we just wanted a little bit of a fair deal. Players had to shorten their careers and rule out cricket in their early 30s because they had to maintain their jobs.'

Commitments to playing for state sides further impeded career and financial ambitions, rather than offering steady employment in the manner of English county cricket. Greg Chappell, who played in the Sheffield Shield for a princely sum of A$8 per day, admitted, 'I was being paid by work, I wasn't being paid a lot by cricket. It was very hard to justify the time away. I really didn't want to admit it to myself but I could see this wasn't going to last for very long because I couldn't afford to do it.' When the SACA, under the rule of Sir Donald Bradman, refused to create an improved financial package for him, the only way he could justify his career was to move to Queensland to become captain.

When it came to its latest big-name acquisition, Jeff Thomson, the QCA felt obliged at the end of the season to 'record its sincere appreciation to Austral Motors and Radio Station 4IP who have assisted with regard to employment for him'.

Edwards, meanwhile, was ostensibly working for a firm of chartered accountants. 'I had just finished qualifying before I went on tour in '72,' he explained. 'I went to England and we didn't have much time before we played Pakistan and went to the West Indies. I was only working part-time as an accountant. Once the season started and you were playing Test matches you don't have much time because you are playing Shield matches as well. For a period from '72 to the end of '75 I think I had about ten weekends at home, and on only about two was there no cricket. We weren't professional cricketers; we weren't getting subsistence wages. The number of cricketers who had to retire because they were financially struggling was substantial. Eventually, I couldn't keep playing because I had a wife and two children.'

Marsh, employed by property developers, reckoned that out of 80 days between October and January in his summer of 1974-75 only eight were not taken up by cricket. He used them to 'put in an occasional appearance at my office and to renew acquaintances with my wife and children'. He counted himself lucky that his two children were 'young enough not to be harmed by my almost continuous absence' and that his employers were 'understanding enough to carry me through this absence in return for the value I could be to them when I was able to be there'. The fact that they paid him his full salary regardless of attendance saved him from 'financial disaster'.

There might have been a lot of flaws in the English practice of awarding benefit seasons to county veterans, but Marsh viewed this sometimes undignified money-grabbing with some envy. 'I have often wondered why the state associations do not follow the

English county system,' he said. 'It is a good way of honouring a player and recognising his contribution to a state side, with an added advantage that most of the benefit money comes from the public as gate money from special benefit matches and from other fund-raising schemes.'

Marsh also believed that the government could help players make their touring fee – A$2,700 for the upcoming visit to England – stretch further. 'It is not particularly good money for 16 weeks, especially if the player is married with a family and is not being paid by his firm while he is away. On A$170 a week he is going to have a struggle. One solution would be for the Australian government to reduce the tax on that income and one could, of course, extend this to all other sportsmen representing Australia overseas. It does not seem unreasonable to me that the government should in fact, subsidise sportsmen in this way and it would certainly go a long way to improving the position of the players.'

Self-employed Redpath would absent himself from the once-in-a-lifetime World Cup and Ashes trip to England later 1975 because he needed to focus on his antiques business. 'I am missing work and my wife said to me, "You are just playing for fun." All I could say was yes. There wasn't a financial incentive. I had two children and one on the way and I was running my own business. I just couldn't keep going, even though I was playing pretty well.'

Ian Chappell not only failed to see why it should be down to his own endeavours to ensure that cricket indirectly offered him some kind of living wage beyond the 'fish and chip money' he got for actually playing, he also knew that most teammates did not share his fortunate circumstances. He chose the issue as the subject of his first column in the inaugural edition of Australia's *Cricketer* magazine in November 1973. 'You're an Australian cricketer,' he wrote. 'You play roughly ten four-day matches a season (more for Test players), you are not exceptionally well-paid, you love the game, but it eats into your family and business life. What are your chances of becoming a full-time professional cricketer?' He went on to suggest that 'we will never see the game in Australia – from Sheffield Shield level up – fully professional'.

Most Test players relied on sympathetic employers who liked the idea of an Aussie international on the payroll; not something that could be taken for granted as unemployment rose throughout the first half of the decade. Redpath had at least extended his international career into his 30s. Many, frightened that the job market would leave them behind, never made it that far.

Oddly, ACB chairman Tim Caldwell, recently retired as an executive at the ANZ Bank, appeared to blame the employers' inconsistent treatment of their cricket-playing staff for the dissatisfaction in the Australia team. 'Some of our players are on full pay whether they are playing or not. Others are not on full pay. And this is the problem.' He gave no indication of recognising that his own organisation bore any responsibility for their financial welfare. 'I would think the general attitude in our community now as I see it is, provided the player is not at a disadvantage, I don't think we in Australia are particularly keen – nor do I think we should be – in trying to compete on professional lines. I think our players are getting more than a fair go.'

Marsh, one of the higher-profile members of the team, could not have disagreed more strongly. He looked at the A$12,000 a year he earned from the country's most popular sport and wondered how his less famous brother, Graham, could be earning ten times that amount on the professional golf circuit.

As the fourth Test approached, Lillee was quoted in the newspapers saying that Australian team members should be earning contracts worth at least A$25,000 per year. He followed up with columns under his own name, complaining about the players' poor reward for the riches they were earning for the Board. A lowly office worker earned more, he argued. It was never likely to be well received by the ACB, whose executives were themselves enthusiastic amateurs, happy to fulfil their roles for the prestige they offered. Caldwell told Chappell, 'You'd better tell your fast bowler to back off with his columns.' Chappell's response was, 'Tim, why don't you tell him yourself? I happen to agree with him.'

Chappell remembered, 'That gives you an idea of how things had really escalated. We had a group who weren't "yes sir, no sir" boys. They were going to speak their mind and they would speak it to anybody who wanted to ask the question. Our major players, Stackpole, Marsh, Greg, Redpath in his own quiet way, even Doug Walters if you asked him face to face, would have told them. By 1974-75 we were becoming quite vocal about it.'

Such was the environment into which Test newcomer McCosker arrived at Sydney. 'Looking back there was a bit of an undercurrent, but I wasn't aware of it at the time. Being a new kid I was just happy to be part of the scene and lapping it all up and happy with my lot. I felt very comfortable playing under Ian, even though I wasn't always comfortable with some of the things he did off the field. He was very forthright in his opinions and never afraid to challenge authority. Being a new guy on the team, I found it a little difficult at times but I knew he was doing it for the right reasons; because he wanted the best for his team and for cricket in general. I knew his motives were right; just sometimes his methods were a little bit different to what I would have used.

'As time went on and I went on a couple of tours, I realised that cricket was becoming very time consuming. I had a young family and so it was very difficult trying to hold down employment because you were being asked to play more and more cricket and not being paid much for it.'

However strong their own feelings, the Australian players were fortunate that Chappell happened to see the role of unofficial shop steward as part of his remit as captain, rather than an unwanted burden. 'My attitude was that I am expecting 100 per cent from the players on the field – and in my opinion that is what they gave me – therefore it is my job to fight for them off the field because we didn't have a players' association,' he said. 'To be honest, I think that probably played a role in me reading where people say the team would have run through a brick wall for me. I don't know I necessarily agree with that, but I have the feeling that the main players would have done that bit extra for me because they knew I had their back and would support them.'

Chappell also believes that his DNA played a role in his eagerness to challenge authority. 'I suppose it comes from the family I grew up in and the fact that my grandfather captained Australia,' he said. 'Vic was very much a cop-no-crap captain, and a cop-no-crap person and I have always said I am more Richardson than I am Chappell. When I read about Vic after I finished playing, I would often laugh at something that had happened and say, "Ah, that is where it came from." I copped a lot of Vic's traits and he was very much a players' man. He died in 1969 when I was 26, so I was well and truly old enough to understand about him. I used to see him a lot so I am sure some of him filtered into my thinking and was probably in my personality anyhow.'

Meanwhile, Lillee was driven by his recent history of financial antagonism with the ACB, resulting from their tardiness in settling his medical bills during his rehabilitation. Only a week before the Australian team for the first Test was to be announced, he'd had to remind ACB secretary Alan Barnes that a sum of around A$100 remained outstanding to surgeon Bill Gilmour. He threatened not to play and to tell the media why if the situation was not resolved. 'It was a strong reaction but I was so annoyed because the bills had been sent to them right through my rehabilitation and they were dragging their feet,' he explained. 'It was not a lot of money to the Board but it was a lot for me and I could hardly afford it.' There was a strong matter of principle at stake, too. Lillee felt that he had been injured in his nation's cause, so the ACB could bloody well pay for it. 'The whole thing left a nasty taste in my mouth,' he said.

Things might have been coming to a head in the summer of 1974-75, but the relationship between the Board and the players had been less than harmonious for much of Chappell's time in the Australian team. 'Up to 1968 I was really just trying to stay in the side,' he said. 'I had a good series in England in '68 and I will never forget the team dinner at the end of the tour at the Waldorf, where we used to stay. Bob Parish was the tour manager and chairman of the Board and was very influential. The usual drinkers were in the bar having a beer and Bob Cowper was among us. I always looked up to him as a player and as a thinker on the game and I never forget he said to us as a group, "You bastards shut up. None of you speak before me." He actually spoke before Bill Lawry. Bob got up and he absolutely shat on the Board in front of Parish. To hear from Bob like that set me thinking.'

Then there was the tour to India in 1969-70, when the quality of the travel and accommodation overseen by the ACB was so bad that Stackpole said of one hotel, 'You wouldn't let a pig loose in there.' Skipper Lawry's highly critical end-of-tour report was thought by many to have been the root of the shoddy manner of his dismissal as captain a year later. 'Things got worse and worse,' Chappell recalled.

'The Board sold us up the river by going to India and then straight on to South Africa.'

Chappell and his colleagues had grown weary of the ACB's apparent reluctance to discuss players' grievances and find grounds for compromise. 'Inept, niggardly, and heartless,' was historian Haigh's description of the organisation.

'It wasn't just financial,' said Greg Chappell. 'It was about being treated like second-class citizens, not being given the credit for knowing a bit about our sport and what was good for us. Generally the attitude of the administrators to players was very much a master and servant attitude. We were given no say in anything and very little pay ... The cricket board's responsibility was to the development of cricket around Australia so the money went back to the states and then to the clubs, and that was always their argument – that their role was to develop the game and not to pay the players; in other words, "Go away and just play."'

If Australia's cricketers needed affirmation in the early days of 1975 that the time for militancy had arrived, they needed only to look at the country's industrial relations environment. 'The decade from the late 1960s in Australia was far and away the most significant period of trade union power and activism in that country,' according to Immanuel Ness, professor of political science at Brooklyn College, New York. 'That seemingly inalienable right of bosses, managers and governments to control the lives of working people was openly challenged.'

Many of the fans baying for Pommie blood were likely to have been committed trade unionists, membership among Australia's workforce having risen from 49 to 56 per cent in the first half of the decade. Some of those in Sydney might even have come from down the New South Wales coast in Clifton, whose miners in 1972 became the world's first to dismiss their bosses and take control of their own mine.

A national strike in 1969 had effectively ended the use of penal laws that punished industrial action through fines and arrests, while the arrival of a new Labour government under Gough Whitlam in 1972 heralded a period of cooperation with the unions, even a threat that non-union members would forfeit a week of annual leave. Progressive reforms and notable pay rises followed, including the Transport Workers' Union winning a wage increase of almost one third in 1974.

It all put into perspective the shabby A$20 increase in match fees that the Australian Test team had been granted since 1970. As referenced by Haigh, Braham Dabscheck of the University of New South Wales calculated that the Australian tourists to India and South Africa in 1969-70 had a weekly income 66 per cent above the average male weekly earnings. By the time they set off for England in 1975 that estimate had fallen to 13 per cent.

'Workers were infused by a new mood of rebellion and defiance,' recorded author Sam Oldham in *Without Bosses*, his study of Australian trade unionism during that decade. 'The 1970s tell a story of ordinary people who by organising at their workplaces and coordinating action across industries and trades, challenged systems of exploitation and oppression through direct actions.'

Unions had become powerful enough that Chappell was advised by Bob Hawke, president of the Australian Council of Trade Unions and future prime minister, to steer clear of the term when discussing the formalisation of the players' attempt to improve their lot. 'We had a meeting with Bob Hawke because we were pretty pissed off with the way things were going. I don't know how but I knew him a little bit and I asked, "Can I bring Greg along because he is probably going to take over from me and I am not sure how much longer I will be captain." He was very helpful with what we needed to do but the thing that sticks in my mind was that he was adamant that we should not call it a players' union because it would immediately get the board's back up and make them think we have come for a fight. That is why we called it a players' association.'[36]

A similar path had recently been trodden by the part-time professionals of the country's major Australian rules competition, who had formed the Victorian Football League Players' Association in 1973. While not subjected to the months away from work without pay that caused such problems for their cricketing counterparts, footballers still faced the kind of balancing act that led Michael Green, champion with Richmond Tigers in 1967 and 1969, to quit

---

36 The Australian Cricketers' Association is registered as an incorporated association rather than a trade union.

the sport in 1972 at the age of 23 to focus on his career in law – before being enticed back a year later. 'Footy' players also had the advantage over cricketers of a competitive market for their services, and a greater 'freedom of contract' environment in order to exploit that was among the biggest priorities for the new organisation.

Australia's sports stars might not have been the 'ordinary people' referred to by Oldham, but the cricketers' concerns, in particular, reflected those of the wider workforce. And the comments of Alan Barnes on the first morning of the Sydney Test certainly had Chappell thinking of 'direct action' of his own. 'These are not professionals,' Barnes was quoted as saying in *The Australian*, pointing out condescendingly that the team had been invited to play. 'There are 500,000 cricketers who would love to play for Australia for nothing,' was his incendiary conclusion. According to Greg Chappell, 'If we didn't think we were disrespected before, that comment united us.'

The editorial column in the subsequent edition of *Cricketer* called Barnes's remarks 'the bluntest, most disturbing salvo fired in the war of words about today's most touchy subject in cricket… money.' It went on to refer to a 'sneering, dismissive comment' and accuse Barnes of 'the gravest piece of administrator bungling yet in a game which possesses an almost unique record for its scant treatment of players, press and other non-entities who come within its dealings.'

Ian Chappell was in a filthy mood in the SCG nets. Every ball he belted back at the bowlers had the face of Barnes on it. He finished his knock early, partly to get changed for the toss and also in the hope of confronting Barnes over his comment. 'I would have throttled him,' he recalled. But in the end he didn't need to. Having won the toss, he returned to the pavilion to find the usually mild-mannered Redpath holding Barnes against a wall, his hand upon his throat, growling, 'You bloody idiot. Of course 500,000 people would play for nothing, but how bloody good would they be?'

Chappell must have felt that recourse to physical threats would be more profitable than attempts at reasoned negotiation. As Richie Benaud noted, the skipper's meetings with the Board were 'extraordinarily unproductive'. There was one occasion when every time Chappell made a financial suggestion to chairman Caldwell, the voice of Bradman, attending in his role as President of the SACA, would chime in, 'No, son, we can't do that.' Chappell felt that Bradman treated the Board's money as though it was his own.

Greg Chappell ran into the same resistance once he inherited the captaincy when his brother stepped down on his own terms ahead of the 1975-76 season. Even though the new skipper felt he was only asking for 'a pittance' on behalf of the players, he recalled 'one particular individual' who controlled the discussion and 'slammed the door very firmly in my face'.

In the short term, however, enough muscles appear to have been flexed to achieve some concessions. Fearful of the players' power and eager not to kill the golden goose – merely to keep it shackled while the eggs were laid – the ACB met prior to the sixth Test in Melbourne in early February. The Board made sure to set expectations by noting that of the receipts of A$220,00 from the Boxing Day Test in Melbourne, only A$44,000 remained after all the grounds and personnel costs were paid. Even so, Barnes emerged from the meeting to explain that the players would be awarded 'a reasonable bonus' for their efforts in the Ashes series, which was reported to be on course to yield a profit approaching A$160,000 (close to £100,000 at the time).

Additional amounts would also be added to their provident fund, the pot of money established in order to create savings that players could withdraw two years after their retirement. The scheme called for A$200 to be put aside for each player for every Test he played above 20, with A$100 being awarded per Test until then. *Cricketer* had hailed it ahead of the summer as 'the most eventual cricket achievement of season 1974-75 – if not of an entire decade or more', although the players might have disagreed with the description of the fund as 'the final realisation that Test cricketers deserve a fair and adequate reward for the time they devote to the most demanding form of cricket'.

The same ACB meeting confirmed that the 16 men heading to England later in the year would receive A$2,734 each, while the ACB was looking forward to making a profit of A$35,000 from that tour. Test match appearances and prize money might nudge individual earnings up by a couple of thousand but Marsh pointed out, 'However you look at it, A$4,700 is not very good money for

16 weeks, especially if the player is married with a family and is not being paid by his firm while he is away.'

For now it was a truce of sorts. Yet it was the injustices highlighted by the 1974-75 season that ensured that the Australian cricketers' desire for payment worthy of their status would match the ambition of Kerry Packer to make the ACB pay for its refusal to countenance a television contract with his Channel 9 station two years later. Packer's own World Series Cricket would provide him with matches to fill his air time and offer the elite players of Australia, and elsewhere in the world, the level of remuneration – often $25,000 per year and upwards – that had been unattainable via the establishment.

According to Edwards, one for whom WSC represented a late-career windfall, 'That was fundamentally a movement created by dissatisfaction of the players a few years beforehand. It was not just the money, but the way the players were treated. Mate, it was diabolical.'

12
ASHES TO ASHES

> *Coming fresh to this Test series is like walking into a pitched battle between the Mafia and the IRA. You knew they'd been at each other's throats but you couldn't believe it was this uncompromising, this violent or this uncouth.*
> **Ian Wooldridge, *Daily Mail***

The Ashes were surrendered by England at three minutes before six on the final day of the fourth Test. Despite isolated moments of resistance it was the outcome that had been widely expected since Australia unleashed Jeff Thomson and Dennis Lillee on the second day of the series back in Brisbane.

Yet there were plenty of observers who felt that something else – the intangible 'spirit of cricket' perhaps – had been lost in the fierce and frenzied environment of the Sydney Cricket Ground, where a venue-record 178,027 turned up to cheer their Aussie heroes and pelt the poor old Poms with abuse and beer cans, 864,000 of which were cleared away during the match.

Over the course of five days, bowlers from both sides were warned about intimidatory bowling, including Lillee on multiple occasions; two more England batsmen received damaging blows; tailenders were left thanking the heavens for lucky escapes; and bad-tempered exchanges between opponents were dotted throughout. Former England captain Sir Len Hutton remarked that if 1932-33 had been 'bodyline' then this must be 'headline'.

By the time the teams had arrived at the SCG on the first morning, thousands of fans were making their way into the ground, preparing for a heavy day ahead. 'Going to the Sydney Cricket Ground was fantastic in the days of the Hill,' said an interviewee in Allison Pressley's Australian-published book, *Living in the 70s*. 'Everyone would take an esky[37] with two dozen cans and two chickens. That was your day's supply per bloke. You'd line your esky up in the queue – the queue would actually be eskies – then you'd just mill around. But everyone knew which esky was his, even though they all looked the same. Then you'd move it up and eventually get in.'

It quickly became clear that overnight rain would delay the start, for half an hour it transpired. It was an academic detail for Mike Denness, who changed into his kit, went out and practised with his teammates and absorbed the full impact of his decision to miss the match. Determined not to sit around feeling sorry for himself, he showered after the first few overs of the match and helped the other reserve players work out the day's duty rota. Wearing casual clothes, he made his way into the stands to watch from behind the bowler's arm, accepting good wishes from those spectators who recognised him and chatting with the former Australia and Essex batsman Bruce Francis. Denness's original intention had been to get away from the ground for periods of relaxation, but the course of events meant he felt a responsibility to be available in the dressing room as much as possible. Proudly bearing his red and yellow-trimmed MCC match blazer, John Edrich had attended the toss in Denness's place and called 'heads'. His luck was no better than his colleague, whose commitment to 'tails' had let him down three times. This time Ian Chappell chose to bat, despite the sultry atmosphere and possibility of further rain. What made up his mind was a hard playing surface that had lost much of the grass of a day earlier.

Left back in the England dressing room with the non-playing tourists was an angry Chris Old. Included at Perth after originally being told he was not required, he had just found that his place in this Test had been snatched away by another last-minute change of heart. 'The night before Sydney I was playing,' he explained. 'That morning I went into the nets with light shoes on, bowled a few overs and walked back into the dressing room. I could see a discussion going on and I was told that I wasn't playing. Bernard Thomas shepherded me out of the dressing room because I was not very happy. They thought it might turn later on so they played two spinners.'

---

37 Australian term for a portable cooler or ice box, deriving from the word 'Eskimo'.

Old felt the decision was indicative of the mood of desperation that descended on the MCC party. 'I think it was grasping at straws. It did not happen on previous tours or on any tour I went on afterwards. You knew the day before whether you were playing or not, unless things drastically changed overnight.' The irony of Edrich being criticised as the match progressed for relying too much on his seamers was not lost on the Yorkshireman.

If some players had got their way, England's new-ball attack would have been strengthened by the man who was flitting between press box and commentary booth. The idea of calling up John Snow had been percolating among the tourists for some time and at the end of the third Test in Melbourne senior players Edrich and Tony Greig had approached Denness with the proposal. The captain duly discussed it with Alec Bedser, but it never became an official agenda item at a selection meeting. Denness not only felt that belatedly picking Snow would undermine the efforts of those already on tour – even though injury to Mike Hendrick offered plenty of justification – but he knew that Bedser could hardly go back to Lord's and plead again for a player about whom objections had been so stridently outlined in the original selection. Condemned to five days of watching, Old decided that he could at least share the load of chores customarily born by reserve wicketkeeper Bob Taylor, the forgotten man of many a tour while Alan Knott was in his prime. 'Bob was wonderful off the field,' said Old, 'because that was the second time he went through a tour of Australia without playing in Test matches. He was brilliant at looking after players, picking them up, making sure they got everything they wanted in the dressing room. You really do need people like that who accept what their role is going to be.

'I remember Bernard Thomas turned to me once and said, "There's going to be a time on this tour when Bob is going to go missing and we have got to try and cover for him so that he can go off and do what he wants to do." At Sydney I kind of took over Bob's role. I can remember someone saying, "I thought Bob would be around," and I said, "No, Bob has gone away to do something privately. Don't worry because whatever you want, we'll cover it." It was well deserved when Bob got his chance in the team when Knotty went to World Series Cricket.'

Meanwhile, the result of the toss meant an instant introduction to Test cricket for Rick McCosker. Prolific throughout the season for New South Wales after being promoted from number six to three by skipper Doug Walters, he was now required to open for his country. A 28-year-old bank clerk, with an upright bearing and the sensible clean-cut grooming one might expect to confront when applying for a loan, McCosker was playing only his 12th game of first-class cricket.

'I don't think I ever gave up hoping to play for Australia,' he said. 'I'd given myself a goal to get into the New South Wales team and then decided I needed to give myself another goal, which was two years to get into the Australian side. I was very fortunate that there was a spot open for me at the right time as Wally Edwards hadn't had the success he was hoping for. When I looked at Ian Chappell, Greg Chappell, Ross Edwards and Doug Walters I knew I wasn't going to displace any of those guys. There was one place left so that was where I went. I had been batting at three for New South Wales for a while and I had opened a little bit for my club side some time ago. If I wanted an Aussie cap that was the only way I was going to get it.

'I wasn't waiting on the end of the phone, It was a bit embarrassing to a certain extent because there were people in the media who were talking me up and it was the last thing I wanted. All I wanted to do was keep scoring runs; that was what I was focusing on. But when I got the call I was ready to go.'

Geoff Arnold, who bowled three overs at either end early on, had the ball moving around and beating the edge of both McCosker and Ian Redpath as though at home on a county green-top. 'He was difficult,' McCosker remembered, 'particularly early in the innings when there was a little bit of moisture in the wicket.' But as they had frequently failed to do in previous games, the Australian openers remained together beyond the tricky opening exchanges, McCosker eventually hooking Greig for the first boundary well beyond the hour mark. Bob Willis made the mistake of thinking the new man was as vulnerable against the short ball as Wally Edwards and saw two bouncers in the same over disappear behind square leg to take Australia to 62 without loss at lunch.

McCosker, who batted with a closed stance, proved just as strong on the drive when Willis began his afternoon work by over-pitching.

He had been at the crease a little over two hours when he marked his debut by reaching a half-century with a well-timed push through midwicket. It was far from being a chanceless innings – Knott missing a low catch off Greig when he was 10 and Edrich spilling a gully chance off Willis at 43 – but that did not stop the crowd rising to its local hero as cheers cascaded from the top of the green-roofed pavilion to the foot of the Hill.

'It was the perfect time for me to be selected,' McCosker explained. 'I have seen a lot of guys selected before the right time. I was fortunate that I went into a very established team that was playing well and they welcomed me, particularly the captain. And the first Test I played was on my home ground so that made a big difference. I remember walking out and looking round and the SCG was pretty full and I thought, "Wow, this is all new." But I felt confident; nervous but not overawed because this was my home ground. I knew the conditions and the wicket. I had a good partner and a strong batting side coming in. It was a clear, sunny day and a beautiful batting wicket. Everything went well.'

The Sydney fans were more generous towards their own man than to Redpath, who had not yet reached 20 but whose presence had doubtless been an assurance to his new colleague. The rowdier patrons had taken to giving Redpath the slow handclap and chanting, 'We want Walters.' More disturbing was the five-minute delay caused when they began hurling cans, not all of them empty, at Greig as he fielded near the boundary. Advised by Bedser to tone down his pantomime villain act in such a potentially volatile environment, Greig seemed relatively unconcerned for his safety. Nevertheless, it was an unwelcome echo off our years earlier when Ray Illingworth had been forced to lead his team from the SCG field when bottles and cans were hurled – with greater intent than on this occasion – at Snow after his bouncer hit Terry Jenner.

With 33 to his name, the usually phlegmatic Redpath was out in untypical fashion, brushing the stumps as he attempted an ungainly pull against Fred Titmus when the partnership was four short of 100. After that, McCosker and Ian Chappell progressed busily at a run a minute, with 26 coming of one sequence of three overs. It tested the athleticism of the tourists to the full, England having omitted five players who would likely have made their best fielding eleven.

McCosker hooked another four against Arnold and then applauded at the non-striker's end when his skipper advanced to drive Titmus to the straight boundary. No one bowled particularly badly, but the conditions and the batsmen's confidence made it hard for new skipper Edrich to see where a wicket might come from. Once again, it was golden boy Greig who delivered. Having tempted McCosker outside the off stump on a couple of occasions he got him to edge to Knott for 80 in the next over as he tried to force the ball off the back foot.

'I didn't think of missing out on a hundred at the time because I didn't realise I was that close,' McCosker said. 'I saw a ball to try and hit and didn't do it right. When I was walking off I was thinking that this is the first day of a Test match and we have got off to a good start. I had done my job so I was fairly comfortable with that.'

After Chappell swept Underwood for two boundaries, tea was taken at 162 for 2. Those on the Hill who were bored enough and emboldened enough by their consumption of alcohol spent the interval pelting the giant scoreboard with bottles and other missiles. The scoreboard did not survive unscathed; nor did the pockets of several of the offenders who were ultimately fined for their actions.

An England fan, quoted by Pressley, remembered, 'Going to Test matches at Sydney Cricket Ground when England was involved was an absolute nightmare. You were lucky to get out alive. If you were English you were really stupid to go on the Hill, so I did, but I'd go with Australian friends and sit in the middle of them so they could protect me. And I just couldn't believe what was happening on the Hill during a cricket match: copulation, defecation, you name it. Every known bodily function. There was no limit on what drink you could take in. I've seen a coffin used as an esky. People would get there at half past ten, and by lunchtime most of them were drunk and not particularly interested in the cricket. They were more interested in fighting and throwing full cans of beer at other people.'

The old-school Cowdrey felt the beer cans were a distraction even when not being used as missiles. 'The crowds have always been vociferous in that part of the world,' he conceded, 'but the tin can chorus which used to strike up mid-afternoon, the banging together of empty beer cans at the slightest excuse, was a new and unattractive feature of a Test match day.'

EW Swanton, who watched part of the Test as guest of the Sydney Cricket Ground Trust and suggested that the Hill was 'urgently in need of more civilised facilities', observed that behaviour had been better in the days 'when the popular sections could not afford the vast quantities of beer which are now consumed'.

ACB chairman Tim Caldwell shrugged, 'I think we've got a community which has set up a permissive society, and this is going to cause people to be more unruly. People can demonstrate in the streets and do the various things the community is able to do. If you pick up that community and put them into a cricket ground as spectators I wouldn't expect them to behave in any other fashion.'

The editorial column of the *Sydney Morning Herald* was less forgiving, suggesting that the solution to all this 'loutish behaviour' might be found in radical action 'The time has surely come for the SCG Trust and the NSW Cricket Association to give urgent consideration to banning beer cans from the ground,' it proposed. 'If the game is not to be spoilt for the majority of spectators they now have little option.' Yet on the evidence of the mountain of cans cleared away over five days, the majority must have been happily quaffing their lagers without turning ugly and would have considered their experience vastly diminished without such refreshment. The newspaper, however, argued that the right to consume alcohol came with an assumption of 'an irreducible minimum of civilised behaviour. Unfortunately it is clear that this assumption is no longer valid.'

There was plenty to be cheered – whether fuelled by beer or not – as Chappell accelerated to a 77-ball fifty early in the final session. Again it was a surprise when Arnold got one to seam away enough to achieve a straightforward edge. For the remaining hour and a quarter of the day, Greg Chappell and Ross Edwards strengthened their team's position against an England attack that had been unable all day to follow up one success with another. Chappell, who had been suffering from a rash and the symptoms of a virus before the start of play, was mostly unobtrusive in the way he accumulated his runs, although he unfurled his signature on-drive and the occasional less cultured shot as he reached an inevitable half-century.

Edwards suffered by stylistic comparison, as most of Chappell's partners did, and benefitted from the premature decision of Titmus and Edrich to dispense with a slip, where one fine cut would certainly have landed. He looked as though he had survived to face the new ball on the second day until, with three balls remaining, he was tucked up by Greig and chopped on to his stumps. At 251 for 4, the day had been won by the home side, who stood poised for the kind of total that had so far proved beyond their opponents.

And so to the second day, whose unholy events made no concession to the fact that it was the Sabbath. 'Practically none of the traditional courtesies of cricket survived,' said *Daily Mail* chief sports writer Ian Wooldridge, while Peter Laker told *Daily Mirror* readers, 'In one of the ugliest days I can recall in any sphere of cricket, Australian fast bowler Dennis Lillee yesterday dragged the fourth Test – and with it this bitterly physical Ashes series – to the brink of total warfare.'

In *The Times*, John Woodcock was moved to write, 'This was one of the noisier days of Test cricket and not one of the more attractive. Just as in football, the turbulent behaviour of the players communicated itself to the crowd, who responded on the Hill as they might on the Kop.' Christopher Martin-Jenkins felt he had witnessed 'a nasty day', noting that 'tempers and bouncers flew; blood boiled and spilt'.

The new ball was taken immediately and, and as so often, instantly did for Walters, trapped in front by a nip-backer from Arnold. Again, England could not achieve a quick follow-up as Greg Chappell, gracefully, and Rodney Marsh, bullishly and sometimes streakily, drove their way to a 50-run partnership. It ended when Marsh missed a drive at Greig and found his middle stump cartwheeling back towards the wicketkeeper.

Having moved into the 80s, Chappell was out in the next over, the irrepressible Greig diving low to his left at second slip after Arnold found the edge. Lillee joined Max Walker and, far from quietly petering out, the Australian innings now went into its most contentious period.

Greig bowled short on a wicket that had become noticeably faster since the first day. Lillee went back but found the ball following him, smacking him painfully on the left elbow. The Aussie dropped his bat, ignored his partner's call for a leg bye, and made a great show of clutching the affected area with his right glove.

From his position at slip, Keith Fletcher retrieved the bat and could not help but succumb to *schadenfreude* as he offered it to his opponent. He knew he had nothing to lose. 'Obviously, it didn't make any difference whether I said anything him, he was still going to be the same, so I might as well say what I felt like.' Despite his place in the firing line, Fletcher had felt that England's bowlers let Lillee get away with too much. 'If I had been a fast bowler, the first delivery I bowled at him would have been straight at his throat,' he said. He welcomed Greig's combative approach and wished others had been as bold. Witnesses to the incident recall Fletcher making sure that Lillee could hear him congratulating Greig on the delivery and urging, 'Let him have another one,' which, according to Ian Chappell, 'wasn't a really smart thing to say'.

Offering Lillee his bat, Fletcher suggested it was a shame that the wrong elbow had been struck. Not only was that an echo of Chappell to Derek Underwood earlier in the series but was exactly the remark now made jokingly by Bill Lawry on the television commentary. According to some, Fletcher might also have suggested that Lillee now knew how it felt. 'He went off like a firecracker,' said Fletcher. 'Aiming a stream of abuse at me so unexpected and uncalled for that I threw his bat back on the grass and walked off.'

Greig gave Lillee more short deliveries in the next over, one causing the ball to be fended away from his face in a flurry of gloves and leaving Lillee glaring down the track. Umpire Tom Brooks decided this was the moment to admonish Greig. Edrich arrived on the scene to be informed by his bowler, 'I've been told that is enough of the short-pitched balls.'

It was ironic to see the medium pacer, whose intention was to elicit a false shot, being warned after the serious jeopardy Lillee and Thomson had created for the England batsmen throughout the series. Martin-Jenkins called it an 'extraordinary misjudgement' and Woodcock described the umpire's action as 'rather pedantic'. That view bridged national prejudices, with *Melbourne Age* writer Percy Beames saying, 'It was a frivolous decision to rule [it] intimidatory,' and Richie Benaud noting in the *Sydney Daily Mirror* that he had 'absolutely no sympathy with the lower half of the Australian order when they complain about an excess of short-pitched bowling against them'.

Perhaps, though, by laying down this particular marker the umpires would also curb Australian excesses. 'Better that way than to risk the game becoming a rough house,' suggested Woodcock.

Dennis Amiss, meanwhile, understood the warning to Greig but felt that subsequent attempts to control the number of short-pitched deliveries at lower-order batsman led to 'confusion', which was 'typical of the inconsistent attitude to this type of bowling'.

When Lillee was bowled by Arnold in the next over, the way in which he stopped mid-stride as he began the walk back to the pavilion made it clear that more had been said to which he took offence. And Arnold, hardly known for his outwardly fiery demeanour, was soon in the thick of things with new batsman Ashley Mallett.

Firstly, the pair exchanged words when Arnold asked Mallett not to stand so wide at the non-striker's end that he was blocking mid-on. That caused an initial intervention from umpire Robin Bailhache. Then an Arnold delivery climbed towards Mallett's ribs and caused the bat to tumble from his grasp as he tried to play it away. A run was completed with the bat left unattended at the striker's end. When Arnold got another, shorter, ball to lift even more, Mallett flipped the bat out of his hand in the vague direction of the ball before ripping off his glove, making as if to advance down the wicket towards the bowler and delivering what might have been interpreted as a V-sign.

'Oh, Ashley. What are you doing?' groaned Lawry. 'It's cream puff pace.' Again, it was serious enough for the umpire to respond, Bailhache the one to issue the warning about intimidatory bowling this time.

It all obscured some questionable captaincy on the part of Edrich, who opted for extended persistence with seamers Arnold and Greig under heavy fire from the tail-enders. Even though the pair finished with five and four wickets respectively, Greig's line had become wayward and it might have been better to force the lesser batsmen to take their chances against the slow bowling of Underwood and Titmus. 'I thought we worked well together,' said the Middlesex spinner, expressing his own surprise at Edrich's strategy. The field placings, too, were perplexing. Benaud shared with TV viewers his confusion over the shortage of catchers as yet another ball squirted through the gully region, and Lawry added, 'I am not sure how they expect to get Walker out if they don't have men in catching positions.' And no sooner had guest commentator Snow added to the chorus of demands for a third slip, so Thomson edged Willis for four through that exact spot.

With Walker and Mallett having both thrashed their way into the 30s and Thomson striking four fours in his 24, Australia's final total of 405 meant that the last three wickets had added 95 runs, all but removing victory from the tourists' scope of ambition.

England began their reply against Thomson at his most unpredictable. Having started with a wide he shocked Amiss with a ball that exploded from short of a length and flew over Marsh's head for four byes. Seaming another delivery to beat Amiss's edge and giving up another bye, he completed his opening over by flinging one outside David Lloyd's leg stump to the fine leg boundary. Ten extras in all.

'I just don't know how to bowl with the new ball,' he explained, 'because with my slinging action it slips out of my hand and goes anywhere. But once the ball has worn a bit and I can get a proper grip I find I have better control.'

Lillee was more predictable, but no less unplayable. 'Both men banged the ball in short,' wrote Martin-Jenkins, 'the sky was menacing and overcast, the atmosphere heavy and the pressure on Amiss and Lloyd intense.'

Lloyd was forced to spring out of the way of a scary Lillee bouncer and lucky to survive after missing two fizzing seamers. Fired up by the sting in his left elbow and the chants of the crowd, this was the fastest Lillee had yet bowled in the series. 'He has come in like a steam train,' Lloyd remembered.

Having 'really let myself go for the first time that season', Lillee was 'well pleased with the result in terms of the speed I was able to build up and the fact that I pulled up so well afterwards.' From his unaccustomed view up in the stands, Denness noted, 'By the third and fourth Tests [Lillee] was back to his old self again. [At] Sydney the boys reckoned that he was even quicker than Thomson.'

Marsh said he was still standing a yard further back for Thomson than Lillee but was now further back for the senior bowler than he had been in 1972.[38] As proof of the speed he was having to deal with he allowed photographers to capture the shattered finger protection inside his gloves. Describing his day's work as 'hammering your hands with a sledgehammer once a minute for six hours' he added, 'Every time I've crouched down behind the stumps I've wondered to myself if this will be a blow to put me out of the game.'

But Marsh was in awe of the purpose of his bowling, as well as the pace. 'I feel now I know precisely what he is aiming to do with every ball,' he said. 'There is a decided plan to his bowling. I can sense what he is planning to do with a particular delivery. He knows he must conserve himself in certain ways, including a slightly modified action to put less strain on his back, so he has made up for it in other ways, perhaps more subtle ways.'

The wicketkeeper was also well positioned to observe the strengthening strategic bond between the men terrorising the England batsmen. 'Watch them when one is bowling and the other is fielding at mid-on or mid-off. The fielding member of the duo will pick up the ball, perhaps give it a quick shine, walk back with the other, talking all the time about the ball coming up, about methods of attack, just trying to give the other guy that extra confidence or edge to take a wicket. Dennis and Two-up[39] are forever discussing tactics and bowling between themselves. Sitting in a corner you'll see them taking about individual batsmen, about ways of improving their fitness or stamina, about their gear, about particular deliveries. They are dedicated to each other's success.'

The restoration of Lillee alongside the terrifying Thomson left Amiss with 'certain reservations about the game I was supposed to be playing'. He remembered, 'Very often it was not cricket, not when I had to spend so much time defending myself. Many a time I walked out to the middle in a Test match knowing it was virtually a waste of time carrying a bat. I knew it would be used not so much to make strokes as to defend the ball off my body.'

---

38 Rudimentary film analysis of the Perth Test had suggested that Thomson was bowling three miles per hour faster than Lillee.

39 Thomson's nickname among his teammates. Two-up was an illegal gambling game involving spinning two coins, played most notably at 'Thommo's Two-up School' in various venues in uptown Sydney.

After Thomson was clipped through midwicket and cut square by Lloyd, his removal from the attack brought Australia an immediate breakthrough when an unsettled Amiss drove loosely at Walker's second ball and Mallett pulled off yet another outstanding diving catch to his left at gully. More brilliant fielding removed Lloyd in Lillee's first over after tea, Thomson reacting smartly at backward short leg, where he had not long since been placed by his skipper.

What Chappell loved as much as anything about Lillee was that he would never ask for a field placing designed to save runs. If he wanted a change it would be for an extra slip or to 'get that bloody bat-pad fielder in closer'. The idea of a sweeper on the boundary was anathema. Besides, Lillee's pace made significant scoring shots in front of the wicket almost impossible, with both Cowdrey and Edrich happy to squirt the ball down to the fine leg boundary.

Discussing his approach decades later, Edrich explained, 'When you first went in against someone like Lillee or Thomson, for the first few overs it is their game. You try to keep out of the way as much as possible, then you hope you might get a few balls you can score off. That is what one tried to do. Sometimes it worked and sometimes it didn't.

'Thommo was the worst to face, because of this slinging action with the high bounce. And he kept going. He was quick and I am not very tall so I spent most of my time trying to get out of the way unless he bowled it down the leg side. Dennis had such a wonderful action and he tended to attack you a lot on off stump or just outside. I always found it easier to play bowlers who had a good action because you picked them up at the start and you could get the line.'

Cowdrey's relief at edging four runs off Thomson dulled some of the pain of two blows on the body but lasted only until he fended the ball off his midriff into the hands of McCosker at forward short leg. The Australian newcomer was in the same position when Edrich flicked Walker off his pads with a full swing of the bat and the ball clanged into his forehead, almost ending up in Mallett's hands at gully on the rebound.

The fielder was helped from the field, but it was the arrival a few minutes earlier of Fletcher – a 'picture of misery' according to Woodcock – that appeared to have placed the scent of blood in

Lillee's nostrils, and those of thousands of fans. Chants of 'kill, kill, kill' swept from the stands, Fletcher sensing that the crowd was 'verging on hysteria'. Thomson recalled of the incoming batsman, 'You have never seen a bloke walk out there so slowly in his life.'

Denness, who as a Scot had the 'Hampden Roar' as his benchmark for crowd engagement, said, 'The crescendo of noise from the massed fans on the Hill came very near to matching it. It started from the moment Lillee stepped off on his long run to the wicket and as his pace increased so did the build-up of noise from the Hill, with the fans in the other parts of the ground joining in the chanting of Lillee's name. By the time he was just about to deliver the ball it had reached its peak. It was very disconcerting for a batsman.'

On this occasion it turned out to be Edrich who bore the brunt of Lillee's wrath. After a series of short balls the umpires made their third intervention of the day, Bailhache issuing the warning.

'One tour too many, Fletch,' Edrich confided in his partner at one point. 'One tour too many.'

Once England had reached the close at 106 for 3, it was the match officials' door to whom reporters beat a path, eager for the background to such a turbulent day. Neither umpire was in the mood to elaborate, Brooks saying he would not comment, while Bailhache offered, 'You can ask questions, but I am not answering them.'

The manner in which the officials monitored the fast bowlers' intent to deliberately intimidate the opposition had been under scrutiny since Brisbane, with some blaming them for indulging Lillee and Thomson's assault on the England batsmen. During the third Test, *Daily Mirror* columnist Frank Taylor had written, 'Cricket is being slowly murdered in Melbourne. What is happening in Australia this winter has no place in the sporting calendar. This is surely all part of the modern image of sport – to win, win, win at all costs and damn the entertainment.'

A similar view was offered by David Frith, editor of *The Cricketer*. 'The foul language from several players, the glares, the waving of arms, the pointing of fingers towards the dressing room. This is not entertainment. It is the petulance of the immature.'

What many saw as a further deterioration at Sydney appeared finally to have emboldened the umpires, although according to Bailhache they had been deliberating the subject throughout the series. 'Lillee and Thomson were getting plenty of attention for their so-called intimidatory bowling and we were copping it for allegedly doing nothing about it,' he said. 'Tom and I had numerous discussions about it and we felt we handled the issue evenly and adequately. During the series we both warned the bowlers on both sides on several occasions about the over-use of short-pitched deliveries. Whenever we did ask a fast bowler to ease up, the request was not well received. Law 46 [governing and unfair play][40] wasn't very explicit then, so there was no real good guideline about intimidation. Tom was generally a little more lenient than I was, being an ex-fast bowler. I think I worried a little more than he did. It was very prevalent, and I didn't envy the English batsmen at all. A couple of them started playing Thommo from square leg. They weren't happy out there and you can't blame them.'

Bedser had enough empathy with the officials to note that it was 'all too easy to make umpires the scapegoats'. He believed, 'The captain is more culpable if he allows his bowlers too free a rein. He has the power to defuse inflammatory situations,' but said he had 'little faith in the desire of so many captains to control what they see as an advantageous position'. He knew that Ray Illingworth had not attempted to shackle Snow four years earlier, so he could hardly expect Ian Chappell to show mercy.

The Australian captain's 'rule one of Test cricket' was, 'When you've got 'em – fast bowlers – hand it out, because when you haven't got 'em you are going to be on the receiving end.' It was, after all, an attitude ingrained in his DNA. It had been his grandfather, Vic Richardson, who had spoken up during the Bodyline series, urging captain Bill Woodfull in vain to instruct Australia's bowlers to give the English batsmen the same treatment that Harold Larwood and his colleagues were administering to the home team.

In later years, Bedser was critical of the Australian board for not intervening in the 'wider interests of cricket' and described the bowling of the home team as 'provocative and unnecessary',

---

40 The revision of the Laws in 1980 reduced their number to 42, the last of which addressed 'Unfair Play'. Currently, Law 41 governs 'Unfair Play', including short-pitched bowling, and Law 42 concerns 'Player Conduct'.

although he also conceded, 'I was one of the old stagers and it was popular stuff, lapped up by the mob . . . Maybe cricket reflects the general violence of the age, but I will always contend that Dennis was one of the greatest fast bowlers and had such high tactical instincts that he lowered himself to try to scare opponents out, especially the tailender.'

What made the whole debate about intimidatory bowling less conclusive was the fact that Thomson continued to inflict most of his damage not via short-pitched balls but through his ability to achieve startling lift from close to a good length. So much so that Denness would comment, 'Even though they were bowling bouncers we were hoping the umpires wouldn't tell them they were bowling too many because they weren't bothering us.'

Willis was among those who felt the laws covering intimidation needed to be more flexible rather than focusing purely on bouncers that passed above shoulder height. 'The law is an ass,' he argued.'Many a vicious delivery has been bowled, even to me, without passing anywhere near as high as my shoulder. The law should be altered to give the umpire complete responsibility to decide when a bowler is deliberately trying to intimidate and the umpire should then be strong enough to interpret the law and act firmly.' He felt that Brooks and Bailhache 'never moved a muscle to restrain the use of the short ball'.

Denness's verdict was that Lillee and Thomson were 'without a doubt' guilty of intimidation. 'If you look over the records, how many times were they likely to have hit the stumps? The answer was nothing at all,' he said. 'They were hoping our concentration would go or we would play a false shot.'

Daily Mail correspondent Alex Bannister suggested, 'If Dennis Amiss, Colin Cowdrey and Keith Fletcher were not subjected to intimidation at the crisis point then I do not know the meaning of the word.'

Lillee, of course, felt that the bowling remained within acceptable boundaries and saw no real difference from the average Sheffield Shield match. 'I don't remember bowling more short balls than I usually did,' he said, adding with some justification, 'I think England got to the stage where they were mentally defeated and played a lot of short balls they should have left.'

The umpires felt they couldn't win and Bailhache eventually lost patience with the media. 'The press had a habit of giving us a pounding one day, but during the next day at lunch, if something has happened, the whole pack waits outside your door. As soon as you have had lunch they come barging in, asking what the hell happened. Towards the end of the series this happened again and I'd had enough. I told them, "You guys aren't welcome. Get out," and slammed the door in their faces. Tommy was saying, "Don't say that; don't do that." The heading in the paper the next day was, "Umpire has had a gut's full."'

Yet Bailhache, who recalled that he had already started receiving 'cranky mail', had worse than persistent reporters to worry about. 'I was doing the Test match in Sydney and my family [wife Josephine and daughters Catherine, Susanne and Belinda] was still in Adelaide,' he explained. 'I got a threatening phone call from someone saying they were going to harm the kids. My wife got in touch with the South Australia Cricket Association and they got the police to keep an eye on my place for the rest of the match.'

The umpires' handling of the bowlers was not a topic that was going to be quickly put aside. The next day's events saw to that. With England's innings in its death throes, Lillee was given another talking to by Brooks after a short ball speared in painfully at Underwood's chest, hitting him just above the heart and bringing boos from the few English supporters in the ground.

Two balls later he let loose a ball that whistled past Willis's waist without bouncing. Willis's was the latest bat to be discarded in protest, while Marsh's act of rolling the ball at the stumps and Lillee's appeal for stumping did nothing to lighten the Englishman's mood. Lillee insisted that he had not committed the heinous act of bowling a deliberate beamer, saying later, 'I may play it tough, but not that tough.'

Robin Marlar, in a guest column for the *Sydney Morning Herald*, suggested, 'If a stallion played up in the stables as Lillee has at this match he would be gelded by nightfall.' By now, though, it was not just the English who were questioning Lillee's antics. After another warning on the fourth day, Bill O'Reilly wrote in the same paper, 'If the talented Australian speedster finds it impossible to control himself under such circumstances there's very little chance of him controlling his bowling either.'

O'Reilly sympathised with the umpires because the sport had made it customary never to fully implement the 'dust-covered rule' designed to protect batsmen. 'Our legislators, charged with conducting Test cricket in the best possible manner to satisfy the public's and participants' interests, have no hope whatever of formulating rules to handle intimidatory bowling.' It was, he suggested, down to the players to police themselves.

Woodcock, meanwhile, felt the umpires 'lacked the conviction to follow the procedure laid down in the laws for dealing with persistent short-pitched fast bowling', suggesting that quiet words with the bowlers should have been replaced by formal sanctions. 'Instead, they introduced a kind of handicap system whereby, for example, Lillee was allowed three bumpers an over at Greig but Greig could only bowl one at Lillee. There is no way on earth that such a scheme, arbitrarily operated, can be satisfactory.'

England's inevitable plunge towards a decisive first-innings deficit continued in the second over of the third day, although by then Edrich had already been dropped by Ian Chappell at first slip off Thomson. Fletcher added only one run to his overnight 23 before clipping Walker cleanly off his legs, straight to the safe-handed Redpath round the corner. Greig remained long enough only to connect with a couple of typically ambitious cut shots, before pushing defensively at a full ball from Thomson and offering a sharp low catch to Greg Chappell.

Edrich and Knott, both renowned battlers, came together at 123 for 5, at which point the 206 total needed to avoid the follow-on seemed challengingly distant. At least when they were parted just under an hour and a half later, that target was only 26 runs away.

Having had success with scoring deliberate runs over the slip cordon, Knott edged inadvertently through the same region off both front and back foot against Walker. Edrich scored fours against the same bowler through square leg and mid-off before gratefully accepting gifts from Ian Chappell and Walters, who were killing overs before lunch, to reach his fifty. But with eight minutes of the morning remaining he made the unforgiveable – in the context of the ongoing battle – mistake of glancing Walters down the leg side to a surprised and delighted Marsh. In a change to the norm, four of the England top six had been out to close catches on the leg side rather than off the outside edge.

Knott, 26 at lunch, re-emerged at his creative, impish best, adding 56 runs in the space of 43 balls in an hour. Clipping anything full off his legs and lifting short balls in the region of third man, he needed an inside edge off Walters to become England's first batsman to reach 50 three times in the series, but his confidence clearly impacted Titmus, who drove happily to score 22 runs of his own. The partnership had reached 60 when, with the new ball looming, Titmus aimed an uncontrolled slash at Walters and was caught behind.

Lillee's first delivery with the new ball was driven through mid-off by Knott, who helped himself to 14 off the over, including three twos and a thump to the straight boundary that had the air of a pre-meditated one-day shot. The bold Underwood, who seemed to have faced as much new-ball bowling in the series as some of England's openers, responded with clubbing drives off both Lillee and Thomson. The hour and five minutes since lunch had produced 95 runs when Thomson bowled Knott, whose horrible slog was unworthy of the innings he'd played until then.

After their encounters with Lillee, Willis lost his leg stump trying to belt Thomson, and Underwood saw new partner Arnold struggle to fend off another dangerously rising ball from the same bowler. The innings ended at 295 when Underwood drove Lillee to Walker at mid-off, his contribution 27 more valuable runs.

A lead of 110 meant that Australia's second knock was an inevitable march towards the declaration that would set up the opportunity for their bowlers to bring home the Ashes. The early loss of Ian Chappell, opening in place of the groggy McCosker, did nothing to change that.

It needed an umpires' conference to rule that Lloyd had taken a clean catch at leg gully, but Greg Chappell made few demands on the officials. He struck the ball out of the middle of the bat, missed virtually nothing and, with England quickly on the defensive, made brisk, untroubled progress to a 66-ball half-century. By close of play, a partnership of 108 with Redpath had taken the home team to 123 for 1.

The possibility of afternoon thunderstorms when play resumed after the rest day pressed Australia into renewed urgency once they had safely negotiated the first half-hour against refreshed bowlers. Chappell began his acceleration by driving Willis on the rise through the covers and demonstrated his comfort at the crease with a glorious on-drive past bowler Greig. Appropriately, it was one of his signature front-foot shots through midwicket – a mere push that made it almost to the boundary – that completed his century in 203 minutes and 161 balls.

He followed up by scoring 35 more in the final five overs of the morning, taking liberties of power and placement with the bowling of Titmus, Greig and, in particular, Willis. Even the arch-competitor Greig could only muster a shrug when Underwood dropped Chappell on the hook at long leg, and there was muted celebration when the centurion eventually skied Arnold to Lloyd at midwicket shortly after lunch. His 144 had included 16 fours, and the stand of 220 with Redpath was his country's highest second-wicket effort in home Tests against England.

With Walters quick to follow him back to the pavilion, it was now a question of how quickly Redpath could achieve his own three figures and clear the path to a declaration. He was apparently in no great hurry, making mostly laboured progress. When he finally worked Arnold to the midwicket boundary and then swept Underwood to reach 103, he had batted two hours longer for his hundred than Chappell. There was no denying that it was a deserved landmark, however, after the unselfish and unspectacular contributions he had made throughout the series. Once he had offered a high catch to substitute fielder Old, the declaration was quick in arriving. Ian Chappell set England 400 to win, or four and a bit sessions to endure in order to achieve the draw that would keep the series alive for the fifth Test in Adelaide. The latter part of the equation was immediately aided, however, by the promised thunder and rain, which delayed England's reply until only 55 minutes were left in the day.

Amiss, who knew that Lillee would have grown impatient but would now be able to go at full pelt until stumps, took guard and prepared for another test of survival. 'You talk to yourself,' he explained. 'You say, "Stand still, keep your head still, watch the ball, watch the ball, watch the hand. Watch the ball from the hand" – that is one of the big things. You have a little bit of a plan: leave it alone, get out of the way. It's a lively wicket. You are just devising in your mind what you are going to play. Try and get over the new ball. Is it swinging? Is it bouncing? Getting the pace and bounce of the wicket. Once you stay there you do get used to it, which helps you to mentally prepare yourself for any shot you are going to play. But if you have got them coming at you both ends, like Lillee and Thomson, you have not got much time to switch off.'

Lillee instantly gave Amiss no time for any thought or action other than to flinch away from a bouncer. Then he had him groping at one that moved away in the air and off the seam. When the batsman made clean contact with a clip off his pads against Thomson, he was denied runs when the ball thudded into the groin of poor old McCosker, who had bravely returned to short leg. 'I'd had a couple of days in bed because I had terrible headaches and vomiting,' recalled the Australian, who, after this match, 'made it very clear that I was never going to field at short leg again in my life'.

Lloyd slapped a four when Thomson's bouncer sat up enticingly outside off stump, but there were no such gifts from Lillee. He sprinted in like an Olympian to send down a ball that struck Amiss on the back of the left shoulder as he turned away in self-preservation. Even when he slowed his approach somewhat, the ball rose past the peak of Amiss's cap and was taken by Marsh at full stretch above his head. Bailhache had seen enough, offering Lillee what was now becoming a daily warning to curb the short stuff.

England got to the close unscathed with 33 on the board, helped by Walters missing a difficult opportunity to remove Lloyd off Lillee. 'We rolled ten Englishmen in one day in the first Test and we'll have to do it again,' a confident Ian Chappell told journalists after play. Edrich sounded a little less optimistic when he said, 'We will set out to try to bat well and see what happens after that.' Richie Benaud told viewers that the pitch was still good and he could see no reason why England could not save the game if they showed 'enough courage and application'.

Amiss, who allowed himself to be struck on the back yet again by Thomson, began the final morning like a man who had impossible victory on his mind. His 23 runs off 16 balls, taking him to 37, were accumulated with a confidence symbolised by the easy, well-timed drive he sent back past Thomson. Lloyd cracked Lillee square for four, although Henry Blofeld would write in *The Guardian* that 'his courage was more admirable than his technique'. With the total on 68, Lloyd could only get the toe end of the bat to a wide delivery from Thomson and Greg Chappell accepted yet another slip catch. In that moment, the breeziness of England's opening half-hour was blown to the corners of distant memory.

Cowdrey arrived with his customary casual air. 'Dennis, what is happening?' he asked.

'Well, if it's short, it is going up and over and I'm trying to leave it as much as I can,' was the reply. 'And if it's up, well, it is a really good wicket.'

Amiss watched Cowdrey take guard. 'The next thing I know the ball was short and it didn't get up and it hit Colin,' he recalled. 'He looks at me as if to say, "Your bloody information isn't any good."'

And in the next over, Lillee served up a snorter that, far from passing at a safe height, was heading for Amiss's jaw until his neck flicked back. The gloves that had been involuntarily raised in defence delivered the faintest deflection to Marsh.

'I thought I was playing as well as I have ever played,' Amiss remembered. 'I got runs at Melbourne, but Sydney was the best I ever played Lillee and Thomson. There was a bit of bounce in the wicket and I was leaving the ball well. I was really disappointed when I nicked Dennis again because I was thinking, "Come on, you can do this. I should get a big one here."'

Edrich replaced Amiss and badly misjudged his first delivery. Lillee had again struck the pitch short of a length, but not enough to justify Edrich ducking and taking his eye off the ball, which smashed sickeningly into his ribcage. 'Dennis always used to try to bowl you a bouncer or a short-pitched ball first ball to let you know he was around,' Edrich explained years later. 'It was uneven bounce and he banged it in and I can see it now. I thought I would let it go but it didn't bounce and it hit me in the ribs. It was my fault. I pre-empted it going over my head.'

Lillee demonstrated obvious concern as Edrich knelt in pain. 'I've always admired Eddie as a courageous and very competent player and I was not surprised, but rather relieved, when he came back later in the innings,' he admitted.

Assisted by Bernard Thomas and Bob Taylor, Edrich returned slowly to the dressing room. An initial medical examination and x-ray determined he had suffered only bruising, much to the surprise of Denness, who had been present when Edrich removed his shirt and was convinced he could discern an indentation in his ribs, 'almost as if the ball was still lodged in there'.

As Edrich might have predicted, Lillee welcomed Fletcher with a short ball. It was easily avoided, but then he beat his edge with an outswinger that left the bowler giving the batsman a sideways look that veered between contempt and sympathy. Meanwhile, Cowdrey, with one run to show for 37 minutes' batting, ended his ordeal with an unnecessary jab at Walker that went to Ian Chappell at first slip. Four England batsmen had now made their way back to the pavilion in the space of six runs. Greig opted for his usual aggressive response to crisis, with his burst of fours in the direction of third man coming via both aerial and ground routes.

Fletcher, who looked accomplished enough when Thomson pitched full, was squared up horribly by another short delivery. 'If you freeze you are certain to get hit,' he explained, admitting that it happened on this occasion. 'For some inexplicable reason, my reactions just did not work in time.' His hands went up in front of his face, but the ball was simply too quick, flicking his glove and hitting him on the badge of his MCC cap with such force that it only just dropped short of Edwards at cover.

'Crikey, he's knocked St George clean off his 'orse,' Arnold gasped to colleagues watching in the pavilion.

Obviously unsettled, Fletcher might have been better advised to join those teammates for a while. Instead he got behind the next ball before pushing at the one after that to be caught by Redpath. England took lunch at 103 for 4, with Greig and Knott apparently holding the hopes of prolonging the Ashes battle in their hands.

Despite being coupled in England's batting order as surely as Morecambe and Wise in BBC's television schedules, Knott recalled, 'We never batted together that much. We didn't have too many partnerships. Either he got runs or I got runs.' This series was proof of that. In the four innings in which Greig passed 50, Knott averaged

7.75, only a fifth of his overall series average. Greig's mark when Knott achieved a half-century was 20, less than half his mark for the series. On this occasion it was Knott's turn to perish early, pushing the spin of Mallett into the sure grasp of Redpath at short leg.

Greig continued with his combination of responsible defence and reckless assault. Not content with subjecting Thomson to his usual array of cuts, he planted a long stride down the track and drove over extra cover with the fullest of swings. He went to 51 with a slightly more unbalanced version of the same shot, sending the ball squarer but with the same result, his ninth four in two hours at the crease.

With 3 p.m. approaching, five wickets remaining and news arriving that Edrich was likely to be able to resume his innings, English survival was still a realistic outcome. Which made it difficult to understand the unbalanced sweep that Titmus aimed at Mallett and all the more disappointing for the tourists when the ball plopped gently into the hands of Thomson.

Ten minutes later, Greig, who had already shown signs of losing his patience with Mallett, shimmied down the wicket and missed the drive he was aiming over mid-off. Marsh removed the bails as Greig flailed around in an attempt to regain his ground. It wasn't long before Underwood, who'd had his greatest success with the bat when relying on his eye rather than his defence, drove the ball straight back to the bowler, Walker. Three self-inflicted wickets for 19 runs in less than half an hour to add to the earlier failings of the top order.

'SUICIDAL,' would be the headline verdict of the *Daily Mirror*, with the sub-heading, 'We batted like a rabble of village-green hotheads.' In his report, Peter Laker described Greig's 'horrifying, irresponsible end'.

'Greigy, what were you doing?' Edrich asked his teammate later. 'We had to try to bat out the day.'

'I thought I'd try to get a few more runs before Lillee and Thomson came back on,' was the less than convincing reply.

Edrich, who'd received a generous welcome back from the 14,000 in attendance, continued to grit his teeth and play shots that were excruciatingly painful, in spite of the tablets he'd taken. He did not know it yet, but his ribs had been broken, as colleagues had suspected. Willis, after scoring two fours in the first over he faced, joined his captain in an exhibition of post-tea obduracy that in a stretch of 13 overs yielded nine maidens and four scoring shots. Having delayed for 15 overs while Mallett bowled to four short legs, Ian Chappell eventually called for the new ball. Lillee beat Willis's hopeful bat with a succession of balls outside off stump before removing him with a straight, fast and full delivery. England were now 201 for 9 in the fourth of the final 15 overs.

The first ball of Arnold's innings would be remembered by witnesses down the years with an accompanying cold sweat. Short, lightning quick, rising; how it ended up missing the number eleven's unprotected head on its way to the boundary for four byes was anyone's guess. According to Willis, 'He appeared to be a fraction of an inch from death and would have been able to do absolutely nothing to get out of the way.'

Bedser described it as 'one of the worst moments of the 1974-75 tour', further indication that the 'atmosphere became overcharged' during this match. 'If the terrifying delivery had struck his head there was no way he could have avoided serious injury or even worse. The England dressing room was amazed, and my personal opinion was that it was nothing short of disgraceful.'

Fletcher remembered, 'The ball was through him before he knew it, searing through the tiny gap between bat and head. It was small wonder, seeing things like that occur, that our tailenders expressed an honest reluctance to get into line. With their limited techniques, they were unlikely to last long anyway, and physical injury or worse was never far from anyone's mind.'

Although admitting that 'we loved it and even frightened their tailenders with the odd short ball', even Lillee had to confess, 'I was relieved that one missed.' He explained, 'When I let fly at Geoff Arnold it was because he had already fired a couple at me. But I'm bloody glad I didn't hit him because I think it might have killed him.' For the fourth consecutive day, Lillee was reminded by the umpires of his obligation not to threaten the lives of his opponents.

By this time, Lillee was coming to regret the now infamous comments he'd made in his book. His intention, he argued later, had been to explain that a bouncer was most effective if it was aimed at the batsman's body; not that he actively hoped to strike his opponent, especially not in the head. It was a distinction that was mostly ignored – unsurprisingly given the language he used. Besides, he would also add, 'I also said bouncers should be bowled only to those batsmen who appear capable of handling them, but I have to confess I did not always follow those noble words. Sometimes my judgment would let me down.'

Gallantly, Arnold proceeded to stick around; long enough to force the reintroduction, amid growing tension, of Mallett. He had just taken his score to 12 with a four and a two off the spinner when, at six minutes to six, he pushed forward and diverted the ball via the inside edge into the outstretched hand of Greg Chappell at forward short leg. Up went the ball in celebration and the Australian players began skipping their way towards the boundary as young fans came to greet them. 'I was aware of Rod and Ian jumping up and down and the whole team letting off a huge amount of pent up desire,' said Chappell.

The Ashes had returned to Australian custody on the same ground that had seen them taken away by the English four years earlier in Ian Chappell's first match as captain. 'Since then, he's worked for today, to win back the Ashes,' Benaud said in summary of the match. 'He did it here at the SCG and he is the cricket success story for Australia for the 1970s.'

'We've got the bastards back,' a beaming Marsh reminded his skipper as they ran from the field.

McCosker recalled, 'I remember how the guys really celebrated and they were just so rapt. Not being involved in the first part of the series, it wasn't until we got back to the dressing room and everyone was carrying on and Ian was handing out the cigars that I suddenly realised we had won the Ashes, not just a Test match. You think, "This is a pretty easy game."'

Mallett's fourth wicket had seen England dismissed for 228. Even though they had been only a few minutes and 5.3 overs from safety, the deficit of 171 runs and the Aussies' unassailable 3-0 series lead both offered an accurate reflection of the home team's dominance.

13

ADVANCE AUSTRALIA FAIR

It's time to create new opportunities for Australians, time for what we can achieve in this generation.
Prime Minister Gough Whitlam (election address, 1972)

The timing of the exchange of the Ashes, two weeks before the fifth Test was contested, meant there was plenty of opportunity for English eyes to begin their examination of what had gone so wrong. For the Australians, it was an occasion for celebrating and gloating.

Over communal beers in the Australian dressing room at the Sydney Cricket Ground, Doug Walters delighted in playing clips from 'The Ashes Song' – a victory ditty Ray Illingworth's team had recorded at the Decca studios in London four years earlier. Over and over, Walters cued up the opening line, 'We've brought the Ashes back home'.

On the back of such an ill-tempered match, not every English player found it easy to smile through Walters's antics and offer congratulations. Several made a brisk departure for the team hotel, while the triumphant Australians got their party started properly at the Koala Motel, a mile or so away from the ground. It continued into the night at The Different Drummer, a bar in the heart of the city's night life in Kings Cross.

The copies of the *Sydney Morning Telegraph* that the late revellers were able to pick up on their way home in the early hours featured pictures of a beleaguered Brit for whom the past few weeks had been the stuff of nightmares. For once it was not Mike Denness in the frame, but Labour MP John Stonehouse, who had spent more than a month in hiding. While Denness escaped the SCG for an hour on the final afternoon of the Test to take a walk round the Royal Sydney Golf Club, Stonehouse had made the journey from Melbourne to Sydney Airport under the assumed name of Taylor with the intention of disappearing from public view once more. After the London Capital Group issued legal proceedings against him over financial irregularities, Stonehouse had gone missing from a beach in Miami, Florida, on 20 November, attempting to fake his own death by leaving behind a pile of clothes. He was eventually arrested on Christmas Eve in Melbourne as a possible illegal immigrant (although police initially thought he might be Lord Lucan, missing since the brutal death of his family's nanny) and had gone to ground again after his release a couple of days before New Year.

While the reports of Stonehouse's death proved to be premature, there was no holding back the obituaries for England's cricketers. Political and sports cartoonist Paul Rigby had drawn for the *Sydney Sunday Telegraph* a picture of the English lion wrapped in bandages and being borne in a coffin by funeral directors. 'Ashes to Ashes, Dust to Dust,' read the caption. 'If Thomson don't get ya, Lillee must.'

It was a good time for Pom bashing. Even Stonehouse, who argued that he'd been a victim of conspiracy rather than a perpetrator of fraud, was seen as a heroic figure by some Aussies for taking a shot at the British establishment. After all, Australians had never before felt so removed from their nation's colonial past, so eager to tread their own global path and forge their own destiny. And even if you didn't see thrashing the old enemy at cricket as symbolic of a new period of Anglo-Australian relations, well it was still bloody good fun.

Bill O'Reilly, the former Australian Test player writing for the *Sydney Morning Herald*, expressed his surprise at the way his sport had suddenly become the hottest of cultural properties. 'It took an outstanding cricket revival, like the one we are drooling over this season, to make us sit up and really take notice of the game's attractive scene,' he said. 'No one could have imagined that our ancient game, so often the butt of tormentors who delight in bashing down our sacred cows, would wage a revival that leaves entrepreneurs green with envy.'

But while that was true to the extent that the breathtaking spectacle of Dennis Lillee and Jeff Thomson had taken Aussie fans as much by surprise as it had English batsmen, conditions were already in place for an unashamed celebration of Australia, and the kind of out-and-out Australianness embodied by the pair of tearaway pacemen.

A nation whose modern history began with the immigration of around 350,000 settlers from Britain – a mixture of convicts and free citizens – in the 18th and 19th centuries had seen its relations with the 'mother country' becoming strained since the early 1960s. At the heart of it was the 'Turn to Europe' pursued initially by Harold McMillan's Conservative UK government in the form of its application to join the European Economic Community in 1961. Along with that very clear signal of Britain's intention to redefine its post-imperial place in the world was the decision to end significant military involvement in the Far East by 1968.

Such policies created irreconcilable differences and left Australia feeling isolated from the nation whose Queen was its head of state. Under Harold Wilson's Labour government, in power from 1964 to 1970, Britain's lack of desire to maintain a politico-military role in South-East Asia conflicted with Australia's priorities, including its deepening involvement in the conflict in Vietnam. The Australian government in Canberra saw British disengagement as undermining its own strategy and potentially creating further destabilisation of a volatile region.

And once Britain achieved acceptance into the EEC under Prime Minister Edward Heath – at the third attempt in January 1972 – it meant that military disassociation was followed by an inevitable severing of trade relations. Faced with an uncertain outlook for its farm exports, The Australian government of Liberal leader William McMahon had no choice but to announce the abolition of trade preferences granted to British imports and the end of the UK-Australia trade agreement. Instead, the country's trading priorities shifted towards the Asia-Pacific region. As author Andrea Benvenuti noted in his study of the two nations in that period, 'The ties of empire which had once bound Australia and Britain became practically inconsequential by the early 1970s.'

Labor leader Gough Whitlam captured the mood in his 'It's Time for Leadership' pre-election speech in November 1972, when he called for the nation to support 'a new team, a new programme' and make the most of the opportunities offered by its release from empirical shackles. 'That whole Labour campaign of 1972 was just terrific,' said an interviewee in *Living in the 70s*. 'It was a new Australia, a new life. It was the start of Australia as an independent nation, not part of Great Britain, not a slave to the United Sates. That's how it appeared to me.'

Having been duly voted into power, Whitlam's administration put into place several symbolic measures that, by the time the MCC party arrived in October 1974, demonstrated the increased emphasis on Australian identity. British royal honours were abolished and replaced by the Order of Australia, while the words 'British subject' disappeared from Australian passports. Perhaps most significantly, on Australia Day in January 1973 Whitlam had outlined his intention to replace 'God Save The Queen' as national anthem. 'We feel it is essential that Australians have an anthem that fittingly embodies our national aspirations and reflects our status as an independent nation,' he said. 'We need an anthem that uniquely identifies our country abroad and recalls vividly to ourselves the distinctive qualities of Australian life and the character and traditions of our nation.'

Research by Australian Public Opinion Polls revealed that only 50 per cent of the nation were initially supportive of a new anthem, although that percentage rose to 65 per cent in those under the age of 30. A clear leader among the songs suggested as anthem was 'Advance Australia Fair', whose 53 per cent mark was well ahead of second-placed 'Waltzing Matilda' on 19 per cent. A wider survey of 60,000 people, conducted for the government by the Australian Bureau of Statistics, showed 51.4 per cent support for the song, which was formally named national anthem in April 1974.[41]

'Gough promoted the place of Australia in the world so gracefully,' said Rale Rasic, a former Yugoslav immigrant who coached Australia to their first qualification for the FIFA World Cup finals in 1974. 'People became dreamers. Not convicts, dreamers.'

According to Lilee, 'You grow up with wanting to beat the Poms . . . wanting to say, "You sent us out here and now we are better than you." I used it a bit in my psyche when I was training.'

Future rugby professional and global head of his sport, Brett Gosper, added, 'We all grew up with the outlook that it was all

---

41 The song, first performed in 1878, was replaced by 'God Save The Queen' for royal and certain other occasions by the Liberal government of Malcolm Fraser in 1976. It was reinstated as the national anthem by the Labour government under Bob Hawke in 1984, with the former anthem played alongside it on royal occasions.

about beating England. When any other team turned up it was good to win, but it wasn't like when England turned up. You always wanted to stick it up the English. They were the old colonial home, and you like to give your parents a little bit of a lesson. Then the Whitlam government brought in a very high level of nationalism, of pride in country, with debates about the national anthem and so forth. He also funded the arts a lot more.'

Such investment, including in the Australian Film, Television and Radio School, led to what became known as the Australian New Wave of cinema, with the country's movies mirroring the success of its cricket team by achieving worldwide popularity. An industry that had all but died in the 1960s now had directors such as Peter Weir and Bruce Beresford taking on the heavyweights of Hollywood. It was also only a little more than a year since Sydney Opera House had finally opened, its distinctive architecture and multi-use venues enhancing the nation's reputation in the world of performing arts.

But, above all, it was sport that Whitlam understood occupied a place at the heart of Australian identity and could be a driver of dreams – even though he was no great lover of it himself, despite wife Margaret having swum for her country in the 1938 Empire Games.[42] In his election address he identified the need for more people to be energised by sport and to take to the country's playing fields. 'There is no greater social problem facing Australia than the good use of expanding leisure,' he said. 'For such a nation as ours, this may very well be the problem of the 1980s.' He gave sport an important place on his government's agenda with several initiatives: the creation of a Department of Tourism and Recreation; programmes aimed at increasing fitness levels in the community; grants at the elite level; and a new emphasis on sports management and science.

Invited by Clem Jones to open The Gabba's new stand at the first Ashes Test in Brisbane, Whitlam admitted, 'Unfortunately I don't get to cricket matches as often as I should. My distinguished predecessor, Sir Robert Menzies,[43] was a great lover of the game. I don't know whether he ever actually played cricket, but he used to

---

42 Now the Commonwealth Games

43 Australia's longest-serving Prime Minister, in office 1939-1941 and 1949-66

watch it at Lord's whenever he went to London, which was quite often. He had a longer innings in politics than anyone, so perhaps there is a lesson somewhere. A prime minister should either follow cricket or go overseas. If he does both it is very hard to get him out.'

Despite the achievements of Rasic's 'Socceroos', it was cricket that remained the one truly national sport among the various regionally favoured versions of oval-ball games; the only major sport that was played in every state, featured national competition and had a national team. It was cricket stadia that housed the nation's biggest sporting events, including the Melbourne Cricket Ground's role as principal stadium for the 1956 Olympic Games.

The Australian cricket team, in fact, was older than the nation itself. It was not until 1901 that the six British colonies of New South Wales, Victoria, Queensland, South Australia (which also governed the Northern Territory), Western Australia and Tasmania united to form the Commonwealth of Australia. By that time Australia's cricketers had contested the first Test match, in 1877, and taken part in 14 Ashes series.[44] The Australian Cricket Council, the first national administrative body for the sport and forerunner of the Australian Cricket Board, had been formed in 1892.

Cricket was in Australia's soul, as well as its soil. No wonder the triumph of Ian Chappell's team was celebrated with such vigour.

According to *The Observer*'s, Tony Pawson, 'The sight of Thomson and Lillee bouncing cricket balls past, or against, the heads of a bunch of plainly nervous Englishmen stirs up some profound emotions: sensations of revenge, in part for having been patronised over the years by English governor generals, English State governors, English visitors and even English migrants.' While his contention that Chappell's team 'applied balm to a deep Australian wound' might have been an over-simplification, it had its basis in truth. And while Chappell felt the crowd's support owed more to identification with the players than nationalism in the blood, there is no doubt that it reflected the country's enhanced sense of self. And then there

---

44 The Ashes were first contested 1882-83, resulting from Australia's victory in a solitary Test at The Oval in 1882, after which the *Sporting Times* posted a mock obituary for English cricket, declaring, 'The body will be cremated and the ashes taken to Australia.'

was the shadow of Bodyline, brought into sharper relief by the fact that it was more fearsome fast bowling that had set up Australia's success and so upset sensitive English souls four decades later. Even those Aussies who had no personal recollection of Harold Larwood aiming balls at the torsos of their batsmen – with the intention of inducing catches in a packed leg-side field – knew the tale and felt the resentment. Part of their Ashes education was learning about the indignation the Poms exhibited when the Australian cricket authorities dared to cable MCC headquarters complaining that the tactics directed by captain Douglas Jardine were 'unsportsmanlike'.

What right had the English to whinge about the trajectory of Lillee and Thomson's bowling when one remembered their response to Australia's complaints 42 years earlier? 'Undignified snivelling,' was how English newspaper *The Daily Herald* had described the home team's grievances back then. *The Times* had maintained, 'It is inconceivable that a cricketer of Jardine's standing ... would ever dream of allowing or ordering the bowlers under his command to practise any system of attack that, in the time-honoured English phrase, is not cricket.' Without first-hand experience to call upon, having chosen not to spend the money to send its own correspondent to Australia, the publication blamed the furore on 'irresponsible chatter of elderly critics in the pavilion and in the press'.

In his book *Anglo-Australian Attitudes*, author Michael Davie noted, 'The ill-feeling and mistrust engendered by Bodyline . . . did not come out of nowhere.' His conclusion, strengthened by the events of 1974-75, was, 'Anglo-Australian competition at cricket has always caused bad blood.'

For the vanquished MCC party, meanwhile, there was always the refuge of humour. And in David Lloyd the downtrodden tourists had someone always willing to provide it. In the SCG dressing room he'd informed teammates that he had written a letter home beginning, 'Dear Mother. I received a half-volley today – in the nets.' And when a young fan at Sydney Airport sought an autograph from Keith Fletcher, still shaken by his blow on the head, Lloyd chimed in, 'What are you signing, Keith? Nat Lofthouse?'

It was same quality for self-deprecation and acceptance of long hours of suffering that underpinned Richard Stilgoe's ditty about 'Lillian Thomson' for BBC's evening current affairs show. 'The nearest thing I had to a job at the time was working for *Nationwide* and doing a song for them every week,' he explained. 'You had to find a subject for a song every week and sometimes that was the editor's idea and every now and again I would put something forward. This was one of the rare times, I think, when I said, "Look, for once cricket is not just a dull thing that nobody is interested in. It is the Ashes series, people are interested, and the reasons they are interested is that there are these two incredible guys who between them make the most frightening woman fast bowler the world has ever seen.'

Yet the English publications saw no cause for jocularity. In-depth post-mortems would be carried out at the conclusion of the tour, but in the meantime correspondents were called upon to deliver an interim diagnosis of the team's ailments. 'English cricket has been in decline for five years and there is no disguising its nakedness any longer,' said Pawson, citing recent home and away defeats against India and the 1973 battering by the West Indies, which signalled the end of Ray Illingworth's captaincy. Suggesting 'the problem starts in the schools, where cricket lost its hold in the Sixties', he gloomily reported the findings at a junior cricket festival in Sussex, where only 40 per cent of 1,000 participants described themselves as 'warm or enthusiastic' about the sport.

In *The Guardian*, Henry Blofeld argued, 'The root of the problem lies in the state of domestic cricket in England.' He felt that restricting the first innings of County Championship matches to 100 overs, and the need for teams to chase bonus points therein, had made it difficult for batsmen to play the kind of innings required in Test matches and had discouraged attacking fast and spin bowling.

Ian Wooldridge suggested in the *Daily Mail* that English players were becoming weary of an excess of cricket. 'To play for Australia remains the ultimate ambition of any male child born in this fiercely chauvinistic and still insular country,' he said. 'To play for England, I am sorry to say, is beginning to look just another day's work.'

Winning Ashes captain Illingworth, meanwhile, called for more 'hard and fast pitches' in England. 'It must be the duty of every county committee to insist they are prepared. Our batsmen lacked the technique, particularly in their footwork and positioning, to deal with Thomson and Lillee largely because they have lacked experience of playing fast bowling in this country. We will never produce our own fast bowlers capable of blasting back unless they are reared in these types of wickets. How can anyone expect a fast bowler to develop in this country if he comes up at full pace on the first day of a county match only to see the ball bounce half-stump high?'

Elsewhere, the quality and focus of English coaching was questioned. At a time when the sport had a more widespread coaching system in place than ever before, the national team was in a slump and the country was struggling to unearth new talent. Flair was being eradicated, so the argument went, in favour of conformity and steady contributors. 'It's lucky for Thomson that he's an Australian,' said former England captain Peter May. 'Over here, he'd have been criticised for his run-up and his delivery and he'd be back in coaching school or playing for Hertfordshire.' Rodney Marsh, who would become part of the England coaching and development set-up in the 21st century, noted in the early 1980s that 'individuality has been the beauty of the Australian game when compared with the English style, which has been more or less stereotyped over the years'.

MCC was the keeper of the sport's accepted coaching manual – *The MCC Cricket Coaching Book*, first published in 1952 – but seemed more interested in winning a proprietary battle than ensuring it reflected the needs of a sport that was modernising rapidly. At MCC's November 1974 committee meeting, treasurer and former England captain Gubby Allen reported that he had been involved in revising the book in a working party with the National Coaches Association, but clearly felt the coaches were attempting to flex too much muscle. He 'found himself in trouble on occasions as he did not fully agree with some of the proposed amendments for the manual'. He sought assurances of the 'full support and active collaboration of the MCC committee' if it came to the point where 'an acceptable compromise in views could not be reached'.

Meanwhile, the tabloids were more interested in personality than squabbles over structure and instruction manuals. 'England's crying need in these dark days is for a leader in the uncompromising image of Australia's Ian Chappell. And that's [Tony] Greig,' said the *Daily Mirror*'s Peter Laker, who was prepared to overlook the former vice-captain's baiting of opponents and fans at the SCG, where he had even hurled an orange back into the crowd.

Former England paceman Fred Trueman, still at that time the Test record-holder with 307 wickets, said in his *Sunday People* column, 'It's time Alec Bedser and his three selectors were out of the firing line – and shot out. Bedser cannot duck out of trouble this time.'

It was, after all, a significant period for leadership at home. On the final day of the Sydney Test, Nottingham Forest's footballers had been pictured on the back pages celebrating their FA Cup upset against Tottenham Hotspur with new manager Brian Clough. On the news pages, former education minister Margret Thatcher was among those challenging Edward Heath for leadership of the Conservative Party. In the first week of February, she would gain more votes than Heath in the first ballot of MPs and then finish off former Cabinet ministers William Whitelaw, Geoffrey Howe, James Prior and James Peyton by winning 53 per cent support in the second vote. Two of the dominant characters of British society were taking up their defining appointments. It would be a few weeks after England returned from Australia with the Ashes four years later that 'The Iron Lady' became Prime Minister and 'Old Big 'Ead' champion of Europe.

Trying to block out the distracting noise of discontent among the press was a minor consideration for the England players when compared to the exhausting problems posed by their on-field opponents. 'By now we were all so jaded mentally and physically that we would have given anything for a break,' said Dennis Amiss of the condition of the MCC party after the Sydney Test. 'Trouble was that our tour itinerary was so tight that we had scarcely had a day off. Tasmania would have provided the ideal opportunity to wind down if we could have played just one game and not two against the same team.'

Denness looked increasingly likely to be the leader of England's Test team once more, even if it was only in the short term and because other batsmen were out of form or injured. The week in Tasmania, from which Greig, Alan Knott, Bob Willis and Fred Titmus were excused, saw him grab the opportunity to make some confidence-boosting runs. Christopher Martin-Jenkins, making his first visit to the island, which was then still something of a cricketing outpost,[45] noted its 'climate and scenery in the south very reminiscent of Scotland's'. Lanarkshire's Denness certainly looked at home in two first-class matches.

Having made a useful 42 in a rain-ruined draw at Hobart, he scored an unbeaten 157 at Launceston to confirm his reinstatement. The opposition might not have been of the highest calibre, and nor was the wicket, which added some credibility to an innings in which he struck 24 fours. The surface had been so unpredictable that Denness had taken off Peter Lever on the first day and ordered Geoff Arnold and Chris Old to bowl medium pacers for the safety of the home batsmen.

Denness's innings came in between his bowlers dismissing Tasmania cheaply twice to set up and secure victory by an innings and 72 runs. His only concern was the sight of Edrich, after 43 minutes at the crease, having to retire on 35. 'He found it virtually impossible to run between the wickets,' Alec Bedser informed the press. 'It will be a few days before we know his prospects for the fifth Test.'

Another tourist for whom the Tasmania trip had provided a needed pick-me-up was Bob Taylor, given the chance to play in back-to-back first-class games for the first time on the tour – although he didn't bat in either match.

It was inevitable that Taylor would occasionally betray the frustration of playing the good tourist. 'If the MCC asked me to play every day, seven days a week, for a five-month tour I would enjoy that more than sitting around the dressing room,' he admitted. 'I keep fit and do my practice and see that the lads get their practice before each game. Possibly, I do more bowling than our bowlers before a Test, giving our batsmen practice in the nets.'

Disappointed not to have been given the chance to play in the solitary one-day international of the tour, he continued, 'Mental tiredness is the main concern I have by not playing regularly. Knotty could go and break a finger as easily in Warrnambool as in a Test match. I'm a professional cricketer and it would be expected of me to go out and take over and do the job well for the team.'

---

[45] Tasmania was not admitted to the Sheffield Shield, the country's state competition, until 1977.

Playing in Tasmania had made him feel more valued. 'Getting changed, having a beer after the match, and going out in the bus to the airport was satisfying to me. I was involved again. Sitting around the dressing room makes you feel lethargic. Even being 12th man, you sometimes feel as though you've been idle, which you have not.'

A former inside-forward who had played semi-professionally at Stoke City, Taylor's serious football aspirations had ended at Burton Albion, where he was released by manager Peter Taylor, future right-hand man of Brian Clough. Cricketing achievement had come more readily, but still he could be left feeling like the invisible man. 'People see the MCC blazer, then don't recognise the name,' he explained. 'There is some attention at the start of the tour but when you are not in the Test team you don't get much publicity. When people don't know you and haven't heard of you, that hurts. I let it ride, of course. To a point, I accept I'm not in the Test side.'

With the MCC party reunited in Sydney to face New South Wales, encouraging happenings on the field were mixed with worrying medical reports. Amiss and Lloyd raced to 92 in the first hour of the match against an opening attack that, while bearing no resemblance to Australia's, did feature Test men in Gary Gilmour and David Colley. Lloyd benefited from some extraordinary luck when Gilmour's seventh ball hit the stumps without displacing the bails and continued to ride his good fortune. Michael Carey wrote in *The Guardian*, 'Lloyd's policy of playing a shot at anything that moved made compulsive watching, just as you watch a trapeze artist waiting for him to slip.'

After both openers were out shortly after reaching half-centuries, Fletcher and Denness put on 140 in close to even time. The former was out for 85, while the captain, dropped twice early in his knock, was caught in the gully one run short of another hundred. His three innings since missing the Sydney Test had now brought him 298 runs, which offered little indication of how he might fare when confronted by Lillee and Thomson but at least meant he would do so in a more positive frame of mind.

After an overnight declaration, MCC ran through their opponents for 157, with Old taking seven wickets on his best day of the tour. Accurate in his line and length and finding awkward movement, it was a performance that Martin-Jenkins felt proved he was 'too useful to be left out of the England side as often as he was on this tour.'

Yet there was rarely a day on this tour that did not reveal some kind of health scare, and when Lloyd left the field with what was reported to be a ricked neck he became the latest player facing a battle to be fit for Test duty. 'It all happened fielding at short leg to Bob Willis,' he explained almost half a century later, the enduring pain and discomfort an unwanted reminder. 'The batsman might have been Alan Turner. I was taking evasive action and my neck gave way. I have had brain scans, neck scans and visited the osteopath twice a week to get some mobility in my neck. It all stems from that injury. I have got degenerative bones in my neck which are grinding together, and it is bloody agony. When I drive I wear a neck brace, which keeps my head in position, and it all stems back to that injury. It turned out I had a bulging C5-C6 disc and I was never the same after that.'

Lloyd was put in a neck collar by hospital staff and sent in advance to Adelaide. Cowdrey was identified as the potential replacement opener, rather than the discarded Brian Luckhurst or the recuperating Edrich. Meanwhile, MCC proceeded to turn their strong position into a 187-run win after Amiss scored 124 in the second innings and the bowlers shared out the wickets to wrap things up with a day to spare.

Amid the parks and churches of Adelaide, any hopes of a stress-free approach to the renewal of international hostilities continued to be undermined by medical matters. Lloyd received hourly traction treatment in the hope of relieving the pressure on the nerve in his neck, while Edrich had to abort training after a few gentle throw-downs from the scorer. 'I had that much pain I couldn't throw the ball,' he said. 'I just had to pack it in.' With two days left before the fifth Test, Edrich was sent for another x-ray. Two weeks after the initial examination had found no serious damage, he was now revealed to have two cracked ribs.

Meanwhile Knott was nursing a sore neck after being in a minor car accident in Sydney, and Old, having at last achieved notable success, departed early from practice, complaining of sore heels. 'Everything was right in Sydney,' Old recalled, 'but I had never played on a pitch that was so hard. After the match I struggled to get a pair of shoes on. I had to walk around in my flip-flops all the time because my feet were just burning and so sore. It was hard to put any weight on my feet at all.'

The wicket at the Adelaide Oval had been one of Australia's most placid throughout the summer, no longer as conducive to slow bowling as in recent seasons. The red Wunderlich tile-making clay that had formed the base of the pitch for several summers had been replaced by black Athelston clay, offering less assistance to the South Australian duo of Ashley Mallett and Terry Jenner. 'This factor, together with the ejection of football, promised a batsman's delight as a pitch,' Frank Tyson reported.

It was clear, however, that groundsman Arthur Lance intended to liven things up by leaving more grass on the track than usual. That, coupled with events in Sydney, ensured that Dennis Lillee was the man the media wanted to speak to on the eve of the fifth Test.

'I admit I tend to blow my top on the field,' he told journalists. 'Because I try so bloody hard every minute I'm out there. So hard that it hurts.' With his recovery from injury proven, and the need to wind up the opposition apparently gone now that the Ashes were won, he felt able to soften some of the pre-series invective. 'I can honestly say that it doesn't thrill me at all to hurt anyone,' he said, although making it clear that he was not about to take a gentler approach to his work. 'To me [bouncers] are a legitimate part of a fast bowler's armoury. If I bruise a batsman in the process then he's got to accept that.'

The performance of the pitch and the behaviour of the champion bowler remained a mystery for at least one more day when an inch of overnight rain soaked the outfield and found its way under the covers. Much of the blame centred on the night security guards who neglected to inform anyone on the grounds crew that part of the square covering had been blown away.

The umpires delayed only until noon before informing the big Saturday crowd that there would be no play on the first day. The decision cost the ACB A$25,000 in lost revenue, although Richie Benaud told viewers, 'I can't have any great sympathy for them because their inadequate covering and inattention to detail meant that neither side could get out on the field.'

The delay made no difference to England's team selection. Lloyd was in and Edrich, of course, was out. So, too, was Old, even with another day to rest. There was a sense, though, that the Yorkshireman's sore feet had saved the MCC tour selectors a tough choice. With Greig not having bowled his slower style often enough or well enough to be considered a second spinner, Old's inclusion – merited on the strength of his recent seven-wicket performance – would have meant upsetting the balance of the attack or choosing between Arnold and Willis. Australia, meanwhile, with the cushion of a series victory and the possibility of a damp wicket offering help to the spinners, brought back Jenner in place of batsman Ross Edwards.

Jenner, twelfth man in the previous three Tests and expecting to be fulfilling the same role again, had welcomed the 24-hour delay. 'Doug Walters was my roommate,' he explained. 'Wet weather was predicted and we both thought we could gamble on some rain and have a late one.' Jenner met up with friends and 'burnt the midnight oil', adding that 'Dougie had a late one too'. He added, 'In those days nobody even questioned your right to have a drink. In fact it was almost expected that you be at The Lion or the Arkaba[46] having a beer.'

When the toss was belatedly conducted on Sunday morning, Denness called correctly and at last England were able to dictate terms, putting their hosts into bat. The pitch was still soft and a damp patch was in evidence at the southern end of the strip. With Derek Underwood, the greatest exploiter of such conditions, in his ranks, the England skipper finally felt as though fortunes were turning in his direction.

---

46 Popular drinking venues in Adelaide.

14
THE SAME OLD SCENE

There would have been no way of knowing from the way they played that this was a Test match. Either the will to resist has gone or they feel they must live dangerously before Lillee or Thomson gets them.
John Woodcock, *The Times*

Australians hardly needed Richie Benaud's reminder that they were about out to face 'the greatest exponent of slow left-arm bowling on a damp pitch in the cricket world'. Anyone who could remember a couple of years previously knew that.

It had been Derek Underwood, then 27 years old and six years on from his Test debut, who had effectively retained the Ashes in 1972 when his six second-innings wickets bowled England to a three-day victory and a 2-1 series lead in the fourth Test. On that occasion, the Headingley wicket was found to have been infected by a fungus called fusarium after heavy rain in the build-up to the match. And there was no bowler in the world, of any speed or style, better at converting a helpful pitch into one that was downright 'Deadly', as he had become known in the game.

Four years prior to his Headingley heroics he had been the beneficiary of the famous mopping up job by fans on the final day of the fifth Test at The Oval, where his seven soggy wickets bowled Australia out in the second innings and provided one of the sport's most famous still images, with all 11 England players in shot around the bat as the final dismissal was achieved. And during the most recent English summer a malfunctioning cover at Lord's had left the Pakistan batsmen at his mercy, leaving him to add Test-best figures of 8 for 51 to a five-wicket first innings haul.

Despite all that, and even though retrospective ICC rankings have since stated that he was the world's top-ranked bowler for much of the period from 1969 to 1973, Underwood was not always guaranteed his place in the team. Until the fourth Test of 1972, his first appearance in that Ashes contest, he had been losing out to fellow left-armer Norman Gifford for the best part of two summers. Gifford's more traditional flight and turn was considered a better option for all conditions than Underwood's quicker style, which relied more on his ability to cut the ball than impart a high number of revolutions.[47] There were times when Underwood could not help being irked that his reputation for destructiveness in certain conditions was sometimes interpreted as lack of effectiveness in others. Even on this tour, the MCC selectors had decided as early as the second Test in Perth that he was not the man for that particular surface. How often had he heard so-called experts urging him to find more variation in methods, greater flexibility of thinking, a more aggressive approach? His current manager and chairman of selectors, Alec Bedser, had explained previous omissions from the England team by telling him to bowl slower. 'Unless I switch to right-arm there is nothing left to experiment with,' was one of Underwood's frustrated responses.

Such arguments could be put aside in Adelaide, where the prospect of what Underwood might do on a damp surface meant that he was a certain starter. Mike Denness brought him into the attack at the Cathedral End after only half an hour. Geoff Arnold switched to the City End to accommodate him and enjoyed a first hour in which he beat both opening batsmen with some regularity.

Rick McCosker got himself into a tangle of bat and pads in Underwood's fifth over and was grateful to receive a long-hop that he slapped to the midwicket fence. Yet he became the Kent man's first victim one over later when he pushed forward to a flighted delivery and found the ball spinning across him, allowing Colin Cowdrey to pocket a simple chance at second slip. McCosker's 35 had formed the bulk of an opening partnership of 52.

Ian Chappell, his form up and down since the first Test, lasted only three balls. The second had lifted and straightened and the next one, unintentionally dragged shorter, popped at the batsman's chest. Trying to swivel out of its way, Chappell saw the ball loop to Alan Knott off the top edge.

---

[47] Gifford never achieved a five-wicket haul in 11 home Test matches, his best figures of 5-55 coming in Karachi early in 1973

The dismissal of brother Greg was achieved in Underwood's next over, as the batsman followed his usual tactic of trying to deny the bowler the opportunity to settle into a rhythm against him. Umpire Tom Brooks might have been a little generous in his decision when Chappell misjudged his shot and was struck on the pad by a delivery that threatened to miss leg stump – and might also have pitched outside it.

At 58 for 3, Underwood's field indicated the extent to which England were on top after he'd taken three wickets without conceding a run. While Keith Fletcher hovered at wide first slip, with Cowdrey outside him at second, Tony Greig either occupied gully or took a step towards the bowler to stand under the batsman's cap at silly point. The surprise was Denness's approach at the other end, where Arnold and Greig had shared duties and Fred Titmus was given one token over a few minutes before lunch. What Denness chose to ignore was that the drying pitch meant that the window of maximum effectiveness for his spinners was closing and that it was worth at least giving the off-spinner an early opportunity. Henry Blofeld called it a 'sad mishandling of his resources' and John Woodcock 'scarcely believable', while former Test spinners Bill O'Reilly and Jim Laker chuntered their disapproval to those in the press box. Laker would later go in front of the cameras to call it 'the most incredible piece of captaincy I have seen in Test match cricket in over 100 matches. I felt they should have been bowled out for 120.'

Titmus got three balls to lift and turn, although Doug Walters, who had come out intent on disturbing Underwood's rhythm, swept him for four. There was still time for one final morning strike by Underwood, who added gully Bob Willis and short leg David Lloyd to the group of close catchers. Ian Redpath had dead-batted his way through two boundary-less hours, but Underwood again achieved turn from a line on leg stump and Greig extended an arm to grab the ball. There was a delay while the protagonists waited for Brooks to raise his arm in recognition of an edge before they trooped off for lunch.

Rodney Marsh lasted less than ten minutes of the afternoon, clubbing Underwood high towards the deep midwicket fence. Greig steadied himself before making a last-second adjustment to his right, catching the ball as he tumbled to his knees. The boisterous reaction of colleagues indicated that this was still an age where any outfield catch beyond the routine was considered noteworthy.

The counter-attacking method of Walters consisted of going after anything full around leg stump and trying to play off the back foot wherever possible. New bat Terry Jenner copied the latter tactic to move into double figures as an important partnership took form. Walters pushed onto his front foot for an all-run four and swung Underwood cleanly through midwicket, although he could only gasp in surprise at a ball that spat so exaggeratedly that Knott required the springiest of heels to gather it.

Jenner, meanwhile, hit three fours in an Arnold over, including a head-in-the-air back-foot drive through the covers as the partnership reached 50 in only 32 minutes. The seagulls who'd been spending a quiet day in the outfield were becoming increasingly unhappy with the more frequent interruptions. At least when Titmus was brought on for only his second over of the day they were able to watch undisturbed as the ball flew towards the red roof of the stand via Walters, whose punch into the covers off a Greig full toss gave him the single he needed for 50.

The absence of Titmus from the attack had grown harder to fathom with every step of Australia's recovery. Christopher Martin-Jenkins recorded, 'At lunch and throughout the long, hot and disastrous afternoon, as England watched the match slip like wet soap through their fingers, everyone except the captain, it seemed, was thinking the same thing.' Dennis Amiss, for example, found it 'hard to understand' why Titmus was held back.

Offering some defence of his skipper, Knott recalled, 'Doug Walters, one of the best players of off-spin, was not so good when the ball was swinging and seaming.' He added, 'When Titmus did come on the ball was not turning so much. It certainly isn't easy being a captain at times.'

Yet Denness, a captain who could usually be seen conferring with senior colleagues, was on this occasion treading a stubbornly solitary path; one whose only possible destination, many believed, was defeat in this match and eventual removal from the captaincy. It was not as though the alternatives to Titmus were bowling particularly well. Arnold looked unthreatening and Greig, in a mixture of bowling styles, was hopelessly inaccurate, going at more than six runs per over. 'The man who had saved his captain's bacon in Trinidad cooked his goose in Adelaide,' Martin-Jenkins noted.

Denness would harbour greater regret about the timing of lunch than about his own on-field choices. 'Had we been able to bowl on during the luncheon interval it would have been different, but in those 40 minutes the wicket dried out sufficiently to benefit the batsman,' he argued. 'Underwood was always going to bowl into the end which was completely wet and he exploited those conditions brilliantly as it dried. It might have seemed logical to have Titmus bowling at the other end but as the dry area into which he would have been bowling was not the right length for him I decided to use instead the medium pace of Arnold and Greig hitting the seam roughly where the wet and dry areas merged.' According to Denness, his explanation was accepted reluctantly by Titmus – 'although he did say he was disappointed not to be given an opportunity to bowl.'

Meanwhile, Willis looked increasingly forlorn and was heading for a second-innings breakdown. A sporadic presence in England's team – because of form and fitness – since his debut four years earlier, he would admit, 'I had once again been exposed as physically ill-prepared for the job.' Ian Chappell remarked during the series that Willis was a force before lunch but easily dealt with later in the day. 'No doubt I bridled indignantly at this slur when I read it, being still at the immature age of finding excuses whenever I bowled badly,' he remembered, 'but the plain fact of the matter is that I was not resilient enough.'

His knees had been aching for the duration of the tour and by the time the MCC squad arrived in Adelaide he was stiffening up so much that he was having to pull himself up the hotel staircase on the banister rail. He would bowl only five overs in the second innings of this fifth Test and was flying home before the conclusion of the sixth.

Willis managed to play a role in the dismissal of Walters soon after the batsman's personal landmark, making ground to his left to take a diving catch after the ball looped behind the bowler off a leading edge. Underwood had now taken all six wickets, but a partnership of 80 had almost doubled the total to 164 and given Jenner the confidence to continue the charge, especially when the ball was given a little more air. Having survived an lbw appeal, he reached his half-century off 70 balls by forcing Greig over mid-on for three runs.

Willis, a spectator for most of the day before reintroduction right before tea, brought boos from the crowd with a bouncer that cleared Jenner's head at a harmless height. When the ball was within distance Jenner carved and drove his way into the 70s, while Max Walker continued his series-long enjoyment of the England bowlers. The pair had added 77 runs when Jenner swung across Underwood's flighted ball and was bowled.

Dennis Lillee was given his customary welcome by Greig, who forced him to glove a short ball from in front of his face. It was Lillee's eagerness to face Greig, though, that did for Walker, who had pushed the ball to Denness in the covers and ignored his partner's charge for a single. With both men at the batting crease, Greig gathered Denness's gentle toss and knocked off the bails. Lillee made to leave in sacrifice, but the umpires decided that Walker had stepped down the track enough for the batsmen to have crossed, necessitating his departure for 41.

England's good fortune turned into further frustration as 45 more runs were scored, mostly from the bats of Lillee and Ashley Mallett, before Willis and Arnold each picked up a wicket with the new ball to end the innings at 304. Amiss reckoned it was twice as many runs as should have been allowed and was certainly a score that seemed beyond Australian hope when they were 84 for 5. It had a value in demoralising the England team well beyond the mere mathematics of the match.

England's openers survived the final two overs of play, but Amiss was dismissed for a duck on the third ball of a clear, warm and sunny third day. Having shown up in the mood for a suitable celebration of Australia Day, the capacity crowd was not kept waiting long as Lillee induced a straightforward edge from Amiss's defensive bat.

Cowdrey pulled the first two runs of the day to long leg as part of an eventful beginning to his innings. Lillee's charge to the wicket had gathered speed as each passing Test bolstered his confidence in his fitness, and this was to be the first innings in the series in which he took more wickets than Thomson. He was convinced he'd had Cowdrey caught behind but the batsman stood unmoved by the vociferous appeals, as did umpire Robin Bailhache. There was no debate when an almost identical delivery shot towards the slips, but this time it was just beyond Ian Chappell's outstretched right hand.

Once more, Cowdrey relied on using his opponents' pace for his most productive shots, helping Thomson's bouncer to the boundary. When one ball failed to lift as much, he got underneath it just enough to clear Walker as he ran back from short leg. Meanwhile, Lloyd had a brief and uncomfortable experience against Lillee, being struck on the body before he steered another rising ball off his waist down the leg side to Marsh, leaving England 19 for 2.

Denness had decided that a one-match absence from the Test team was not enough time to attempt any change of technical approach at the crease. As usual, his initial step was to move his back foot towards the leg side, giving himself room to play the cut. He profited more often on this occasion, although four of his runs came via an ungainly hook against Walker. He and Cowdrey had advanced the score to 66 when the veteran encountered a nasty lifter from Thomson, once more bowling quicker in his second spell of the day. Cowdrey kept the ball from his ribs but Walker skipped back from short leg and leapt to pull off his catch.

'Colin's form slipped towards the end of the tour,' Redpath observed, 'but even then he made no sign of backing away. He was always behind the ball and at all times gave the impression that he was trying to blunt our attack.'

Having driven Walker for four, Denness's footwork might have brought his downfall when Thomson followed him with a short ball. Unbalanced, Denness almost ended up stepping on his leg stump as he lifted his bat to protect his head. Another cut for four against Thomson and a single off Jenner saw him to his first fifty of the series, which was greeted generously amid the more amiable atmosphere of this match. It was hardly a surprise, however, when he reached an ugly end, slashing at Thomson once more and giving a crisp nick to Marsh. The bowler's 32nd wicket of the series meant he had surpassed by one the totals of John Snow and Lillee in the previous two Ashes series.

Lunch, taken at 95 for 4, was followed by a series of boundaries; Greig pulling Jenner and cutting Lillee, and Fletcher taking three fours off Jenner's fifth over, including one particularly graceful drive.

Jenner admitted to becoming rattled after being denied Greig's wicket when he thought he had got him to edge his slider into Marsh's gloves. Tom Brooks disagreed.

'Fuck!' Jenner exclaimed.

'Don't use that word on my oval,' the umpire warned.

'With all due respect, Tom, this is my fucking oval,' the disgruntled South Australian bowler reminded him.

Walters would spend years reminding Jenner of the incident by arguing, 'You realise, TJ, that Tom actually won that match for Australia . . . when Tom gave Tony Greig not out it changed the game. If he had given him out, the captain would have had to keep you on.'

Greig was eventually out at the other end, caught when he edged a wide Lillee delivery that he should have ignored. Fletcher was then dumped on his backside by the same bowler's bouncer. To his credit, he dusted himself off and clipped the next ball off his legs for four.

Knott suffered an uncharacteristically weak dismissal when he pulled Mallett, who had replaced Jenner, directly to Lillee behind square leg; not the kind of end that justified his assertion that night that the Australian was 'the best off-spinner I have ever played against'. Then Fletcher was caught in the slips when he aimed the kind of ugly head-up swipe at Thomson that belonged in the Sunday League. Underwood survived only one ball before falling to a sharp catch by Lillee as he swept at Mallet, and Titmus was caught on the midwicket boundary by Greg Chappell after he swung hard at the off-spinner. When Arnold lost his stumps to the pace of Lillee, England were all out for 172, their last six wickets having fallen for 42 runs in 79 minutes.

'There was some feeble batting,' Benaud observed. 'It wasn't very good to watch and it was in keeping with the way England has batted through this series.' According to Henry Blofeld, 'Technique, resolve and concentration were all missing.'

Those waking in England and switching on radios to hear about this latest collapse had to wait through typically grim news bulletins. More bombs had been going off around England as the third day's play began. At shops in Bond Street, Kensington, Victoria and Manchester and at a chemical factory and a gasworks in Enfield. Further devices were discovered and defused in Putney and Hampstead. Only the coded warnings delivered in advance by telephone kept the casualties down to six people injured. The speculation was that this was a show of strength by the Provisional IRA ahead of more ceasefire talks.

When the current affairs updates gave way to live commentary of the final stages of the day's play, English ears were forced to listen to the description of Australia's relentless journey towards another inevitable declaration that would set them up for victory. England had yet to bowl out the home side twice in the series, and by the time stumps were reached at 111 for 2 it was clear that the trend was unlikely to change.

An early tea had followed the conclusion of England's innings, after which Australia moved briskly to 16 in only the third over when Arnold moved the ball away from McCosker into the gloves of Knott, who gathered low to his right. The delay before England's appeal was answered suggested McCosker had not got a touch, but Bailhache was merely keen to check with Brooks that the ball had carried. Redpath also edged, against Willis, but Fletcher could not hold on to a low chance.

England's seamers were punished when they pitched short and it was left to Underwood to slow the scoring until Ian Chappell decided to swing him over the midwicket fence. But, having moved to 41 later in the same over, he could only send the ball spinning vertically when he attempted the same shot and Knott waited patiently for it to drop into his grasp.

The idea of a 'rest day' was anathema to a natural athlete and competitor such as Jeff Thomson. He had no intention of using the trip made by players of both teams to the Yarumba winery in the Barossa Valley merely to sit in a deckchair sipping the local produce. Instead, having made use of the swimming pool, he took his turn on the grass tennis court, even though it was a sport he had barely ever played in his life.

Thomson was not a man to mess around and play for laughs. Whether it was bowling at Pommie batsmen, chasing wild boars or playing amateur soccer – from which he was banned for several years after punching a referee on the nose – sport meant the challenge of securing victory. So when his match reached a critical point, he wound up to launch the biggest serve he could muster. Pain tore through his right shoulder and his racquet fell to the ground. He had still managed to serve an ace, though.

A visit to a specialist revealed damaged tendons. His Ashes series was over.

Perhaps, then, if England could delay Australia's declaration long enough, they might be able to hold out for a draw against a depleted attack. The occupants of the press box clearly did not believe so and set about submitting their entries for a sweepstake on what time on the final day the match would end.

Willis's absence and Greig's ineffectiveness, which saw him bowl only two second-innings overs, meant England's bowling was weakened even more than the home team's. It made their efforts early on a hot, windless day even more creditable, with Underwood removing both overnight batsmen and the support of Arnold helping him to restrict the scoring to 24 in an hour.

Redpath, not long after reaching a half-century, was bowled when he attempted to smother the turn and saw the ball spinning back from his bat to hit the stumps. Walters survived a confident lbw shout the very next ball, but Underwood had to wait only for his next over to pick up his tenth wicket of the match when Greg Chappell drove loosely and Greig held the ball low at mid-off.

England's hopes of a deferred declaration dissipated over the next couple of hours, though, as Walters and Marsh mounted a three-figure partnership at a run a minute. While Marsh bludgeoned down the ground and cut crisply when given width, Walters swung vigorously for the short leg-side boundary, hitting a four and a six off successive Underwood deliveries. After lunch arrived at 203 for 4, Walters was the first of the pair to reach 50. Having stepped back to cut Underwood to the unprotected fence he achieved his milestone with a single and then helped Marsh take an all-run four as the left-armer's first over after the break went for 11 runs. Marsh's half-century was reached with customary belligerence, the ball sailing over Greig on the midwicket boundary for six off Underwood.

Marsh edged high into the air when he tried the same shot to the next ball, but Knott, racing towards square leg with arms outstretched could not quite get his gloves underneath the falling ball. Two balls later, Marsh went for it again, this time landing the ball comfortably in the grasp of the distant figure of Greig. Underwood's match haul of 11 wickets had only been bettered by an Englishman in Australia on five occasions.

At 3 p.m., shortly after Walters had pulled Arnold to take the lead past 400, Ian Chappell declared, setting England 405 to win – an 'academic question', Benaud told viewers. There was a sense that English eyes had seen this movie too often in the recent weeks, but the opening scenes in the brief session before tea were to be even more unwatchable than usual.

Lillee made the fourth ball lift and seam and the hapless Amiss could merely look back in the hope that Marsh would spare him by spilling the chance. He didn't. Amiss, just as on his Ashes debut against Australia in 1968, had bagged a pair, attributing his dismissal on this occasion to 'anxiety to get off the mark'. Greg Chappell would remark, 'I thought Amiss was a very good player but that summer he was good enough to nick everything. The first good ball he got, he'd nick it.'

Having begun the series full of pain-killers and anxiety about whether his back would let him down, Lillee's mastery of the man who had begun the series as the most prolific scorer in Test cricket provided him with the assurance that he was still a force in his sport. 'After an 18-month gap . . . .I was satisfied. Maybe I bowled less quickly than before but I was a lot more accurate. With Amiss, I was getting his wicket from movement caught behind or leg before wicket. I didn't get him out hooking, but nicking edges.'

Walker, experiencing the novelty of a new ball in his hand, offered a generous long hop to Lloyd to begin his innings, but, like Lillee, he had to wait only until his fourth ball for a wicket. Lloyd played with firm feet at a delivery angling across him, failing either to get in line or leave alone, and Walters took the catch at third slip.

Lloyd had suffered his first two single-figure dismissals of a series that, for him, was now over after 196 runs at a 24.50 average. His neck injury would see him on an early flight home, 'shocked and shattered out of Test cricket', according to John Arlott. 'He got it bang on,' Lloyd would admit. 'It is that realisation, "I'm not just good enough." I probably had the stuffing knocked out of me by the pair of them [Lillee and Thomson]. I wasn't prepared for what was coming up.'

Cowdrey had seen enough over the years to be prepared, but further proof that he was simply no longer up to the task was provided when he fell victim to the kind of weary waft outside off stump that he had so doggedly avoided earlier in the series. He guided Lillee to a diving Mallett, brilliant in the gully once again, and England were 10 for 3 in only the third over.

Walker offered sufficient width to allow Fletcher and Denness to find the boundary before tea, and Fletcher even had the confidence to cut Lillee for four in front of square immediately after the break. But Denness, having failed to add to his 14 runs since the resumption, fell into Ian Chappell's trap of posting Jenner at fly slip when he slashed Lillee directly to the fielder.

All four wickets, which had fallen for 33, were off the edge. 'This was a demoralised side,' said Martin-Jenkins, 'going through the motions of challenging Australia but doing so no longer with any real hope of conviction.'

The same old images were recurring, Fletcher narrowly avoiding a brutal Lillee bouncer and Greig bursting out of disciplined defence by going hard at anything wide. He had scored a couple of boundaries when Walker cut one in and it pinned him lbw for 20. Fletcher took a pair of comfortable fours off Mallett and Walker to move to 39 and Knott nudged and scampered as usual as England reached the close of play at 94 for 5.

It had been another feeble response to Australia's dominance, especially in light of Thomson's absence and the favourable state of the wicket. 'The most calamitous day for England in this whole depressingly uneven series,' was EW Swanton's verdict in *The Daily Telegraph*. Even Woodcock was uncharacteristically mocking in tone when he suggested to *The Times* readers, 'Surround England by green caps and anyone, it seems, could bowl them out at the moment.'

The *Daily Mirror* was typically blunt. 'HUMILIATION' it screamed in giant back-page capital letters, while reporter Peter Laker said that the Australian players displayed 'undisguised contempt' for their opponents.

It meant that the final day began with what Blofeld called 'a lackadaisical air of inevitability' and ended at around 3 p.m. By then Knott had once more exempted himself from the blanket condemnation of England's performance, having scored only their second hundred of the series to add to his half-centuries in each of the previous three Tests.

Fletcher, too, managed a personal milestone, his first fifty, which he reached via three fours in Lillee's first over of the day; a clip off his legs and two square cuts. Lillee was switched after only two overs to the Cathedral End, from where he ended Fletcher's innings on 63. Four balls after allowing the batsmen the freedom to find the boundary behind point once more, he sent down an inswinging yorker that resulted in a simple lbw verdict.

Knott's partnership of 68 with Fletcher was replicated exactly in tandem with Titmus, whose tenacity, rather than technique, saw him stick around so that the wicketkeeper could continue his progress towards a third Test match century. Quick to pick up the length of the spinners and Walker's medium pace, Knott's habit of standing with feet planted well outside leg stump gave him the best opportunity to execute his array of dabs, cuts and slices against Lillee. His fifty arrived after 100 minutes' batting and he was on 72 when lunch was taken at 198 for 6, his quest for three figures the only real issue of intrigue remaining in the match.

Jenner tried coming round the wicket to Knott, who immediately seemed to lose concentration and came close to offering a catch to square leg. He gathered himself by sweeping the next ball for four. Titmus's method against Jenner's line of attack was to pad up to three consecutive deliveries – the ire of the bowler growing with each refused appeal – but when he was deceived by the leg-spinner's googly Bailhache ruled in the Australians' favour.

Underwood quickly offered Ian Chappell an easy slip catch off Mallett – giving him a five-ball pair in the match – and Arnold's walk to the middle was interrupted by a fan running to the field to give him a home-made bat roughly twice the width of the stumps.[48] He lasted only long enough to see Knott swat a Jenner full toss to the midwicket boundary before he played down the wrong line against Mallett; the third England man to fail to score in either innings.

It was down to Willis to accompany Knott through the final 15 runs to his ton, although the manner in which Knott charged at

---

48 The gesture was repeated in the English summer of 1976, when a West Indian fan gave a similar piece of woodwork to John Edrich.

Mallett suggested no great confidence in his partner's durability. He was on 92 when Lillee was given the new ball, nine overs after it had become due, but a two, a late cut for four and an uppercut over the slips to the fence at third man brought him his landmark, begrudged by no one in the last-day crowd of just over 20,000. No England batsman in the series had been more deserving of a piece of personal glory among the collective chaos. For good measure he repeated the last of those strokes for his ninth boundary in a score of 106.

Willis, relieved of responsibility for his colleague, survived an edge against Walker before losing his middle stump to a ball that kept low. Australia were winners by 163 runs, going 4-0 up in the series, and England – all out for 241 – had managed a match tally of only 413, their lowest at Adelaide in 18 tours since 1994-95. In ten innings they had yet to reach 300.

While former Australian Test captain Lindsay Hassett collected his winnings from the press box sweepstake, Jim Laker was summoned for a television interview in which he concluded, '[England's] tactics have been pathetic,' and warned, 'A few heads have got to fall after this debacle.'

Denness 'had hoped for better from the side' after winning two state matches and rediscovering some confidence. 'We returned to square one again,' he said, 'let down by batting failures.' As much as he had been floundering at the crease, so he was now struggling for answers when questioned by the media. 'We need a lot of application, dedication and hard work,' he offered, in line with previous post-match scripts. When he was pressed by what he actually meant, he admitted forlornly, 'I just don't know. I wish I knew the complete answer.'

When he offered the assertion that 'we'll climb back up again' it sounded blindly optimistic. But England and their skipper were about to find some blessed relief.

15
THE DAY OF DENNESS

He will attack with stylish strokes and, against ordinary bowling on attacking wickets, he will score runs.
John Arlott, *The Guardian*

A five-month Ashes tour could seem even longer when it was characterised by heavy defeat after heavy defeat; when batsmen had to worry about physical safety more than they were able to celebrate personal achievement; and when bowlers found that however gamely they tried, their efforts barely created puffs of smoke in comparison to the fireworks of their opposition counterparts. 'I doubt whether it is possible for any touring team to feel more dejected than we were when we arrived at Melbourne for the sixth Test,' remembered Dennis Amiss.

Yet Mike Denness insisted after England had gone 4-0 down in the series that 'there is a lot of humour around' in the England squad, offering an illustration years later. 'If you have got people in your dressing room like David Lloyd . . . terrific sense of humour and great in the hospitality room. He would just take the mickey, which was brilliant. The humour was something that would keep you going, and bear in mind you are talking about nigh on six months of a tour.'

There was no disguising that Jeff Thomson's injury, which the Australian selectors quickly announced would preclude him for selection for the final Test, helped to further lighten the mood. Meanwhile, Denness was confident that despite 'dejection in our camp' over results, he could count on the professional pride of the players to carry them through the final days in Australia. And with no Thomson to contend with he knew that 'here was our big chance of success. I wanted this so desperately for myself and my team after all we had been through.'

To some of those travelling alongside the MCC party and observing from close quarters, however, there remained a suspicion that there was a little too much contentment and high spirits; a sense that the team's fate had been too readily absorbed. Henry Blofeld observed as the sixth Test approached, 'The defeats have been accepted or digested just as a visit to the cinema might be. Around the corridors in the hotel come the same smiling benign faces, as often as not with a couple of children in tow. It is all so unreal, for the humiliation of it all seems to have passed most players by – Greig excepted, of course. But it would not be surprising if even he has said to himself, "To hell with it."'

Such comments were undoubtedly valid, yet they also hint at the frustration of the English press when faced with the task of finding new ways to describe recurring batting collapses, new angles upon which to discuss upcoming Tests. 'By the time a sixth Test match comes along, with one side leading 4-0, the material for a preview has inevitably become somewhat limited,' admitted EW Swanton, about to report on his final Test for *The Daily Telegraph* before retirement. 'The various hopes and possibilities are apt to have exhausted themselves.'

Creatively, John Woodcock recalled a previous tour of India when several people were forced to endure six injections after exposure to a dog with rabies. The final shot, he explained, was far less painful than the previous five; just as he hoped England's experience in the sixth and final Test would be.

Yet with more fitness concerns presenting themselves ahead of the Melbourne match, Blofeld voiced further frustration with the manner in which medical bulletins had been shared throughout an injury-hit tour. 'Too many people in a position to give a definitive answer have been unwilling to commit themselves on anything much more demanding than the time of day,' he complained. 'And once or twice relations between press and management have been needlessly stretched.'

The days between the fifth and sixth Tests offered nothing in the way of new storylines. Newcastle, 100 miles up the coast from Sydney, was the setting for a three-day game against Northern New South Wales. Although performances there did not count in first-class records, the match provided an opportunity for several players to prove their fitness, others to improve their form, and some to remind themselves they were still part of the tour party.

In the first category, John Edrich scored 66 not out and 40 as he tested his mending ribs, while Mike Hendrick's wicketless return in both innings was accompanied by enough tenderness in his hamstring to rule him out of the Test. Of those looking for a boost in confidence, Dennis Amiss followed his two ducks in Adelaide with a first-innings 74 and Colin Cowdrey made his highest score of the tour when his second-innings 85 steered MCC to a four-wicket victory.

Meanwhile, forgotten batsman Brian Luckhurst passed 50 twice in the match, while Hendrick's ongoing problems and Bob Willis's breakdown offered Peter Lever an opportunity to press for his first Test appearance since the opening match of the series with two wickets in each innings.

While MCC were thus engaged, their opposition for a 40-over game when they arrived in Melbourne was determined by New Zealand beating Western Australia by eight wickets in the final of the local version of the Gillette Cup. The match, played at a near-empty MCG, was settled when the state side crumbled to 26 for 8. The MCC tour schedule had called for a meeting with the tournament champions, meaning that the game against New Zealand was not treated as an official one-day international.

An unresponsive public, only 3,462 of whom were sprinkled around the cavernous arena, and an apparently uninterested MCC team reflected the game's lack of meaningful status. Yet it could not dissuade the watching English journalists from offering more scathing reviews after a 66-run defeat.

And this was not a case of tabloid reporters pouncing on an insignificant game to perpetuate the narrative desired by blood-hungry sports desks. This was Woodcock of *The Times* reporting that MCC's performance 'had nothing: no skill, no defiance, no cricketing common-sense'. He began his account with, 'MCC showed they can lose a limited-over match with just as little difficulty as they can a five-day Test,' and reckoned that their effort 'rates as low as anything they have done' on the tour. *The Guardian*'s Blofeld was in accord, arguing that 'there was no excuse for the apathetic way in which they approached the match' and castigating them for 'indifferent bowling and atrocious fielding'.

Denness was questioned for allowing New Zealand to bat first in perfect conditions, generosity they accepted by scoring 262 for 8.

Typical of MCC's performance in the field was the over from Fred Titmus in which Kiwi wicketkeeper Ken Wadsworth was dropped three times in the outfield – by Keith Fletcher and twice by Chris Old – and by the carelessness of Geoff Arnold in bowling two no-balls in the final over. 'At times MCC were embarrassing to watch,' concluded Woodcock, who was also unable to fathom why Tony Greig did not bat until the match was slipping away at 47 for 4. 'At times one cannot help wondering what Denness is thinking about,' he wrote, although by then he had been influenced by seeing Greig score 79, for which he was given the consolation of the Man of the Match award.

There was another prize coming Greig's way before the final Test, when he was honoured at a champagne breakfast at the Hilton Hotel as joint winner, with Dennis Lillee, of Personality of the Series. In his light-hearted acceptance speech he promised he would 'be coming back to Australia and that we're going to thrash the pants off your fellows'.

From the wreckage of England's latest beating emerged the likely line-up for the sixth Test. Willis, Hendrick and Lloyd were not fit enough, and Luckhurst was apparently not considered as the latter's replacement as opener, a role that would fall again to Cowdrey. As temperatures topped 100 degrees Fahrenheit on the eve of the match, fanned by a hot northerly wind, a squad of 12 that effectively picked itself was announced. The final choice, it was assumed, lay between Lever and Old, who was reported to be suffering from a cold. 'He always has something as a Test match approaches,' Woodcock grumbled.

In the end, though, both seamers played and Titmus stood down, his unexpected Ashes adventure ending with the kind of bowling average, 51.42, that was a long way from justifying the selectors' decision to include him. Lever apparently received confirmation of his participation on the morning of the match, when wife Barbara handed him the local paper over breakfast in bed at the Windsor Hotel and said, 'Look, you're playing.'

Conditions had set the MCC selection committee on a course of playing three specialist seamers. During the one-dayer against New Zealand, the surface for the Test had been barely distinguishable from the green outfield and while plenty of grass had come off since then the wicket was likely to have retained some life. 'I always felt because they had the fastest bowlers there was always a little bit more grass left on their wickets,' argued Amiss. 'John Inverarity always challenges me on that, but he didn't play. I'm sure the grass was a bit longer than what you would want in England.' Fletcher would claim that a 'sequence of bad pitches' had been prepared for the series. 'Many were simply not flat,' he said, describing patches of brown, where the mower had removed too much grass, mixed with 'valleys of green', which had been ignored.

Australian captain Ian Chappell seemed no less happy with the state of the playing surface. He would comment during the match, 'I am thoroughly sick and tired of having to play on Australian wickets which are wet or in some ways affected by water.'

As well as discussing the pitch, many of the English newspaper previews reminded readers that Freddie Brown's England team of 1950-51 had won the final Test of their series after losing the first four, which at least offered hope to Denness's team, similarly 4-0 down. Current manager Alec Bedser, it was noted in the search for omens, had taken ten wickets in the match. With Thomson's place going to the left-arm fast-medium of Geoff Dymock, Woodcock sounded positively cheery when he predicted, 'So long as England still have the spirit for it they should, in one innings or another, make a long score.'

Denness was not sorry to lose the toss, knowing that he ought to bat but tempted by the green of the track. There was also a small, troublesome-looking damp patch at the southern end, caused by water falling as the covers were being removed. But it remained baking hot, meaning it could potentially be a long day in the field if the batsmen got themselves in. Ian Chappell, his batting line-up strengthened by the return of Ross Edwards for Terry Jenner, made the safe choice and told his openers to get their pads on.

With the Ashes secured, the Australian captain had allowed himself a little pre-match indulgence. 'I guess it says a bit about my temperament,' Chappell explained, 'because the night before that Test [rock singer] Billy Thorpe played in a band at the Doncaster Hotel, which is in a suburb of Melbourne. I always liked Billy and so did Rodney Marsh, so I said to him, "Come on, why don't we go and listen to Billy Thorpe?" Rodney said, "Mate, we have got a Test to play tomorrow, we can't do that. It will be a late finish." I said, "Bugger it, let's go." I will never forget Rodney said to me afterwards, "You can get fucked, mate. I am not doing that ever again."

'That was probably a pretty stupid decision on my part, but probably also tells you a bit about how I thought. My line of thinking was that if you play five Tests and win three of them it doesn't matter what happens in the other two. A lot of people might think that is a stupid way of thinking, but to me it wasn't. It also belies the fact that most people who don't know me say I am ruthless. I am not ruthless. If you want ruthless, you go and talk to Greg about batting. I don't even think I was a ruthless batsman. In my opinion, I certainly wasn't a ruthless captain because, one, I liked a contest and, two, I was silly enough to do something like that.'

In what was generally assumed to be his final Test match – it had been decided that he would not be going on to New Zealand – Cowdrey was given the honour of leading the England team on to the MCG field. A rousing welcome rose up from a first-day crowd that would reach 32,515. In their midst was a home-made banner that said, 'Melbourne Cricket Ground fans thank Colin – six tours.'

Arnold, bowling into a northerly breeze, opened with a maiden over in which he troubled Ian Redpath; and then it was time for Lever's dramatic re-entrance to the series. After a wicketless performance in the first Test, the man who would explain that he had come to feel 'like a leper' on the tour needed only four balls to remove Rick McCosker, caught by Tony Greig at second slip after he edged a rising outswinger that he could easily have left alone.

Australia had to wait until the fifth over before scoring a run as England's new-ball bowlers enjoyed the humid conditions. They had still managed only five when, after 35 minutes, Redpath fell in similar fashion to his opening partner, another wicket for Lever, whose deliveries were leaving visible marks on the still-moist area of the pitch.

Greg Chappell was hit on the side of the face by a ball that Lever got to lift from short of a length, causing a delay of several minutes before he could resume. In the same bowler's next over, he failed to get fully to the pitch of the ball and edged to Denness in the gully, putting his dismissal down to the earlier blow he'd taken. 'It didn't do me any damage physically, but psychologically I was a bit rattled and next over I was caught.'

Edwards survived only a matter of minutes and a handful of balls before glancing Lever to Amiss chest-high at leg slip. Australia were 23 for 4, with a sweat-soaked Lever responsible for all the wickets. Denness, who admitted 'I had to keep kicking myself to believe it was all happening', gave Lever a deserved rest after seven overs, but Old immediately removed Doug Walters from the other end when the ball popped from a good length and John Edrich, diving forward from gully, took the catch.

Ian Chappell, meanwhile, had played some firm shots on the leg side but he, too, could have gone when Denness failed to hold a square cut off Arnold. He defended sturdily to take his team into lunch at 66 for 5 and reached his 79-ball fifty in the first over of the afternoon before hooking and driving Greig for a pair of leg-side boundaries.

The wicket settled down as the day advanced, but the damage had already been done. Even Chappell's rearguard ended when, on 65, Robin Bailhache ruled that he had glanced a leg-side ball from Old into Knott's gloves, although television replays suggested the ball had brushed his hip. Chappell looked disappointed but left the crease, while Marsh showed his disapproval by tossing down his batting gloves. 'I didn't have a high regard for Bailhache as an umpire, but I respected his decision,' Chappell remembered.

Christopher Martin-Jenkins called it 'the first of several questionable decisions made in the match by two umpires who were clearly tired after wrongly being asked to adjudicate the entire series'.

Marsh was as keen as ever to counter-attack, connecting with a few drives before a ball from Old hit his middle stump through the gap between bat and pad. Walker, straight and resolute, again batted with skill and common sense for 70 minutes, prompting Robin Marlar of the *Sunday Times* to observe, 'Walker is an architect and if his buildings are as indestructible as his innings they may last forever.'

Meanwhile, Dennis Lillee twice forced Old to the fence before slashing at Lever and edging to Knott. Maintaining his pace and bounce, Lever then found Ashley Mallett shuffling towards the leg side and took out his middle stump to claim his sixth wicket. 'Neutral, I feel no elation,' was how Lever described his emotions.

'After losing the Ashes it seems to me almost a useless performance. But I hope it taught one or two people one or two things.'

Dymock was the last man out just before tea when he edged Greig. Australia's 152 was their lowest score of the series; England's excellent catching and attacking field placement mirroring their opponents in the earlier matches. 'It was a sign of how things could have been,' said Amiss. 'Our bowlers had some help from the conditions and all the edges went to our fielders, who held everything.'

Yet thoughts that this might be a complete role reversal were put on hold when England's reply began after a delay caused by gathering rain clouds. With only the fourth ball, Lillee trapped Amiss on the back foot with an inswinger and the man who had led all Test match run-scorers in 1974 was on his way with a third consecutive duck in the series – all inflicted by Lillee. 'I don't think I have ever played against such sustained hostile bowling in my life,' Amiss recalled. 'Dennis goes down in my book as being the best I have ever played against, and there were some good bowlers in those West Indies sides over the years. He would give 120 per cent and his back stood up to it, which we didn't think it would.' And he was forced to admit, 'Lillee had built up a massive stranglehold over me.'

Worsening light and persistent drizzle ended the day's play during the seventh over of the innings, England happy to miss out on a further 42 minutes' examination of their batting in unfavourable conditions. Cowdrey went to sleep that night with high hopes of a grand finale to his career on a ground where he had scored three Test centuries. He'd felt his feet moving quickly into correct positions and had little trouble evading or playing safely the more awkward deliveries.

But when Walker resumed his interrupted over the following morning it was a different story. Cowdrey survived a difficult chance in the gully before the next ball lifted surprisingly to meet his glove and then settle in those of Marsh. Cowdrey, ever the gentlemen, did not bother to wait for the decision before leaving the crease for what ended up being the final time in his unexpectedly prolonged Test career.

It was difficult to offer a true assessment of his tally of 165 runs in the series. At times it appeared that the example his batting set

– in its discipline and doggedness – was more important than the number up on the scoreboard. Yet it was impossible not to question the wisdom of picking a player for whom success was sticking around for scores of 20 and 40. The Australians certainly failed to see what there was to be lost by putting in a youngster who might have got nought or 100. The way England saw it, a series average of 18.33 was neither here nor there to Cowdrey at the end of his illustrious career; but might have been highly damaging to someone close to the start of their journey as an international cricketer.

For Denness, who had championed Cowdrey's inclusion, the debate could wait. As he replaced his county colleague, he had his own demons to deal with: the fact that he'd already batted four times on this ground without success. For once, he was greeted by some good fortune. Having employed his usual technique against Lillee of staying inside the line and aiming shots square of the wicket – 'not two of the best overs I have ever played' – he saw the fast bowler trudge away at the end of his second over of the day, and sixth of the innings, flexing his right ankle in discomfort.

During the course of Walker's next over, in which Denness scored freely in his favoured region behind point, Lillee adjusted his boot and examined his foot. England's batsmen walked over to where the bowler sat in time to hear him tell the umpires he was going off for treatment. Like partner Jeff Thomson, his series was done. He left the ground for an X-ray that revealed severe bruising on the ball of his right foot.

Dymock took over at the Pavilion End and suddenly it was an entirely different contest. It was appropriate that the front page of the next day's *Daily Mirror* would scream 'CEASEFIRE' in giant capital letters. It referred to the Provisional IRA's decision to temporarily halt its bombing in Northern Ireland and on the British mainland, but on the MCG field, too, it felt like hostilities had ended. Now when Denness laid back to cut he had enough time for the ball to find the middle of the bat and reach the fence in front of square. Suddenly he appeared in control of his actions instead of being a party to involuntary footwork and a blade guided purely by reflex. Half-volleys could be anticipated, and short balls looked forward to as opportunities to score rather than potential for injury.

With the role of third seamer falling to Walters, who would bowl 23 overs in the innings[49], Edrich enjoyed the opportunity to drive off the front foot, although he did come close to playing on when caught in two minds about the length of a ball from Dymock. Denness, too, had an escape on 36 when he clipped Walters to a butter-fingered McCosker at midwicket, before bringing up England's 100 by thumping a Walker full toss to the extra cover boundary. In the next over, he steered Mallett past gully to reach his half-century.

Edrich's fifty had to wait until immediately after lunch had been taken at 120 for 2, turning Mallett for two behind square to get to his milestone. The manner in which he thrashed Walker through cover shortly afterwards illustrated the joy England had at last found in their batting, as did Denness's nimble feet against Mallett. The Australian total of 152 was soon left behind.

The century that seemed a just reward for Edrich's stoicism throughout the tour was denied him, however, when he flashed at Walker and Ian Chappell's sharp catch at first slip dismissed him for 70 after a partnership of 149 with his skipper.

Denness approached his century with a back-foot drive off Walker that sped to the boundary but he was fortunate not to come up short when he failed to anticipate Redpath getting down to a similar shot and would have been run out by a distance if the throw to the bowler's end had hit the stumps. On 98, he managed to catch up with a Dymock delivery outside leg stump, although it was not until Tom Brooks signalled four that the crowd could be sure he had made contact and could embark on their warm acknowledgement of his feat, achieved in 221 minutes from 203 balls. This was no time for the 43,332 in the ground, or Denness himself, to consider that he had not been facing Australia's best bowlers. For the leader of such a wretched tour it was simply time to enjoy a moment that, during the dark days of early New Year, could not have seemed further away. Even the Australian players didn't begrudge him his moment. 'He didn't blow up,' said Redpath. 'A lot of other men would have done so under the circumstances. Even though he had a frightful tour he was always able to smile and take the good with the bad.'

---

49 It was the only time Walters ever bowled 20 overs in a Test innings.

Tea offered Denness a chance to compose himself and prepare to build on England's lead, knowing the new ball would be arriving shortly. Even that, of course, was a different prospect now and Keith Fletcher quickly took advantage of Walker's inswing to guide a series of shots into the leg side. Sensing his own opportunity, Fletcher was content to proceed with caution, reaching his fifty in a little under three hours shortly before the close, having struck only two boundaries.

Meanwhile, Denness was dropped by Ian Chappell when he drove wearily at Dymock on 121 and he added four to his score when he aimed an even looser shot – feet in the air Caribbean-style – and the ball flew to the third-man fence. Struggling to maintain his concentration after the relief of reaching three figures and the unaccustomed fatigue of a long innings, he gloved an attempted hook against the left-armer and was relieved to see the ball drop short of Marsh's dash towards the stumps.

'Keith Fletcher did a first-class job talking me through that very difficult period,' he recalled. 'In between overs he came down the wicket offering encouraging words, which was certainly a great help.' The sight of a healthy scoreboard fortified him further and he was happy to go quietly to stumps at 133 not out from a total of 273 for 3. He knew that the day might not have saved his status as long-term England captain, nor erased the negative numbers in the ledger of his tour, but, golly, it felt good. For once the mood the dressing room was relaxed and happy. 'It was a day we were all enjoying for a change.'

While Denness's early-tour failures had been back-page lead material in the *Daily Mirror*, the story of his redemption was buried underneath the racing cards on an inside page, although Peter Laker did acknowledge, 'Whatever the freakishness of his luck yesterday you cannot take glory from a man who, in eight previous Test innings, had aggregated three runs fewer than he scored in this one spell-binding attempt.'

Denness had become only the fourth England captain, after Andrew 'AE' Stoddart, Archie MacLaren and Peter May, to score a Test century in Australia, and the third day saw him advance his final total to 188, the highest by an England player in an away Ashes contest since Wally Hammond's 231 during the 1936-37 tour. By lunch, he had scored 53 of his team's 78 runs in the session in a chanceless couple of hours, marching past 150 with a pair of boundaries against Dymock.

The sight of Walters's long hops being forced through gaps in the field re-emphasised the holes in the Australian attack, as did the presence of Thomson in the press box sharing his thoughts on events with his ghost-writer. Denness, having achieved the highest score of his first-class career, was eventually dismissed in the third over after lunch. Giving himself room to target the off side once again, Walker's delivery was straighter than he expected and when he slapped it back down the track the bowler dropped to his knees, stuck out his right arm and held onto the ball.

Having shared a partnership of 192 with his skipper, Fletcher was now happy to play a supporting role in a two-hour stand of 148 runs with Greig. He preferred to lean, rather than launch, into his attacking shots, although a satisfying crack went around the ground when he stepped back to force Ian Chappell to the cover boundary and reach his century after 337 minutes at the crease. It was his first hundred in 39 first-class innings over two Australian tours.

Mostly, Fletcher was content to enjoy the sight of Greig cracking 13 boundaries in a 94-ball innings of 89. A couple of ungainly swipes against Chappell demonstrated the all-rounder's intent rather than producing results, but once he found his range the ball began speeding to boundaries in all areas of the ground. Laker described him as 'using his bat like a navvy's pick-axe', but that did little justice to some of the straight drives and delicate late cuts. It was, however, an accurate way of conveying some of the blasts he aimed at Chappell and Walters, the latter having three consecutive deliveries pounded to the leg-side fence as the partnership reached three figures in 72 minutes.

Fletcher finished his afternoon's work with a crisply driven four off Dymock and a hook that was less elegant but equally productive, England going to the break at 496 for 4. From then on, it was a procession of wickets, triggered by Greig's flailing at Walker and skying the ball to mid-off. Looking for the boundary that would have taken him to 150, Fletcher advanced against Walker but could not beat the reach of Redpath at wide mid-on. Dymock hurried one through's Old's defences and three wickets had fallen for a single run. Knott and Arnold both presented Marsh with easy catches off Walker, who collected his eighth wicket and ended England's innings on 529 when Underwood missed a swish to leg.

Australia made it through the final hour of play without losing a wicket, knocking 32 off their first-innings deficit of 377, although McCosker had to survive appeals for a slip catch off Arnold and an lbw to Lever.

When play continued after the rest day, Lever made it through less than half an hour before having to leave the field with flu symptoms. He had gone for 27 runs in three ragged overs since the restart, McCosker hitting him for three fours in the second of them as he advanced to a 63-ball half-century. It left England, like Australia, a bowler short, but at least they had a bank of runs to bolster them and a pitch that, although slow, offered some variable bounce.

Old was guilty of giving the batsmen too much width, but when Arnold replaced him it was further temptation outside the off stump that found McCosker cutting and edging sharply to the alert Cowdrey at third slip.

Arnold was aggrieved that Brooks turned down a pair of lbw appeals against Ian Chappell, shirt unbuttoned lower than ever in the MCG heat. The Australian skipper almost chopped onto his stumps as he attempted to drive Arnold, who then got one to lift from a length to strike him painfully on the hand. From the same end, Old left Redpath, who had reached a painstaking fifty in almost four hours, rubbing his ribs. Either side of that blow, however, Redpath cut and drove for four.

Greig had bowled his off-spin – with five men crouched around the bat – so well that Denness delayed the introduction of Underwood until well after lunch. Chappell, struck on the hand again by Old, looked more at ease against the left-armer, profiting with the drive and the sweep. One of the latter stokes went fine to the boundary to take Australia past 200 in the 53rd over and a repeat saw them to tea at 206 for 1, with Chappell one short of a fifty he duly completed.

Greig had switched to the Pavilion End to take advantage of the unpredictable bounce enjoyed by his colleagues and Redpath edged perilously close to Cowdrey when the ball climbed at him. Greig changed to seam after tea, striking Redpath on the pads before Arnold spilled the ball at long leg when the batsmen got underneath his pull shot. Greig, bowling as well as at any time in the series, finally got some reward when Chappell slid across the crease and Brooks ruled that the ball had been touched to Knott as it passed outside leg stump. It looked, at best, a marginal decision.

'I was out both times caught by Knott down the leg side and I didn't hit either of them,' Chappell recalled. 'I was pissed off, but I always accepted the decision. I think Mike Brearley was writing about the match and said that no one at the ground would have known I got two bad decisions.'

What angered Chappell equally on this occasion was the umpires' reaction to an exchange with Greig that was evident to the crowd, Chappell delivering some words to the bowler over his right shoulder as he departed. 'As I was walking off, Greigy told me to piss off at some point. Stupidly I turned round and said, "Why don't you go and get rooted?" Tom Brooks said, "Ian, watch your language." I said, "Tom, why don't you listen to what he said first."'

It was almost the final moment of contention for an umpiring team who had come to look more jaded than England's beleaguered batsmen. *Wisden*'s verdict on Brooks and Bailhache was that 'their umpiring fell short of required standards'. As well as questioning the 'lack of protection afforded to England's batsmen', the piece said, 'Their judgement of lbw and legside catches seemed at times to bear little relation to reality. Batsmen sometimes appeared to be immune from lbw decisions unless they were right back on their stumps with the ball keeping low. England's bowlers seemed to suffer more in that respect, but Australia had their share of controversial decisions.'

Redpath drove Underwood for four; then survived an appeal for a silly point catch by Greig, who just managed to stop himself throwing the ball down in disgust; and was struck on the thigh by another awkward ball from Greig. The erratic bounce looked as though it was on Greg Chappell's mind when he edged through the slips for four and his third boundary in that same over could also be classed as an escape as he gloved a hook not far from the reach of Amiss at leg slip. A couple of overs later, however, Amiss was positioned perfectly to pouch the ball at backward square leg when Redpath tried to hook Greig. His 83 runs had been compiled in six hours, and his series average of 42.90 and scoring rate of 13 runs per hour offered a perfect snapshot of his contribution to his team's success.

Edwards, uncomfortable and tentative, was hit flush on the pads by Greig and the uncertain bounce was the only possible explanation for Brooks refusing to give what seemed a certain lbw. Greg Chappell, meanwhile, played with growing confidence, guiding Australia to stumps at 274 for 3.

Lever's incapacitation had persuaded Denness to delay the second new ball until four overs before the close of play, but the Lancashire paceman was back on the field for the final day, albeit with heavy-looking legs. It was Arnold who extracted enough life in the fourth over to get the ball bouncing at the ribs of Edwards, who fended it down the leg side to Knott. He also had Chappell hooking the ball well above head height for the two runs that took him to 50.

The reluctance of Brooks to expose his finger to fresh air had saved new batsman Walters when Lever cut the ball into his pads about half-way up the stumps. But, one ball after inside-edging into his pads, Walters lost his bail to one that seamed away sharply. Marsh lingered only briefly before driving at a wide delivery from Lever and offering Denness a catch at fourth slip.

The third wicket to fall for 17 runs in half an hour had virtually ended any debate over the outcome of the match. Even Greg Chappell, quick to punch anything short through the off side and fluent in his driving on both sides of the wicket, appeared to have accepted the futility of the situation as he accelerated his rate of scoring in search of a century before running out of partners.

Walker at least accompanied him past lunch, aided by Brooks's continued reluctance to recognise the validity of any lbw appeal after Old thumped him on the pads. There was no reprieve, though, when Walker didn't pick up the slower ball and drove a comfortable return catch into the welcoming grip of Greig.

Chappell by now needed only four for his ton and Australia ten from the last three wickets to make England bat again. Chappell was struck on the foot by a Lever yorker before manoeuvring Greig to fine leg for the boundary that took him into three figures. Not only was he the sole batsman to have achieved the feat twice in the series, he had done so without ever being completely free of the viral symptoms that had dogged him throughout the summer.

His dismissal for 102, bowled when playing across the line to Lever, precipitated a swift end to the match. With the score still on

373, four short of parity, Dymock was ruled to have feathered an edge to Knott off Lever, before Mallett gave Greig his fourth wicket via a bat-pad catch to Edrich at short leg. Neither batsmen thought very much of the umpires' decisions.

A cheerful Denness grabbed a stump from Bailhache and made a point of seeking out Lillee for a handshake as he led his triumphant team from the field. He was still clutching the stump when the team were pictured in a chaotic changing room enjoying their long-awaited moment of triumph. 'It had not happened to us before and we made the most of it,' he remembered. Victory, he felt, was no more than they deserved for the way in which they had battled through sickness, injury and ill-fortune. 'They never gave up,' he said of his men, 'fighting against adversity all the time.'

No one was pretending in the midst of all this happiness that any slates had been cleaned. As Blofeld noted, the result was 'neither a justification for the way England have played and particularly batted out here, nor is it a sign that all is not as bad with England's cricket as it has seemed over these last months'. He warned. 'It was the manner of the defeat which was so sad and which must not be forgotten following this Test match.'

Yet the circumstances of Australia's defeat in the final Test did allow the development of the narrative emphasising that Lillee and Thomson represented the most important difference – some felt the only difference – between the two teams. 'Yes. That's the only answer I can give you,' was the definitive response from Lever when asked if he agreed with that historical perspective. 'Clive Lloyd would say the same; they are the quickest he has ever seen. We were racing to get to Lillee's end because Thommo was just so frightening. There was always a bit of fear. It was the fact that you weren't good enough to contend with it. You couldn't do anything about it because of your lack of skill, particularly down the order. It was bad enough for the first five, let alone numbers nine or ten.'

Immediately after England's victory, Bedser said, 'Our batting suddenly looked world-class because without all that pressure we were playing a different game. We can criticise our blokes for not getting into line, for pulling their heads away from the bat and all the rest of it. But, over the years, it's always been the same story as soon as you have two high-class fast bowlers about. The reason is simple. They are such a rare breed that when they come out of the blue no coaching manual is going to help you.'

Denness had been told by Cowdrey that Lillee and Thomson were the 'most difficult and unpredictable' pair of fast bowlers he had ever encountered and years later the England captain contended, 'In conversation with Ian Chappell I said that I would have liked to see it reversed and Lillee and Thommo on our side and see how your lads got on. Ian would have said, "It wouldn't have made any difference; we still would have got runs." I have to question that because on those pitches we played on I think even the Aussies' top six batsmen would have struggled against them. It did make the difference . . . if there was a change in bowling there was always a batsman rushing to get down to that end to avoid Thommo and Lillee.'

Fletcher would recall, 'Those two weren't there and we absolutely annihilated them then. They were the difference between the two sides by a long chalk.' Or, as Woodcock noted, 'Thomson and Lillee are no ordinary pair and Australia without them are no extraordinary side.'

Of course, that the Lillee-Thomson combination was the greatest differentiating feature of the Ashes combatants is indisputable. At the same time, it is an over-simplification to offer events of the sixth Test as the sole evidence. England's consolation victory in Melbourne was not merely a question of not having to face those two. Lillee's injury early in the match meant that Australia were a bowler short, regardless of identity. It is much harder to imagine England winning by an innings had Lillee been ruled out before the start and a replacement fast bowler, someone such as Victoria's Alan Hurst, had been able to offer the home team a fully stocked attack.

'We were we pissed off about the loss,' said Ian Chappell, who admitted that he thought the series overall would be closer than transpired. 'But we were also pragmatic and we didn't have Thommo and then Dennis's foot gave out after six overs. If Dennis wasn't playing you would have hoped they would have picked Hurst and he was pretty quick. He was no Dennis Lillee, but still I think England would have had a bit of a hangover from previous matches. I bowled 12 overs and if that happens we are in deep shit.

'But I go back to what I said to the guys, "You learn a hell of a lot more from a loss than from a win," so there were things there to be learned. But I would be a fool if I said we weren't pissed off about losing.'

Lillee's limited participation in the match perhaps softened the blow for him. 'Such a comprehensive defeat did little if anything to take the gloss off our 4-1 win over England in the series,' he reflected. 'It had been a rough and tough series, with many tense moments as the bumper war raged pretty well throughout. But at the end of it all there was great satisfaction.'

Meanwhile, Denness was torn out of the joy of England's moment to tackle inevitable questions about his Test future. 'That's not my jurisdiction,' he responded. 'I'm just doing a job on this tour and everything will be reviewed in April.'

While he spoke to the press, Cowdrey, the man whose future had already been determined with the decision to send him back to England rather than to New Zealand, stood in a straw hat in front of the spectators' sign on the boundary, contentedly signing autographs and posing for photos. He had been 'quite overcome' by the goodwill of the Melbourne crowd and was happy to do whatever he could to show his appreciation.

That Cowdrey had somehow become the face of this England team to the Australian public was both an indictment of the tourists' performance and policy of selection and an indication of how crazy his participation in the series was in the eyes of home fans brought up with an understanding that the promise of future feats would invariably be favoured over past glories when teams were chosen.

As Blofeld observed of the England team in signing off his report in *The Guardian*, 'They will go leaving behind them an Australian public who are obviously amazed that the present state of English cricket should be such that the party out here are the best players in England.'

ASHES SERIES AVERAGES

Australia Batting

	M	I	NO	HS	Runs	100	50	Avg.
GS Chappell	6	11	0	144	608	2	5	55.27
TJ Jenner	3	3	1	74	100		1	50.00
MJN Walker	6	8	3	41*	221			44.20
IR Redpath	6	11	1	105	472	1	3	42.90
KD Walters	6	11	2	103	383	1	3	42.55
RD McCosker	3	5	0	80	202		2	40.40
IM Chappell	6	12	1	90	387		4	35.18
RW Marsh	6	11	2	55	313		1	34.77
R. Edwards	5	9	1	115	261	1	1	32.62
JR Thomson	5	5	2	24*	65			21.66
DK Lillee	6	8	2	26	88			14.66
AA Mallett	5	7	2	31	61			12.20
WJ Edwards	3	6	0	30	68			11.33
G. Dymock	1	2	0	0	0			0.00

Australia Bowling

	O	M	R	W	BB	Avg.
JR Thomson	175.1	34	592	33	6-46	17.93
AA Mallett	140.6	47	339	17	4-21	19.94
DK Lillee	182.6	36	596	25	4-49	23.84
MHN Walker	218.7	46	684	23	8-143	29.73
KD Walters	56.3	14	175	5	2-13	35.00
TJ Jenner	42	10	136	3	2-45	45.33

Also Bowled: IM Chappell 22-3-83-1; G. Dymock 39-6-130-1.

England Batting

	M	I	NO	HS	Runs	100	50	Avg
JH Edrich	4	7	1	70	260		2	43.33
AW Greig	6	11	0	110	446	1	3	40.54
APE Knott	6	11	1	106*	364	1	3	36.40
KWR Fletcher	5	9	0	146	324	1	1	36.00
MH Denness	5	9	0	188	318	1	1	35.33
D Lloyd	4	8	0	49	196			24.50
DL Amiss	5	9	0	90	175		1	19.44
MC Cowdrey	5	9	0	41	165			18.33
FJ Titmus	4	8	0	61	138		1	17.25
CM Old	2	3	0	43	50			16.66
RGD Willis	5	10	5	15	76			15.20
BW Luckhurst	2	4	0	27	54			13.50
DL Underwood	5	9	0	30	111			12.33
P. Lever	2	4	2	14	24			12.00
M. Hendrick	2	4	2	8*	12			6.00
GG Arnold	4	7	1	14	22			3.66

England Bowling

	O	M	R	W	BB	Avg.
P Lever	61	8	214	9	6-38	23.77
RGD Willis	140.4	15	522	17	5-61	30.70
DL Underwood	185	42	595	17	7-113	35.00
CM Old	51.6	4	210	6	3-50	35.00
GG Arnold	141.1	23	528	14	5-86	37.71
AW Greig	167.5	19	681	17	4-56	40.05
FJ Titmus	122.3	30	360	7	2-43	51.42
MJ Hendrick	34.6	6	119	2	2-64	59.50

16
ESCAPE TO VICTORY

As the plane left Australia for New Zealand, some of the lads said they were glad to get out alive.
Mike Denness

Another flight. This one, heading for Wellington on the south-western tip of New Zealand's north island, had the feel of military personnel being airlifted to safety beyond enemy airspace. Mike Denness, who'd had cause to examine his leadership plenty of times during four months in Australia, heard the comments of teammates relieved to be in one piece and wondered if he should have been more aware of the extremity of their collective state of mind under heavy bombardment from Dennis Lillee and Jeff Thomson.

Yet hadn't he spent much of the previous four months, like his teammates, trying to deny the sheer bloody terror of facing those two without helmets? Hadn't he gone along with the party line that batsmen's concerns were more focused on the technique required to avoid dismissal than the fear of serious injury? Denness might have done some things wrong on this tour, but he could probably cut himself some slack on this occasion.

'They didn't come back to you and openly say, "I am worried about my health here," but where I did appreciate [it] was on the flight to New Zealand,' he remembered. 'A number of them said, "Thank goodness we got out of there alive." That is where it made me think that one or two of these lads were very serious about getting hit on the head.'

Denness had acknowledged after the sixth Test that 'our batsmen just didn't get enough runs; we encountered a new degree of pace out here and had no rest from it'. But it had taken escape from Australia for some to realise the burden under which they had been labouring. According to Dennis Amiss, 'It wasn't until we moved on to New Zealand that I personally felt the oppressive weight of Australia's yoke of pressure lifted from my shoulders.'

As New Zealand hove into view, Denness realised that the public would never understand the harrowing experience of batting under the conditions that had prevailed in Australia. All he and his teammates could do was prove that the runs they'd finally scored in Melbourne were more indicative of their abilities than the earlier collapses.

In truth, the two Test matches that could provide such an opportunity were not exactly being eagerly anticipated by the remaining MCC tourists. 'I think after that last match in Melbourne all we wanted to do was go home,' said Chris Old. In the end the two games added to the argument for removing England matches in New Zealand from the fag-end of an Ashes tour and giving them more prominence in their own right. Not, however, because they were compelling contests; more because a rain-hit two-match series proved so unsatisfactory. Even though Denness and Keith Fletcher continued their rehabilitation as international batsmen and England achieved one comprehensive victory, the series would have been erased instantly from memory if not for the near-tragic events on the final morning of the first Test.

David Lloyd and Bob Willis were already at home nursing injuries when the MCC players landed in New Zealand, almost four months after they had left England. Colin Cowdrey, meanwhile, had taken the gratitude and respect of management and teammates with him on his early journey back to England.

With Denness and Fletcher, the two heavy run-scorers in the final Australian Test, being given some rest and Peter Lever nursing an injured toe it meant that the team for the three-day match against Wellington saw Alan Knott playing as a specialist number five batsman and assistant manager AC Smith making up the numbers. As it transpired, play was only possible on the first two days, during which nothing of great note occurred, other than a fifty for Knott and a couple of low scores by Brian Luckhurst.

A new batsman was on his way to join the party in Auckland, venue for the first Test. Mentioned as candidates had been Peter Denning of Somerset and Nottinghamshire's Derek Randall, both considered rising talents. But the call went out to Lancashire's experienced opener Barry Wood, who had been making some good scores for an English Counties XI in the West Indies. He got to New

Zealand 63 hours after leaving the Caribbean. 'To show how tired I was,' he recalled, 'I got there in the afternoon and organised a net with a guy called Gary Troup.[50] He hit me on the fucking hand and I didn't think I was going to be able to play in the Test. I went back to the hotel and I slept for 24 hours.'

The fact that Wood was inked in to play despite jet-lag and bruising angered Luckhurst, a forgotten man since opening in the first two Test matches of the tour. 'It became blindingly obvious to me that I would not get a Test recall when we went on to New Zealand,' he recorded. Having been out for 23 and 9 against Wellington and seen Wood selected ahead of him, Luckhurst asked the tour management if he could take an early flight home. Permission was refused and he ended up fulfilling 12th-man duties in the first Test. 'The four-month tour felt like four years to me,' he said. 'It was a shame that my England career had to end that way, and I felt I should have been given the opportunity – like the other top-order batsman in the squad – of being able to score runs against New Zealand after battling so hard in Australia.'

Having watched closely the events across the Tasman Sea, as well as scoring their own limited-overs victory over the MCC tourists in Melbourne, New Zealand had high hopes of achieving the nation's first Test victory over England. They had come close at Trent Bridge and Lord's on their 1973 tour and, in Glenn Turner, had one of the world's finest opening batsmen, a man accustomed to piling up runs against English bowlers for Worcestershire. He had scored 1,332 runs at an average of 60.54 in the most recent county season. The home side would, however, be without promising young opening bowler Richard Hadlee because of injury. England, meanwhile, selected three specialist seamers, leaving Tony Greig to offer the spin-bowling support to Derek Underwood.

In front of an Eden Park crowd rendered teetotal by the banning of alcohol at the ground for the duration of the match, Denness won the toss and chose to bat, although New Zealand captain Bev Congdon preferred to field first anyway. By the end of the first day, it was Denness's judgement that was vindicated, with his team 319 for 3 and his own score an unbeaten 149.

---

50 Left-arm seamer who would make his New Zealand Test debut the following year.

On an easy-paced pitch with little of the Australian bounce the England batsmen knew they could play forward without any concerns. And when the ball was short, Denness, who could not lose his habit of making an initial movement of his back foot towards leg, had time to get back in line against the slower New Zealand seamers for his favoured square cut. Interestingly, the fact that he was spending long periods at the crease by this stage of the tour allowed for closer scrutiny of his technique, which was not necessarily favourable. *The Guardian*'s Henry Blofeld, for example, clearly hated some of what he was seeing. He said of Denness's cut, 'It is a stroke he plays with almost no control. He hits it with a flat bat, arms outstretched, not always along the ground, and he plays the delivery in such a way that if the ball should suddenly bounce unexpectedly he is unable to check the stroke.'

England's openers both missed out, with new arrival Wood remembering. 'I got a second-baller, one that reared off a length from Dayle Hadlee.' His memory flatters him, having been dismissed on his first ball, which was sure to have irked Luckhurst even more. John Edrich made 64 and shared a century stand with Denness, who was accompanied by Fletcher through to the close, by which time the Essex man was 76 not out.

Fletcher reached his century during a flurry of 30 runs in the first half-hour of the second day, the confidence that had gone missing until the final Test in Australia now coursing through every effortless cover drive. Denness, unable to recapture the fluency of the first day, fell just short of a double hundred for the second successive innings, skying Congdon to mid-on for 181 and ending the fourth-wicket partnership at 266.

Fletcher gave only one half-chance to the wicketkeeper before he was dismissed for 216, his highest score for England. His 443 minutes at the crease included 29 boundaries. With Greig having contributed a half-century, Denness was able to declare at 593 for 6 and see his team capture the important wicket of Turner prior to the close of the second day.

A third-day crowd of 22,000 saw Worcestershire batsman John Parker stubbornly resist England's bowlers, of whom Lever was conspicuously guilty of bowling too short to be effective. Parker reached stumps unbeaten on 121 out of 285 for 5, but with the wicket producing uneven bounce and signs of turn as the match progressed New Zealand had all but lost the match 24 hours later.

Greig, with five wickets, and Underwood, three, were able to exploit the conditions to hasten the home side to 326 all out late on the fourth morning. Following on, the home side offered up five more victims to the varied flight and spin of Greig and might have lost before stumps had the clocks not gone back the previous night, ensuring that bad weather denied England the final few minutes of scheduled play. Instead, New Zealand survived at 161 for 9, still 106 behind, meaning everyone having to traipse back to the ground after a belated rest day for England to take one wicket. As Blofeld noted, it left 'only the barest of formalities to be completed'. Little did anyone know the turn those formalities would take.

Old was excused the chore, having also missed the fourth day. 'I had been unwell on the rest day. I was very light-headed and was all over the place and it wasn't until a week later that the doctor told me that it was bronchial pneumonia. I got up to go for a walk on the morning of the rest day and had to walk around the hotel holding on to the wall to get myself back to bed.'

Two New Zealand debutants, batsman Geoff Howarth and seam bowler Ewen Chatfield, began the final day at the crease, having survived 30 minutes on the fourth evening. They had taken their partnership to 44 by the time Lever began his fifth over of the day.

Having seen Chatfield almost glove the ball to short leg, Lever and Denness brought in additional close fielders on either side of the wicket. 'This is the way to get him,' Lever told himself. When the fifth ball of Lever's over was pitched short, the Kiwis' number 11, an industrial chemist from Wellington, found it rearing towards his face. His left elbow went up instinctively and the ball deflected off his glove into his left temple. 'I lost sight of it and I knew it had hit me on the head,' said Chatfield, who staggered towards Edrich at short leg before slumping to his knees. Just as it looked as though he was about to lift himself to his feet his body went limp, as if he had gone to sleep. Which, in a sense, he had. His heart had stopped.

'He had just been playing forward and the bowler obviously thought a bouncer might make him play differently,' recalled Knott, who was one of the first England players to hurry to the batsman's aid. 'It was so slow to rise that it was almost like a slow-motion replay. Chatfield had a habit of turning his head to the side and ducking so that his eyes were not on the ball at all.'

The sight that greeted England's players was unforgettable and unsettling. 'When he turned I saw that his face had actually collapsed on one side like dissolving wax,' Knott continued. 'Next thing he was lying on the ground and because of his face I felt that he was in serious trouble.'

According to Denness, 'When someone has a stroke their whole face becomes distorted. When we pulled him over that is what it looked like. His body started to have convulsions.'

The New Zealand team had no medical staff on duty, not even a physiotherapist. While players called for help and Denness and others attempted to straighten Chatfield's legs, Bernard Thomas realised that it was down to him to act, running to the field with a local ambulance worker, John May. 'I was aware I was a guest and it was a New Zealand Cricket situation,' he recalled. 'But there was no doctor on the ground as the authorities had believed that as a swift finish was expected, it was not needed.'

Old remembered, 'I was sat in the crowd outside the dressing room watching when Chatfield got hit. The thing about it was that it wasn't a particularly quick bouncer. Bernard was out there like a shot because we knew something was serious and he did a wonderful job.'

Denness continued, 'We did not know what was happening to his tongue, whether he was losing it or not. His face was changing colour the whole time. After what seemed a long time, but was probably only a matter of seconds, his body suddenly stopped.'

Thomas realised quickly that Chatfield had swallowed his tongue but was informed that the stadium had no resuscitation equipment. He administered mouth-to-mouth resuscitation and heart massage. 'It was the worst case I have seen,' said Thomas, who had spent the previous three months on the edge of his seat, fearing he might be called to the aid of an England batsman in similar straits at any moment. 'His heart had stopped beating and technically that's the sign of dying.'

May added, 'If we hadn't got there when we did, he could have died. It was as serious as that.'

Denness called it 'the most terrible experience I have ever had on a cricket field'. While there had been no specific instruction to bowl bouncers at Chatfield, there had been general agreement about the need to keep him playing on the back foot, so effective had his forward defensive proved.

It was even worse for the bowler, Lever, who was on his knees and in tears, fearful that he had caused the death of an opponent. 'I bowled the ball too straight and he couldn't get out of the way,' he explained. 'When they were working on Ewen, it was the closest I had come to praying for a long time. I honestly thought I had killed him as I saw him lying there in convulsions. I felt sick and ashamed at what I had done and all I could think when I got back to the pavilion was that I wanted to retire.' Denness got some teammates to escort Lever from the field and gave instructions that nobody was to be allowed to talk to him.

In the meantime, it was down to the England players to inform others how serious the situation was. Denness was shocked at how unconcerned local officials appeared, and at how long it took for an ambulance to arrive – around 15 minutes. 'There was no apparent emergency about anything,' he said.

Knott recorded, 'When we were standing outside the dressing room some of the New Zealand team asked how Chatfield was. I replied that he could be dead and their horrified reaction brought tears to my eyes. I went into our dressing room and cried.' The enormity of a player facing such a trauma when the game was effectively won hit him hard. 'When you are immersed in a game you don't give a thought to any such injury occurring,' he said.

Meanwhile, local television had broadcast the incident but ended coverage soon afterwards with news that Chatfield had been rushed to hospital. Watching at home, Chatfield's parents made frantic and fruitless telephone calls trying to find out what was going on. In the end they called the police, who were able to identify the hospital being used. Chatfield's father, Neville, eventually managed to talk to a nurse who asked if he wanted to speak to his son. 'If I could have reached down the phone and kissed her, I would have,' he recalled.

Lever showered and left for the hospital, along with Thomas. Several members of the England team had a stiff drink in the dressing room to calm themselves, giving a toast of thanks when news came through via Thomas that Chatfield had recovered consciousness after about 20 minutes and was even able to recall the score. That Chatfield's retirement had given England victory by an innings and 83 runs seemed an irrelevant detail. Denness and Alec Bedser visited the hospital a couple of hours later. By that time, Chatfield, who was diagnosed with a hairline fracture of the skull, was able to sit up and talk to his visitors.

The next day he told reporters, 'My reflexes are not that quick. It's not really [Lever's] fault. I should have been able to get out of the way.' He even said of his opponent, 'He's a very nice fellow.' In future years Chatfield acknowledged, 'If it hadn't been for Bernard there's a good chance I wouldn't be around today', although he admitted to *Wisden* obituarist Richard Whitehead at the time of Thomas's death in 2018 that he had never discussed the incident with him, even when he had made subsequent tours of England.

Lever, meanwhile, made no attempt to disguise his own distress. 'All through your cricket life you wonder about the possibilities of somebody getting hurt,' he said. 'I don't feel like playing in the next Test and I won't be bowling any bouncers for a while.'

Coming so soon after the MCC batsmen's escapes against the Australian fast bowlers, not only did the irony register of it being England who inflicted the most serious blow of the tour, but the debate about short-pitched bowling was given fresh impetus. Only a few days earlier, Pakistan captain Intikhab Alam, no mean batsman, had been unable to avoid being stuck on the head by a bouncer from West Indies paceman Andy Roberts in Lahore.

TCCB secretary Donald Carr's response merely highlighted the difficulty in effectively policing the issue. 'This seems to have been purely an accident, but there has been a tendency throughout the world for an increasing use of short-pitched balls,' he noted. 'They are an accepted part of the fast bowler's armoury but should be strictly controlled by the umpires. It is impossible to legislate against all such deliveries but a procedure is laid down for the umpire to deal with intimidatory bowling. The difficulty is to obtain a consistent interpretation. This subject is of constant concern and nearly always a subject for discussion at the International Cricket Conference. I have no doubt it will be on the agenda of this year's meeting at Lord's this summer. One of the biggest difficulties is the variety in pitches in different parts of the world.'

EW Swanton highlighted an article attributed to Greg Chappell in *The Australian* only a few days before the Chatfield incident as evidence of the need for greater clarity and firmer application of the laws. Chappell had said, 'Perhaps a legislation could be passed clearly defining the umpires' actions. If, for example a bowler was felt to be bowling an excess of intimidatory deliveries he could be warned twice and then if he persisted prevented from bowling again in the innings.' Swanton was aghast that a senior player could apparently be ignorant that such a regulation already existed. 'There can only be two explanations of this extraordinary passage,' he said in *The Cricketer*. 'Either the Australian team were ignorant of the penalty, which in theory at least their fast bowlers might have brought upon themselves, or else (though this I hate to suggest) young Chappell might have been assisted by a ghost [writer] unfamiliar with cricket.'

Lever and Knott were among those suggesting that batsmen should wear protective headwear,[51] although Denness feared it might simply stir fast bowlers to bowl even more bouncers. Such comments from those at the heart of the debate were at least taken more seriously than that of Britain's sports minister, Dennis Howell, who said that his Labour government would look into including short-pitched fast bowling in public health and safety legislation.

In the meantime, cricket went on, of course, which in the case of the England team meant a second Test in Christchurch. After rain prevented any play on the first two days it was decided to start play the next day, which had originally been scheduled as the rest day – although not before complaints by the tourists to Bedser.

Acknowledging New Zealand's reliance on revenue from Test matches to finance its cricket, Bedser was keen to help out, but he recalled, 'To my dismay some of the England players opposed the plan, complaining they were at the end of a gruelling tour and were physically and mentally spent. I listened to the arguments and decided we would play and added that I did not think it too much of a hardship as they had not had to perform for two days. To be fair, spirits were low after being beaten by Australia and

---

51 Knott would be among the first players to try out the cumbersome motorcycle-style crash helmets experimented with in World Series Cricket in 1977-78.

the players wanted to get home but I thought it was not much to expect.'

He wrote in his autobiography, 'Top players sometimes overlook the fact that a large part of their livelihood springs from Test matches and tours, not to mention their commercial spin-off value, all against countries largely run by dedicated unpaid officials willing to give up their leisure for the benefit of the game at all levels.'

Denness, fighting for the rights of his players, offered a very different view, of course. When it was suggested to him by Bedser and Walter Hadlee, chairman of the New Zealand Cricket Council, that the rest day could be foregone, creating a six-day Test, he expressed concern at setting a precedent for future Tests. 'They refused to take no for an answer,' he said, adding, 'I had to safeguard the interests of a very tired touring party.'

Denness assumed he would be involved in discussion with Lord's before any decision was made but was informed by Bedser on the morning of the scheduled rest day that his men were required to play. 'I was staggered,' he said, mystified why he'd heard nothing from Lord's. 'I felt that a great deal more attention should have been paid to my views, which also expressed the feelings of the players.' And the New Zealand players, it might be added. For a while, he considered resigning as captain on the spot.

With play still not beginning until after lunch and the scheduled final day also being a victim of the weather, the match drifted towards a draw. Denness put New Zealand in and saw Geoff Arnold dismiss John Morrison with the first ball of the match. But by the time the home side were all out for 342 in the final session of the fourth day, there already appeared little prospect of a result.

'We only went through the motions,' Denness admitted, 'and I found it extremely difficult to motivate our players.' The length of the tour, the battering in Australia and the trauma of Auckland had taken their toll. Denness had 'little enthusiasm' for the match.

When England batted, Amiss took the opportunity to restore his battered confidence by scoring an unbeaten 164 out of 272 for 2, an innings full of his typically crisp drives. 'It didn't compensate for my feeling that I hadn't proved myself against the best in the world,' he confessed. Denness fought off his own lethargy to be 59 not out when the match was forced to a premature conclusion. Since dropping himself in Sydney he had scored 804 first-class runs in nine innings at an average of nearly 115. And still the cricket continued, with four matches left for the tourists to play. After rain wrecked two scheduled one-day internationals against New Zealand in Dunedin and Wellington the tourists began their journey home when they flew out of Auckland on 10 March. But after landing at Hong Kong's Kai Tak Airport there was no chance of a quick turnaround and a departure for England. Not until two more matches had been played – and won – against a Hong Kong President's XI and a Hong Kong XI could they resume their journey on 14 March, with Greig heading to South Africa to see family and join the DH Robins XI touring team.

The headlines that greeted the returning MCC party were not so different from the ones that sent them on their way five months earlier. IRA leaders were ordering their men 'back into action' after two members were shot dead by British troops in Belfast – in 'gross violation' of the month-old truce, they argued – while a 38-year-old Protestant was killed in County Down and five soldiers were injured by a landmine in Newry. The Chancellor of the Exchequer, Denis Healey, was said to be buoyed by February figures that showed a decreasing monthly trade deficit and raised hopes of improving Britain's economy without adding to inflation. Exports were reported to have risen 1.5 per cent in the previous three months, while imports had fallen 5 per cent.

On the industrial front, troops were to be deployed in Glasgow to remove the 70,000 tons of rubbish that had accumulated during the work stoppage by dustcart drivers, while the government was being advised by Sir Don Ryder, head of the National Enterprise Board, to support British Leyland workers' future pay claims only in return for union promises to keep factories free of wildcat strikes.

Northern Ireland, the economy, industrial relations. Five months away might have seemed an eternity when another daunting confrontation with Australia's fast bowlers was looming, but the

MCC players must have felt like they had barely left, so little had changed outside of the touring bubble.

Yet the 1974-75 Ashes tour had set in motion a period of great change in their own sport, the impact of which would be felt beyond just the celebrations of the Australians and the inquests of the English.

17
FOLLOWING ON

> *Watching the two [Lillee and Thomson] in action, it was easy to believe they were the fastest pair ever to have coincided in a cricket team. They would have been too good for better batting sides than Denness's. It is doubtful whether an England side could have been selected that might have given Australia a run for their money, no matter who the captain was.*
> **Wisden Cricketers' Almanack, 1976**

'Welcome Back!' read the purple italic type above the picture of the MCC squad, taken in whites and blazers while in Australia. What else could the menu for the post-tour dinner have said? 'Well done' would hardly have been appropriate; not with so many words dissecting the shortcomings in Australia being prepared for print since the players had returned almost two weeks earlier. In the rural setting of the Great Danes Hotel in Hollingbourne, Kent – a short trip for many of the squad – war stories were shared patiently with the guests, who included other county cricketers, MCC members, and major figures of the sports world, such as Frank Bough and Brian Johnston.

As well as this event, held to raise funds for Derek Underwood's benefit season, the players' post-tour commitments included dinner with Prime Minister Harold Wilson at Downing Street. It was a sombre event that bore little resemblance to the meeting of hungover and, in some cases, still inebriated members of the triumphant England team with Tony Blair after the historic 2005 Ashes.

This was not, after all, a time for celebration. It was an opportunity for polite condolences on the part of those meeting the vanquished troops and, for those able to operate from the bunkers of their studies and newspaper offices, a chance to fire their missiles of criticism and volleys of suggestions about where English cricket should go from here; to follow up on those on-the-spot verdicts during the tour with deeper, more damning assessment.

'There were even calls for a public inquiry to be established and explore how and why it all went so horribly wrong,' Dennis Amiss remembered. 'More column inches in the media seemed to be devoted to analysis of the tour than any other topic of the day, including Margaret Thatcher's defeat of Ted Heath in the Conservative Party leadership election.'

One of the tour's most consistent critics was the *Daily Mirror*'s Peter Laker, even if some of the time he'd been simply fulfilling his role as tabloid mouthpiece for change. 'The greatest English cricket disaster since the squires of Broadhalfpenny Down invented the game,' was one of his descriptions of the tour, calling the England team 'an apathetic bunch who have theorised themselves silly off the field and performed like clowns in the middle'.

In another piece, he argued, 'What has been lacking is the knowing guidance of a qualified someone in immediate touch with the modern game, if only to rekindle a flagging team spirit that was evident in the hands of a few isolated individuals.' Describing AC Smith's assistant manager role as 'superfluous' and recognising that Alec Bedser's duties had failed to extend beyond that of a tour administrator, he suggested that someone such as Ray Illingworth, Micky Stewart, Ken Barrington or Norman Gifford – all still or recently active in the game – should be guiding the England team.

Henry Blofeld focused once more on the batting failures. 'Players with the ability to bat for four or five hours and make 70 or so would have made Australia's task harder,' he said. On only one occasion in the first five Tests of the series – Greig's century at Brisbane – did an England batsman spend four hours at the crease. 'It has also cast doubt on the actual structure of domestic cricket in England,' he added.

The publication with the greatest space for reflection was *The Cricketer*, England's monthly publication on the sport. It duly presented a 'Think Tank' in which 27 ex-players, umpires, administrators, journalists and celebrity fans were invited to pass judgement on the state of English cricket. The gallery of headshots accompanying the piece, which stretched over multiple pages, betrayed the ageing profile of the panel. It would have been instructive to have heard from, say, a county professional, but none were included. Instead, a very old-school series of opinions were presented to readers.

Former England all-rounder Trevor Bailey, a *Test Match Special* radio regular, felt that 'our batting against pace, both technically and morally, had been cruelly exposed long before the advent of Thomson' and blamed too many overseas imports, the lack of facilities at schools, examination dates, and the bonus points system in county cricket. He also lamented the state of county coaching, saying, 'Only last summer a good young batsman, whom many believed would make the England team, complained that he had learned nothing in his two years on the staff.'

Charlie Elliott, a recently retired Test umpire, cited too much one-day cricket, too many overseas players in the English game and suggested that the sport was not as financially attractive as in 1930 when he began his career. Rather than calling for cricket to create a broader base from which to produce its players, he complained, 'Today's socio-political attitudes with regard to university entrance have dried up the flow of Oxbridge players to the top level.'

Sir Leonard Hutton blamed the 'shortage of good young players' on, among other things, 'full employment' – even though the number of jobless people in the UK had risen by a third since late 1973 and was, by April 1975, running at around 4.5 percent of the workforce.[52]

Within weeks, both Elliott and Hutton would be able to voice their views in England selection meetings.

Ted Dexter stuck to safer ground by saying that the right players existed but had not been picked, often being kept waiting in county cricket. 'The longer they compete only at county level without a taste of the big stuff the more stereotyped and unsuited to Test cricket they can easily become.'

Australian Neil Hawke, playing league cricket in England, thought it 'highly significant' that 'a great many average cricketers,

---

52 A figure that would climb to more than 10 percent early in the 1980s.

rejected by one county, all too easily find second careers with other counties to the exclusion of the new blood so urgently required'.

Tom Graveney complained that England's batsmen had no knowledge of where their off stump was, while more than one old-timer dated England's batting decline to the change in the lbw law in the 1930s, which offered a batsman immunity to dismissal if playing a shot outside off stump. CJ Barnett, the ex-Gloucestershire and England batsman, even called for the use of experienced players from the 'great days of the 1920s and early 1930s who played with and understood how Wally Hammond commanded the bowlers with his perfect back play' to tutor the modern generation.

Even that sounded reasonable when set against the eccentric call of broadcaster and writer for *The Times*, Alan Gibson, who urged, 'Sack the selection committee, sack the players, sack all those elitist writers whose newspapers sell less than two million a day.'

The final word went to comedian Tim Brooke-Taylor of *The Goodies* fame. 'Asking me for my views on the decline of English cricket is a bit like asking a navvy for his views on the Royal Ballet,' he admitted. Instead he offered a light-hearted view that England's batsmen were too intelligent for their own good, doing the sensible thing of moving away from the ball when Thomson bowled it. 'That fault lies with the education system,' he joked. 'Debase this and we can have a whole new breed.' It barely qualified as the most irrational opinion offered as the tour went into the history books.

Given their own time for contemplation, England's batsmen would take mixed memories into their retirements. Brian Luckhurst might well have remembered it as one tour too many for him, but David Lloyd, participating in his only England trip, would 'recall it fondly', even though it was 'a chastening experience'.

Even Amiss said, 'I don't regret being on the trip, even though it knocked my Test career for six to a certain extent. Even though I came back, it scarred me for a long time. When I played against Australia again it all came back, what we'd been through.' And he admitted, 'Whenever I see John Inverarity he says, "How are the nightmares going?"'

The 1975 summer schedule ensured that England would have to go through it all again very soon. On the strength of his runs in the latter part of the tour, Mike Denness narrowly retained his place as captain for the inaugural 60-over World Cup, staged over two weeks in England. The new selection panel – on which Barrington joined Hutton and Elliott under chairman Bedser after the removal of Jack Bond, Brian Taylor and Ossie Wheatley – had been split on that issue. Bedser favoured the retention of Denness and was supported by Hutton, while Barrington and Elliott wanted Greig, who'd also been championed by John Woodcock in *The Times*. 'The fortunes of the England team could benefit from a change of captain,' he wrote. 'Greig is a unifying figure, He has the ear of the players, too.'

It was entirely consistent with England's apparently disjointed management in the mid-1970s that Bedser was picking a team charged with winning a limited-overs World Cup immediately after being removed from the Benson and Hedges Cup's panel of man-of-the-match adjudicators because of his public criticism of one-day cricket. While in Wellington he had said, 'I was against it when it came in and I am still against it. I realise we need the money, but personally I never watch it. If you want cricket like that you might as well watch baseball.'

Bedser attempted to backtrack by claiming he had made his comments in a 'flippant manner', but it was an embarrassment that the sponsors of one of English cricket's major tournaments decided they could do without. Heaven knows what the England players thought of having their participation in cricket's first global one-day competition determined by a man who claimed never to watch them play the format.

Given a favourable draw, England qualified comfortably for a semi-final meeting with Australia, which must have sent shivers through a batting line-up that still included Denness, Amiss and Keith Fletcher. Under Headingley clouds and on a green pitch, it was left-arm swing bowler Gary Gilmour who skittled England, striking six times to leave the hosts 36 for 6. 'It was as black as arseholes and you couldn't see anything,' said Barry Wood. 'At Headingley they had no sight screen for Test matches and big one-day matches. They did for county matches, but for big games they took them away. Frank Hayes and I were both out offering no shot because we hadn't seen the ball.'

England were all out for 93, before Gilmour rescued Australia from 39 for 6 after destructive spells by Chris Old and John Snow, who was once again considered suitable to be picked at home. Denness had told the new selectors, 'Bowlers. First on my agenda is John Snow. Does anyone have any objections?'

After Australia lost a memorable Lord's final against West Indies, it was time for a four-Test Ashes rematch, for which Denness's status as captain was confirmed only for the first game at Edgbaston. 'I think they wanted Denness to fail just to get someone new in,' suggested Geoff Arnold, who would be playing in his final Test match. 'I think they felt they should give "Haggis" a last chance. The real nail in the coffin was when he stuck them in.'

With heavy rain heading for Birmingham, Denness consulted his senior players after winning the toss and invited Australia to bat. 'I remember him talking to Dennis Amiss for a long, long time about what to do,' said Derek Underwood. 'Dennis said that if the wicket had got anything in it, then it was going to be first thing on the first morning. Then, of course, it rained.'

Delaying the reacquaintance with Dennis Lillee and Jeff Thomson put England at risk of being caught on a wet track; these being the days when pitches were left uncovered after the start of the day's play. Boosted by some big hits from their lower order, Australia reached 359 in dry conditions before being dismissed on the second day.

And after one over of England's reply in mid-afternoon a storm drenched the wicket, leaving it in a treacherous state when play resumed later in the day. England were 83 for 7 by stumps, on their way to 101 all out and a heavy defeat. Amiss, Fletcher and Denness re-lived their winter horrors and Essex batsman Graham Gooch bagged a pair on his Test debut.

Ian Chappell had little sympathy for his opposite number. 'I never went and asked anybody about the toss,' he said. 'I don't necessarily think this would have happened in the Australian side, but it might: if you speak to the bowlers they will tell you to bat; you go to the batsmen and they will tell you to bowl. So why talk to them? You have got to make up your mind about how you are going to win the game.

'At Edgbaston it was black as buggery. I was told it was raining everywhere but at the ground. In the morning, before the game, I see Mike going round the ground. They have appointed him for only one game, which was diabolical. He is talking to the batsmen and talking to the bowlers and I am thinking. "Shit, mate, you are in trouble." We get to the middle and toss and he wins, and I am thinking, "This will be interesting," and he says, "You can have a hit."

'We would have batted anyway because I had one theory on captaincy in England and that was if it wasn't raining you had to bat because of that diabolical law that you couldn't cover the pitch until play was called off for the day, but you could cover the bowlers' run-ups. I mean, if you could think of a more stupid playing condition I would like to hear about it. You can't have bowlers running up on dry run-ups bowling on to a wet pitch. It doesn't make any sense at all. I certainly always believed that was there for Derek Underwood.

'For some reason it never rained while we batted. We were bowled out on the second morning and then it absolutely bucketed down. We are not talking English rain, we are talking Brisbane rain. To make matters even better for us, they had decided we could extend play at the end of the day if the light was good. So it thumped down for 45 minutes, which meant we now have Lillee and Thomson bowling on dry run-ups onto a wet pitch, and we are also going to extend play. It was bright sunshine late into the evening. We pissed them out for 101, won by an innings and they dropped Denness.'

So hurt was Denness by the reaction to his insertion of Australia that he'd spoken to Bedser before the end of the match and told him he was stepping down. Jim Laker had claimed in the *Daily Express* that one of the selectors had told him he was opposed to the captain's decision at the toss, which Denness saw as a serious breach of confidence.

A phone call was made to Greig. 'I have got something I would like to ask you,' said Bedser. 'Would you accept the captaincy for the rest of the series?'

Greig took up the offer and led England to three evenly-contested draws over the remainder of the summer. With unheralded Northamptonshire batsman David Steele becoming a national hero with the blunt, no-nonsense manner in which he took on Lillee and Thomson, and Greig displaying the charismatic leadership his supporters knew he possessed, English cricket had managed to save some face.

Chappell returned home with the Ashes still in Australian possession and his own future settled in his mind. During the 1974-75 series he'd spoken of 'the stresses of captaincy' and admitted, 'I've never felt a series weighing me down as much.'

He explained, 'I am not a confrontational person but if you push me I am going to push back. That is part of the reason why I resigned as captain: one, because of what I always said about the bastards not getting me; and two, I was rooted, mate. The changing bowlers, moving the field around, pinning up the batting order up, that doesn't wear you out. But I always felt captaincy was two parts. Captaincy was on-field leadership and also off the field. I always felt that I had put a lot of time into that, which I was prepared and happy to do because I quite enjoyed sitting around talking with the guys because they were good company. But by the end of it I was absolutely rooted and a lot of that was down to the constant fighting with the Board.

'I always felt that if I'd had six months between the end of the 1975 series and the start of the next series I might have made it, but I knew that I had no chance of being the captain that I had to be against the West Indies. I felt the only way we were going to beat them was by attacking them and I was worn down. I am not going to be as attacking as I think I need to be. I had seen the West Indies in that final in '75 and I knew how good they were. Unfortunately for them I don't think they knew how good they were in '75-76 but they learned pretty bloody quickly. The constant fight had worn me down.'

It would be brother Greg who led his country to a series win over West Indies even more emphatic than that of the previous season. Thomson took 29 wickets and Lillee 27 as Australia stormed to their 5-1 victory. West Indies captain Clive Lloyd would soon resolve to base his attack purely on pacemen; the more the merrier.

So it was that Greig's second summer as England captain began with the ill-judged promise to make West Indies 'grovel', and ended with him on his knees in front of celebrating Caribbean fans at The Oval after a four-man fast attack secured the tourists' 3-0 series win in a five-match summer. The fifth Test had at least seen redemption achieved by Amiss, who, after a year out of the England team, returned with an exaggerated back-and-across technique that earned him a double-century against an attack that featured a rampant Michael Holding on his way to 14 wickets in the match.

'I have often been asked how a batsman whose record against the West Indies, Pakistan, New Zealand and India was as good as the best of his generation could fail so spectacularly and consistently over the years against Australia,' Amiss pondered in his autobiography more than four decades later. 'I was never able to overcome the psychological advantage that the Aussies established over me.'

Amiss would be back at the top of the English order as Greig's team achieved an impressive 3-1 series win in India in 1976-77, by which time Fletcher – discarded after Edgbaston in 1975 – had regained his place as an expert against spin. It meant that there were familiar faces in the Australian bowlers' sights when England travelled from the subcontinent to Melbourne for the Centenary Test in March 1977, although Amiss was shielded from the new ball by being placed at number four in the order.

By this time, though, Thomson was an absentee from the Australian team, his best Test years behind him after a collision with Alan Turner in the field against Pakistan dislocated his right shoulder. Never again would England face him and Lillee in harness. Woodcock had shown considerable prescience when he wrote of Lillee and Thomson in his summary of the 1974-75 series for *Country Life* magazine, 'To get them simultaneously as fit as they were for most of the winter is never going to be easy and once the edge goes off their fitness they are not such a redoubtable pair.'

The celebratory atmosphere around the Melbourne contest – which saw the home team replicate their 45-run victory of the first Test a century earlier – lasted only until the early stages of Australia's Ashes tour that summer, when news of Kerry Packer's plan for World Series Cricket emerged. The seeds sown by Australian cricket's profits in the 1974-75 Ashes series had blossomed in the garden of Packer's grudge against the ACB for not giving him the chance to bid for its television rights. The fruit they bore proved toxic to cricket's establishment, which would now lose its star players to Packer's employ. Ironically, there would also be a role in WSC for Denness, who was employed as manager of the World XI side that would compete against Packer's Australian and West Indies teams over a series of 'Supertests' and one-day matches.

The fall-out from the breaking news and the discussion of its implications for global cricket provided an unavoidable backdrop to the 1977 Ashes series. Greig was stripped of the England captaincy for his role as World XI leader and Packer recruiter and saw his successor, Mike Brearley, win back the urn with a 3-0 victory over a distracted Australian team.

Returning to the England side with a century in the third Test was a certain Geoffrey Boycott, who proceeded to score his 100th first-class century in the fourth Test on his home ground of Headingley. It was a reminder to Denness of the talent he had been unable to call upon almost three years earlier. Fletcher, who never believed the accusations that Boycott's absence was a result of deliberately avoiding the fastest bowlers, said, 'At the very least he would have been obdurate, although given how many balls wide of the stumps Thomson delivered, the rate of scoring would have been excruciatingly slow.'

When Brearley's team went on to defeat a second-string Australia 5-1 in the 1978-79 Ashes, it proved too much for the ACB's finances to bear, especially with WSC, after a shaky start, finally beginning to win the hearts of the Australian fans in its second season. The introduction of floodlit cricket with white balls and coloured kits, the stamp of authenticity offered by the use of Sydney Cricket Ground, and a public relations assault spearheaded by the infuriatingly catchy 'C'mon Aussie C'mon' song meant that the ACB was ready to give Packer what he wanted in order to get its players back.

Packer, who was easily able to absorb the A$6 million his venture had cost, was not only given the right to televise Test cricket on his Channel 9 network, but his subsidiary company, PBL Sports Pty Ltd, was granted exclusive promotional rights to Australian cricket for ten years for A$1.7 million per year. One-day internationals would be played under the World Series Cricket banner, part of a packed programme of Tests and one-day internationals that mirrored the WSC season format.

For the Australian players, a more appropriate level of compensation had been established under Packer; in effect the financial victory Ian Chappell had gone looking for. But for some there was a price to pay. Greg Chappell blamed the exhausting merry-go-round of high pressure matches and constant travel for being so 'strung out' that he instructed brother Trevor to bowl the final ball underarm to ensure an Australian victory against New Zealand in one of the World Series Cup finals of 1980-81. 'I wasn't fit to captain a row boat,' he admitted.

'When I saw the 1980-81 programme I felt that World Series Cricket had got us nowhere,' he explained. 'It was absolutely mad. Travel days, when you might have to make two connecting flights from one side of Australia to the other, were seen as days off for us. It was ridiculous, verging on a form of punishment.' He would stay at home when Australia returned to England in 1981 to lose a series dominated by the heroics of Ian Botham, who at times treated a 32-year-old Lillee with the same contempt that the bowler had shown for England's batsmen in 1974-75.

Yet Chappell's discontent with the new structure of Australian international cricket had no more impact on the game's rulers than his brother's complaints about low pay had in the previous decade. The game had changed irrevocably. It was reaching the levels of commerciality that Ian Chappell had always known it could exploit; it had a new on-field look thanks to batsmen now being wise enough to protect their heads against the type of bowling Lillee and Thomson had normalised; and was played against the rowdy, rumbunctious backdrop that had been established in 1974-75.

The revolution was not merely televised by Packer but accompanied by a soundtrack featuring two of the key insurgents, Ian Chappell and Tony Greig, who would trade insults and opinions in the commentary booth for three decades as fiercely as they had fought on the field. Their voices were a continual reminder of how deeply the sport, as it moved into the 21st century, had been shaped by one unforgettable Ashes series.

ACKNOWLEDGEMENTS

An author who was only 13 years old at the time and half a world away from the events about which he is writing inevitably relies heavily on the experiences of others. Thank you, therefore, to those I have spoken to about the 1974-75 Ashes series, either specifically for this book or in connection with previous titles, and whose insight and memories have helped shape much of this story: Dennis Amiss, Geoff Arnold, Robin Bailhache, Ian Chappell, Ross Edwards, Brett Gosper, Alan Knott, Peter Lever, David Lloyd, Rick McCosker, Chris Old, Ian Redpath, Barry Wood, and the late Mike Denness, John Edrich, Tony Greig, Derek Underwood and Bob Willis. I am also indebted to Bryan Henderson at Sky Sports for giving me access to an archive of interviews with players involved in the series, most of which have never been broadcast.

The wealth of written material I have consulted during my research is acknowledged in this book's bibliography. My apologies for any omissions – which also applies to the list of people who have helped in various other ways, including Jennie Decker, David Kelly, Tom Rawlings, John Rolfe, Gerry Schembri and Jon Surtees. The staff at the MCC Library at Lord's were wonderfully helpful in digging scorebooks, committee meeting minutes and other assorted documents out of their vaults.

Richard Whitehead was a constant sounding board and even suggested the title, while Matt Thacker and his team at Fairfield Books shared my vision for the book from its very beginnings. My great thanks are due to Stephen Chalke for casting his expert eye over the text and making numerous valuable suggestions. My agent, David Luxton, has guided the project with his usual expertise and I thank him and his colleagues at DLA for their continued support.

I must also recognise the patience and friendship of Andrea and Mark Hallam. A good portion of this book was written during the months I spent flat on my back in their spare room while waiting for, and recovering from, spinal surgery – at a time when our own house was being renovated. The regular arrival of tea and biscuits was welcomed in the manner I imagine England's batsmen seized upon drinks intervals in the heat of their battles against the Aussie fast bowlers.

Thank you as always to my family: daughters Amy, Sarah, Laura and Karis, grandchildren Jacob, Oscar and Heidi, and especially my wife, Sara. Far from having more of me to herself since I left full-time employment she has had to become even more indulgent of my passions for writing and cricket. That she does so with the grace and humour of Colin Cowdrey in the face of onslaught by Jeff Thomson is more than I deserve.

MCC TOUR RESULTS, 1974-75

(For full Ashes Test match details, see Scorecards section that follows).

Match 1: v South Australian Country (not first-class), Port Lincoln. SA Country XI 7-1. *Match Abandoned.*

Match 2: v South Australia, Adelaide. South Australia 247 (JE Nash 67, M Hendricks 57; DL Underwood 4-64) and 320 (IM Chappell 78, GJ Cosier 65; M Hendrick 5-68); MCC 349-9 dec, (JH Edrich 58, AW Greig 54; TJ Jenner 5-110) and 82-3. *Match Drawn.*

Match 3: v Victorian Country XI (not first-class), Warrnambool. MCC 158 for 4 dec. (BW Luckhurst 94); Victorian Country XI 83-5 (C Gaut 50). *Match Drawn.*

Match 4: v Victoria, Melbourne. Victoria 293-8 dec. (WL Stillman 61, RJ Bright 53) and 174-8; MCC 392-9 dec. (DL Amiss 152, BW Luckhurst 116; MHN Walker 4-71). *Match Drawn.*

Match 5: v Capital Territory and Southern NSW XI (not first-class), Canberra. MCC 159-2 dec. (D. Lloyd 66, JH Edrich 51); Capital Territory XI 58-1. *Match Drawn.*

Match 6: v New South Wales, Sydney. NSW 338 (IC Davis 91, A Turner 72, GJ Gilmour 59*; CM Old 4-64) and 174 (RB McCosker 56; AW Greig 5-55); MCC 332-7 dec. (KWR Fletcher 79, AW Greig 70) and 181-4 (D Lloyd 80, KWR Fletcher 57*). *MCC won by 6 wickets.*

Match 7: v Queensland Country XI (not first-class), Nambour. *Match Abandoned*

Match 8: v Queensland, Brisbane. MCC 258 (FM Francke 4-93) and 175 (G. Dymock 5-48); Queensland 226 (GS Chappell 122; M Hendrick 4-49) and 161 (GS Chappell 51; CM Old 4-44). *MCC won by 46 runs.*

Match 9: v South Queensland Country XI (not first-class), Southport. South Queensland Country XI 52 (AW Greig 5-1); MCC 53-0. *MCC won by 10 wickets.*

MATCH 10: FIRST TEST v Australia, Brisbane. *Australia won by 166 runs.*

Match 11: v Western Australia, Perth. Western Australia 265-8 dec. (WJ Edwards 50) and 346-5 dec. (RJ Inverarity 99, GD Watson 86*, RS Langer 62*); MCC 314-5 dec (AW Greig 167*, APE Knott 62) and 177 (AW Greig 57; RG Paulsen 7-41). *Western Australia won by 120 runs.*

Match 12: v Western Australian Country XI (not first-class), Geraldton. MCC 214-6 dec. (BW Luckhurst 76*); WA Country XI 153-9. *Match Drawn.*

MATCH 13: SECOND TEST v Australia, Perth. *Australia won by 9 wickets.*

Match 14: v South Australia, Adelaide. South Australia 270-6 dec. (GJ Cosier 75, AJ Woodcock 62; DL Underwood 5-58) and 222-6 dec. (RH Drewer 61); MCC 277-2 dec. (MH Denness 88*, MC Cowdrey 78, DL Amiss 73) and 210-6 (DL Amiss 57). *Match Drawn.*

MATCH 15: THIRD TEST v Australia, Melbourne. *Match Drawn.*

Match 16: v Australia (One-Day International, 40 overs), Melbourne. Australia 190 (CM Old 4-57); England 191-7 off 37.1 overs (DL Lloyd 49, DL Amiss 47). *England won by 3 wickets.*

MATCH 17: FOURTH TEST v Australia, Sydney. *Australia won by 171 runs.*

Match 18: v Tasmania, Hobart. MCC 204-4 dec. (BW Luckhurst 59); Tasmania 189-5. *Match Drawn.*

Match 19: v Tasmania, Launceston. Tasmania 164 and 105; MCC 341-4 dec. (MH Denness 157*, BW Luckhurst 74). *MCC won by an innings and 72 runs.*

Match 20: v New South Wales, Sydney. MCC 315-5 dec. (MH Denness 99, KWR Fletcher 85, DL Amiss 52, D Lloyd 51) and 266-7 dec. (DL Amiss 124, APE Knott 79); NSW 157 (CM Old 7-59) and 237 (DJ Colley 90). *MCC won by 187 runs.*

MATCH 21: FIFTH TEST v Australia, Adelaide. *Australia won by 163 runs.*

Match 22: v Northern New South Wales XI (not first-class), Newcastle. Northern NSW XI 251-5 dec. (C. Baker 73*, OJ Bush 63) and 270-6 dec. (G Davies 82, R, Haworth 65*, OJ Bush 50); MCC 281-5 dec. (DL Amiss 74, JH Edrich 66*, BW Luckhurst 50) and 242-6 (MC Cowdrey 85, BW Luckhurst 58). *MCC won by 4 wickets.*

Match 23: v New Zealand, Gillette Cup winners (not first-class, 40 overs), Melbourne. New Zealand 262-8; MCC 196 (AW Greig 79). *New Zealand won by 66 runs.*

MATCH 24: SIXTH TEST v Australia, Melbourne. *England won by an innings and 4 runs.*

Match 25: v Wellington, Basin Reserve. MCC 218 (APE Knott 56) and 52-1; Wellington 188-6 dec. (JFM Morrison 80; GA Newdick 57). *Match Drawn.*

Match 26: v New Zealand, First Test, Auckland. England 593-6 dec. (KWR Fletcher 216, MH Denness 181, JH Edrich 64, AW Greig 51*); New Zealand 326 (JM Parker 121, JFM Morrison 58; KJ Wadsworth 58; AW Greig 5-98) and 184 (JFM Morrison 58; GP Howarth 51*; AW Greig 5-51). *England won by an innings and 83 runs.*

Match 27: v New Zealand, Second Test, Christchurch. New Zealand 342 (GM Turner 98, KJ Wadsworth 58); England 272-2 dec. (DL Amiss 152*, MH Denness 59*). *Match Drawn.*

Match 28: v New Zealand (One-Day International), Dunedin. England 136; New Zealand 15-0. *Match Abandoned.*

Match 29: v New Zealand (One-Day International), Basin Reserve, Wellington. New Zealand 227 (BE Congdon 101; P. Lever 4-35); England 35-1. *Match Abandoned.*

Match 30: v Hong Kong Cricket Association President's XI (not first-class), Hong Kong. MCC 239-3 dec. (KWR Fletcher 103); President's XI 155 (KWR Fletcher 4-36). *MCC won by 84 runs.*

Match 31: v Hong Kong (not first-class), Hong Kong. MCC 234-3 dec. (DL Amiss 101, B. Wood 68); Hong Kong 132 (DL Underwood 4-13, FJ Titmus 4-43). *MCC won by 102 runs.*

BIBLIOGRAPHY

Amiss, Dennis, with James Graham-Brown, *Not Out at Close of Play: A Life in Cricket* (The History Press, 2021)

Arlott, John, *The Ashes 1972* (Pelham Books, 1972)

Bedser, Alec, *Twin Ambitions: An Autobiography* (Stanley Paul, 1986)

Benvenuti, Andrea *Anglo-Australian Relations and the Turn to Europe, 1961-72* (Royal Historical Society, 2008)

Boycott, Geoffrey, *Boycott: The Autobiography* (Macmillan, 1987)

Brayshaw, Ian, *Lillee and Thommo: The Deadly Pair's Reign of Terror* (Hardie Grant, 2017)

Cashman, Richard, *'Ave a Go, Yer Mug!'* (Harper Collins Australia, 1984)

Chappell, Greg, with Malcolm Knox, *Fierce Focus* (Hardie Grant, 2012)

Cowdrey, Colin, *MCC: The Autobiography of a Cricketer* (Hodder and Stoughton, 1976)

Cowdrey, Colin, *Tackle Cricket* (Stanley Paul, 1964)

Davie, Michael, *Anglo-Australia Attitudes* (Martin Secker & Warburg, 2000)

Denness, Mike, *I Declare* (Arthur Baker, 1977)

Eddy, Dan, *Brilliance and Beauty: Richmond, Carlton and the Grand Finals of 1969, 1972 and 1973* (Slattery Books, 2023)

Fletcher, Keith, *Ashes to Ashes: The Rise, Fall and Rise of English Cricket* (Headline, 2005)

Fletcher, Keith, *Captain's Innings: An Autobiography* (Stanley Paul, 1983)

Haigh, Gideon *The Cricket War: The Inside Story of Kerry Packer's World Series Cricket* (The Text Publishing Company, 1993)

Jenner, Terry with Ken Piesse, *T.J. Over The Top: Cricket, Prison and Warnie* (Information Australia, 1999)

Knott, Alan, *It's Knott Cricket: The Autobiography of Alan Knott* (Macmillan, 1985)

Lillee, Dennis with Ian Brayshaw, *Back to the Mark* (Staney Paul, 1974)

Lillee, Dennis, *Menace: The Autobiography* (Headline, 2003)

Lillee, Dennis, *My Life in Cricket* (Methuen Australia, 1982)

Lloyd, David, *The Ashes According to Bumble* (HarperSport, 2013)

Luckhurst, Brian with Mark Baldwin, *Boot Boy to President* (KOS Media, 2004)

Mallett, Ashley, *Thommo Speaks Out: The Authorised Biography of Jeff Thomson* (Allen & Unwin, 2009)

Mallett, Ashley with Ian Chappell, *Hitting Out: The Ian Chappell Story* (Orion, 2005)

Marsh, Rodney, *The Gloves of Irony* (Pelham Books, 1982)
Marsh, Rodney with Ian Brayshaw, *You'll Keep* (Hutchinson Publishing, 1975)
Martin-Jenkins, Christopher, *Assault on the Ashes (Macdonald and Jane's, 1975)*
Oldham, Sam, *Without Bosses: Radical Australian Trade Unionism in the 1970s* (Interventions Inc., 2020)
Pressley, Alison, *Living in the 70s: Being Young in Australia in an Extraordinary Decade* (Random House Australia, 2002)
Redpath. Ian with Neill Phillipson, *Always Reddy* (Garry Sparke and Associates, 1976)
Snow, John, *Cricket Rebel* (Hamlyn, 1976)
Swanton, EW, *Swanton in Australia: With MCC 1946-1975* (William Collins Sons & Co, 1975)
Thomson, Jeff with David Frith, *Thommo* (Angus & Robertson, 1980)
Titmus, Fred, *My Life in Cricket* (John Blake, 2005)
Tossell, David, *Grovel! The Summer and Legacy of 1976* (Know The Score, 2007)
Tossell, David, *Tony Greig: A Reappraisal of English Cricket's Most Controversial Captain* (Pitch Publishing, 2011)
Turbervill, Huw, *The Toughest Tour: The Ashes Away Series Since The War* (Aurum, 2013)
Tyson, Frank, *Test of Nerve: Test Series 1974-75, Australia versus England* (Manark Pty, 1975)
Walters, Doug, with Ken Laws, *The Doug Walters Story* (Rigby Publishers, 1981)
Whitehead, Richard (editor), *The Times on The Ashes* (The History Press, 2015)
Willis, Bob, *Lasting the Pace* (Willow Books, 1985)
Willis, Bob with Patrick Murphy, *The Cricket Revolution: Test Cricket in the 1970s* (Sidgwick & Jackson, 1980)

Other publications
Canberra Times, *Country Life*, *Cricketer* (Australia), *Daily Express*, *Daily Herald*, *Daily Mail*, *Daily Mirror*, *Melbourne Age*, *Sunday Telegraph*, *Sydney Daily Mirror*, *Sydney Morning Herald*, *Sydney Sunday Telegraph*, *The Cricketer*, *The Australian*, *The Daily Telegraph*, *The Guardian*, *The Independent*, *The Observer*, *The Sun*, *The Times*, *Time* (Australia), *Wisden Cricketers' Almanack* (various years).

Websites
Cricket Archive, ESPNCricinfo.

ASHES SCORESHEETS, 1974-75
(UNOFFICIAL)

AUTHOR'S NOTE

In the days before computerised scoring, it is inevitable that over an intense five days of Test cricket the scorers were prone to very occasional lapses. Anyone who has had their concentration broken while doing a stint in the scorebook for their club side must marvel at the focus achieved by men such as JE Sandes, who scored the MCC tour without recourse to technological aids, relying more on a pencil sharpener and an additional red biro.

In digging into the official scorebooks and footage of the 1974-75 series to construct completely unofficial linear scoresheets – the style made famous around that time by Bill Frindall – I unearthed occasional minor inconsistencies, usually in the total of individual balls faced compared to official records. In such instances I re-checked my ball-by-ball reconstructions multiple times, especially where Mr Sandes's less than pristine numerical notations were at their most impenetrable. Balls faced by the batsmen are not logged in the official scorebook and appear to have been calculated by some other method.

One obvious error is in the second innings of the fourth Test, where David Lloyd is credited in the official records with facing eight balls fewer than he did, the scorer seemingly having forgotten to factor in a maiden over in calculating his balls faced.

There are also instances where the official scorebook records either seven-ball or nine-ball overs, including one of each in Australia's second innings in the third Test. I had to gauge whether that was umpire or scorer error using available information. Where it appears to be down to the umpire – as in most instances – I retained the nine or seven balls in my scoresheets. Incidentally, in that same match, England's Mike Hendrick broke down after six balls of an over and play resumed with a fresh over, rather than another bowler completing Hendrick's set of eight balls.

The biggest challenge was in Australia's first innings at the fourth Test, where the official MCC bowling and batting scoresheets contradict each other. Greg Chappell is noted in the scorebook as being 9 not out at tea, which is correct according to the ball-by-ball bowling details I used to construct my own scoresheets. Yet the scorebook also notes him having started his innings 3, 2, 2, 4 – which means he would never have been 9 not out. More importantly, a single early in the innings of Ross Edwards seems to have been incorrectly credited to Chappell, and this was adopted by TV and newspapers etc. I found no evidence of an incident that would account for this. Without giving the single to Edwards, you no longer have the batsmen at the correct end for subsequent events. Curiously, although the single is missing from Edwards's tally in the scorebook, it does not appear on Chappell's ledger either. The only reason Chappell's score in the official book adds up to the accepted tally of 84 (rather than my 83) is because of that misrepresentation early in his innings.

Confused? Imagine how I felt. Anyway, I followed my policy of entering my own figures in my scoresheets and innings summaries. I was most relieved when I checked the Australian scorer Charles Davis's website [*https://www.sportstats.com.au/bloghome.html*] and found that his own records had uncovered the same mistake. He also notes various similar problems of apparent miscalculation and almost illegible scorebook entries. Incidentally, even Frindall's published scorebooks of subsequent Test series show discrepancies with the official statistics.

All of this is by way of explaining some minor differences to the published records in my scorecards rather an attempt to denigrate the work of Mr Sandes. It is thanks to his assiduous recording of so much detail, such as timing of bowling changes, that I was able to attempt a linear reconstruction from the traditional scorebook. That I did so was initially for my own benefit, to immerse myself in the ebb and flow of play and to create a more authentic narrative around the action. Having done so, and given the publication of Frindall's scoresheets in the latter half of the 1970s – beginning with the Ashes series of 1975 – I thought it would be of interest to the more statistically-minded reader to have them reproduced here.

Those familiar with the Frindall scoresheets will see some differences in presentation; for example, a running tally of the bowlers' figures on the ball-by-ball sheets in order to save space rather than on a separate page. Most notably, producing them on a keyboard rather than by hand meant some compromise on symbols used. Those you will see most frequently here are: n = no ball (n3, for example, means three runs were scored off a no-ball); L = leg bye; b = bye; + = wide). Anything else should be obvious in context.

As a reminder, at the time of the 1974-75 tour, wides and no-balls did not count against the bowlers' individual figures, which is why you will see maiden overs recorded when such extras have been conceded. Also, when runs were scored off a no-ball only the runs scored by the batsmen were recorded, not an additional extra, which is why the running tally of no-balls bowled in some innings is higher than the runs from no-balls recorded in the extras column.

FIRST TEST MATCH

AUSTRALIA v **ENGLAND** at THE GABBA, BRISBANE on NOVEMBER 29-30, DEC 1, 3, 4 1974

1st DAY TIME	BOWLERS Stanley Street (S) NAME	BOWLERS Vulture Street (N) NAME	BATSMEN UMP: T. BROOKS (S) NAME	B	4/6	BATSMEN UMP: R. BAILHACHE (N) NAME	B	4/6	NOTES	AUSTRALIA 1ST Toss AUS O	R	W	LBat	RBat	Ext
			REDPATH			W.EDWARDS								
11:00	WILLIS		.2.....	8						1	2	0	2	2	
	1-0-2-0	LEVER				.n......2	9		nb1	2	5	0	2	2	1
	WILLIS	1-0-2-0	....	16					M1	3	5	0	2	2	
11:19	2-1-2-0	HENDRICK				...2.W	15			7	1	2	4		
11:20		1-0-5-1				I.CHAPPELL									
			.3	18						4	10	1	5	0	
11:23	WILLIS		..W	21							10	2	5	0	
11:24	3-2-2-1		G.CHAPPELL												
			.....	5					M2	5	10	2	0	0	
		HENDRICK				....	8		M3	6	10	2	0	0	
	WILLIS	2-1-5-1	1	6		....	15			7	11	2	1	0	
	4-2-3-1	HENDRICK	1 ...1	11		..1	18			8	14	2	3	1	
	LEVER	3-1-8-1	..3 ...3	18		1	19			9	21	2	9	2	
	2-0-9-0	HENDRICK	.......n 1	27					nb2	10	23	2	10	2	2
	LEVER	4-1-9-1	1	28		....	26			11	24	2	11	2	
12:00	3-0-10-0	HENDRICK	....n.2 2.	37					nb3	12	29	2	15	2	3
	WILLIS	5-1-13-1				1	34			13	30	2	15	3	
	5-2-4-1	GREIG	.....	42		..1	37			14	31	2	15	4	
	WILLIS	1-0-1-0				.....2..	45			15	33	2	15	6	
	6-2-6-1	GREIG	1	49		.	46			16	34	2	16	6	
	UND'WOOD	2-0-2-1	1	54		...	49			17	35	2	17	6	
	1-0-1-0	GREIG	....2...	62						18	37	2	19	6	
	UND'WOOD	3-0-4-0				....	57		M4	19	37	2	19	6	
	2-1-1-0	GREIG	2......3	70						20	42	2	24	6	
	HENDRICK	4-0-9-0	.....4 2.	78	1				1st 4	21	48	2	30	6	
	6-1-19-1	GREIG				4.......	65	1		22	52	2	30	10	
	HENDRICK	5-0-13-0	...1 2..	85		1	66			23	56	2	33	11	
1:04	7-1-23-1		LUNCH			LUNCH									
1:41		GREIG	.1	87		..1 .6.	72	1/1	1st 6	24	64	2	34	18	
	LEVER	6-0-21-0	...4...L	95	2				lb1	25	69	2	38	18	4
	4-0-14-0	GREIG	.4..4...	103	4					26	77	2	46	18	
	LEVER	7-0-29-0	..1	106		1	77			27	79	2	47	19	
	5-0-16-0	GREIG	4 3	108	5	......	83		50:123m 107 balls	28	86	2	54	19	
	LEVER	8-0-36-0	2 n......1	116		.	84		nb4	29	90	2	57	19	5
	6-0-19-0	GREIG	....	124					M5	30	90	2	57	19	
	LEVER	9-1-36-0	....	128		.4 2 1	88	2/1		31	97	2	57	26	
	7-0-26-0	GREIG				...4.2.3	96	3/1		32	106	2	57	35	
	HENDRICK	10-1-45-0	..1	131		..1 .1	101			33	109	2	58	37	
2:36	8-1-26-1	UND'WOOD	W	132		.1	103		• 100 p		110	3	58	38	
		3-1-3-1	R.EDWARDS												
2:40			1	5						34	111	3	1	38	
	HENDRICK		1	12		1	104			35	113	3	2	39	
	9-1-28-1	UND'WOOD				...4..4 1	112	5/1		36	122	3	2	48	
	HENDRICK	4-1-12-1	....	16		.2.3	116		50:177m 114 balls	37	127	3	2	53	
	10-1-33-1	UND'WOOD	2 1	18		1	122			38	131	3	5	54	
	WILLIS	5-1-16-1	...1	22		4...	126	6/1		39	135	3	6	58	
	7-2-11-1	UND'WOOD	1	23		....	133			40	136	3	7	58	
	WILLIS	6-1-17-1	..1 ...1	30		1	134			41	139	3	9	59	
	8-2-14-1	UND'WOOD	.n......1	38		n.	136		nb6	42	143	3	10	59	7
	LEVER	7-1-18-1	..1 ..	43		..1	139			43	145	3	11	60	
	8-0-28-0	UND'WOOD				....(n4).4 n..	149	8/1	nb8	44	154	3	11	68	8
	LEVER	8-1-26-1	1	50		1	150			45	156	3	12	69	
	8-0-30-0	UND'WOOD				.1	152			46	157	3	12	70	
3:44		9-1-27-1	TEA			TEA									
	HENDRICK					....	160		M6	47	157	3	12	70	
	11-2-33-1	UND'WOOD	...3	60		....	164			48	160	3	15	70	

Time	Bowler	Figures	Bowler	Figures	Over	Runs	Extras	Wkt	Score	Wkts	Batter1	Batter2	Extras
	HENDRICK	10-1-30-1	....		68			M7	49	160	3	15	70
		12-3-33-1	UND'WOOD			...4 4...	172	10/1	50	168	3	15	78
	HENDRICK	11-1-38-1	.L 2.		72	1	176	lb2	51	172	3	17	79	9
		13-3-36-1	UND'WOOD			..2....1	184		52	175	3	17	82
	WILLIS	12-1-41-1	2....L	77		1..	187	lb3	53	179	3	19	83	10
		9-2-17-1	UND'WOOD	4.....4.	85	2			54	187	3	27	83
	WILLIS	13-1-49-1	...2	89		...3	191		55	192	3	29	86
		10-2-22-1	GREIG	..	91	1	197		56	193	3	29	87
	WILLIS	11-1-46-0	...L	95		..1 2	201	lb4	57	197	3	29	90	11
		11-2-25-1	GREIG	....	103			M8	58	197	3	29	90
5:05	WILLIS	12-2-46-0				.W	203			197	4	29	90
		12-3-25-2				WALTERS							
5:06				....	109			M9	59	197	4	29	0
			GREIG	. 2 .	112	3	5		60	202	4	31	3
5:15	WILLIS	13-2-51-0				W	6			202	5	31	3
		13-3-27-3				MARSH							
5:17				...1	116	..1	3		61	204	5	32	1
5:26			UND'WOOD	.W	118	1	9			205	6	32	2
				JENNER					62	205	6	0	2
5:28			WILLIS	.1	2	..1 ...	15		63	207	6	1	3
		14-3-29-3	UND'WOOD	....	10			M10	64	207	6	1	3
			LEVER	15-2-50-2	.2	12	1	21		65	210	6	3	4
			10-0-33-0	HENDRICK			.../....2	29	/new ball	66	212	6	3	6
			LEVER	14-3-38-1	4....1	18	1	.1	31		67	218	6	8	7
			11-0-39-0	HENDRICK			1	39		68	219	6	8	8
6:04				15-3-39-1	STUMPS		STUMPS			ATTENDANCE: 15,303
11:00	WILLIS					1	45		69	220	6	8	9
			15-3-30-3	HENDRICK	4	27	2	3	46		70	227	6	12	12
11;13	WILLIS	16-3-46-1	W	28		.1	48			228	7	12	13
			16-3-32-4		LILLEE								
11;14						1	53		71	229	7	0	14
11;20			HENDRICK			....W	58			229	8	0	14
			17-3-49-2			WALKER							
11;21				.3	2	.	1		72	232	8	3	0
	WILLIS			.1	9	1	2		73	234	8	4	1
		17-3-34-4	HENDRICK			..2....1	10		74	237	8	4	4
	WILLIS	18-3-52-2	1 1	11		..4.1 1	16	1	75	245	8	6	10
		18-3-42-4	HENDRICK	.4..1 .4	18	2	3	17		76	257	8	15	13
			LEVER	19-3-64-2			....	25		M11	77	257	8	15	13
11;44		12-1-39-0	GREIG	.W	20					257	9	15	13
			14-2-55-1	THOMSON									
11;45				..4...	6	1				78	261	9	4	13
	LEVER			1	11	1 ..	28		79	263	9	5	14
		13-1-41-0	GREIG	2..1	15	..4.	32	2	80	270	9	8	18
	LEVER	15-2-62-1	.1 ...	20		..1	35		81	272	9	9	19
		14-1-43-0	GREIG			4......4	43	4	82	280	9	9	27
	LEVER	16-2-70-1	3	25		4..	46	5	83	287	9	12	31
		15-1-50-0	UND'WOOD	....	33			M12	84	287	9	12	34
	LEVER	16-3-50-2	.....	38	.n.3	50	nb9	85	291	9	12	34	12
		16-1-53-0	UND'WOOD			....	58		M13	86	291	9	12	34
	WILLIS	17-3-50-2	..2.2.1	45		.	59		87	296	9	17	34
		19-3-47-4	UND'WOOD	....	53			M14	88	296	9	17	34
	WILLIS	18-3-50-2	..1	56		1	64		89	298	9	18	35
		20-3-49-4	UND'WOOD	....	64			M15	90	298	9	18	35
1;01		19-3-50-2	LUNCH			LUNCH							
1:40	WILLIS			.1	66	.1 4...	70	6	91	304	9	19	40
		21-3-55-2	UND'WOOD	.4......	74	2				92	308	9	23	40
1:50	WILLIS	20-3-54-2	..RO	77	.1	72			309	10	23	41
		21.5-3-56-4											

2nd DAY	BOWLERS Stanley Street (S)	BOWLERS Vulture Street (N)	BATSMEN UMP: T. BROOKS (S)			BATSMEN UMP: R. BAILHACHE (N)			NOTES	ENGLAND 1ST TOTALS AT END OF OVER					INNINGS
TIME	NAME	NAME	NAME	B	4/6	NAME	B	4/6		O	R	W	LBat	RBat	Ext
			AMISS			LUCKHURST									
2:02	LILLEE		..+..4...	8	1				wd1	1	5	0	4	0	1
	1-0-4-0	THOMSON				....	8		M1	2	5	0	4	0	
	LILLEE	1-1-0-0	1	9		....	15			3	6	9	5	0	
	2-0-5-0	THOMSON	. 1	15		. 1	17			4	8	0	6	1	
	LILLEE	2-1-2-0				....	25		M2	5	8	0	6	1	
2:32	3-1-5-0	THOMSON	... 1	19		. W	27				9	1	7	1	
		3-1-3-1				EDRICH									
2:33						..	2			6	9	1	7	0	
	LILLEE		....	27					M3	7	9	1	7	0	
2:44	4-2-5-0	THOMSON	... W	31		... 1	6			8	10	2	7	1	
		4-1-4-2	DENNESS												
2:45	LILLEE					....	14		M4	9	10	2	0	1	
	5-3-5-0	THOMSON	......n..	9					M5; nb1	10	11	2	0	1	2
	LILLEE	5-2-4-2				.4.4.2..	22	2		11	21	2	0	11	
	6-3-15-0	WALKER	.. 1	12		..2..	27			12	24	2	1	13	
	THOMSON	1-0-3-0	. 1	14		....4.	33	3		13	29	2	2	17	
3:17	6-2-9-2	WALKER	..4..W	20							33	3	6	17	
		2-0-12-1	FLETCHER												
3:19			1	1		4	34	4		14	38	3	1	21	
	THOMSON		..4.....	9	1					15	42	3	5	21	
	7-2-13-2	WALKER	3	15		. 1	36			16	46	3	8	22	
	THOMSON	3-0-16-1	...4..1	22	2	.	37			17	51	3	13	22	
	8-2-18-2	WALKER	1	30						18	52	3	14	22	
3:40		4-0-17-1	TEA			TEA									
4:00	WALTERS		2 1 ...	34		.. 1	40			19	56	3	17	23	
4:10	1-0-4-0	LILLEE	.....W	40		1	41				57	4	17	24	
		7-3-16-1	GREIG												
4:11			..	2						20	57	4	0	24	
	WALKER					1	49			21	58	4	0	25	
	5-0-18-1	LILLEE				....	57		M6	22	58	4	0	25	
	WALKER	8-4-16-1	....	10					M7	23	58	4	0	25	
	6-1-18-1	LILLEE				....	65		M8	24	58	4	0	25	
	WALKER	9-5-16-1	.4...4..	18	2					25	66	4	8	25	
	7-1-26-1	LILLEE				....	73		M9	26	66	4	8	26	
	WALKER	10-6-16-1	2...4..1	26	3					27	73	4	15	26	
	8-1-33-1	THOMSON	....n n...1	36					nb3	28	76	4	16	25	3
	WALKER	9-2-19-2	1	37		L	80		lb1	29	78	4	17	25	4
	9-1-34-1	THOMSON				....2 n...	89		nb4	30	81	4	17	27	5
	WALKER	10-2-21-2	. 1	39		....	95			31	82	4	18	27	
	10-1-35-1	THOMSON	...n..2..	48					nb5	32	85	4	20	27	6
	WALKER	11-2-23-2	......	54		. 1	97			33	86	4	20	29	
	11-1-36-1	THOMSON	..	56		.+n 2.2 1	103		wd2;nb6	34	93	4	20	34	8
	WALKER	12-2-28-2	. 2	58		3	109			35	98	4	22	36	
	12-1-41-1	WALTERS	.. 1	61		1	114			36	100	4	23	37	
	JENNER	2-0-6-0	....4...	69	4					37	104	4	27	37	
	1-0-4-0	WALTERS	...1	73		1 ...	118			38	106	4	28	38	
	JENNER	3-0-8-0	....	81					M10	39	106	4	28	38	
	2-1-4-0	WALTERS	1	82		....1 ..	125			40	108	4	29	39	
	LILLEE	4-0-10-0	...4.1.	89	5	1	126			41	114	4	34	40	
	11-6-22-1	THOMSON				....	134			42	114	4	34	40	
6:03		13-3-28-2	STUMPS			STUMPS				ATTENDANCE: 15,597					
11:00	LILLEE		....1 .	95		. 1	136			43	116	4	35	41	
	12-6-24-1	THOMSON	4 2...	100	6	.. 1	139			44	123	4	41	42	
	LILLEE	14-3-35-2	1 .	102		..1 ..3	145			45	128	4	42	46	
11:18	13-6-29-1	THOMSON				2 W	147				130	5	42	48	
		15-3-37-3				KNOTT									
11:20						......	6			46	130	5	42	0	
	LILLEE		..2...4.	110	7					47	136	5	48	0	
	14-6-35-1	THOMSON				.2......	14			48	138	5	48	2	
	LILLEE	16-3-39-3	. 1	112		......	20			49	139	5	49	2	

Time	Bowler figures	Bowler	Balls	Runs	Wkt	Bowler figures 2	Balls 2	Wkt 2	Notes	Total	Wkts	Score1	Score2	Extra
	15-6-36-1	THOMSON	..1 1	116		...1	24		50: 155m 115 balls	50	142	5	51	3
		LILLEE	17-3-42-3	1	124					51	143	5	52	3
	16-6-37-1	WALKER	1	131		1	25			52	145	5	53	4
		JENNER	13-1-43-1			...4...4	33			53	153	5	53	12
	3-1-12-0	WALKER	...1	135		....	37			54	154	5	54	12
		JENNER	14-1-44-1	...4..4.	143	9				55	162	5	62	12
12:13	4-1-20-0	WALKER				. W	39				162	6	62	12
			15-1-46-2			LEVER								
12:15						....2.	6			56	164	6	62	2
		JENNER		1	144	2......	13			57	167	6	63	4
12:26	5-1-23-0	WALKER	..1	147		. W	15				168	7	64	4
			16-1-51-3			UND'WOOD								
12:28						4	3	1		58	172	7	64	4
		LILLEE		..4.....	155	10				59	176	7	68	4
	17-6-41-1	WALKER		..1	158	.1 ...	8			60	178	7	69	5
		JENNER	17-1-53-3	...1	162		....	12			61	179	7	70	5
	6-1-24-0	THOMSON	........n.	171					nb7	62	180	7	70	5	9
	WALKER	18-4-42-3	...L	175		...1	16		lb2	63	182	7	70	6	11
	18-1-54-3	THOMSON	.n........	184					M12;nb8	64	183	7	70	6	12
1:00			19-5-42-3	LUNCH		LUNCH								
1:40	WALKER			..	186	....2 1	22			65	186	7	70	9
	19-1-57-3	THOMSON	..+1	189		/.1 ...	27		/new ball wd3	66	189	7	71	10	13
	WALKER	20-5-44-3	...1	193		....	31			67	190	7	72	10
	20-1-58-3	THOMSON	4 2 .1	197	11	.2 4 2	35	2		68	205	7	79	18
	WALKER	21-5-59-3	2 1 1	200		,1 ...	40			69	210	7	83	19
	21-1-63-3	LILLEE	4 .1	203	12	2	45			70	217	7	88	21
	WALKER	18-6-48-1	.1	205		....4.	51	3		71	222	7	89	25
	22-1-68-3	LILLEE	4	213	13					72	226	7	93	25
2:23	WALTERS	19-6-52-1				W	52				226	8	93	25
2:24	5-1-10-1					WILLIS	7		M13	73	226	8	93	0
		LILLEE	4 4 ..1	218	15	...	10		100:281m 215 balls	74	235	8	102	0
	WALTERS	20-6-61-1	....4 4..	226	17					75	243	8	110	0
2:44	6-1-18-1	LILLEE	.(b4) W	229		1	15				248	9	110	1
			21-6-62-2	HENDRICK										
2:47				.	1				b4	76	248	9	0	1	17
	WALKER					....4...	23	1		77	252	9	0	5
	23-1-72-3	LILLEE	.....4..	9	1					78	256	9	4	5
	WALKER	22-6-66-2	..	11		......b	29		M14;b5	79	257	9	4	5	18
	24-2-72-3	LILLEE	....	15		.4.3	33	2		80	264	9	4	12
3:11	WALKER	23-6-73-2	. W	17		..1	36				265	10	4	13
	24.5-2-73-3			TEA		TEA								

3rd DAY	BOWLERS Stanley Street (S)	BOWLERS Vulture Street (N)	BATSMEN UMP: R. BAILHACHE (S)			BATSMEN UMP: T. BROOKS (N)			NOTES	44 AHEAD AUSTRALIA 2ND INNINGS TOTALS AT END OF OVER					
TIME	NAME	NAME	NAME	B	4/6	NAME	B	4/6		O	R	W	LBat	RBat	Ext
			REDPATH			W.EDWARDS									
3:32		WILLIS	. 4	8	1					1	4	0	4	0	
	LEVER	1-0-4-0	. . . . . .	14		. 1	2			2	5	0	4	1	
	1-0-1-0	WILLIS	. . . .			. . . .	10		M1	3	5	0	4	1	
	HENDRICK	2-1-4-0	 1	19		. . 1	13			4	7	0	5	2	
	1-0-2-0	WILLIS	. 1	22		. 1 . . L	18		lb1	5	10	0	6	3	1
	HENDRICK	3-1-6-0	. . 2	25		 1	23			6	13	0	8	4	
4:08	2-0-5-0	WILLIS	1	26		. . . . 1 W	29				15	1	9	5	
		4-1-9-1				I.CHAPPELL									
4:10						1	1			7	16	1	9	1	
	HENDRICK					. . . . . .	9		M2	8	16	1	9	1	
	3-1-5-0	WILLIS	. . . .	34					M3	9	16	1	9	1	
	HENDRICK	5-2-9-1	. 4 1	37	2	4 . . 1 .	14	1		10	26	1	14	6	
	4-1-15-0	LEVER	. 2 . . 1	42		. . .	17			11	29	1	17	6	
	HENDRICK	2-0-4-0	1 . 3	45	3	4 1 . . .	22	2		12	38	1	21	11	
	5-1-24-0	LEVER	. . . . n . .	54					M4; nb1	13	39	1	21	11	2
4:50	UND'WOOD	3-1-4-0				. . . W	27				39	2	21	11	
	1-1-0-1					G.CHAPPELL									
4:52						. . .	3			14	39	2	21	0	
		LEVER	1 . . . n . .	58		. . . . n . 1	10		nb3	15	43	2	22	1	4
	UND'WOOD	4-1-6-0	. . . . .	63		. . 1	13			16	44	2	22	2	
	2-1-1-1	LEVER				. . . .	21		M4	17	44	2	22	2	
	UND'WOOD	5-2-6-0	. . . .	71					M5	18	44	2	22	2	
	3-2-1-1	LEVER				2	29			19	46	2	22	4	
	UND'WOOD	6-3-8-0	. . . .	79					M6	20	46	2	22	4	
	4-3-1-1	LEVER				. . . .	37		M7	21	46	2	22	4	
	UND'WOOD	7-4-8-0	. . . .	87					M8	22	46	2	22	4	
	5-4-1-1	WILLIS				. . . .	45		M9	23	46	2	22	4	
	UND'WOOD	6-3-9-1	2	95						24	48	2	24	4	
	6-4-3-1	WILLIS				. . . . . . 2 .	53			25	50	2	24	6	
	UND'WOOD	7-3-11-1	. . . .	103					M10	26	50	2	24	6	
	7-5-3-1	WILLIS	. . . .	107		. . . 1	57			27	51	2	24	7	
6:00		8-3-12-1	STUMPS			STUMPS				ATTENDANCE: 17,127					
11:00	UND'WOOD		. . . . . .	113		. 1	59			28	52	2	24	8	
	8-5-4-1	WILLIS	. . . . . .	119		. 1	61			29	53	2	24	9	
	UND'WOOD	9-3-13-1	. 1	121		. . . 4 . . 1	67	1		30	59	2	25	14	
11:15	9-5-10-1	WILLIS	. . . W	125							59	3	25	14	
		10-3-14-2	R.EDWARDS												
11:17			. . . 1	4						31	60	3	1	14	
	UND'WOOD		. 2	12						32	62	3	3	14	
	10-5-12-1	WILLIS	1	13		1 1	74			33	65	3	4	16	
	UND'WOOD	11-3-17-2	. .	15		 1	80			34	66	3	4	17	
	11-5-13-1	WILLIS	. . . . . .	21		4 1	82	2		35	71	3	4	22	
	UND'WOOD	12-3-22-2				. . . . 4 . . .	90	3		36	75	3	4	26	
	12-5-17-1	LEVER	1	26		2 . 1	93			37	79	3	5	29	
	UND'WOOD	8-4-12-0	. . 1	29		. . . . (n1) .	99		nb4	38	81	3	6	30	
	13-5-19-1	LEVER	. . . 3	33		. . . .	103			39	84	3	9	30	
	HENDRICK	9-4-15-0	. . . .	41					M11	40	84	3	9	30	
	6-2-24-0	LEVER	. (n1)	43		. . . 1 . . n .	111		nb6	41	87	3	10	31	5
	HENDRICK	10-4-17-0	. . . 2 . . 1	50		.	112			42	90	3	13	31	
	7-2-27-0	LEVER	. . 2 2 1	55		. 2 .	115			43	97	3	18	33	
	HENDRICK	11-4-24-0	1	56		 L	122		lb2	44	99	3	19	33	6
	8-2-28-0	GREIG	. . 2 . 1	61		1 . .	125			45	103	3	22	34	
	HENDRICK	1-0-4-0	2 . 1 .	65		. . . 3	130			46	109	3	25	37	
	9-2-34-0	GREIG	. 2 1	68		. 1 . . .	135			47	113	3	28	38	
	UND'WOOD	2-0-8-0	. 1	75		1	136			48	115	3	29	39	
	14-5-21-1	GREIG	. . . 1	78		. . . 4 1	141	4		49	121	3	30	44	
	UND'WOOD	3-0-14-0	. 4 . .	86	1		149			50	125	3	34	44	
1:00	15-5-25-1		LUNCH			LUNCH									
		GREIG	. .	88		 1	155			51	126	3	34	45	
		UND'WOOD	4-0-15-0	. 4 .	91	2	 L	160		lb3	52	131	3	38	45	7

Time	Bowler1	Bowler2	Balls1	Runs1	Over	Balls2	Runs2	Notes	Score	Wkt	Bat1	Bat2	Extra
	15-6-36-1	THOMSON	..1 1	116		...1	24	50: 155m 115 balls	50	142	5	51	3
		LILLEE	17-3-42-3	1	124				51	143	5	52	3
		16-6-37-1	WALKER	1	131		1	25		52	145	5	53	4
		JENNER	13-1-43-1			...4...4	33		53	153	5	53	12
		3-1-12-0	WALKER	...1	135		....	37		54	154	5	54	12
		JENNER	14-1-44-1	...4..4.	143	9				55	162	5	62	12
12:13	4-1-20-0	WALKER				. W	39			162	6	62	12
			15-1-46-2			LEVER							
12:15						....2.	6		56	164	6	62	2
		JENNER		1	144	2......	13		57	167	6	63	4
12:26	5-1-23-0	WALKER	..1	147		. W	15			168	7	64	4
			16-1-51-3			UND'WOOD							
12:28						..4	3	1	58	172	7	64	4
		LILLEE		..4.....	155	10				59	176	7	68	4
		17-6-41-1	WALKER	..1	158		.1 ...	8		60	178	7	69	5
		JENNER	17-1-53-3	...1	162		....	12		61	179	7	70	5
		6-1-24-0	THOMSON	........n.	171				nb7	62	180	7	70	5	9
		WALKER	18-4-42-3	...L	175		...1	16	lb2	63	182	7	70	6	11
		18-1-54-3	THOMSON	.n	184				M12;nb8	64	183	7	70	6	12
1:00			19-5-42-3			LUNCH	LUNCH						
1:40	WALKER			..	186		....2 1	22		65	186	7	70	9
	19-1-57-3	THOMSON	..+1	189		/.1 ...	27	/new ball wd3	66	189	7	71	10	13
	WALKER	20-5-44-3	...1	193		....	31		67	190	7	72	10
	20-1-58-3	THOMSON	4 2 .1	197	11	.2 4 2	35	2	68	205	7	79	18
	WALKER	21-5-59-3	2 1 1	200		,1 ...	40		69	210	7	83	19
	21-1-63-3	LILLEE	4 .1	203	12	2	45		70	217	7	88	21
	WALKER	18-6-48-1	.1	205		....4.	51	3	71	222	7	89	25
	22-1-68-3	LILLEE	4	213	13				72	226	7	93	25
2:23	WALTERS	19-6-52-1				W	52			226	8	93	25
2:24	5-1-10-1					WILLIS	7	M13	73	226	8	93	0
		LILLEE	4 4 ..1	218	15	...	10	100:281m 215 balls	74	235	8	102	0
	WALTERS	20-6-61-1	....4 4..	226	17				75	243	8	110	0
2:44	6-1-18-1	LILLEE	. (b4) W	229		1	15			248	9	110	1
			21-6-62-2	HENDRICK									
2:47				.	1			b7	76	248	9	0	1	17
	WALKER					....4...	23	1	77	252	9	0	5
	23-1-72-3	LILLEE	.....4..	9	1				78	256	9	4	5
	WALKER	22-6-66-2	..	11		......b	29	M14;b5	79	257	9	4	5	18
	24-2-72-3	LILLEE	....	15		.4 .3	33	2	80	264	9	4	12
3:11	WALKER	23-6-73-2	. W	17		..1	36			265	10	4	13
		24.5-2-73-3		TEA		TEA							

4th DAY — 333 TO WIN ENGLAND 2ND INNINGS

TIME	BOWLERS Stanley Street (S) NAME	BOWLERS Vulture Street (N) NAME	BATSMEN UMP: T. BROOKS (S) NAME	B	4/6	BATSMEN UMP: R. BAILHACHE (N) NAME	B	4/6	NOTES	O	R	W	LBat	RBat	Ext
			AMISS			LUCKHURST									
5:30		LILLEE	. + 4 3	7	1	.	1		wd1	1	8	0	7	0	1
	THOMSON	1-0-7-0	. . . . . 2 . .	15						2	10	0	9	0	
5:41	1-0-2-0		BAD LIGHT			BAD LIGHT									
5:45			STUMPS			STUMPS				ATTENDANCE: 8,675					
11:00		LILLEE	. . . . . .	21		. 1	2			3	11	0	9	1	
	THOMSON	2-0-8-0				. . . .	10		M1	4	11	0	9	1	
	2-1-2-0	LILLEE	. . . 4	29	2					5	15	0	13	1	
		THOMSON	3-0-12-0			. . . . . 2 . .	18			6	17	0	13	3	
11:27	3-1-4-0	LILLEE	. . . 1	33		. W	20			18	1	14	3		
		4-0-14-1				EDRICH									
11:29						. 1	2			7	19	1	14	1	
	THOMSON					 4	10	1		8	23	1	14	5	
	4-1-8-0	LILLEE	. . . 1	37		. . . .	14			9	24	1	15	5	
	WALKER	5-0-15-1	. . . .	45					M2	10	24	1	15	5	
	1-1-0-0	LILLEE	. . 1 .	49		. . L L	18		lb2	11	27	1	16	5	3
	WALKER	6-0-16-1				. . . .	26		M3	12	27	1	15	5	
	2-2-0-0	THOMSON	. 2 (b4). . . 2 1	57					b4	13	36	1	21	5	7
	WALKER	5-1-13-0	. . . . . 2 1	64		1	27			14	40	1	24	6	
12:12	3-2-4-0	THOMSON				. W	29			40	2	24	6		
		6-1-15-1				DENNESS									
12:14						. . . . 2 .	6			15	42	2	24	2	
	WALKER		1	65		. . . . . .	14			16	43	2	25	2	
	4-2-5-0	THOMSON	. n W	68					nb1	44	3	25	2	8	
		7-1-16-2	FLETCHER												
			 1	5		.				17	45	3	1	2	
	WALKER		. 1 . .	9		. 4 . 1	18	1		18	51	3	2	7	
	5-2-11-0	THOMSON	. n . + . 2 .	15		. . L	21		lb3; nb2; wd2	19	56	3	4	7	
	WALKER	8-1-18-2	. 1	17		2 3 . . 4 4	27	3		20	70	3	5	20	
	6-2-25-0	LILLEE	2	25						21	72	3	7	20	
	JENNER	7-0-18-1				. . . . . 4 . .	35	4		22	76	3	7	24	
	1-0-4-0	LILLEE	1 2	31		. 1	37			23	80	3	10	25	
1:00		8-0-22-1	LUNCH			LUNCH									
	JENNER		. . .	34		 1	42			24	81	3	10	26	
1:40	2-0-5-0	THOMSON	. 4 n . . 2 1	41	1	1 .	44		nb3	25	90	3	17	27	
	JENNER	9-0-26-2	. . . . 2 . . .	49						26	92	3	19	27	
1:55	3-0-7-0	THOMSON				. W	46			92	4	19	27		
		10-0-28-3				GREIG									
1:57						. . . 2 . .	6			27	94	4	19	2	
2:04	JENNER		. . . . W	56						94	5	19	2		
	4-1-7-1		KNOTT												
2:05			.	1						28	94	5	0	2	
2:07		THOMSON				W	7			94	6	0	2		
		11-0-29-4				LEVER									
2:09						. . . . . . n 1	8		nb4	29	97	6	0	1	9
	JENNNER		 3	8		1	9			30	100	6	3	2	
	5-1-11-1	THOMSON	 1	15		.	10			31	101	6	4	2	
	JENNER	12-0-30-4	. . . 1	19		. . 4 .	14	1		32	106	6	5	6	
	6-1-16-1	LILLEE	. . . .	27					M4	33	106	6	5	6	
	JENNER	9-1-22-1				. . . . . . 2 .	22			34	108	6	5	8	
	7-1-18-2	LILLEE	. . . . 1 . .	34		1	23			35	110	6	6	8	
	JENNER	10-1-24-1	.	35		. . . . 4 . 1	30	1		36	115	6	6	14	
2:48	8-1-23-1	LILLEE				. W	32			115	7	6	14		
		11-1-25-2				UND'WOOD									
2:50						 1	6			37	116	7	6	1	
	JENNER					. . . .	14		M5	38	116	7	6	1	
	9-2-23-1	LILLEE	. . . .	43					M6	39	116	7	6	1	
	JENNER	12-2-25-2				. . . . . 4 . 4	22	2		40	124	7	6	9	
	10-2-31-1	WALKER	. . . .	51					M7	41	124	7	6	9	
	JENNER	7-3-25-0				. 4	30	3		42	128	7	6	13	
	11-2-35-1	WALKER	. . 4 . 1	56	1	. 2 .	33			43	135	7	11	15	

	JENNER	8-3-32-0	4 . . . . . 4 .	64	3				44	143	7	19	15
		12-2-43-1	WALKER			. . . .	41		M8	45	143	7	19	15
		WALTERS	9-4-32-0	. . . .	72				M9	46	143	7	19	15
		1-1-0-0	THOMSON			. . . . (b4) .	49		M10;b8	47	147	7	19	15	13
		WALTERS	13-1-30-4	. . . .	80				M11	48	147	7	19	15
3:40		2-2-0-0		TEA		TEA								
4:00			THOMSON			. 4 . . . 4 4 2	57	6		49	161	7	19	29
	JENNER	14-1-44-4	. . . .	88				M12	50	161	7	19	29
		13-3-43-1	THOMSON			 1	65			51	162	7	19	30
4:17		JENNER	15-1-45-4			. . . . W	70				162	8	19	30
		14-3-43-2				WILLIS								
4:19				. . .	91				M13	52	162	8	19	0
4:24			THOMSON	. . W	94	. . . (n1)	4		nb5		163	9	19	1
			16-1-46-5	HENDRICK										
4:25				. .	2					53	163	9	0	1
	JENNER				 2	12			54	165	9	0	3
		15-3-45-2	THOMSON	n	11			M14;nb6	55	166	9	0	3	14
	JENNER	17-2-46-5				. . . .	20		M15	56	166	9	0	3
4:40		16-4-45-2	THOMSON	. . . . W	16						166	10	0	3
			17.5-2-46-6	**AUSTRALIA WON BY 166 RUNS**						ATTENDANCE: 5,017				

AUSTRALIA FIRST Innings

IN	OUT	MINS	NO	BATSMAN	HOW OUT	BOWLER	RUNS	WK	TOTAL	BALLS	4s	6s	NOTES
11:00	11:23	23	1	IR REDPATH	BOWLED	WILLIS	5	2	10	21			Played around fast, straight yorker
11:00	11:19	19	2	WJ EDWARDS	CT AMISS	HENDRICK	4	1	7	15			Hurried, top-edged hook to fine leg
11:20	5:05	289	3	IM CHAPPELL	CT GREIG	WILLIS	90	4	197	203	10	1	Top-edged pull to square leg
11:24	2:36	155	4	GS CHAPPELL	CT FLETCHER	UNDERWOOD	58	3	110	132	5		Edged defensive prod to slip
2:40	5:26	147	5	R EDWARDS	CT KNOTT	UNDERWOOD	32	6	205	118	2		Edged forward defensive to keeper
5:06	5:15	9	6	KD WALTERS	CT LEVER	WILLIS	3	5	202	6			Skied pull to wide mid-on
5:17	11:20	67	7	RW MARSH	CT DENNESS	HENDRICK	14	8	229	58	2		Skied off drive to extra cover
5:28	11:13	49	8	TJ JENNER	CT LEVER	WILLIS	12	7	228	28	2		Skied pull to wide mid-on
11:14	11:54	40	9	DK LILLEE	CT KNOTT	GREIG	15	9	257	20	6		Gloved attempted hook to keeper
11:21		110	10	MHN WALKER	NOT OUT		41			72			
11:55	1:50	76	11	JR THOMSON	RUN OUT		23	10	309	77	2		Direct hit on quick single to mid-off
					EXTRAS		12			LB 4, NB 8			
					TOTAL	(ALL OUT, 92.5 OVERS)	309						

BOWLER	O	M	R	W	NB/W
WILLIS	23.5	3	56	4	
LEVER	16	1	53	0	3/
HENDRICK	19	3	64	2	2/
GREIG	16	2	70	1	
UNDERWOOD	20	6	54	2	4/

Runs	Mins	Overs	Last50
50	100	21.1	100
100	169	31.4	69
150	234	43.6	65
200	317	59.5	83
250	417	75.5	100
300	490	90.4	73
350			
400			
450			
500			

LUNCH 56-2
23 overs

TEA 157-3
46 overs

STUMPS DAY 1:
219-6 68 overs

LUNCH 289-9
90 overs

• Chappell/Chappell 100 partnership in 154 min

Wkt	Partnership		RUNS
1	Redpath	Edwards	7
2	Redpath	Chappell	3
3	Chappell	Chappell	100
4	Edwards	Chappell	87
5	Edwards	Walters	5
6	Edwards	Marsh	3
7	Jenner	Marsh	23
8	Lillee	Marsh	1
9	Lillee	Walker	28
10	Thomson	Walker	52

ENGLAND FIRST Innings

IN	OUT	MINS	NO	BATSMAN	HOW OUT	BOWLER	RUNS	WK	TOTAL	BALLS	4s	6s	NOTES
2:02	2:44	42	1	DL AMISS	CT JENNER	THOMSON	7	2	10	31	1		Lifting delivery off glove to gully
2:02	2:32	30	2	BW LUCKHURST	CT MARSH	THOMSON	1	1	7	27			Fended short ball off hip to keeper
2:33	11:18	191	3	JH EDRICH	CT I.CHAPPELL	THOMSON	48	5	130	147	4		Steered to first slip
2:45	3:19	32	4	MH DENNESS	LBW	WALKER	6	3	33	20	1		Offered no shot to in-swinger
3:19	4:10	31	5	KW FLETCHER	BOWLED	LILLEE	17	4	57	40	2		Played on trying to force through off
4:11	2:44	296	6	AW GREIG	CT MARSH	LILLEE	110	9	248	229	17		Thin-edge drive to keeper
11:20	12:13	53	7	APE KNOTT	CT JENNER	WALKER	12	6	162	39	2		Offered easy catch to gully
12:15	12:26	11	8	P LEVER	CT I.CHAPPELL	WALKER	4	7	168	15			Flat-footed prod to first slip
12:28	2:23	75	9	DL UNDERWOOD	CT REDPATH	WALTERS	25	8	226	52	3		Drive into the hands of extra-cover
2:24	3:11	47	10	RGD WILLIS	NOT OUT		13			36	2		
2:47	3:11	24	11	M HENDRICK	CT REDPATH	WALKER	4	10	265	17	1		Back-foot drive to cover point
					EXTRAS		18						B 5, LB 2, W 3 NB 8
					TOTAL		265						(ALL OUT, 80.5 OVERS)

BOWLER	O	M	R	W	NB/W
LILLEE	23	6	72	2	/1
THOMSON	21	5	59	3	9/2
WALKER	24.5	2	73	4	
WALTERS	6	1	18	1	
JENNER	6	1	24	0	

Runs	Mins	Overs	Last50
50	90	16.7	90
100	195	36	105
150	281	53	86
200	361	67.7	80
250	411	76.5	50
300			
350			
400			
450			
500			

TEA: 52-3
18 overs, 257 behind
STUMPS DAY 2: 114-4
42 overs, 195 behind
LUNCH: 183-7
64 overs, 126 behind

Wkt	Partnership		RUNS
1	Amiss	Luckhurst	7
2	Amiss	Edrich	3
3	Denness	Edrich	23
4	Fletcher	Edrich	24
5	Greig	Edrich	73
6	Greig	Knott	32
7	Greig	Lever	6
8	Greig	Underwood	58
9	Greig	Willis	22
10	Hendrick	Willis	17

AUSTRALIA SECOND Innings

IN	OUT	M	NO	BATSMAN	HOW OUT	BOWLER	RUNS	WK	TOTAL	BALLS	4s	6s	NOTES
3:32	11:15	163	1	IR REDPATH	BOWLED	WILLIS	25	3	59	125	3		Beaten by ball that cut in off seam
3:32	4:08	36	2	WJ EDWARDS	CT KNOTT	WILLIS	3	1	15	29			Edge to wicketkeeper
4:10	4:50	40	3	IM CHAPPELL	CT FLETCHER	UNDERWOOD	11	2	39	27	2		Edged prod to diving first slip
4:52	2:47	255	4	GS CHAPPELL	BOWLED	UNDERWOOD	71	4	173	202	7		Missed attempt to turn ball to leg side
11:37	3:17	200	5	R EDWARDS	CT KNOTT	WILLIS	53	5	190	149	4		Thin edge on ball that seamed away
2:49	5:13	126	6	KD WALTERS	NOT OUT		62			96	8		
3:19	5:13	96	7	RW MARSH	NOT OUT		46			57	5	1	
			8	TJ JENNER									
			9	DK LILLEE									
			10	MHN WALKER									
			11	JR THOMSON									
				EXTRAS	B 1, LB 7, W 1, NB 6		15						
				TOTAL	(5 WICKETS, 85 OVERS)		288 DEC						

BOWLER	O	M	R	W	NB/W
WILLIS	15	3	45	3	
LEVER	18	4	58	0	5/1
HENDRICK	13	2	47	0	
GREIG	13	2	60	0	
UNDERWOOD	26	6	63	2	3/

Runs	Mins	Overs	Last50
50	137	24.7	
100	239	44.1	102
150	309	58	80
200	376	70.4	67
250	431	80.3	55
300			
350			
400			
450			
500			

STUMPS DAY 3: 59-2
27 overs, 103 ahead

LUNCH: 125-3
50 overs, 169 ahead

TEA: 211-5
73 overs, 255 ahead

- G.Chappell/Edwards 100 partnership in 149 min

wkt	Partnership		RUNS
1	Redpath	Edwards	15
2	Redpath	Chappell	24
3	Redpath	Chappell	20
4	Edwards	Chappell	114
5	Edwards	Walters	17
6	Marsh	Walters	98
7			
8			
9			
10			

331

ENGLAND SECOND Innings

AUSTRALIA WON BY 166 RUNS

IN	OUT	MINS	NO	BATSMAN	HOW OUT	BOWLER	RUNS	WK	TOTAL	BALLS	4s	6s	NOTES
5:30	12:24	95	1	DL AMISS	CT WALTERS	THOMSON	25	3	92	68	2		Fended rising ball to third slip
5:30	11:27	38	2	BW LUCKHURST	CT I.CHAPPELL	LILLEE	3	1	18	20			Edged tentative prod to first slip
11:29	12:12	43	3	JH EDRICH	BOWLED	THOMSON	6	2	40	29			Beaten for pace, lost off stump
12:14	1:55	61	4	MH DENNESS	CT WALTERS	THOMSON	29	4	44	46	2		Edged to diving third slip
12:26	2:04	58	5	KW FLETCHER	CT G.CHAPPELL	JENNER	19	5	94	56	1		Edged wide ball to second slip
1:57	2:07	10	6	AW GREIG	BOWLED	THOMSON	2	6	94	7			Bowled by leg stump yorker
2:05	4:24	119	7	APE KNOTT	BOWLED	THOMSON	19	9	163	94	3		Inside edge to full ball on off stump
2:09	2:48	39	8	P LEVER	CT REDPATH	LILLEE	14	7	115	32	2		Fended short ball to short leg
2:50	4:17	67	9	DL UNDERWOOD	CT WALKER	JENNER	30	8	162	70	6		Skied slog to mid-on
4:19	4:40	21	10	RGD WILLIS	NOT OUT		3			20			
4:25	4:40	15	11	M HENDRICK	BOWLED	THOMSON	0	10	166	16			Defensive shot beaten by pace
					EXTRAS		18			B 8, LB 3, W 2, NB 5			
					TOTAL		166			(ALL OUT, 56.5 OVERS)			

BOWLER	O	M	R	W	NB/W
LILLEE	12	2	25	1	/1
THOMSON	17.3	5	46	6	6/1
WALKER	9	4	32	0	
JENNER	16	5	45	2	
WALTERS	2	2	0	0	

Runs	Mins	Overs	Last50
50	109	17.4	
100	168	30	59
150	252	48.2	84
200			
250			
300			
350			
400			
450			
500			

STUMPS DAY 4: 10-0
2 overs, 323 to win
LUNCH: 80-3
23 overs, 253 to win
TEA: 147-7
48 overs, 186 to win
MATCH ATTENDANCE: 61,719

wkt	Partnership		RUNS
1	Amiss	Luckhurst	18
2	Amiss	Edrich	22
3	Amiss	Denness	4
4	Fletcher	Denness	48
5	Fletcher	Greig	2
6	Knott	Greig	0
7	Knott	Lever	21
8	Knott	Underwood	47
9	Knott	Willis	1
10	Hendrick	Willis	3

SECOND TEST MATCH

AUSTRALIA v **ENGLAND** at THE WACA, PERTH on DECEMBER 13-15, 17 1974

ENGLAND 1ST INNINGS

1st DAY TIME	BOWLERS Causeway End (S) NAME	BOWLERS Grandstand End (N) NAME	BATSMEN UMP: R. BAILHACHE (S) NAME	B	4/6	BATSMEN UMP: T. BROOKS (N) NAME	B	4/6	NOTES Toss AUS	O	R	W	LBat	RBat	Ext
			LLOYD			LUCKHURST									
11:00	LILLEE		..4.2...	8	1					1	6	0	6	0	
	1-0-6-0	THOMSON				....	8		M1	2	6	0	6	0	
		LILLEE	1-1-0-0	......2.	16					3	8	0	8	0	
	2-0-8-0	THOMSON				....	16		M2	4	8	0	8	0	
		LILLEE	2-2-0-0	....	24				M3	5	8	0	8	0	
	3-1-8-0	THOMSON				......4.	24	1		6	12	0	8	4	
		LILLEE	3-2-4-0	1	32					7	13	0	9	4	
11:39	4-1-9-0	WALKER	.....2..	40						8	15	0	11	4	
		LILLEE	1-0-2-0	.	41	.4..441	31	4		9	28	0	11	17	
	5-1-22-0	WALKER				....	39		M4	10	28	0	11	17	
		LILLEE	2-1-2-0	....	49				M5	11	28	0	11	17	
	6-2-22-0	WALKER				.4....4.	47	6		12	36	0	11	25	
12:06	THOMSON	3-1-10-0	....	57					M6	13	36	0	11	25	
		4-3-4-0	WALKER	...4...	64	2	1	48		14	41	0	15	26	
	THOMSON	4-1-15-0	.2...	69		..1	51			15	44	0	17	27	
12:21	5-3-7-0	WALKER				.W	53				44	1	17	27	
		5-2-15-1				COWDREY									
12:23						......	6		M7	16	44	1	17	0	
	THOMSON								M8	17	44	1	17	0	
	6-4-7-0	WALKER		77		....	14		M9	18	44	1	17	0	
	THOMSON	6-3-15-1	......n...	86					nb1	19	45	1	17	0	1
	7-5-7-0	WALKER				4.......	22	1		20	49	1	17	4	
12:45	LILLEE	7-3-19-1	3 ...1	91		..3	25			21	56	1	21	7	
	7-2-29-0	WALKER	.....4..	99	3					22	60	1	25	7	
	LILLEE	8-3-23-1				.2.+......	33		wd1	23	63	1	25	9	2
1:03	8-2-31-0		LUNCH			LUNCH									
1:40		MALLETT	....442.	107	5					24	73	1	35	9	
	LILLEE	1-0-10-0	....	111		...1	37			25	74	1	35	10	
	9-2-32-0	MALLETT				....	45		M10	26	74	1	35	10	
	LILLEE	2-1-10-0	1	118		.	46			27	75	1	36	10	
	10-2-33-0	MALLETT	.1	120		......	52			28	76	1	37	10	
	LILLEE	3-1-11-0	....	128					M11	29	76	1	37	10	
	11-3-33-0	MALLETT				..4...	60	2		30	80	1	37	14	
2:13	THOMSON	4-1-15-0	4+...21	134	6	..	62		wd2	31	88	1	44	14	3
	8-5-14-0	MALLETT	....	142					M12	32	88	1	44	14	
	THOMSON	5-2-15-0				....	70		M13	33	88	1	44	14	
	9-6-14-0	MALLETT	.1	144		.4....	76	3		34	93	1	45	18	
	THOMSON	6-2-20-0	1	150		.1	78			35	95	1	46	19	
2:35	10-6-16-0	WALTERS	.3	152		..1 ...	84			36	99	1	49	20	
2:45	THOMSON	1-0-4-0	...W	156							99	2	49	20	
		11-6-21-1	GREIG												
2:47			4..n1	5	1				nb2	37	105	2	5	20	4
		WALKER	.4...1	11	2	..	86			38	110	2	10	20	
	THOMSON	9-3-28-1	1	12		.2......	93			39	113	2	11	22	
		12-6-24-1	WALKER	41	14	3	....	99			40	118	2	16	22	
3:06	THOMSON	10-3-33-1	1	15		.W	101				119	3	17	22	
	13-6-29-2					FLETCHER									
3:08						n.4...	6	1	nb3	41	124	3	17	4	5
		WALKER	1	16		....	13			42	125	3	18	4	
	LILLEE	11-3-34-1	3	24						43	128	3	21	4	
		12-3-36-0	WALKER	....	32				M14	44	128	3	21	4	
3:32	LILLEE	12-4-34-1				...,W	17				128	4	21	4	
3:34	13-3-38-1					DENNESS									
						2...	4	1		45	130	4	21	2	
		WALKER	.2......	40						46	132	4	23	2	
3:40		13-4-36-1	TEA			TEA									
4:06	LILLEE					........W	12		M15	47	132	5	23	2	

Time	Bowler1	Bowler	Balls	Runs	Bowler2	Balls	Runs	Extras	Score#	Total	Wkts	B1	B2	Over
	14-4-38-2				KNOTT									
4:12		WALKER	.....W	46						132	6	23	0	
		14-4-38-2	TITMUS											
4:14			. 2	2					48	134	6	2	0	
	LILLEE		.....	7	...+ (n1)	4	1	wd3;nb4	49	136	6	2	1	6
	15-4-39-2	WALKER	...	10	1	9			50	137	6	2	2	
	LILLEE	15-4-39-2	1	11	3 ..4..1	16	2		51	146	6	3	10	
	16-4-48-2	WALKER	..	13	3	22			52	149	6	3	13	
	THOMSON	16-4-42-2			...n....4	31	3	nb5	53	154	6	3	17	7
	14-6-33-2	WALKER	....	21				M16	54	154	6	3	17	
	THOMSON	17-5-42-2	.1 1	24	.(n4)3 .3 .	37	4	nb7	55	166	6	5	27	
	15-6-45-2	MALLETT	....	32				M17	56	166	6	5	27	
	WALKER	7-3-20-0	....	39	1	38			57	167	6	5	28	
	18-5-42-3	MALLETT	......n.	47	1	39		nb8	58	169	6	5	29	8
	WALKER	8-3-21-0	...	50	3	44			59	172	6	5	32	
	19-5-45-3	MALLETT	1	51	....1 4 3	51	5		60	181	6	6	40	
	WALKER	9-3-30-0	...	54	3	56			61	184	6	6	43	
	20-5-48-3	MALLETT	.2	56	....2 1	62			62	189	6	8	46	
	I.CHAPPELL	10-3-35-0	......	62	.1	64			63	190	6	8	47	
5:33	1-0-1-0	WALTERS			.4..W	69	6	50: 84m 66 balls		194	7	8	51	
		2-0-11-1			OLD									
5:35			.	63	.3	2			64	197	7	8	3	
5:39	I.CHAPPELL				...4 W	7	1			201	8	8	7	
	2-0-10-1				ARNOLD									
5:42					1RO	1				202	9	8	1	
					WILLIS									
5:43					4	2	1		65	206	9	8	4	
		WALTERS	.2 W	66						208	10	10	4	8
		2.3-0-13-2												

AUSTRALIA 1ST INNINGS — 1st DAY

TIME	BOWLERS Causeway End (S) NAME	BOWLERS Grandstand End (N) NAME	BATSMEN UMP: R. BAILHACHE (S) NAME	B	4/6	BATSMEN UMP: T. BROOKS (N) NAME	B	4/6	NOTES	O	R	W	LBat	RBat	Ext
5:58	WILLIS		REDPATH 1	7		W.EDWARDS .	1			1	1	0	1	0	
6:02	1-0-1-0		STUMPS			STUMPS					ATTENDANCE: 16,264				
11:00		ARNOLD	...2....	15						2	3	0	3	0	
	WILLIS	1-0-2-0	.1.	18		.(L2).1 1	6		lb2	3	8	0	4	2	2
	2-0-4-0	ARNOLD	......	24		.3	8			4	11	0	4	5	
	WILLIS	2-0-5-0	1 . 2	27		...3 3	13			5	20	0	7	11	
	3-0-13-0	ARNOLD	3 ..	30		2.1 .1	18			6	27	0	10	15	
	WILLIS	3-0-12-0	...1	34		.4.1	22	1		7	33	0	11	20	
	4-0-19-0	ARNOLD	.3 .4.	39	1	..1	25			8	41	0	18	21	
	WILLIS	4-0-20-0	.2	41		1	31			9	44	0	20	22	
	5-0-22-0	ARNOLD	1	42		1 ....4 1	38			10	51	0	21	28	
11:48	OLD	5-0-27-0	3	47		1 ..	41			11	55	0	24	29	
11:58	1-0-4-0	GREIG	4.1 2 1	52	2	1 W	43				64	1	32	30	
		1-0-9-1				I.CHAPPELL .	1			12	64	1	32	0	
12:00	OLD		1	58		.2	3			13	67	1	33	2	
	2-0-7-0	GREIG	.2......	66						14	69	1	35	2	
	OLD	2-0-11-0	..2.2..	73		1	4			15	74	1	39	3	
	3-0-12-0	GREIG				4..4.4..	12	3		16	86	1	39	15	
	OLD	3-0-23-0	....	81					M1	17	86	1	39	15	
	4-1-12-0	GREIG				.(b4)..4..4	20	5	b4	18	98	1	39	23	6
	OLD	4-0-31-0	.....2..	89						19	100	1	41	23	
12:39	5-1-14-0	TITMUS	.	90		1	27			20	101	1	41	24	
	OLD	1-0-1-0	.W	92		....	35		M2	21	101	1	41	24	
12:47	6-2-14-0	TITMUS									101	2	41	24	
		2-0-5-1	G.CHAPPELL ....4.	6	1										
12:49							43		M3	22	105	2	4	24	
	OLD					....	43			23	105	2	4	24	
	7-3-14-0	TITMUS	1	13		.	44			24	106	2	5	24	
	OLD	3-0-6-1	.....2..	21		LUNCH				25	108	2	7	24	
1:02	8-3-16-0		LUNCH												
		TITMUS	1	28		1	45			26	110	2	8	25	
1:47	ARNOLD	4-0-8-1	3	29		..W	48				113	3	11	25	
	6-0-32-1					R.EDWARDS ...2	4			27	115	3	11	2	
1:49		TITMUS	....	37					M4	28	115	3	11	2	
	ARNOLD	5-1-8-1	...1	41		...1	8			29	117	3	12	3	
	7-0-34-1	TITMUS	2..1 ..	47		.1	10			30	121	3	15	4	
	ARNOLD	6-1-12-1	....	51		...1	14			31	122	3	15	5	
	8-0-35-1	TITMUS				.....2..	22			32	124	3	15	7	
	ARNOLD	7-1-14-1	4 1	53	2	....2.	28			33	131	3	20	9	
	9-0-42-1	TITMUS	1	59		..	30			34	132	3	21	9	
	ARNOLD	8-1-15-1	1	60		....	37			35	133	3	22	9	
	10-0-43-1	TITMUS	.....4 1	67	3	.	38			36	138	3	27	9	
	ARNOLD	9-1-20-1	......2.	75						37	140	3	29	9	
	11-0-45-1	TITMUS	1	76		.....1 .	45			38	142	3	30	10	
	ARNOLD	10-1-22-1	...1 .4	82	4	.1	47			39	148	3	35	11	
	12-0-51-1	TITMUS	..1	85		(b3)	52		b7	40	152	3	36	11	9
2:43	WILLIS	11-1-23-1	..3 .	89		...3	56			41	158	3	39	14	
	6-0-28-0	TITMUS	.1	91		1	62			42	160	3	40	15	
	WILLIS	12-1-25-1	.2.1	95		2...	66			43	165	3	43	17	
	7-0-33-0	TITMUS	..1	98		2....	71			44	168	3	44	19	
	WILLIS	13-1-28-1	....2...	106						45	170	3	46	19	
	8-0-35-0	TITMUS				....	79		M5	46	170	3	46	19	
	WILLIS	14-2-28-1	4 1 .	109	5	1	84		50:105m 107 ball	47	176	3	51	20	
	9-0-41-0	TITMUS				......4.	92	7		48	180	3	51	24	
	WILLIS	15-2-32-1	.2 3	112		.....	97			49	185	3	56	24	
3:24	10-0-46-0	GREIG	...4.1	118		..	99			50	190	3	61	24	
3:33	WILLIS	5-0-36-1	..1 ...W	125		1	100			51	192	4	62	25	
	11-1-48-1		WALTERS												

335

Time	Batsman 1	Bowler	Balls 1	Runs 1	O	Balls 2	Runs 2	Total	Wkt	Notes	Ball#	Score	W	R1	R2	Ov
3:35		TITMUS	..2.1	5		.1 1	103				52	197	4	3	27	
	WILLIS	16-2-37-1				...4....	111		2		53	201	4	3	31	
3:43	12-1-52-1		TEA			TEA										
4:00		GREIG	..4.1 3	11	1	.1	113				54	210	4	11	32	
	OLD	6-0-45-1	......4.	19	2						55	214	4	15	32	
	9-3-20-0	GREIG	1 3	21		....1 1	119				56	220	4	19	34	
	OLD	7-0-51-1	.2 3	24		.....	124				57	225	4	24	34	
	10-3-25-0	GREIG	.2 4 1	28	3	....	128				58	232	4	31	34	
	OLD	8-0-58-1	4....1	34	4	..	130				59	237	4	36	34	
	11-3-30-0	GREIG	..4 1	39	5	1 4.	133	3			60	248	4	42	39	
	OLD	9-0-69-1	4	47	6						61	252	4	46	39	
	12-3-34-1	TITMUS	..4.4 1	53	8	1 .	135			50:48m 50 balls	62	262	4	55	40	
	OLD	17-2-47-1	.2.....1	61							63	265	4	58	40	
	13-3-37-0	TITMUS	...4 1	66	9	...	138				64	270	4	63	40	
	OLD	18-2-52-1	.2....4.	74	10						65	276	4	69	40	
	14-3-43-0	TITMUS	.1	76		...1 4.	144				66	282	4	70	45	
	OLD	19-2-58-1	.1 .1	80		.L ..	148			lb3	67	285	4	72	45	10
	15-3-45-0	ARNOLD	1 .	82		.2/2...1	155			50:171m 155 balls /new ball	68	291	4	73	50	
	WILLIS	13-0-57-1	..1	85		...1 1	160			•100p	69	294	4	74	52	
	13-1-55-1	ARNOLD	1 .1	88		..1 1 1	165				70	299	4	76	55	
	WILLIS	14-0-62-1	1	89		..L	172			lb4	71	301	4	77	55	11
	14-1-56-1	ARNOLD	..2.1 1	95		1 2	174				72	308	4	81	58	
	WILLIS	15-0-69-1	L	96		..2 2 2.1	181			lb5	73	316	4	81	65	12
	15-1-63-1	ARNOLD	.1 1	99		2 4 1 1 .	186	4			74	326	4	83	73	
	WILLIS	16-0-79-1	.2..1	104		...	189				75	329	4	86		
	16-1-66-1	ARNOLD	.2.2.2 1	111		1	190				76	337	4	93	74	
	WILLIS	17-0-87-1	4....6	117	11/1	2 3	192			100:133m 117 balls	77	352	4	103	79	
6:05	17-1-81-1		STUMPS			STUMPS				ATTENDANCE; 23.303						
11:00		ARNOLD				2 2 2 2 2 ...	200				78	362	4	103	89	
11:07	WILLIS	18-0-97-1	.W	119								362	5	103	89	
	18-1-83-2		MARSH													
11:09			2.....	6							79	364	5	2	89	
		ARNOLD	.....	11		...n (n3)	205			nb2	80	368	5	2	92	13
	WILLIS	19-0-100-1	.1	13		....1 .	211				81	370	5	3	93	
	19-1-85-2	ARNOLD	....1 .	19		.1	213				82	372	5	4	94	
	WILLIS	20-0-102-1	2....	24		..1	216				83	375	5	6	95	
	20-1-88-2	ARNOLD	.4.1	28	1	...1	220				84	381	5	11	96	
	WILLIS	21-0-108-1	1	35		.	221				85	382	5	12	96	
	21-1-89-2	OLD	4..4.1	42	3	1	222				86	392	5	21	97	
	WILLIS	16-3-55-0	L .	44		...1 .1	228			lb6	87	395	5	21	99	14
	22-1-91-2	OLD	....	51		1	229			100:293m 229 balls	88	396	5	21	100	
	ARNOLD	17-3-56-0				2..2.4.2	237	5			89	406	5	21	110	
	22-0-118-1	OLD	...L 1	56		1 ..	240			lb7	90	409	5	22	111	15
	ARNOLD	18-3-58-0	..2.....	64							91	411	5	24	111	
	23-0-120-1	TITMUS	.1	66		...2 1 1	246				92	416	5	25	115	
12:23	ARNOLD	20-2-63-1				W	247					416	6	25	115	
	24-1-120-2					WALKER										
12:25						....	7			M6	93	416	6	25	0	
		TITMUS	4..L	70	4	. (L2) .	11			lb10	94	423	6	29	0	18
	ARNOLD	21-2-67-1	4....1	76	5	.1	13				95	429	6	34	1	
	25-1-126-2	TITMUS	...(L2) .2	82		.3	15			lb12	96	436	6	36	4	20
	ARNOLD	22-2-72-1				2	23				97	438	6	36	6	
	26-1-128-2	TITMUS	1	87		..	25				98	439	6	37	6	
	ARNOLD	23-2-73-1	1	88		.n	32			nb3	99	441	6	38	6	21
	27-1-129-2	TITMUS	.1 ..1	93		.L ..	35			lb13	100	444	6	40	6	22
1:02		24-2-75-1	LUNCH			LUNCH										
	OLD		1	94		.2.2...	42				101	449	6	41	10	
1:47	19-3-63-0	TITMUS	W	95								449	7	41	10	
		25-3-75-2	LILLEE													
1:49			....	7						M7	102	449	7	0	10	
	OLD		2 3	9		...1 ..	48				103	455	7	5	11	

	20-3-69-0	TITMUS	. . . 4	17	1				104	459	7	9	11	
2:02	OLD	26-3-79-2	2 . W	20		1	52			462	8	11	12	
	21-3-72-2		MALLETT											
2:95			. W	2						462	9	0	12	
			THOMSON											
2:07			. .	2					105	462	9	0	12	
		TITMUS				. . . 2	60		106	464	9	0	14	
	OLD	27-3-81-2	. . . 3 L	7		1 2 .	63	lb14	107	471	9	3	17	23
	22-3-78-2	TITMUS	1	8		. 2	70		108	474	9	4	19	
2:23	OLD	28-3-84-2	. 4 2 1	12		. W	72			481	10	11	19	
	22.6-3-85-3													

3rd DAY

273 BEHIND ENGLAND 2ND INNINGS

UMP: T. BROOKS (S) — UMP: R. BAILHACHE (N)

TIME	BOWLERS Causeway End (S) NAME	BOWLERS Grandstand End (N) NAME	BATSMEN NAME	B	4/6	BATSMEN NAME	B	4/6	NOTES	O	R	W	LBat	RBat	Ext
			LLOYD			COWDREY									
2:35	LILLEE		....	8					M1	1	0	0	0	0	
	1-1-0-0	THOMSON				......+..	8		M2;wd1	2	1	0	0	0	1
	LILLEE	1-1-0-0	1	16						3	2	0	1	0	
	2-1-1-0	THOMSON	....	24					M3	4	2	0	1	0	
	LILLEE	2-2-0-0	......	30		. 1	10			5	3	0	1	1	
	3-1-2-0	THOMSON				4	18	1		6	7	0	1	5	
	LILLEE	3-2-4-0	....	38					M4	7	7	0	1	5	
	4-2-2-0	WALKER	...4	42	1	..2 3	22			8	16	0	5	10	
	LILLEE	1-0-9-0	......	49		1	23			9	17	0	5	11	
	5-2-3-0	WALKER				..4..2..	31	2		10	23	0	5	17	
	LILLEE	2-0-15-0	....	57					M5	11	23	0	5	17	
	6-3-3-0	WALKER				...2....	39			12	25	0	5	19	
	THOMSON	3-0-17-0	..1	60		......	44			13	26	0	6	19	
3:42	4-2-5-0		TEA			TEA									
4:00		WALTERS	....4...	68	2					14	30	0	10	19	
	THOMSON	1-0-4-0				...4....	52	3		15	34	0	10	23	
	5-2-9-0	WALTERS	....	76					M6	16	34	0	10	23	
	THOMSON	2-1-4-0				4....2..	60	4		17	40	0	10	29	
	6-2-15-0	WALTERS	1	77		...4....	67	5		18	45	0	11	33	
	THOMSON	3-1-9-0	.n....2..	86					nb1	19	48	0	13	33	2
	7-2-17-0	WALTERS				....	75		M7	20	48	0	13	33	
	THOMSON	4-2-9-0	1	91		...	78			21	49	0	14	33	
	8-2-18-0	WALTERS	.2...1	97		..	80			22	52	0	17	33	
4:42	THOMSON	5-2-12-0	. RET HURT	98					Groin						
	9-2-23-0		DENNESS												
4:47			1	1		....4.	86	6		23	57	0	1	37	
		WALTERS	....	9					M8	24	57	0	1	37	
5:03	THOMSON	6-3-12-0				n.....4 W	94	7	nb2		62	1	1	41	3
	10-2-29-1					GREIG									
5:05						2	1			25	64	1	1	2	
		WALKER	....	17					M9	26	64	1	1	2	
	THOMSON	4-1-17-0	.2 4 2.	22	1	..1	4			27	73	1	9	3	
	11-2-38-1	WALKER	......	28		.1	6			28	74	1	9	4	
	LILLEE	5-1-18-0				4.....4.	14	2		29	82	1	9	12	
	7-3-11-0	WALKER	....	36					M10	30	82	1	9	12	
	LILLEE	6-2-18-0	.	37		....4.3	21	3		31	89	1	9	19	
	8-3-18-0	WALKER				......4.	29	4		32	93	1	9	23	
	LILLEE	7-2-22-0	2.....2.	45						33	97	1	13	23	
	9-3-22-0	WALKER				..4....	37	5		34	101	1	13	27	
	LILLEE	8-2-26-0	....	53					M11	35	101	1	13	27	
	10-3-22-0	MALLETT	....	57		...1	41			36	102	1	13	28	
6:00		1-0-1-0	STUMPS			STUMPS				ATTENDANCE: 23,940					
11:03	THOMSON					4....W	47	6			106	2	13	32	
	12-2-42-2					LLOYD									
11:05						..	100			37	106	2	13	17	
		LILLEE	.1 ..3	62		.n 1 2	104		nb3	38	114	2	17	20	4
	THOMSON	11-3-29-0	3	63		1	111			39	118	2	20	21	
	13-2-46-2	LILLEE				....4..2	119	3		40	124	2	20	27	
11:24	THOMSON	12-3-35-0	..W	66							124	3	20	27	
	14-3-46-4		FLETCHER												
11:26			W	1							124	4	0	27	
			KNOTT												
11:28			.n..n.	6					M12;nb5	41	126	4	0	27	6
		LILLEE	1	11		L ..	122		lb1	42	128	4	1	27	7
	THOMSON	13-3-36-0	..4.4.n..	20	2				nb6	43	137	4	9	27	8
	15-3-54-4	LILLEE				.2....4.	130	4		44	143	4	9	33	
	THOMSON	14-3-42-0	2 4 3	23	3	...2.	135			45	154	4	18	35	
12:00	16-3-65-4	LILLEE	........W	31						46	154	5	18	35	
			15-3-42-1			LUCKHURST									
12:02	WALKER					....	143		M13	47	154	5	0	35	
	9-3-26-0	LILLEE	1	5		...	146			48	155	5	1	35	

Time	Bowler 1	Bowler 1 analysis	Balls 1	Runs 1	W1	Bowler 2	Balls 2	Runs 2	W2	Notes	O	R	W	LBat	RBat	Ext
12:15	WALKER	16-3-43-1	. 1	7		. W	148				156	6	2	35		
		10-3-27-1				TITMUS										
12:17						. . . .	4				49	156	6	2	0	
			MALLETT	. . . .	15					M14	50	156	6	2	0	
	WALKER	2-1-1-0				. . . .	12			M15	51	156	6	2	0	
	11-4-27-1	MALLETT	. . . .	23						M16	52	156	6	2	0	
	WALKER	3-2-1-0	. . . .	27		 L	16			M17;lb2	53	157	6	2	0	9
	12-5-27-1	MALLETT	. n . 2 . . .	35		3	17			nb7	54	163	6	4	3	10
	WALKER	4-2-6-0	4 2	42	1	1	18				55	170	6	10	4	
	13-5-34-1	MALLETT				. . . 4 n . 4 . .	27	2		nb8	56	179	6	10	12	11
	WALKER	5-2-14-0	. . . .	50						M18	57	179	6	10	12	
	14-6-34-1	MALLETT				. . . 4	35	3			58	183	6	10	16	
	WALKER	6-2-18-0	. 1	52		. . . . . .	41				59	184	6	11	16	
	15-6-35-1	MALLETT	. . . .	60						M19	60	184	6	11	16	
1:00		7-3-18-0	LUNCH			LUNCH										
	WALKER					. . . .	49			M20	61	184	6	11	16	
	16-6-35-1	WALTERS	. . . .	68						M21	62	184	6	11	16	
	WALKER	7-4-12-0				 1	57				63	185	6	11	17	
	17-6-36-1	WALTERS				 4	65	4			64	189	6	11	21	
	WALKER	8-4-16-0	. . 1	71		 1	70				65	191	6	12	22	
	18-6-38-1	WALTERS	. . . . .	78		. . 1	73				66	192	6	12	23	
	LILLEE	9-4-17-0	. . . .	82		/ . . . 1	77			/new ball	67	193	6	12	24	
	17-3-44-1	THOMSON	2 4 . . n .	88		. . . (n1)	81			nb10	68	201	6	18	25	12
	LILLEE	17-3-72-4	. .	90		 1	87				69	202	6	18	26	
	18-3-45-1	THOMSON	.	91		. . . . . n . 3	95			nb11	70	206	6	18	29	13
	LILLEE	18-3-75-4				. . . . . . 4 .	103	5			71	210	6	18	33	
	19-3-49-1	WALKER	. . . . . 2 .	99							72	212	6	20	33	
	LILLEE	19-6-40-1	1	100		. . . 1 . . .	110				73	214	6	21	34	
	20-3-51-1	WALKER	. . . . . 2 .	108							74	216	6	23	34	
2:58	LILLEE	20-4-42-1	W	109		 3	117				75	219	7	23	37	
	21-3-54-2		OLD													
3:00			WALKER			. 4	125	6			76	223	7	0	41	
	LILLEE	21-4-46-1	 3	5		2 . .	128				77	228	7	3	43	
	22-3-59-2	WALKER	. . . . . 4 2 .	13	1						78	234	7	9	43	
	THOMSON	22-4-52-1				 1	136				79	235	7	9	44	
	19-3-76-4	WALKER				 4	144	7			80	239	7	9	48	
	THOMSON	23-4-56-1	. . 4	21	2						81	243	7	13	48	
	20-3-80-4	WALKER	2 4 . . 4 6 1	28	4/1	3	145			50:151m 145 balls	82	263	7	30	51	
	THOMSON	24-4-76-1	. . 1	31		. . . . . .	150				83	264	7	31	51	
3:40	21-3-81-4		TEA			TEA										
4:00			MALLETT	. . . 1	35		. . . 1	154				84	266	7	32	52	
	THOMSON	8-3-20-0				 1	162				85	267	7	32	53	
	22-3-82-4	MALLETT				. . . . . 2 . .	170				86	269	7	32	55	
	THOMSON	9-3-22-0	. . . .	43						M22	87	269	7	32	55	
	23-4-82-4	MALLETT				. . . n	179			M23 nb12	88	270	7	32	55	14
	THOMSON	10-4-22-0	4 1	45	5/1	. . . 2 . .	185				89	277	7	37	57	
4:24	23-4-89-4	MALLETT	(L2) 6 W	48	5/2					lb4		285	8	43	57	16
		11-2-32-1	ARNOLD													
4:26						. . . 4 .	190	8			90	289	8	0	61	
4:32	THOMSON		. . 4 . . . . W	8	1						91	293	9	4	61	
	24-3-93-5		WILLIS													
4:35			MALLETT			W	191					293	10	0	61	
		11.1-2-32-2														

4th DAY TIME	BOWLERS Causeway End (S) NAME	Grandstand End (N) NAME	BATSMEN UMP: T. BROOKS (S) NAME	B	4/6	UMP: R. BAILHACHE (N) NAME	B	4/6	NOTES	21 to win AUSTRALIA SECOND INNINGS TOTALS AT END OF OVER				
										O	R	W	LBat	RBat	Ext
			REDPATH			W.EDWARDS									
4:45	WILLIS		4	8	1					1	4	0	4	0	
4:53	1-0-4-0	ARNOLD				. . W	3				4	1	4	0	
		1-0-2-1				I.CHAPPELL									
4:55			. . 1	11		1 .	2			2	6	1	5	1	
	WILLIS		. . 1 . .	16		. . 3	5			3	10	1	6	4	
5:07	2-0-8-0	ARNOLD	. . 2 . 4	21	2	4 3	7	1			23	1	12	11	
		1.7-0-15-1	AUSTRALIA WON BY 9 WICKETS							ATTENDANCE: 12,481					

ENGLAND FIRST Innings

IN	OUT	MINS	NO	BATSMAN	HOW OUT	BOWLER	RUNS	WK	TOTAL	BALLS	4s	6s	NOTES
11:00	2:45	187	1	D LLOYD	CT G.CHAPPELL	THOMSON	49	2	99	156	6		Edge to second slip's left hand
11:00	12:21	81	2	BW LUCKHURST	CT MALLETT	WALKER	27	1	44	63	6		Low diving catch at gully
12:23	3:06	125	3	MC COWDREY	BOWLED	THOMSON	22	3	119	101	3		Full ball, bowled behind legs
2:47	4:12	65	4	AW GREIG	CT MALLETT	WALKER	23	6	132	46	3		Edged back foot drive to gully
3:08	3:32	24	5	KW FLETCHER	CT REDPATH	LILLEE	4	4	128	17	1		Edged push to gully
3:34	4:06	12	6	MH DENNESS	CT G.CHAPPELL	LILLEE	2	5	132	12			Slash to second slip
4:08	5:33	85	7	APE KNOTT	CT REDPATH	WALTERS	51	7	194	69	5		Back-foot drive, diving catch at gully
4:14	5:47	93	8	FJ TITMUS	CT REDPATH	WALTERS	10	10	208	66			Cut to gully
5:35	5:39	4	9	CM OLD	CT G.CHAPPELL	I.CHAPPELL	7	8	201	7	1		Clipped to short mid-wicket
5:41	5:42	1	10	GG ARNOLD	RUN OUT		1	9	202	1			Failed to beat throw going for two
5:43	5:47	4	11	RGD WILLIS	NOT OUT		4			2	1		
					EXTRAS		8			W 3, NB 5			
					TOTAL	(ALL OUT, 65.3 OVERS)	208						

BOWLER	O	M	R	W	NB/W
LILLEE	16	4	48	2	/2
THOMSON	15	6	45	2	4/1
WALKER	20	5	49	2	
MALLETT	10	3	35	0	1/
WALTERS	2.3	0	13	2	
I.CHAPPELL	2	0	10	1	

Runs	Mins	Overs	L50
50	107	20.1	107
100	189	36.5	82
150	282	52.4	93
200	341	64.4	59
250			
300			
350			
400			
450			
500			

LUNCH: 63-1
23 overs

TEA: 132-3
46 overs

Wkt	Partnership		RUNS
1	Lloyd	Luckhurst	44
2	Lloyd	Cowdrey	55
3	Greig	Cowdrey	20
4	Greig	Fletcher	9
5	Greig	Denness	4
6	Greig	Knott	0
7	Titmus	Knott	62
8	Titmus	Old	7
9	Titmus	Arnold	1
10	Titmus	Willis	6

AUSTRALIA FIRST Innings

IN	OUT	MINS	NO	BATSMAN	HOW OUT	BOWLER	RUNS	WK	TOTAL	BALLS	4s	6s	NOTES
5:58	12:07	111	1	IR REDPATH	ST KNOTT	TITMUS	41	2	101	92	2		Out of ground after missed drive
5:58	11:58	62	2	WJ EDWARDS	CT LLOYD	GREIG	30	1	64	43	2		Hit short ball to cover point
12:00	1:47	64	3	IM CHAPPELL	CT KNOTT	ARNOLD	25	3	113	48	5		Touched down leg side to keeper
12:49	3:33	126	4	GS CHAPPELL	CT GREIG	WILLIS	62	4	192	125	6		Ricochet between two gully fielders
1:49	12:23	322	5	R EDWARDS	BOWLED	ARNOLD	115	6	416	247	6		Played on from outside off stump
3:35	11:07	140	6	KD WALTERS	CT FLETCHER	WILLIS	103	5	362	119	11	1	Edged seaming delivery to first slip
11:09	1:47	120	7	RW MARSH	CT LLOYD	TITMUS	41	7	449	95	5		Skied full toss to deep mid-off
12:25	2:23	80	8	MHN WALKER	CT KNOTT	OLD	19	10	481	72	1		Thing edge trying to force to off
1:49	2:02	13	9	DK LILLEE	BOWLED	OLD	11	8	462	20	1		Swung across in-swinging delivery
2:04	2:05	1	10	AA MALLETT	CT KNOTT	OLD	0	9	462	2			Edged cut to wicketkeeper
2:07	2:23	16	11	JR THOMSON	NOT OUT		11			12	1		
				EXTRAS			23						B 7, LB 14, NB 2
				TOTAL	(ALL OUT, 108.6 OVERS)		481						

BOWLER	O	M	R	W	NB/W
WILLIS	22	0	91	2	
ARNOLD	27	1	129	2	3/
OLD	22.6	3	85	3	
GREIG	9	0	69	1	
TITMUS	23	8	84	2	

Runs	Mins	Overs	Last50
50	51	9.7	
100	99	19.6	48
150	186	39.1	87
200	241	52.2	55
250	286	61.0	45
300	335	70.3	49
350	374	77.0	39
400	437	88.4	63
450	509	102.4	72
500			

LUNCH 108-2
25 overs, 100 behind

TEA 201-4
53 overs, 7 behind

STUMPS DAY 2: 352-4
77 overs, 144 ahead

LUNCH 444-6
100 overs, 236 ahead

• R Edwards/Walters 100 partnership in 85 min

wkt	Partnership		RUNS
1	Redpath	Edwards	64
2	Redpath	Chappell	37
3	Chappell	Chappell	12
4	Chappell	Edwards	79
5	Walters	Edwards	170
6	Marsh	Edwards	54
7	Marsh	Walker	33
8	Lillee	Walker	13
9	Mallett	Walker	0
10	Thomson	Walker	19

ENGLAND SECOND Innings

IN	OUT	MINS	NO	BATSMAN	HOW OUT	BOWLER	RUNS	WK	TOTAL	BALLS	4s	6s	NOTES
2:35	12:15	180	1	D LLOYD	CT G.CHAPPELL	WALKER	35	6	156	148	4		Cut wide delivery to second slip
2:35	5:03	131	2	MC COWDREY	LBW	THOMSON	41	1	62	94	7		Moved across crease, beaten by pace
4:47	11:24	97	3	MH DENNESS	CT REDPATH	THOMSON	20	3	124	66	1		Fended rising ball to fourth slip
5:05	11:03	58	4	AW GREIG	CT G.CHAPPELL	THOMSON	32	2	106	47	6		Edged drive to second slip
11:25	11:26	1	5	KW FLETCHER	CT MARSH	THOMSON	0	4	124	1			Thin edge to wicketkeeper
11:28	12:00	32	6	APE KNOTT	CT G.CHAPPELL	LILLEE	18	5	154	31	3		Slashed drive to second slip
12:02	2:58	136	7	BW LUCKHURST	CT MALLETT	LILLEE	23	7	219	109	2		Edged defensive push to gully
12:17	4:35	198	8	FJ TITMUS	CT G.CHAPPELL	MALLETT	61	10	293	191	8		Down the wicket, drove to mid-off
3:00	4:24	64	9	CM OLD	CT THOMSON	MALLETT	43	8	285	48	5	2	Skied top-edge to mid-wicket
4:26	4:32	6	10	GG ARNOLD	CT MALLETT	THOMSON	4	9	293	8	1		Diving catch in the gully
4:34	4:35	1	11	RGD WILLIS	NOT OUT		0						

EXTRAS LB 4, W 1, NB 11
TOTAL (ALL OUT, 91.1 OVERS) 293

BOWLER	O	M	R	W	NB/W
LILLEE	22	5	59	2	2/1
THOMSON	25	4	93	5	7/1
WALKER	24	7	76	1	
WALTERS	9	4	17	0	
MALLETT	11.1	4	32	3	

TEA: 26-0
13 overs, 247 behind

STUMPS DAY 3: 102-1
36 overs; 171 behind

LUNCH: 184-6
60 overs; 89 behind

TEA: 264-7
83 overs; 9 behind

Lloyd ret. hurt, 4:42 (52-0)
until 11:05 (106-2)

Runs	Mins	Overs	L50
50	106	21.2	106
100	176	33.3	70
150	219	44.3	43
200	341	67.6	122
250	418	81.3	77
300			
350			
400			
450			
500			

Wkt	Partnership		RUNS
1	Lloyd/Denness	Cowdrey	62
2	Denness	Greig	44
3	Denness	Lloyd	18
4	Fletcher	Lloyd	0
5	Knott	Lloyd	30
6	Luckhurst	Lloyd	2
7	Luckhurst	Titmus	63
8	Old	Titmus	66
9	Arnold	Titmus	8
10	Willis	Titmus	0

AUSTRALIA SECOND Innings

AUSTRALIA WON BY 9 WICKETS

IN	OUT	MINS	NO	BATSMAN	HOW OUT	BOWLER	RUNS	WK	TOTAL	BALLS	4s	6s	NOTES
4:45		22	1	IR REDPATH	NOT OUT		12			21	2		
5:45	4:53	8	2	WJ EDWARDS	LBW	ARNOLD	0	1	4	3			Trapped in front by full delivery
4:55		12	3	IM CHAPPELL	NOT OUT		11			7	1		
				GS CHAPPELL									
				R EDWARDS									
				KD WALTERS									
				RW MARSH									
				MHN WALKER									
				DK LILLEE									
				AA MALLETT									
				JR THOMSON									
				EXTRAS									
				TOTAL	(1 WICKET, 3.7 OVERS)		23						

BOWLER	O	M	R	W	NB/W
WILLIS	2	0	8	0	
ARNOLD	1.7	0	15	1	

Runs	Mins	Overs	Last50
50			
100			
150			
200			
250			
300			
350			
400			
450			
500			

MATCH ATTENDANCE: 73,988

wkt	Partnership		RUNS
1	Redpath	Edwards	4
2	Redpath	Chappell	19
3			
4			
5			
6			
7			
8			
9			
10			

THIRD TEST MATCH

AUSTRALIA v **ENGLAND** at MELBOURNE CRICKET GROUND on DECEMBER 26-28, 30-31 1974

1st DAY TIME	BOWLERS Pavilion End (N) NAME	BOWLERS Southern End (S) NAME	BATSMEN UMP: R. BAILHACHE (N) NAME	B	4/6	BATSMEN UMP: T. BROOKS (S) NAME	B	4/6	NOTES Toss AUS	ENGLAND 1ST O	ENGLAND 1ST R	ENGLAND 1ST W	INNINGS LBat	INNINGS RBat	Ext
			AMISS			LLOYD									
11:00/05	LILLEE		...2..2 W	8						1	4	1	4	0	
	1-0-4-1		COWDREY												
11:06		THOMSON				+2......	8		wd1	2	7	1	0	2	1
	LILLEE	1-0-2-0	....2...	8						3	9	1	2	2	
		2-0-6-1	THOMSON			....	16		M1	4	9	1	2	2	
	LILLEE	2-1-2-0	1	14		.1	18			5	11	1	3	3	
		3-0-8-1	THOMSON			2........	24			6	13	1	3	5	
	LILLEE	3-1-4-0	2.......	22						7	15	1	5	5	
		4-0-10-1	WALKER			....	32		M2	8	15	1	5	5	
	LILLEE	1-1-0-0	....2...	30						9	17	1	7	5	
		5-0-12-1	WALKER			....	40		M3	10	17	1	7	5	
	LILLEE	2-2-0-0	1..1	34		1 ...	44			11	20	1	9	6	
		6-0-15-1	WALKER			....	42		M4	12	20	1	9	6	
	LILLEE	3-3-0-0	..	44		..4..1	50	1		13	25	1	9	11	
		7-0-20-1	WALKER			....	58		M5	14	25	1	9	11	
	THOMSON	4-4-0-0	..1	47		.....	63			15	26	1	10	11	
		4-1-5-0	WALKER	.4......	55	1				16	30	1	14	11	
	THOMSON	5-4-4-0	....	62		1	64			17	31	1	14	12	
		5-1-6-0	WALKER	..	64		1	70		18	32	1	14	13	
	THOMSON	6-4-5-0				....	78		M6	19	32	1	14	13	
		6-2-6-0	WALKER	....	72				M7	20	32	1	14	13	
	THOMSON	7-5-5-0				....	86		M8	21	32	1	14	13	
		7-3-6-0	WALTERS	.1 ...	77		..1	89		22	34	1	15	14	
12:49	THOMSON	1-0-2-0				W	90			34	2	15	14		
		8-3-8-1				EDRICH									
12:50						2	7			23	36	2	15	2	
		WALTERS	....	85					M9	24	36	2	15	2	
	THOMSON	2-1-2-0				4........	15	1		25	40	2	15	6	
1:03		9-3-12-1	LUNCH			LUNCH									
1:40		WALKER	4.......	93	2					26	44	2	19	6	
	THOMSON	8-5-9-0				....	23		M10	27	44	2	19	6	
		10-4-12-1	WALKER	....	101				M11	28	44	2	19	6	
	THOMSON	9-6-9-0	..(4n)..	106		...3	27		nb1	29	51	2	19	9	5
		11-4-15-1	WALKER			....	35		M12	30	51	2	19	6	
	THOMSON	10-7-9-0	..4.....	114	3					31	55	2	23	9	
		12-4-19-1	WALKER	.....	119		..1	38			32	56	2	23	10	
	LILLEE	11-7-10-0	1	120		.1 22...	45			33	62	2	24	15	
		8-0-26-1	WALKER	...(L2)....	131				M13;lb2	34	64	2	24	15	7
	LILLEE	12-7-10-0				..4.....	53	2		35	68	2	24	19	
		9-0-30-1	WALKER	..1	135		...1	57			36	70	2	25	20	
	LILLEE	13-7-12-0	.	136		.....4 1	64	3		37	75	2	25	25	
		10-0-35-1	MALLETT	1 .	138		..1 ..1	70			38	78	2	26	27	
	LILLEE	1-0-3-0	.2...	144		.1	72			39	81	2	28	28	
		11-0-38-1	MALLETT	..	146		...2.3	78			40	86	2	28	33	
	WALTERS	2-0-8-0	..	148		....2 1	84			41	89	2	28	36	
		3-1-5-0	MALLETT			..(n2)..2...	93		nb2	42	93	2	28	40	
	WALTERS	3-0-12-0	....2...	156						43	95	2	30	40	
		4-1-7-0	MALLETT	1	162		.1	95			44	97	2	31	41	
	WALTERS	4-0-14-0	1	163		..2....	102			45	100	2	32	43	
		5-0-10-0	MALLETT	.1 1 ...	167		1 1	104			46	104	2	34	45	
	THOMSON	5-0-18-0				..2..n.	113		nb3	47	107	2	34	47	8
		13-4-21-1	MALLETT	..1	170		1	118			48	109	2	35	48	
3:32	THOMSON	6-0-20-0	W	171		.1	120			110	3	35	49		
		14-4-22-2	DENNESS							49	110	3	0	49		
3:34			.....	5											
3:39		MALLETT				...W	124			110	4	0	49		
		7-1-20-1	TEA			TEA									

344

Time	Bowler1	Analysis1	Balls1	Runs1	Bowler2	Analysis2	Balls2	Bowler3	Analysis3	Over	Score	Wkts	Bat1	Bat2	Extras
4:00					GREIG	. . . .	4	M14		50	110	4	0	0	
	THOMSON		2 1	7		n 4 . . n 4 4 .	12	3	nb5	51	127	4	3	12	10
		15-4-37-2	MALLETT	. . . . 2 . . .	15					52	129	4	5	12	
	THOMSON	8-1-22-1		.	16		. . . 2 . 2 1	19		53	134	4	5	17	
		16-4-42-1	MALLETT				. . . .	27	M15	54	134	4	5	17	
	THOMSON	9-2-22-1		. . . . 2 . . .	24					55	136	4	7	17	
		17-4-44-1	MALLETT	. 1	26		. . 1 2 . .	33		56	140	4	8	20	
	WALKER	10-2-26-1		. . . .	34				M16	57	140	4	8	20	
4:37		14-8-12-0	MALLETT	. . . . W	39		. . 1	36		58	141	5	8	21	
			11-2-27-2	KNOTT											
4:39	WALKER						. . . .	44	M17	59	141	5	0	21	
		15-9-12-0	MALLETT	. 2	8					60	143	5	2	21	
	WALKER	12-2-29-2					. . . . . 4 . .	52	4	61	147	5	2	25	
		16-9-16-0	MALLETT	. . . 3 . 2	14		. 1	54		62	153	5	7	26	
	WALKER	13-2-35-2					. . . . . 2 . .	62		63	155	5	7	28	
		17-9-18-0	MALLETT	. . . . . 2RO>	20						157	5	9	28	
5:03			14-2-37-2			TITMUS										
5:05							. .	2		64	157	6	9	0	
	WALKER			 2	28					65	159	6	11	0	
		18-9-20-0	MALLETT				. . . .	10	M18	66	159	6	11	0	
			LILLEE	15-3-37-2			/ . 2	36	/new ball	67	161	6	13	0	
		12-0-40-1	WALKER				. . 1	13		68	162	6	13	1	
			LILLEE	19-9-21-0			. . 1 2	17		69	166	6	14	4	
		13-0-44-1	WALKER	. 3	47		. . . . . .	23		70	169	6	17	4	
			LILLEE	20-9-24-0			. 1	25		71	171	6	18	5	
		13-0-46-1	WALTERS				2 . . 2 . . . 1	33		72	176	6	18	10	
			LILLEE	6-0-15-0			. . . .	41	M19	73	176	6	18	10	
		15-1-46-1	WALTERS						M20	74	176	6	18	10	
5:59			LILLEE	7-1-15-0			. . . .	61			176	6	18	10	
			16-2-46-2			STUMPS	. . . . W	45				ATTENDANCE: 77,165			
				STUMPS		UNDERWOOD										
							. . . .	4	M21	75	176	7	18	0	
			THOMSON	. . 2 1	65		4 . 2 .	8	1	76	185	7	21	6	
		LILLEE	18-4-53-2	. 2 . 3	69		. . . .	12		77	190	7	26	6	
		17-2-51-2	THOMSON	. n . . 2	78				nb6	78	193	7	28	6	11
		LILLEE	19-4-55-2				2	20		79	195	7	28	8	
		18-2-53-2	THOMSON	. . 4 n . 2 . . 1	87	1			nb7	80	203	7	35	8	12
		LILLEE	20-4-62-3	3 . 4 . . 1	93	2	1 .	22		81	212	7	43	9	
11:38			19-2-62-2	WALKER	. . 1	96	W	23			213	8	44	10	
				21-9-25-1		WILLIS										
11;39							. . . .	4		82	213	8	44	0	
		LILLEE		2 1 . 2 . . .	103		3	5		83	221	8	49	3	
		20-2-70-2	WALKER				. . . . . 4 . 2	13	1	84	227	8	49	9	
11:54	THOMSON	22-9-31-1	1	104		4 W	15	2	50: 134m 104 balls		232	9	50	13	
			21-4-67-3			HENDRICK										
11:55				. . . . .	109					85	232	9	50	0	
			WALKER				. . . . 4 . . .	8	1	86	236	9	50	4	
	THOMSON	23-9-35-1	. . 1	112		. . 4 . .	13	2	87	241	9	51	8	
		22-3-72-3	WALKER	. . 1	115		. . . . .	18		88	242	9	52	8	
12:17	THOMSON	24-9-35-1	. . . W	119							242	10	52	8	12
		22.3-72-4														

345

2nd DAY TIME	BOWLERS Pavilion End (N) NAME	BOWLERS Southern End (S) NAME	BATSMEN UMP: R. BAILHACHE (N) NAME	B	4/6	BATSMEN UMP: T. BROOKS (S) NAME	B	4/6	NOTES	AUSTRALIA 1ST TOTALS AT END OF OVER O	R	W	LBat	RBat	Ext
			REDPATH			W.EDWARDS									
12:28	WILLIS		3	6		.1	2			1	4	0	3	1	
	1-0-4-0	HENDRICK				....	10		M1	2	4	0	3	1	
	WILLIS	1-1-0-0	.4......	14	1					3	8	0	7	1	
	2-0-8-0	HENDRICK	..1	17		..3 .1	15			4	13	0	8	5	
	WILLIS	2-0-5-0	2	18		1	22			5	16	0	10	6	
	3-0-11-0	HENDRICK	..2 L	22		1 .\	24		\Bowler inj.; lb1	6	20	0	12	7	1
1:00		2.6-0-8-0	LUNCH			LUNCH									
1:40	WILLIS		....	30					M2	7	20	0	12	7	
	4-1-11-0	UND'WOOD				....	32		M3	8	20	0	12	7	
	WILLIS	1-1-0-0	.2	38					M4	9	22	0	14	7	
	5-1-13-0	UND'WOOD	.1	40		....1 1	38			10	25	0	15	9	
	WILLIS	2-1-3-0	.	41		.4....1	45	1		11	30	0	15	14	
	6-1-18-0	UND'WOOD	....4..	48	2	1	46			12	35	0	19	15	
	WILLIS	3-1-8-0	..	50		1	52			13	36	0	19	16	
	7-1-19-0	UND'WOOD	......	56		.1	54			14	37	0	19	17	
	GREIG	4-1-9-0	1	57		1	61			15	39	0	20	18	
	1-0-2-0	UND'WOOD	..4 1	62	3	..1	64			16	45	0	25	19	
	GREIG	5-1-15-0	1	67		1 .1	67			17	48	0	26	21	
	2-0-5-0	UND'WOOD	.	68		1	74			18	49	0	26	22	
	GREIG	6-1-16-0				....	82		M5	19	49	0	26	22	
	3-1-5-0	UND'WOOD	...4 1	73	4	...	85			20	54	0	31	22	
	GREIG	7-1-21-0	..1	76		.....	90			21	55	0	32	22	
	4-1-6-0	TITMUS	....	84					M6	22	55	0	32	22	
	GREIG	1-1-0-0	....	88		...1	94			23	56	0	32	23	
	5-1-7-0	TITMUS				....	102		M7	24	56	0	32	23	
	GREIG	2-2-0-0	.1 1 .	92		.3 .1	106			25	62	0	34	27	
3:12	6-1-13-0		LIGHT/TEA			LIGHT/TEA									
4:00		TITMUS	....			....	114		M8	26	62	0	34	27	
	WILLIS	3-3-0-0	....	100					M9	27	62	0	34	27	
	8-2-19-0	TITMUS	.....	105		..1	117			28	63	0	34	28	
	WILLIS	4-3-1-0				...	120				63	0	34	28	
4:10	8.3-2-19-0		RAIN/STUMPS			RAIN/STUMPS				ATTENDANCE: 54,580					
11:00/02	WILLIS		1	106		1 .W	123				65	1	35	29	
	9-2-22-1					G.CHAPPELL									
11:03						1	1			29	66	1	35	1	
		TITMUS	....	113		1	2			30	67	1	35	2	
		5-3-2-0													
11:10	WILLIS					...W	6				67	2	35	2	
	10-2-23-2					R.EDWARDS									
11:11			.	114		..1	3			31	68	2	35	1	
11:16		TITMUS				...W	6				68	3	35	1	
		6-4-2-1				WALTERS									
11:17						......	5		M10	32	68	3	35	0	
	WILLIS		..1	121		1	6			33	70	3	36	1	
	11-2-25-2	TITMUS				....	14		M11	34	70	3	36	1	
	WILLIS	7-5-2-1	....	129					M12	35	70	3	36	3	
	12-3-25-2	TITMUS				....	22		M13	36	70	3	36	3	
	WILLIS	8-6-2-1	1 ..	132		2...3	27			37	76	3	37	8	
	13-2-31-2	TITMUS	.1	134		..1 ..4	33	1		38	82	3	38	13	
	GREIG	9-6-8-1	...1 ..1	141		1	34			39	85	3	40	14	
	7-1-16-0	TITMUS	..1 1	145		...1	38			40	88	3	42	15	
	GREIG	10-7-11-1	..1	148		...2.	43			41	91	3	43	17	
	8-1-19-0	TITMUS	.1 1	151		4..3 .	48	2		42	100	3	45	24	
	GREIG	11-7-20-1	1	156		..1	51			43	102	3	46	25	
	9-1-21-0	TITMUS	.1 ..	161		1 .1	54			44	105	3	47	27	
	GREIG	12-7-23-1	.1 .	165		.1 .1	58			45	108	3	48	29	
	10-1-24-0	UND'WOOD				....	66		M14	46	108	3	48	29	
	GREIG	8-2-21-0	.1 ..3 .	171		1 1	68		50: 221m 170 balls	47	114	3	52	31	
	11-1-30-0	UND'WOOD	....	178		1	69			48	115	3	52	32	

Time	Bowler	Figures	Balls	Runs	Batsman	Balls	Runs		Over	Total	W	Batsman1	Batsman2	
12:36	GREIG	9-2-22-0			. 2 4 W	73	3			121	4	52	38	
	12-1-37-1				I.CHAPPELL									
12:37			. .	180	. 1	2			49	122	4	52	1	
		UND'WOOD			. . . .	10		M15	50	122	4	52	1	
12:48	GREIG	10-3-22-0	3 . . . W	185	. 1	12				126	5	55	2	
	13-1-41-2		MARSH											
12:50			.	1					51	126	5	0	2	
		UND'WOOD			. . . .	20		M16	52	126	5	0	2	
	GREIG	11-4-22-0	. . . .	9				M17	53	126	5	0	2	
1:00	14-2-41-2		LUNCH		LUNCH									
1:40		UND'WOOD	1	10	. . . . 3 . .	27			54	130	5	1	5	
	WILLIS	12-4-26-0	2 . 1	13	. . . . .	32			55	133	5	4	5	
	14-2-34-2	UND'WOOD	. . . .	21				M18	56	133	5	4	5	
	WILLIS	13-5-26-0	.	22	4 . . . 4 . 1	39	2		57	142	5	4	14	
	15-2-43-2	TITMUS			. . . .	47		M19	58	142	5	4	14	
	UND'WOOD	13-8-23-1	 1	28	. . 4	49	3		59	147	5	5	18	
	14-5-31-0	TITMUS	. 1	30	. 2	55			60	150	5	6	20	
	UND'WOOD	14-8-26-1	. 1	32	. . . .	61			61	151	5	7	20	
	15-5-32-0	TITMUS	1	33	. . . 4 . 3	68	4		62	159	5	8	27	
	UND'WOOD	15-8-34-1			. . . 4 . .	76	5		63	163	5	8	31	
	16-5-36-0	TITMUS	 L	38	. . . .	79		M20;lb2	64	164	5	8	31	2
	UND'WOOD	16-8-34-1	. . . 4	46	1				65	168	5	12	31	
	17-5-40-0	TITMUS	. .	48	. . . . 4 1	85	6		66	173	5	12	36	
2:37	WILLIS	17-8-39-1			. / . . W	89		/new ball		173	6	12	36	
	16-2-44-3				WALKER									
2:39			. .	50	. 1	2			67	174	6	12	1	
		GREIG			. . . . . 2 . .	10			68	176	6	12	3	
	WILLIS	15-2-43-2	. 1	52	. . . .	16			69	177	6	13	3	
	17-2-45-3	GREIG	. 1 . .	56	. . . 1	20			70	179	6	14	4	
	WILLIS	16-2-45-2	3 . 1	59	1 . . 3 .	25			71	187	6	18	8	
	18-2-53-3	GREIG	. . . 4 . 1	65	2	. .	27		72	192	6	23	8	
	WILLIS	17-2-50-2	. 1 . . 3	70	. 1 .	30			73	197	6	27	9	
	19-2-58-3	TITMUS	. . . .	78				M21	74	197	6	27	9	
	GREIG	18-9-39-1	. 1	80	1 2	36			75	201	6	28	12	
	18-2-54-2	TITMUS	. 1	82	. . . . . .	42			76	202	6	29	12	
	GREIG	19-9-40-1	1	83	. . . . . .	49			77	203	6	30	12	
	19-2-55-2	TITMUS	. . . . . . (b2) .	91				M22;b2	78	205	6	30	12	4
	GREIG	20-10-40-1			 2	57			79	207	6	30	14	
3:40	20-2-57-2		TEA		TEA									
4:00		UND'WOOD	. . . .	95										
4:02		18-6-40-0	RAIN		RAIN									
4:06			. . . . .	99				M23	80	207	6	30	14	
	GREIG				2	65			81	209	6	30	16	
	21-2-59-2	UND'WOOD	. 2 4 2 . 1	105	3	. .	67		82	218	6	39	16	
	GREIG	19-6-49-0	 2	113					83	220	6	41	16	
	22-2-61-2	UND'WOOD			. 4 . 2	75	1		84	226	6	41	22	
	GREIG	20-6-55-0	1	114	. . . .	82			85	227	6	42	22	
	23-2-62-2	UND'WOOD	. . 1	117	. 4 . . 1	87	2		86	233	6	43	27	
	GREIG	21-6-60-0		118	 1	94			87	234	6	43	29	
	24-2-63-2	UND'WOOD	. . . .	122	. . . 1	98			88	235	6	43	29	
4:44		22-6-61-0	RAIN		RAIN									
4:56	WILLIS		. , 1	125	1	103			89	237	6	44	30	
5:04	20-2-60-3	TITMUS	. . . W	129						237	7	44	30	
		21-11-40-2	LILLEE											
5:05			. . . .	4				M24	90	237	7	0	30	
5:10	WILLIS				. . . . . W	108				237	8	0	30	
	21-3-60-4				MALLETT									
5:11					. . .	2		M25	91	237	8	0	0	
5:16		TITMUS	1	5	. . RO	6				238	9	1	0	
		22-11-42-2			THOMSON									
5:18					2 . . .	4			92	240	9	1	2	
5:24	WILLIS		1	6	. . . . . W	10				241	10	2	2	4
	21.7-3-61-5													

3rd DAY TIME	BOWLERS Pavilion End (N) NAME	BOWLERS Southern End (S) NAME	BATSMEN UMP: T. BROOKS (N) NAME	B	4/6	BATSMEN UMP: R. BAILHACHE (S) NAME	B	4/6	1 AHEAD NOTES	ENGLAND 2ND INNINGS TOTALS AT END OF OVER O	R	W	LBat	RBat	Ext
			AMISS			LLOYD									
5:35	LILLEE		1	5		...	3			1	1	0	1	0	
5:41	1-0-1-0		LIGHT/STUMPS			LIGHT/STUMPS				ATTENDANCE: 39,621					
11:00		THOMSON	..+..4..1	13	1				wd1	2	7	0	6	0	1
	LILLEE	1-0-5-0	..3 1	17		1 ...	7			3	12	0	10	1	
	2-0-6-0	THOMSON	...4 5	22	2	...	10			4	21	0	19	1	
	LILLEE	2-0-14-0	2.......	30						5	23	0	21	1	
	3-0-8-0	THOMSON				...2....	18			6	25	0	21	3	
	LILLEE	3-0-16-0	..3 4.	35	3	..1	21			7	33	0	28	4	
	4-0-16-0	THOMSON	3	36		1	28			8	37	0	31	5	
	LILLEE	4-0-20-0	.4 1 2.	41	4	..1	31			9	45	0	38	6	
	5-0-24-0	THOMSON	.1	43		..1 4..	37	1		10	51	0	39	11	
	WALKER	5-0-26-0	...1 1	48		2.1	40			11	56	0	41	14	
	1-0-5-0	THOMSON	3 1	50		.3 ...4	46	2		12	67	0	45	21	
	WALKER	6-0-37-0	..2..1	57			47			13	70	0	48	21	
	2-0-8-0	THOMSON	2 2.1 .1	63		.3	49		50: 71m 58 balls	14	79	0	54	24	
	WALKER	7-0-46-0	4..1	67	5	2 . 4 .	53			15	90	0	59	30	
	3-0-19-0	MALLETT	..1	71		...1	57			16	92	0	60	31	
	WALKER	1-0-2-0	.3	73		1	63			17	96	0	63	32	
	4-0-23-0	MALLETT	1	76		2 .2 (L2) 1	68		+100 p lb2	18	104	0	64	37	3
	WALKER	2-0-8-0	3	77		.1	75			19	108	0	67	38	
	5-0-27-0	MALLETT	....	85					M1	20	108	0	67	38	
	WALKER	3-1-8-0	1 ...	89		.1 .1	79			21	111	0	68	40	
12:45	6-0-30-0	MALLETT				..4 W	83				115	1	68	44	
		4-1-13-1				COWDREY									
12:47			...	92		1	1			22	116	1	68	1	
	WALKER					......2.	9			23	118	1	68	3	
	7-0-32-0	MALLETT	1	100						24	119	1	69	3	
	WALKER	5-1-14-1	...1	104		....	13			25	120	1	70	3	
1:00	8-0-33-0		LUNCH			LUNCH									
		MALLETT	1	110		.1	15			26	122	1	71	4	
	LILLEE	6-1-17-1	1 1	112		..2 1 1 .	21			27	128	1	73	8	
	6-0-30-0	MALLETT	1	119		.	22			28	129	1	74	8	
1:58	LILLEE	7-1-17-1	.1	121		.(L4).W	26		lb6		134	2	75	8	7
	7-0-31-1					EDRICH									
2:00						..	2			30	134	2	75	0	
		MALLETT	....	129					M2	31	134	2	75	0	
	LILLEE	8-2-17-1	1	134		.1	5			32	136	2	76	1	
	8-0-33-1	MALLETT	.4.3 ..	140	6	.1	7			33	144	2	83	2	
	LILLEE	9-2-25-1	..1 .	144		.1 .1	11			34	147	2	84	4	
	9-0-36-1	MALLETT	...1	148		L ...	15		lb7	35	149	2	85	4	8
2:29	THOMSON	10-2-26-1	..2 1	152		...W	19			36	152	3	88	4	
	8-0-49-1					DENNESS									
2:31		MALLETT	....	160					M3	37	152	3	88	0	
	THOMSON	11-3-26-1	.1	162		.1	6			38	154	3	89	1	
	9-0-51-1	MALLETT	.1 .	165		1	11			39	156	3	90	2	
2:45	THOMSON	12-3-28-1				W	12				156	4	90	2	
	10-0-52-2					GREIG									
2:47			......	171		.(n1)	2		nb1	40	157	4	90	1	
2:55		MALLETT	..W	174		...1	6				158	5	90	2	
		13-3-29-2	KNOTT												
2:56			.	1						41	158	5	0	2	
	THOMSON					...2....	14			42	160	5	0	4	
	11-0-54-2	MALLETT	1	7		..	16			43	161	5	1	4	
3:09	THOMSON	14-3-30-2	..3 W	11		.1	18				165	6	4	5	
	12-0-58-3		TITMUS												
3:11			..	3						44	165	6	0	5	
		MALLETT	......	8		2 1	20			45	168	6	0	8	
	THOMSON	15-3-33-2	......	14		.1	22			46	169	6	0	9	
	13-0-59-3	MALLETT				.2 ..(b2).1	30		b2	46	174	6	0	12	10
	LILLEE	16-3-36-2				2....2..	38			47	178	6	0	16	

348

	10-0-40-1	MALLETT	....	22				M4	48	178	6	0	16
		LILLEE	17-4-36-2			....	46		M5	49	178	6	0	16
3:40	11-1-40-1		TEA			TEA							
4:00/02		MALLETT	. W	24						178	7	0	16
			18-4-40-4										
			UND'WOOD										
4:03/06			...4 W	5	1					182	8	4	16
			WILLIS										
4:07			.	1					50	182	8	0	16
		LILLEE				1	54		51	183	8	0	17
	12-1-41-1	MALLETT	.	2		6.....(n2) 1	62	/1	nb2	52	192	8	0	26
		LILLEE	19-4-49-4			....	70		M6	53	192	8	0	26
	13-2-41-1	MALLETT	....	10					M7	54	192	8	0	26
		LILLEE	20-5-49-4	..1	13	1	75			55	194	8	1	27
4:33	14-2-43-1	THOMSON	..1	16		.....	80			56	195	8	2	27
		LILLEE	14-0-60-3	....	24				M8	57	195	8	2	27
			15-3-43-1	THOMSON			....	88		M9	58	195	8	2	27
		LILLEE	15-1-60-3	.2...4..	32	1				59	201	8	8	27
	16-3-49-1	MALLETT		32		1	96			60	202	8	8	28
		WALKER	21-5-50-4	...1	36		2 1 ..	100			61	206	8	9	31
			9-0-37-0	MALLETT	....	44				M10	62	206	8	9	31
		WALKER	22-6-50-4	...	47	.4..1	105	1/1		63	211	8	9	36
			10-0-42-0	MALLETT	.	48	4..(L2)..1	112	2/1	lb9	64	218	8	9	41	12
		WALKER	23-6-55-4	....+.	53	2.1	115		wd2	65	222	8	9	44	13
			11-0-43-0	MALLETT	....	56	.4..1	120	3/1		66	227	8	9	49
		THOMSON	24-6-60-4	.	57	4./....1	127	4/1	50:142m 121 balls /new ball	67	232	8	9	54
5:38	16-1-65-3	LILLEE				.4.2 W	132	5/1			238	8	9	60
			17-3-55-2			HENDRICK								
5:40						...	3			68	238	9	9	0
5:46		THOMSON		4..2...W	65					69	244	10	15	0	13
			17-1-71-4											

349

4th DAY — AUSTRALIA 2ND INNINGS (246 TO WIN)

TIME	BOWLERS Pavilion End (N) NAME	BOWLERS Southern End (S) NAME	BATSMEN UMP: T. BROOKS (N) NAME	B	4/6	BATSMEN UMP: R. BAILHACHE (S) NAME	B	4/6	NOTES	O	R	W	LBat	RBat	Ext
			REDPATH			W.EDWARDS									
5:57	WILLIS		...(b4)....	8					M1/b4	1	4	0	0	0	4
6:02	1-1-0-0		STUMPS			STUMPS				ATTENDANCE: 36,526					
11:03		GREIG				......W	8			4	1	0	0		
		1-1-1-0				I.CHAPPELL									
11:05						..	2		M2	2	4	1	0	0	
11:10	WILLIS		..L	11		..W	5		lb1	5	2	0	0	5	
	2-2-1-0					G.CHAPPELL									
11:11						..	2		M3	3	5	2	0	0	
		GREIG	1	16		...	5			4	6	2	1	0	
	WILLIS	2-1-1-1	..4.1	21	1	..1	8			5	12	2	6	1	
	3-2-6-1	GREIG	1	27		1 1	10			6	15	2	7	3	
	WILLIS	3-1-4-1	.3	29		....3 .	16			7	21	2	10	6	
	4-2-12-1	GREIG	1	34		2..	19			8	24	2	11	8	
	WILLIS	4-1-7-1	...1	38		....	23			9	25	2	12	8	
12:34	5-2-13-1	TITMUS	...b	42		..2.	27		b5	10	28	2	12	10	6
		GREIG 1-0-2-0	....	50					M4	11	28	2	12	10	
	5-2-7-1	TITMUS	.	51		1	34			12	29	2	12	11	
		GREIG 2-0-3-0	...1	55		1 ...	38			13	31	2	13	12	
	6-2-9-1	TITMUS	..1	58		......	43			14	32	2	14	12	
		GREIG 3-0-4-0	1	63		.2 L	46		lb2	15	36	2	15	14	7
	7-2-12-1	TITMUS	..L	67		.3 .1	50		lb3	16	41	2	15	18	8
		GREIG 4-0-8-0	1	71		1 .2.	54			17	45	2	16	21	
	8-2-16-1	TITMUS	.1	73		1	60			18	47	2	17	22	
		GREIG 5-0-10-0	......	79		.1	62			19	48	2	17	23	
	9-2-17-1	UND'WOOD				4.......	70	1		20	52	2	17	27	
		GREIG 1-0-4-0	1	86		1	71			21	54	2	18	28	
	10-2-19-1	UND'WOOD	1	87		....1 .4	78	2		22	60	2	19	33	
		GREIG 2-0-10-0	..1	90		...n.1	84		nb1	23	63	2	20	34	9
	11-2-21-1	UND'WOOD	..2.	94		...3	88			24	68	2	22	37	
1:00		3-0-15-0	LUNCH			LUNCH									
1:40	WILLIS		..1	97		2...1	93			25	72	2	23	40	
	6-2-17-1	TITMUS	..1	100		.....	98			26	73	2	24	40	
	WILLIS	6-0-11-0	1	108						27	74	2	25	40	
	7-2-18-1	TITMUS	2 1	115		1	99			28	78	2	28	41	
	WILLIS	7-0-15-0	.n	121		..1	102		nb2	29	80	2	28	42	10
	8-2-19-1	TITMUS	..2	124		1	107			30	83	2	30	43	
	WILLIS	8-0-18-0				.....2..	115			31	85	2	30	45	
	9-2-21-1	TITMUS	....	132					M5	32	85	2	30	45	
	WILLIS	9-1-18-0				.2.4..2.	123	3	50: 147m 119 balls	33	93	2	30	53	
	10-2-29-1	TITMUS	..1	135		.4..1	128	4		34	99	2	31	58	
	WILLIS	10-1-24-0	...2..2	142		3	129		• 100p	35	106	2	35	61	
2:33	11-2-36-1	TITMUS				.......W	137		M6	36	106	3	35	61	
						R.EDWARDS									
2:35	UND'WOOD	11-2-24-1	1	149		.	1			37	107	3	36	0	
		4-0-16-0	TITMUS .1 ,,,	154		..1	4			38	109	3	37	1	
	UND'WOOD	12-2-26-1	....	161		3	5			39	112	3	37	4	
		5-0-19-0	TITMUS	164		....	13		M7	40	112	3	37	4	
	UND'WOOD	13-2-26-1	..1 ..	166		..1	16			41	114	3	38	5	
3:00		6-0-21-0	TITMUS (1RO)	167		..4 1	20			42	120	4	39	10	
		14-2-33-1	WALTERS												
3:02			..1	3						42	121	4	1	10	
	UND'WOOD		....	11					M8	43	121	4	1	10	
3:08	7-1-21-0	TITMUS				W	21				121	5	1	10	
		15-2-34-2				MARSH									
3:10			..1	14		(L3) ...	4		lb6	44	125	5	2	0	13
	UND'WOOD		..1	17		2....	9			45	128	5	3	2	
	8-1-24-0	TITMUS	...1	21		....	13			46	129	5	4	2	
	UND'WOOD	16-2-35-2	....	29					M9	47	129	5	4	2	
	9-2-24-0	TITMUS	...1	33		2 1 .	16			48	133	5	5	5	
	UND'WOOD	17-2-39-2	2.1	36		....2 1	22			49	139	5	8	8	

	10-2-30-0	TITMUS	3	37		.1	29		50	143	5	11	9
		UND'WOOD	18-2-43-2	...1	41		...1	33		51	145	5	12	10
3:40	11-2-32-0		TEA			TEA						
4:00		TITMUS	4 1	43	1	...1 ,,	39		52	151	5	17	11
	GREIG	19-2-49-2	2 1 ...1	49		.1	41		53	156	5	21	12
	12-2-26-1	TITMUS	..2.24..	57	2				54	164	5	29	12
4:18	GREIG	20-2-57-2	2 1 W	60		1 3	43			171	6	32	16
	13-2-33-2		WALKER										
4:20			...	3					55	171	6	0	16
		TITMUS				....	51		M10	56	171	6	0	16
	GREIG	21-3-57-2	1			. 2 4	58	1		57	178	6	1	22
	14-2-40-2	TITMUS	....	11					M11	58	178	6	1	22
	UND'WOOD	22-4-57-2	2	16		2.1	61			59	183	6	3	25
	12-2-37-0	TITMUS				....	69		M12	60	183	6	3	25
	UND'WOOD	23-5-57-2	....	24					M13	61	183	6	3	25
	13-3-37-0	TITMUS				4.......	77	2		62	187	6	3	29
	UND'WOOD	24-5-61-2	....	32					M14	63	187	6	3	29
	14-4-37-0	TITMUS	...2..	38		.1	79			64	190	6	5	30
	UND'WOOD	25-5-64-2	....	45		L	80		M15,lb7	65	191	6	5	30	14
	15-5-37-0	TITMUS	......	50		..L	83		M16,lb8	66	192	6	5	30	15
	UND'WOOD	26-6-64-2	1 .	52		1 ..2.1	89			67	197	6	6	34
	16-5-42-0	TITMUS				....	97		M17	68	197	6	6	34
	UND'WOOD	27-7-64-2	..1	55		.....	102			69	198	6	7	34
	17-5-43-0	TITMUS	....	63					M18	70	198	6	7	34
	UND'WOOD	28-8-64-2				....	110		M19	71	198	6	7	34
	18-6-43-0	TITMUS	....	71					M20	72	198	6	7	34
5:34		WILLIS	29-9-64-2	/ .1	73		L ..n.4 2	117	3	lb9, nb3 /new ball	73	207	6	8	40	17
5:43	12-2-43-1	GREIG	.b	75		W	118		b6		208	7	8	40	18
			15-2-41-3				LILLEE							
5:45			.	76		...1	4			74	209	7	8	1
		WILLIS				.4..2.n2.	13	1	nb4	75	218	7	8	9	19
	13-2-51-1	GREIG	2.1 ...3	83		1	14			76	225	7	14	10
		WILLIS	16-2-48-3	..1 ..3	89		.1	16			77	230	7	18	11
	14-2-56-1	GREIG	..1	96		1	17			78	232	7	19	12
	UND'WOOD	17-2-50-3				....	25		M21	79	232	7	19	12
6:21	19-7-43-0	GREIG	.1	98		. (n2) W	28		nb5		235	8	20	14
			18-2-54-3				MALLETT							
6;22			. 2 1	101		.	1			80	238	8	23	0
6;26						**MATCH DRAWN**					**ATTENDANCE: 42,827**			

351

ENGLAND FIRST Innings

IN	OUT	MINS	NO	BATSMAN	HOW OUT	BOWLER	RUNS	WK	TOTAL	BALLS	4s	6s	NOTES
11:00	11:05	5	1	DL AMISS	CT WALTERS	LILLEE	4	1	4	8			Edged away swinger to third slip
11:00	12:49	109	2	D LLOYD	CT MALLETT	THOMSON	14	2	34	90	1		Gloved rising delivery to gully
11:06	3-32	229	3	MC COWDREY	LBW	THOMSON	35	3	110	171	3		Beaten for pace playing back
12:50	3:39	132	4	JH EDRICH	CT MARSH	MALLETT	49	4	110	124	3		Thin edge down leg side
3:34	4:37	42	5	MH DENNESS	CT MARSH	MALLETT	8	5	141	39			Edged attempted cut
4:00	5:03	63	6	AW GREIG	RUN OUT		28	6	157	62	4		Failed to beat throw from third man
4:39	12:17	157	7	APE KNOTT	BOWLED	THOMSON	51	10	242	119	2		Played around straight delivery
5:05	5:59	54	8	FJ TITMUS	CT MALLETT	LILLEE	10	7	176	45			Short ball fended to gully off glove
11:00	11:38	38	9	DL UNDERWOOD	CT MARSH	WALKER	9	8	213	23	1		Edged full ball to wicketkeeper
11:39	11:54	15	10	RGD WILLIS	CT WALTERS	THOMSON	13	9	232	15	2		Skied slog into the off side
11:55	12:17	22	11	M HENDRICK	NOT OUT		8			18	2		
					EXTRAS		11						LB 1, W 1, NB 9
					TOTAL		242						(ALL OUT, 88.4 OVERS)

BOWLER	O	M	R	W	NB/W
LILLEE	20	2	70	2	
THOMSON	22	4	72	4	6/1
WALKER	24	10	36	1	
WALTERS	7	2	15	0	
MALLETT	15	3	37	2	1/

Runs	Mins	Overs	L50
50	141	28.6	
100	216	44.4	75
150	295	61.4	79
200	389	79.3	94
250			
300			
350			
400			
450			
500			

LUNCH: 40-2 25 overs
TEA: 110-4 49.4 overs
STUMPS DAY 1: 176-6 74.4 overs

Wkt	Partnership		RUNS
1	Amiss	Lloyd	4
2	Cowdrey	Lloyd	30
3	Cowdrey	Edrich	76
4	Denness	Edrich	0
5	Denness	Greig	31
6	Knott	Greig	16
7	Knott	Titmus	19
8	Knott	Underwood	37
9	Knott	Willis	19
10	Knott	Hendrick	10

AUSTRALIA FIRST Innings

IN	OUT	MINS	NO	BATSMAN	HOW OUT	BOWLER	RUNS	WK	TOTAL	BALLS	4s	6s	N O T E S
12:28	12:48	242	1	IR REDPATH	CT KNOTT	GREIG	55	5	126	185	4		Edged cut to wicketkeeper
12:28	11:02	136	2	WJ EDWARDS	CT DENNESS	WILLIS	29	1	65	123	1		Cross-batted short ball to cover
11:03	11:10	7	3	GS CHAPPELL	CT GREIG	WILLIS	2	2	67	6			Off shoulder of bat to second slip
11:11	11:16	5	4	R EDWARDS	CT COWDREY	TITMUS	1	3	68	6			Defensive push edged to first slip
11:17	12:36	79	5	KD WALTERS	CT LLOYD	GREIG	36	4	121	73	3		Clipped full ball to square leg
12:37	2:37	80	6	IM CHAPPELL	LBW	WILLIS	36	6	173	89	6		Missed leg-side clip to full ball
12:50	3:40	130	7	RW MARSH	CT KNOTT	TITMUS	44	7	237	129	3		Top-edged sweep into the air
2:39	5:10	115	8	MHN WALKER	CT KNOTT	WILLIS	30	8	237	108	2		Edged defensive shot
5:05	5:24	19	9	DK LILLEE	NOT OUT		2			6			
5:11	5:16	5	10	AA MALLETT	RUN OUT		0	9	238	6			Sent back after looking for single
5:18	5:24	6	11	JR THOMSON	BOWLED	WILLIS	2	10	241	10			Missed fast yorker
				EXTRAS		B 2, LB 2	4						
				TOTAL	(ALL OUT, 92.7 OVERS)		**241**						

BOWLER	O	M	R	W	NB/W
WILLIS	21.7	4	61	5	
HENDRICK	2.6*	1	8	0	
UNDERWOOD	22	6	62	0	
GREIG	24	2	63	2	
TITMUS	22	11	43	2	

*Hendrick injured. Over recorded as complete in team total with no other bowler finishing it

Runs	Mins	Overs	Last50
50	93	19.4	93
100	198	41.7	105
150	284	59.4	86
200	357	75	73
250			
300			
350			
400			
450			
500			

LUNCH: 20-0
6 overs, 222 behind

TEA: 62-0
25 overs, 180 behind

STUMPS DAY 2: 63-0
28.3 overs, 179 behind

LUNCH: 126-5
53 overs, 116 behind

TEA: 207-6
79 overs, 35 behind

Wkt	Partnership		RUNS
1	Redpath	Edwards	65
2	Redpath	Chappell	2
3	Redpath	Edwards	1
4	Redpath	Walters	53
5	Redpath	Chappell	5
6	Marsh	Chappell	47
7	Marsh	Walker	64
8	Lillee	Walker	0
9	Lillee	Mallett	1
10	Lillee	Thomson	3

ENGLAND SECOND Innings

IN	OUT	MINS	NO	BATSMAN	HOW OUT	BOWLER	RUNS	WK	TOTAL	BALLS	4s	6s	NOTES
5:35	2:55	201	1	DL AMISS	CT I.CHAPPELL	MALLETT	90	5	158	174	6		Mistimed shot to mid-wicket
5:35	12:45	111	2	D LLOYD	CT AND B	MALLETT	44	1	115	83	4		Drove straight back to bowler
12:47	1:08	31	3	MC COWDREY	CT G. CHAPPELL	LILLEE	8	2	134	26			Lifter edged high to second slip
2:00	2:29	29	4	JH EDRICH	CT MARSH	THOMSON	4	3	152	19			Edged wide delivery
2:31	2:45	14	5	MH DENNESS	CT I.CHAPPELL	THOMSON	2	4	156	12			Edged seaming delivery to slip
2:47	5:38	151	6	AW GREIG	CT G. CHAPPELL	LILLEE	60	9	238	132	5		Diving catch after steer to gully
2:56	3:09	13	7	APE KNOTT	CT MARSH	THOMSON	4	6	165	11			Diving catch by wicketkeeper
3:11	4:02	31	8	FJ TITMUS	BOWLED	MALLETT	0	7	178	24			Tentative shot to full delivery
4:03	4:06	3	9	DL UNDERWOOD	CT I.CHAPPELL	MALLETT	4	8	182	5	1		Edged forward defensive to slip
4:07	5:46	89	10	RGD WILLIS	BOWLED	THOMSON	15	10	244	65	2		Fast, straight ball on middle stump
5:40	5:46	6	11	M HENDRICK	NOT OUT		0			3			
					EXTRAS		B 2, LB 9, W 2		13				
					TOTAL	(ALL OUT, 69 OVERS)			244				

Runs	Mins	Overs	L50		
50	53	9.6	53		STUMPS DAY 3: 1-0
100	95	17.4	42		1 over; 2 ahead
150	174	34.3	79		LUNCH: 120-1
200	297	58.6	123		25 overs; 121 ahead
250					TEA: 178-6
300					49 overs; 179 ahead
350					+ Amiss/Lloyd 100
400					partnership in 95 min
450					
500					

BOWLER	O	M	R	W	NB/W
LILLEE	19	3	55	2	
THOMSON	17	1	71	4	1/1
WALKER	11	0	45	0	/1
MALLETT	24	6	60	4	1/

wkt	Partnership		RUNS
1	Amiss	Lloyd	115
2	Amiss	Cowdrey	19
3	Amiss	Edrich	18
4	Amiss	Denness	4
5	Amiss	Greig	2
6	Knott	Greig	7
7	Titmus	Greig	13
8	Underwood	Greig	4
9	Willis	Greig	56
10	Willis	Hendrick	6

AUSTRALIA SECOND Innings

MATCH DRAWN

IN	OUT	MINS	NO	BATSMAN	HOW OUT	BOWLER	RUNS	WK	TOTAL	BALLS	4s	6s	NOTES
5:57	3:00	205	1	IR REDPATH	RUN OUT		39	4	121	167	1		Failed to get back for second run
5:57	11:03	5	2	WJ EDWARDS	LBW	GREIG	0	1	4	6			Moved across stumps, trapped
11:05	11:10	5	3	IM CHAPPELL	LBW	WILLIS	0	2	5	5			Beaten by pace on back foot
11:11	2:33	162	4	GS CHAPPELL	LBW	TITMUS	61	3	106	137	4		Missed on back foot, turning to leg
2:35	3:08	33	5	R EDWARDS	CT LLOYD	TITMUS	10	5	120	21	1		Bat-pad catch at short leg
3:02	3:40	56	6	KD WALTERS	CT DENNESS	GREIG	32	6	171	60	2		Driven low to cover
3:10	5:43	133	7	RW MARSH	CT KNOTT	GREIG	40	7	208	118	3		Caught down leg side
4:20	6:26	126	8	MHN WALKER	NOT OUT		23			101			
5:45	6:21	36	9	DK LILLEE	CT DENNESS	GREIG	14	8	235	1	1		Mis-hit to cover
6:22	6:26	4	10	AA MALLETT	NOT OUT		0						

EXTRAS		B 6, LB 9, NB 4	19
TOTAL	(8 WICKETS, 80 OVERS)		234

BOWLER	O	M	R	W	NB/W
WILLIS	14	2	56	1	3/
GREIG	18	2	56	4	2/
TITMUS	29	10	64	2	
UNDERWOOD	19	7	43	0	

Runs	Mins	Overs	Last50
50	100	19.1	100
100	170	34.1	70
150	247	51.5	77
200	342	72.3	95
250			
300			
350			
400			
450			
500			

STUMPS DAY 4: 4-0
242 to win

LUNCH: 68-2
24 overs, 178 to win

TEA: 145-5
51 overs, 101 to win

+ Redpath/Chappell 100 partnership in 158 min

MATCH ATTENDANCE: 250,719

Wkt	Partnership		RUNS
1	Redpath	Edwards	4
2	Redpath	Chappell	1
3	Redpath	Chappell	101
4	Redpath	Edwards	14
5	Walters	Edwards	1
6	Walters	Marsh	50
7	Walker	Marsh	37
8	Walker	Lillee	27
9			
10			

FOURTH TEST MATCH

AUSTRALIA v **ENGLAND** at SYDNEY CRICKET GROUND on JANUARY 4-6, 8-9 1975

1st DAY	BOWLERS Paddington End (N)	BOWLERS Randwick End (S)	BATSMEN UMP: T. BROOKS (N)			BATSMEN UMP: R. BAILHACHE (S)			NOTES	AUSTRALIA 1ST TOTALS AT END OF OVER					INNINGS
TIME	NAME	NAME	NAME	B	4/6	NAME	B	4/6	Toss AUS	O	R	W	LBat	RBat	Ext
11:00			DAMP PITCH			DAMP PITCH									
			REDPATH			McCOSKER									
11:30	WILLIS		L 2	6		.1	2		lb1	1	4	0	2	1	1
	1-0-3-0	ARNOLD				.n.......	11		M1/nb1	2	5	0	2	1	2
	WILLIS	1-1-0-0	1	13		1	12			3	7	0	3	2	
	2-0-5-0	ARNOLD	.L	16		2..n(n1) .1	19		nb3/lb2	4	13	0	3	6	4
	WILLIS	2-1-4-0	...1	20		..+1 .	23		wd1	5	16	0	4	7	5
	3-0-7-0	ARNOLD	1	27		1	24			6	18	0	5	8	
	WILLIS	3-1-6-0	.2...1	33		1 1	26			7	23	0	8	10	
12:08	4-0-12-0	GREIG				......2 1	34			8	26	0	9	13	
	ARNOLD	1-0-3-0	.n..	37		1	39		nb4	9	28	0	8	14	6
	4-1-7-0	GREIG	...3	41		2.1 .	43			10	34	0	11	17	
	ARNOLD	2-0-9-0	...n.1	47		.2.	46		nb5	11	38	0	12	19	7
	5-0-10-0	GREIG	.1 1	50		,4.1 .	51	1		12	45	0	14	24	
	ARNOLD	3-0-16-0	n1	58		1	52		nb6	13	48	0	15	25	8
	6-0-12-0	UND'WOOD				....	60		M2	14	48	0	15	25	
	WILLIS	1-1-0-0	1	59		4 2.4 2..	67	3		15	61	0	16	37	
	5-0-25-0	UND'WOOD	...1	63		....	71			16	62	0	17	37	
	WILLIS	2-1-1-0	....	71					M3	17	62	0	17	37	
1:03	6-1-25-0		LUNCH			LUNCH									
1:40		TITMUS	.	72		1	78			18	63	0	17	38	
	WILLIS	1-0-1-0				......4.	86	4		19	67	0	17	42	
	7-1-29-0	TITMUS	..1	75		1	91			20	69	0	18	43	
	WILLIS	2-0-3-0	..	77		1	97			21	70	0	18	44	
	8-1-30-0	TITMUS	.....	82		..1	100			22	71	0	18	45	
	WILLIS	3-0-4-0				....	108		M4	23	71	0	18	45	
	9-2-30-0	TITMUS	......4.	90	1					24	75	0	22	45	
	ARNOLD	4-0-8-0	..2...	96		.1	110			25	78	0	24	46	
	7-0-15-0	TITMUS	...1	100		...3	114			26	82	0	25	49	
	ARNOLD	5-0-12-0	3..n 2 n n,1	109		.3	116		50:133m 116b/nb9	27	94	0	31	52	11
2:27	8-0-24-0	TITMUS	.2..W	114							96	1	33	52	
		6-0-14-1	I.CHAPPELL												
2:29			...	3						28	96	1	0	52	
	ARNOLD		...1 ..	9		1 1	118			29	99	1	1	54	
	9-0-27-0	TITMUS	..	11		2 1	124			30	102	1	1	57	
	ARNOLD	7-0-17-1				4	132	5		31	106	1	1	61	
	10-0-31-0	TITMUS	....1 .	17		.1	134			32	108	1	2	62	
	UND'WOOD	8-0-19-1				....	142		M5	33	108	1	2	62	
	3-2-1-0	TITMUS	...1 3	22		2.1	145			34	115	1	6	65	
	UND'WOOD	9-0-26-1	1 1	24		....1 4	151	6		35	122	1	8	70	
	4-2-8-0	TITMUS	3 .3 4	28	1	.1 .1	155			36	134	1	18	72	
	GREIG	10-0-38-1				.2 1	163			37	137	1	18	75	
	4-0-19-0	UND'WOOD	...	31		..4.1	168	7		38	142	1	18	80	
3:19	GREIG	5-2-13-0				W	169				142	2	18	80	
	5-1-19-1					G.CHAPPELL									
3:21						....	7		M6	39	142	2	18	0	
		UND'WOOD	.1 ..4.	37	2	.3	9			40	150	2	23	3	
	GREIG	6-2-21-0				..2.....	17			41	152	2	23	5	
	6-1-21-1	UND'WOOD	..2....4	45	3					42	158	2	29	5	
	GREIG	7-2-27-0				....4...	25	1		43	162	2	29	9	
4:02	7-1-25-1		TEA			TEA									
		UND'WOOD	....	53					M7	44	162	2	29	9	
	WILLIS	8-3-27-0	.	55		1	31			45	163	2	29	10	
	10-2-31-0	UND'WOOD				4........	39	2		46	167	2	29	14	
	WILLIS	9-3-31-0	2..3	59		....	43			47	172	2	34	14	
	11-2-36-0	UND'WOOD	...4 2..2	67	4					48	180	2	42	14	
	WILLIS	10-3-39-0				4......4	51	4		49	188	2	42	22	
	12-2-44-0	UND'WOOD	4..1	71	5	....	55			50	193	2	47	22	

Time	Bowler	Figures	Batsman	Scoring	Score		Batsman	Scoring	Score		Notes	Over	Total	W	Bat1	Bat2	Extras
	ARNOLD	11-3-44-0		. 2 . . . 3	77			. .	57		50:110m 77 balls	51	198	2	52	22	
		11-0-36-0	UND'WOOD	. . 1	80			. . . . .	62			52	199	2	53	22	
4:45	ARNOLD	12-3-45-0		. . . W	83								199	3	53	22	
		12-1-36-1					EDWARDS										
4:47				. . . . .	5						M8	53	199	3	0	22	
			UND'WOOD	1 . . .	9			. . 1 (n4) 3	67	5	nb10	54	208	3	1	30	
	ARNOLD	13-3-54-0						. . . 2	75			55	210	3	1	32	
		13-1-38-1	TITMUS	. . 1	12			. . . 4 .	80	6		56	215	3	2	36	
	ARNOLD	11-0-43-1		1	13			. . 4	87	7		57	220	3	3	40	
		14-1-43-1	TITMUS	 4	21	1						58	224	3	7	40	
	ARNOLD	12-0-47-1						. . . .	95		M9	59	224	3	7	40	
		15-2-43-1	TITMUS	. . . .	29						M10	60	224	3	7	40	
	ARNOLD	13-1-47-1		. . . .	36			1	96			61	225	3	7	41	
		16-2-44-1	TITMUS	. 4 1 . . .	42	2		3 3	98			62	236	3	12	47	
	GREIG	14-1-58-1						. . 2 . . 2 . 1	106		50:118m 104 balls	63	241	3	12	52	
		8-1-30-1	TITMUS	. 4 .	45	3		 3	111			64	248	3	16	55	
	GREIG	15-1-65-1						. . . .	119		M11	65	248	3	16	55	
		9-2-30-1	TITMUS	. . . .	53						M12	66	248	3	16	55	
5:56	GREIG	16-2-65-1		. . . W	57			. 3	121				251	4	16	58	
		10-2-33-2		WALTERS													
5:58				. .	2							67	251	4	16	58	
6:00				STUMPS				STUMPS			ATTENDANCE: 52,164						
11:00			WILLIS	1	3			/ . . 1 . . 2 .	128		/new ball	68	255	4	1	61	
11:07	ARNOLD	13-2-48-0		. . . W	7								255	5	1	61	
		17-3-44-2		MARSH													
11:09				. . . .	4							69	255	5	0	61	
			WILLIS	. .	6			2 3	134			70	260	5	0	66	
	ARNOLD	14-2-53-0						. . . .	142		M13	71	260	5	0	66	
		18-3-44-2	WILLIS	. 2 . 4 1	11	1		. . 1	145			72	268	5	7	67	
	ARNOLD	15-2-61-0		1 1	13			. . . . 1 1	151			73	272	5	9	69	
		19-3-48-2	WILLIS	. . 1	20			1	152			74	274	5	10	70	
	GREIG	16-2-63-0						. . . 4 4 . . .	160	9		75	282	5	10	78	
		11-2-41-2	WILLIS	. 2 2 4	28	2						76	290	5	18	78	
	GREIG	17-2-71-0		. . . . 4 2 .	35	3		1	161			77	297	5	24	79	
		12-2-48-2	ARNOLD	2 2 . . . L	41			1 .	163		lb3	78	303	5	28	80	12
12:05	GREIG	20-3-53-2		. 2 W	44								305	6	30	80	
		13-2-54-3		WALKER													
12:07				. 1 . .	4			3	164			79	309	6	1	83	
12:15			ARNOLD					. . . . n . . . W	173			80	310	7	1	83	13
		21-4-53-3						LILLEE									
12:17	GREIG			. . . . . 2 . .	12							81	312	7	3	0	
		14-2-56-3	ARNOLD	. 1	14			. 3	6			82	316	7	4	3	
	GREIG	22-4-57-3		. 3 . . 3	19			. L .	9		lb4	83	323	7	10	2	14
		15-2-62-3	ARNOLD	. . 1	22			 4	14	1		84	328	7	11	7	
	GREIG	23-4-62-3		2 . 1	25			 1	19			85	332	7	14	8	
12:49	16-2-66-3		ARNOLD					. . . W	23				332	8	14	8	
		24-4-62-4						MALLETT									
12:51				. . . .	4						M14	86	332	8	14	0	
	GREIG			 1	33							87	333	8	15	0	
		17-2-67-3	ARNOLD					. . . .	8			88	334	8	16	0	
1:02		25-4-63-4		LUNCH				LUNCH									
1:40	GREIG			. . 1	40			4	13	1		89	339	8	17	4	
		18-2-72-3	ARNOLD	1 . . . 3	45			. 1 1	16			90	345	8	21	6	
	GREIG	26-4-69-4		1	46			4 1 . 2 . 1	23	2		91	354	8	22	14	
		19-2-81-3	ARNOLD	2 . 1	49			1 . . n 2 .	29		nb11	92	361	8	25	17	15
	GREIG	27-4-75-4		. . . 1 1	54			1 . .	32			93	364	8	27	18	
2:12	20-2-84-3		ARNOLD	. . . 3 W	59			1	33				368	9	30	19	
		28-4-79-5		THOMSON													
2:14				. .	2							94	368	9	0	19	
	GREIG			. 1	4			4 1	39	3		95	374	9	1	24	
		21-2-90-3	ARNOLD	(n2) . . 4 . 1	11	1		. .	41		nb12	96	381	9	8	24	
	GREIG	29-4-86-5		1 1	13			. . 4 . 1 .	47	4		97	388	9	10	29	
		22-2-97-3	WILLIS	. 4 . 4 . 1	19	3		. n .	50		nb13	98	398	9	19	29	16
2:41	GREIG	18-2-80-0		. 4 . 1	23	4		2 . W	53				405	10	24	31	
		22.7-2-104-4															

2nd DAY	BOWLERS		BATSMEN					NOTES	ENGLAND 1ST INNINGS					
	Paddington End (N)	Randwick End (S)	UMP: T. BROOKS (N)			UMP: R. BAILHACHE (S)			TOTALS AT END OF OVER					
TIME	NAME	NAME	NAME	B	4/6	NAME	B	4/6		O	R	W	LBat	RBat	Ext
			AMISS			LLOYD									
2:53		LILLEE	...1	4		....	4			1	1	0	1	0	
	THOMSON	1-0-1-0	+1 (b4).b	8		..1 (b4)	8		wd1, b9	2	13	0	2	1	10
		1-0-2-0	LILLEE	1		9	....	15			3	14	0	3	1	
	THOMSON	2-0-2-0	2.2.....	17						4	18	0	7	1	
		2-0-6-0	LILLEE	4...	21	1	...3	19		5	25	0	11	4	
	THOMSON	3-0-9-0				.24....4	27	2		6	35	0	11	14	
		3-0-16-0	LILLEE	..1	24		.....	32		7	36	0	12	14	
3:32	WALKER	4-0-10-0	.W	26							36	1	12	14	
		1-0-1-1	COWDREY												
3:34			1	6						8	37	1	1	14	
		LILLEE	.3	8		......	38			9	40	1	4	14	
3:40		5-0-13-0	TEA			TEA									
4:00	WALKER		1	13		..1	41			10	42	1	5	15	
4:07	2-0-3-1	LILLEE				4..W	45	3			46	2	5	19	
		6-0-17-1				EDRICH									
4:09						....	4			11	46	2	5	0	
	WALKER		1	19		..	6			12	47	2	6	0	
		3-0-4-1	LILLEE	24	27	1				13	53	2	12	0	
	WALKER	7-0-23-1	....	31		...1	10			14	54	2	12	1	
		4-0-5-1	LILLEE			......4.	18	1		15	58	2	12	5	
	WALKER	8-0-27-1	....4...	39	2					16	62	2	16	5	
		5-0-9-1	THOMSON			....	26		M1	17	62	2	16	5	
	WALKER	4-1-16-0	..1 ..1	45		.L	28		lb1	18	65	2	18	5	11
4:47	6-0-11-1	THOMSON	4.W	48	3						69	3	22	5	
		5-1-20-1	FLETCHER												
4:49			B	1		....	32		b10	19	70	3	0	5	12
	WALKER		1	6		...	35			20	71	3	1	5	
		7-0-12-1	THOMSON	......4.	14	1				21	75	3	5	5	
	WALKER	6-1-24-1	L	15		....3 ..	42		lb2	22	79	3	5	8	13
		8-0-15-1	THOMSON	.........(b4)	23					M2;b14	23	83	3	5	8	17
	WALKER	7-2-24-1		24		1	49			24	84	3	5	9	
		9-0-16-1	THOMSON			......2.	57			25	86	3	5	11	
	WALKER	8-2-26-1	....	32					M3	26	86	3	5	11	
		10-1-16-1	LILLEE	...2	36		...1	61			27	89	3	7	12	
	WALKER	9-0-30-1	2...	40		...1	65			28	92	3	9	13	
		11-1-19-1	LILLEE			....	73		M4	29	92	3	9	13	
	MALLETT	10-1-30-1	2.4.2...	48	2					30	100	3	17	13	
		1-0-8-0	LILLEE			....	81		M5	31	100	3	17	13	
	WALTERS	11-2-30-1	..2.4...	56	3					32	106	3	23	13	
6:00	1-0-6-0		STUMPS			STUMPS				ATTENDANCE: 42,176					
11:00		THOMSON	.1	58		..b ...	87		b15	33	108	3	24	13	18
11:07	WALKER	9-2-27-1	...W	62							108	4	24	13	
		12-1-23-2	GREIG												
11:09			...4	4	1					34	112	4	4	13	
		THOMSON				....	95		M6	35	112	4	4	13	
	WALKER	10-3-27-1	...3	8		.2.4	99	2		36	121	4	7	19	
11:24	13-1-32-2	THOMSON	..2.W	13							123	5	9	19	
		11-3-29-2	KNOTT												
11:27			...	3						37	123	5	0	19	
	WALKER		1	4		2...1 ..	106			38	127	5	1	22	
		14-1-36-2	THOMSON	.1	6		.2.2..	112			39	132	5	2	26	
	WALKER	12-3-34-2	1	14						40	133	5	3	26	
		15-1-37-2	THOMSON	..3	17		1	117			41	137	5	6	27	
	WALKER	13-3-38-2	.4....	23	1	.1	119			42	142	5	10	28	
		16-1-42-2	LILLEE			./.....1	127			43	143	5	10	29	
	WALKER	12-2-31-1	.	24		1	134			44	144	5	10	30	
		17-1-43-2	LILLEE	1	25		...1 ...	141			45	146	5	11	31	
	WALKER	13-2-33-1	....	33					M7	46	146	5	11	31	
		18-2-43-2	LILLEE			.....2..	149			47	148	5	11	33	
	WALKER	14-2-35-1	4.1 2.	38	1	..1	152			48	156	5	18	34	
		19-2-51-2	LILLEE	...	41		1	157			49	157	5	18	35	
	WALKER	15-2-36-1	.1	43		...1 .4	163	3		50	163	5	19	40	

358

Time	Bowler1 fig	Bowler2	Balls1	Runs1		Balls2	Runs2		Bowler fig	Over	Score	W	Bat1	Bat2	
	20-2-57-2	WALTERS	....	51					M8	51	163	5	19	40	
	I.CHAPPELL	2-1-6-0	1	57		4 1	165	4		52	169	5	20	45	
	1-0-6-0	WALTERS	1 .	61		4..L	169		lb3	53	175	5	21	49	19
	I.CHAPPELL	3-1-11-0	....4..	68	2	1	170		50;220m 170 balls	54	180	5	25	50	
12:52	2-0-11-0	WALTERS				W	171				180	5	25	50	
		4-2-11-1				TITMUS									
12:54						....	7		M9	55	180	5	25	0	
	I.CHAPPELL		. 1	70		......	13			56	181	6	26	0	
1:00	3-0-12-0		LUNCH			LUNCH									
		THOMSON	4	78	3					57	185	6	30	0	
	WALKER	14-3-42-2	L	79		. 1	19		lb4	58	187	6	30	1	20
	21-2-58-2	THOMSON	....4 2.4	87	5					59	197	6	40	1	
	WALKER	15-3-52-2	..3	90		3 2.4.	24	1		60	209	6	43	10	
	22-2-70-2	WALTERS	..1	93		.4..1	29	2		61	215	6	44	15	
	WALKER	5-2-17-1	.2..1 2	99		1 1	31			62	222	6	49	17	
	23-2-77-2	WALTERS	1	100		..1	38		50: 220m 100 balls	63	224	6	50	18	
	I.CHAPPELL	6-2-19-1	4..1	104	6	4	42	3		64	233	6	55	22	
2:21	4-0-21-0	WALTERS	2.4 1	108		. W	44				240	7	62	22	
		7-2-26-2				UNDERWOOD									
2:23						..	2			65	240	7	62	0	
	LILLEE		/4 2 . 2 . 4 . 2	116	8				/new ball	66	254	7	76	0	
	16-2-50-1	THOMSON	.2 4.	120	9	..4 1	6	1		67	265	7	82	5	
	LILLEE	16-3-63-2				...4... 4	14	3		68	273	7	82	13	
2:45	17-2-58-1	THOMSON	. W	122							273	8	82	13	
		17-3-67-3	WILLIS													
2:47			...1	4		. 3	16			69	277	8	1	16	
	LILLEE		.1 .	7		L ...1	21		lb5	70	280	8	2	17	21
3:01	18-2-60-1	THOMSON	W	8		.. 4 1	25	4			285	9	2	22	
		18-3-72-4	ARNOLD													
3:03			...	3						71	285	9	0	22	
	LILLEE		..1	6		1 ..4.	30	5		72	291	9	1	27	
		19-2-66-1	THOMSON	(L2)....2..	14				lb7	73	295	9	3	27	23
3:16	LILLEE	19-3-74-4				W	31				295	10	3	27	
	19.1-2-66-2														

359

3rd DAY — 110 AHEAD AUSTRALIA 2ND INNINGS

TIME	BOWLERS Paddington End (N) NAME	BOWLERS Randwick End (S) NAME	BATSMEN UMP: R. BAILHACHE (N) NAME REDPATH	B	4/6	BATSMEN UMP: T. BROOKS (S) NAME I.CHAPPELL	B	4/6	NOTES	O	R	W	LBat	RBat	Ext
3:37	WILLIS		.2..1..	7		1	1			1	4	0	3	1	
	1-0-4-0	ARNOLD	1	14		1	2			2	6	0	4	2	
	WILLIS	1-0-2-0	..2..3	20		..	4			3	11	0	9	2	
	2-0-9-0	ARNOLD	.1 ...	25		..3	7			4	15	0	10	5	
3:59	WILLIS	2-0-6-0				.W	9				15	1	10	5	
	3-0-15-1					G.CHAPPELL									
4:02			1	26		.(n4) 1 ...	6	1	nb1	5	21	1	11	5	
		ARNOLD	.1	28		....4.	12	2		6	26	1	12	9	
	WILLIS	3-0-11-0	..n..1	34		..3	15		nb2	7	31	1	13	12	1
	4-0-19-1	ARNOLD	2	40		4 1	17	3		8	38	1	15	17	
	GREIG	4-0-18-0				....	25		M1	9	38	1	15	17	
	1-1-0-0	ARNOLD	.1 ..1	45		..1	28			10	41	1	17	18	
	GREIG	5-0-21-0	1 ..	48		.2..1	33			11	45	1	18	21	
	2-1-4-0	ARNOLD				..2..4.1	41	4		12	52	1	18	28	
	GREIG	6-0-28-0	......	54		4 L	43	5	lb1	13	57	1	18	32	2
	3-1-8-0	ARNOLD	..	56		1	49			14	58	1	18	33	
	GREIG	7-0-29-0	.4.....	63	1	3	50			15	65	1	22	36	
	4-1-15-0	ARNOLD	1	68		4 3	53	6		16	73	1	23	43	
	UND'WOOD	8-0-37-0	3 ..	71		1	58			17	77	1	26	44	
	1-0-4-0	GREIG				..2.2..2	66		50:78min 66 balls	18	83	1	26	50	
	UND'WOOD	5-1-21-0	....4.3	78	2	.	67			19	90	1	33	50	
	2-0-11-0	GREIG	.42.1..	85	3	1	68			20	98	1	40	51	
	UND'WOOD	6-1-29-0	1 1	87		..4 1 3 2	74	7		21	110	1	42	61	
	3-0-23-0	TITMUS	....	95					M2	22	110	1	42	61	
	UND'WOOD	1-1-0-0				....4 4..	82	9	•100p	23	118	1	42	69	
	4-0-31-0	TITMUS	4	103	4					24	122	1	46	69	
	WILLIS	2-1-4-0				....	90		M3	25	122	1	46	69	
	5-1-19-1	TITMUS	1	109		..	92			26	123	1	47	69	
6:00		3-1-5-0	STUMPS			STUMPS			ATTENDANCE: 33,780						
11:00	WILLIS		..2.....	117						27	125	1	49	69	
	6-1-21-1	ARNOLD				....	100		M4	28	125	1	49	69	
	WILLIS	9-1-37-0	.2.1	121		...2	104		50:155m 120 balls	29	130	1	52	71	
	7-1-26-0	ARNOLD	.1 2.	125		...1	108			30	134	1	55	72	
	WILLIS	10-1-41-0	1	126		1	115			31	136	1	56	73	
	8-1-28-0	ARNOLD	.1	128		2....	121			32	139	1	57	75	
	WILLIS	11-1-44-0	....1 ..	134		.1	123			33	141	1	58	76	
	9-1-30-0	ARNOLD	..4.	138	5	...1	127			34	146	1	62	77	
	WILLIS	12-1-49-0	2.1 ..	143		4 1 1	130	10		35	155	1	65	83	
	10-1-39-0	ARNOLD				....	138		M5	36	155	1	65	83	
	GREIG	13-2-49-0	...1 ..	149		..1	140			37	157	1	66	84	
	7-1-31-0	ARNOLD	......	155		.1	142			38	158	1	66	85	
	GREIG	14-2-50-0	.1	157		4 +...1 1	148	11	wd1	39	166	1	67	91	3
	8-1-38-0	ARNOLD	..2.....	164		1	149			40	169	1	69	92	
	GREIG	15-2-53-0				.2.....1	157			41	172	1	69	95	
	9-1-41-0	ARNOLD	..1	167		2..3 1	162		100:203m 161 balls	42	179	1	70	101	
	GREIG	16-2-60-0	...4...	174	6	1	163			43	184	1	74	102	
	10-1-46-0	TITMUS	1 .	176		1 ...4 1	169	12		44	191	1	75	108	
	GREIG	4-1-12-0	..	178		2.2..4 1	175	13		45	200	1	75	117	
	11-1-55-0	TITMUS	..1 ..	183		1 .1	178			46	203	1	76	119	
	WILLIS	5-1-15-0				4 2 4..(n2)..1	187	15	•200p nb3	47	216	1	76	132	
	11-1-52-1	GREIG	...4..	188	7	4.1	190	16		48	225	1	80	137	
1:00		12-1-64-0	LUNCH			LUNCH									
1:40	ARNOLD		1 ..	191		..1 .1	195			49	228	1	81	139	
	17-2-63-0	UND'WOOD				1	203			50	229	1	81	140	
1:54	ARNOLD	5-0-32-0	1 1	193		3 .1 .W	208				235	2	83	144	
	18-2-69-1					WALTERS									
1:56						.	1			51	235	2	83	0	
		UND'WOOD	....	201					M6	52	235	2	83	0	
	ARNOLD	6-1-32-0	1	202		.1 n.....	9		nb4	53	238	2	84	1	4
2:09	19-2-71-1	UND'WOOD				...2 2 W	15				242	3	84	5	

360

		7-1-39-1			EDWARDS								
2:11					. 3	2		54	245	3	84	3	
	ARNOLD				. . . n	11	M7;nb5	55	246	3	84	3	5
	20-3-71-1	UND'WOOD	. 2 . 2 . . . 1	210				56	251	3	89	3	
	ARNOLD	8-1-44-1	. . . 2	218				57	253	3	91	3	
	21-3-73-1	UND'WOOD			. . 4	19	1	58	257	3	91	7	
	ARNOLD	9-1-48-1	. . . 4 . . 1	225	8	.	20		59	262	3	96	7	
	22-3-78-1	UND'WOOD	. 2 . 1 . 4 .	232	9	1	21	100:326m 231 balls	60	270	3	103	8	
	TITMUS	10-1-56-1			. . . .	29	M8	61	270	3	103	8	
	6-2-15-0	UND'WOOD	. . . 1	236		. . . .	33		62	271	3	104	8	
	TITMUS	11-1-57-1	. 1	238	. 2 . 2 . 1	39		63	277	3	105	13	
3:01	7-2-21-0	UND'WOOD	W	239	. . 3	42			280	4	105	16	
		12-1-65-2	MARSH										
3:03			2 2	2	. 1	44		64	285	4	4	17	
	TITMUS		2 1	4	L	45	lb2		289	4	7	17	6
3:10	7.3-2-24-0		DECLARED		DECLARED								

4th DAY	BOWLERS		BATSMEN					400 TO WIN ENGLAND 2ND INNINGS					
	Paddington End (N)	Randwick End (S)	UMP: R. BAILHACHE (N)			UMP: T. BROOKS (S)		NOTES	TOTALS AT END OF OVER				
TIME	NAME	NAME	NAME	B	4/6	NAME	B	4/6		O	R	W	LBat	RBat	Ext
3:20			RAIN/THUNDER			RAIN/THUNDER								
			AMISS			LLOYD								
5:05	LILLEE		....2...	8						1	2	0	2	0	
	1-0-2-0	THOMSON	..(b4)....	15		1	1		b4	2	7	0	2	1	4
	LILLEE	1-0-1-0				..4.....	9	1		3	11	0	2	5	
	2-0-6-0	THOMSON	....	23					M1	4	11	0	2	5	
	LILLEE	2-1-1-0				...2...2	17			5	15	0	2	9	
	3-0-10-0	THOMSON	4....1	29	1	..	19			6	20	0	7	9	
	LILLEE	3-1-6-0	.1	35		.1	21			7	22	0	8	10	
	4-0-12-0	THOMSON				.....4..	29	2		8	26	0	8	14	
	LILLEE	4-1-10-0	3 3	42		1	30			9	33	0	14	15	
	5-0-19-0	WALKER	....	50					M2	10	33	0	14	15	
	LILLEE	1-1-0-0				....	38		M3	11	33	0	14	15	
6:02	6-1-19-0		STUMPS			STUMPS				ATTENDANCE: 35,900					
		THOMSON	..3 b	54		.1 ..	42		b5	12	38	0	17	16	5
	LILLEE	5-1-14-0	3 .3	57		3	47			13	47	0	23	19	
	7-1-28-0	THOMSON	.2 2 1	61		...1	51			14	53	0	28	20	
	LILLEE	6-1-20-0	3	62		.....4.(n1)	59	3	nb1	15	61	0	31	25	
11:29	8-1-36-0	THOMSON	.4 1 1	66		.1 W	62			68	1	37	26		
		7-1-27-1				COWDREY									
11:31						L	1		lb1	16	69	1	37	0	6
11:36	LILLEE		W	67		1	7			70	2	37	1		
	9-1-37-1		EDRICH												
11:38			RET HURT .	1					Ribs	17	70	2	0	1	
			FLETCHER												
11:43		THOMSON				....	15		M4	18	70	2	0	1	
	LILLEE	8-2-27-1	....	8					M5	19	70	2	0	1	
	10-2-37-1	WALKER				....	23		M6	20	70	2	0	1	
	LILLEE	2-2-0-0	n....2.n..	18					nb3	21	74	2	2	1	8
12:08	11-2-39-1	WALKER				..W	26			74	3	2	1		
		3-3-1-0				GREIG									
12:10						.....	5			22	74	3	2	0	
	THOMSON		4.......	26	1					23	78	3	6	0	
	9-2-31-1	WALKER				.....4.4	13	2		24	86	3	6	8	
	THOMSON	4-3-8-1	....3 .	32		.1	15			25	90	3	9	9	
	10-2-35-1	WALKER				..4....	23	3		26	94	3	9	13	
	THOMSON	5-3-12-1	.1	34		.2 n .4..	30	4	nb4	27	102	3	10	19	9
	11-2-42-1	WALKER	1	39		...	33			28	103	3	11	19	
12:47	THOMSON	6-3-13-1	......W	46						103	4	11	19		
		12-3-42-2	KNOTT												
12:49			.	1					M7	29	103	4	0	19	
		WALKER				....	41		M8	30	103	4	0	19	
	THOMSON	7-4-13-1	......4.	9	1					31	107	4	4	19	
1:00	13-3-46-2		LUNCH			LUNCH									
		WALKER	.....	14		2.1	44			32	110	4	4	22	
	LILLEE	8-4-16-1	..4....	21	2	1	45			33	115	4	8	23	
	12-2-44-1	WALKER				.2.2....	53			34	119	4	8	27	
	LILLEE	9-4-20-1	....	29	37				M9	35	119	4	8	27	
	13-3-44-1	WALKER				4	61	5		36	123	4	8	31	
	LILLEE	10-4-24-1	..2.....	37						37	125	4	10	31	
	14-3-46-1	WALKER				1	69			38	126	4	10	32	
	THOMSON	11-2-25-1				..4..2 4..	77	7		39	136	4	10	42	
2:25	14-3-56-2	MALLETT	.W	39						136	5	10	42		
		1-1-1-0	TITMUS												
2:27			......	6						40	136	5	0	42	
	THOMSON		(b4).1	9		...4 L	82	8	lb2, b9	41	146	5	1	46	14
	15-3-61-2	MALLETT	1	14		...	85			42	147	5	2	46	
	THOMSON	2-1-1-1	..2.....	22						43	149	5	4	46	
	16-3-63-2	MALLETT	.	23		1	92			44	150	5	4	47	
	THOMSON	3-1-2-1				..4....1	100	9	50: 122w 95 balls	45	155	5	4	52	
2:58	17-3-68-2	MALLETT	W	24		..1	103			156	6	4	53		
		4-1-3-2	EDRICH												
3:00			....	5						46	156	6	0	53	

	LILLEE		...1	9		..1 .	111			47	158	8	1	54	
3:09	15-3-48-1	MALLETT				....W	108				158	7	1	54	
		5-2-3-3				UNDERWOOD									
3:11						....	4			48	158	7	1	0	
	LILLEE		2....44.	17	2					49	168	7	11	0	
	16-3-58-1	MALLETT	.....2.	24		1	5			50	171	7	13	1	
3:27	WALKER	6-2-6-3				..4....W	13			51	175	8	13	5	
	12-2-29-2					WILLIS									
3:29		MALLETT	....	32					M10	62	175	8	13	0	
	WALKER	7-3-6-3				.n....4.4	9	2	nb5	63	184	8	13	8	15
	13-2-37-2	MALLETT	....	40					M11	64	184	8	13	8	
3:40		8-4-6-3	TEA			TEA									
4:00	WALKER					....	17		M12	65	184	8	13	8	
	14-3-37-2	MALLETT	....	48					M13	66	184	8	13	8	
	THOMSON	9-5-6-3	....	55		1	18			67	185	8	13	9	
	18-3-69-2	MALLETT	1	60		L ..	21		lb3	68	187	8	14	9	16
	THOMSON	10-5-7-3	....	68					M14	69	187	8	14	9	
	19-4-69-2	MALLETT				....	29		M15	70	187	8	14	9	
	WALKER	11-6-7-3	..4.....	76	3					71	191	8	18	9	
	15-3-41-2	MALLETT				....	37		M16	72	191	8	18	9	
	I.CHAPPELL	12-7-7-3	....	84					M17	73	191	8	18	9	
	1-1-0-0	MALLETT				....	45		M18	74	191	8	18	9	
	I.CHAPPELL	13-8-7-3	1	92						75	192	8	19	9	
	2-1-1-0	MALLETT	....	100					M19	76	192	8	19	9	
	I.CHAPPELL	14-9-7-3				....	53		M20	77	192	8	19	9	
	3-2-1-0	MALLETT	....4...	108	4					78	196	8	23	9	
	LILLEE	15-9-11-3	1	113		1 2.	56		Last 15>	79	200	8	24	12	
	17-3-62-1	THOMSON	....	121					M21	80	200	8	24	12	
	LILLEE	20-5-69-2				.../.....n.	65		/new ball M22;nb6	81	201	8	24	12	17
	18-4-62-1	THOMSON	....	129					M23	82	201	8	24	12	
5:17	LILLEE	21-5-69-2				....W	69				201	9	24	12	
	19-5-62-2					ARNOLD									
5:19						(b4)...	4		M24	83	205	9	24	0	21
		THOMSON	...4.1	135	5	..	6			84	210	9	29	0	
	LILLEE	22-5-64-2	1	143						85	211	9	30	0	
	20-5-63-2	WALKER	1	150		4	7	1		86	216	9	31	4	
	LILLEE	16-3-46-2	....2...	158						87	218	9	33	4	
	21-5-65-2	MALLETT				..2...2.	15			88	222	9	33	8	
	THOMSON	16-9-15-3	....	166					M25	89	222	9	33	8	
5:54		23-6-64-2	MALLETT			..42W	20				228	10	33	12	
		16.5-9-21-4		AUSTRALIA WON BY 171 RUNS						ATTENDANCE: 14,007					

363

AUSTRALIA FIRST Innings

IN	OUT	MINS	NO	BATSMAN	HOW OUT	BOWLER	RUNS	WK	TOTAL	BALLS	4s	6s	NOTES
11:30	2:27	140	1	IR REDPATH	HIT WICKET	TITMUS	33	1	96	114	1		Brushed stumps playing pull shot
11:30	319	192	2	RB McCOSKER	CT KNOTT	GREIG	80	2	142	169	7		Edged back-foot drive
2:29	4:45	118	3	IM CHAPPELL	CT KNOTT	ARNOLD	53	3	199	83	5		Edged defensive push
3:21	12:15	216	4	GS CHAPPELL	CT GREIG	ARNOLD	83	7	310	173	9		Edge to left of diving second slip
4:47	5:56	69	5	R EDWARDS	BOWLED	GREIG	16	4	251	57	3		Back foot, played on off inside edge
5:68	11:07	9	6	KD WALTERS	LBW	ARNOLD	1	5	255	7			Trapped by ball that seamed in
11:09	12:05	56	7	RW MARSH	BOWLED	GREIG	30	6	305	44	3		Missed straight drive
12:07	2:12	89	8	MHN WALKER	CT GREIG	ARNOLD	30	9	368	59			Slash to second slip
12:17	12:49	37	9	DK LILLEE	BOWLED	ARNOLD	8	8	332	23	1		Missed defensive shot on back foot
12:51	2:41	72	10	AA MALLETT	LBW	GREIG	31	10	405	53	4		
2:14	2:41	27	11	JR THOMSON	NOT OUT		24			23	4		Moved cross stumps playing to leg
				EXTRAS			16						LB 4, W 1, NB 11
				TOTAL	(ALL OUT, 98.6 OVERS)		405						

BOWLER	O	M	R	W	NB/W
WILLIS	18	2	80	0	1/
ARNOLD	29	7	86	5	11/
GREIG	22.7	2	104	4	
UNDERWOOD	13	3	54	0	1/
TITMUS	16	2	65	1	

Runs	Mins	Overs	Last50
50	80	14.2	
100	148	29.1	68
150	202	39.7	54
200	266	53.3	64
250	329	66.2	65
300	392	77.2	63
350	468	90.2	76
400	515	98.2	47
450			
500			

LUNCH 62-0
17 overs

TEA 162-2
43 overs

STUMPS DAY 1:
251-4 67 overs

LUNCH 334-8
88 overs

Wkt	Partnership		RUNS
1	Redpath	McCosker	96
2	McCosker	Chappell	46
3	Chappell	Chappell	57
4	Chappell	Edwards	52
5	Chappell	Walters	4
6	Chappell	Marsh	50
7	Chappell	Walker	5
8	Lillee	Walker	22
9	Mallett	Walker	36
10	Mallett	Thomson	37

ENGLAND FIRST Innings

IN	OUT	MINS	NO	BATSMAN	HOW OUT	BOWLER	RUNS	WK	TOTAL	BALLS	4s	6s	N O T E S
2:53	3:32	39	1	DL AMISS	CT MALLETT	WALKER	12	1	36	26	1		Diving gully catch off loose drive
2:53	4:00	54	2	D LLOYD	CT THOMSON	LILLEE	19	2	46	45	3		Clipped to backward short leg
3:34	4:47	53	3	MC COWDREY	CT McCOSKER	THOMSON	22	3	69	48	3		Fended ball to forward short leg
4:09	12:52	223	4	JH EDRICH	CT MARSH	WALTERS	50	6	180	171	5		Caught down leg side
4:49	11:07	78	5	KW FLETCHER	CT REDPATH	WALKER	24	4	108	62	3		Clipped to backward short leg
11:09	11:24	15	6	AW GREIG	CT G.CHAPPELL	THOMSON	9	5	123	13	1		Edged low to second slip
11:27	2:45	158	7	APE KNOTT	BOWLED	THOMSON	82	8	273	122	11		Missed slog to leg side
12:54	2:21	47	8	FJ TITMUS	CT MARSH	WALTERS	22	7	240	44	3		Edged back-foot slash
2:23	3:16	53	9	DL UNDERWOOD	CT WALKER	LILLEE	27	10	295	31	5		Drive to wide mid-off
2:47	3:01	14	10	RGD WILLIS	BOWLED	THOMSON	2	9	285	8			Missed swing to leg side
3:03	3:16	13	11	GG ARNOLD	NOT OUT		3			14			
				EXTRAS			23			B 15, LB 7, W 1			
				TOTAL	(ALL OUT, 72.1 OVERS)		**295**						

BOWLER	O	M	R	W	NB/W
LILLEE	19.1	2	66	2	
THOMSON	19	3	74	4	/1
WALKER	23	2	77	2	
MALLETT	1	0	8	0	
WALTERS	7	2	26	2	
I.CHAPPELL	3	0	21	0	

Runs	Mins	Overs	Last50
50	68	13.0	
100	157	29.5	89
150	248	47.1	91
200	302	59.1	54
250	335	65.6	33
300			
350			
400			
450			
500			

TEA: 40-1
9 overs, 265 behind

STUMPS DAY 3: 106-3
32 overs, 299 behind

LUNCH: 181-6
56 overs, 224 behind

Wkt	Partnership		RUNS
1	Amiss	Lloyd	36
2	Cowdrey	Lloyd	10
3	Cowdrey	Edrich	23
4	Fletcher	Edrich	39
5	Greig	Edrich	15
6	Knott	Edrich	57
7	Knott	Titmus	60
8	Knott	Underwood	33
9	Willis	Underwood	12
10	Arnold	Underwood	10

AUSTRALIA SECOND Innings

IN	OUT	MINS	NO	BATSMAN	HOW OUT	BOWLER	RUNS	WK	TOTAL	BALLS	4s	6s	NOTES
3:37	3:01	344	1	IR REDPATH	CT SUB (OLD)	UNDERWOOD	105	4	280	239	9		Hit high to mid-off
3:37	3:59	22	2	IM CHAPPELL	CT LLOYD	WILLIS	5	1	15	9			Low one-handed catch at leg gully
4:02	1:54	252	3	GS CHAPPELL	CT LLOYD	ARNOLD	144	2	235	208	16		Skied to mid-wicket
1:56	2:09	13	4	KD WALTERS	BOWLED	UNDERWOOD	5	3	242	15			Bowled playing across line
2:11	3:10	59	5	R EDWARDS	NOT OUT		17			45	1		
23:03	3:10	7	6	RW MARSH	NOT OUT		7			4			
			7	RB McCOSKER									
			8	MHN WALKER									
			9	DK LILLEE									
			10	AA MALLETT									
			11	JR THOMSON									
				EXTRAS		LB 3, W 1, NB 3	6						
				TOTAL		(4 WICKETS, 64.3 OVERS)	**289** DEC						

BOWLER	O	M	R	W	NB/W
WILLIS	11	1	52	1	2/
ARNOLD	22	3	78	1	2/
GREIG	12	1	64	0	/1
UNDERWOOD	12	1	65	2	
TITMUS	7.3	2	24	0	

Runs	Mins	Overs	Last50
50	66	11.6	
100	115	20.3	49
150	183	34.1	68
200	246	44.6	63
250	304	54.4	68
300			
350			
400			
450			
500			

STUMPS DAY 3: 123-1 26 overs; 233 ahead
LUNCH: 225-1 48 overs, 335 ahead
• Redpath/Chappell 100 partnership in 102 min
• Redpath/Chappell 200 partnership in 231 min

Wkt	Partnership		RUNS
1	Redpath	Chappell	15
2	Redpath	Chappell	220
3	Redpath	Walters	7
4	Redpath	Edwards	38
5	Marsh	Edwards	25
6			
7			
8			
9			
10			

ENGLAND SECOND Innings

AUSTRALIA WON BY 171 RUNS

BATSMAN	IN	OUT	MINS	NO	HOW OUT	BOWLER	RUNS	WK	TOTAL	BALLS	4s	6s	NOTES
DL AMISS	5:05	11:36	93	1	CT MARSH	LILLEE	37	2	70	67	2		Gloved vicious lifting delivery
D LLOYD	5:05	11:29	86	2	CT G.CHAPPELL	THOMSON	26	1	68	62	3		Toe-end edge to second slip
MC COWDREY	11:31	12:08	37	3	CT I.CHAPPELL	WALKER	1	3	74	26			Edged wide delivery to first slip
JH EDRICH	11:36	5:54	155	4	NOT OUT		33			166	5		
KW FLETCHER	11:43	12:47	64	5	CT REDPATH	THOMSON	11	4	103	46	1		Edged full ball to gully
AW GREIG	12:10	3:09	139	6	ST MARSH	MALLETT	54	7	158	108	9		Advanced down track, missed drive
APE KNOTT	12:49	2:25	56	7	CT REDPATH	MALLETT	10	5	136	39	2		Low catch at short leg
FJ TITMUS	2:27	2:58	31	8	CT THOMSON	MALLETT	4	6	156	24			Top edged sweep to mid-wicket
DL UNDERWOOD	3:11	3:27	16	9	CT & BOWLED	WALKER	5	8	175	13	1		Off drive hit head height to bowler
RGD WILLIS	3:29	5:17	88	10	BOWLED	LILLEE	12	9	201	69	2		Full ball, beaten by pace
GG ARNOLD	5:19	5:54	35	11	CT G.CHAPPELL	MALLETT	14	10	228	20	2		Inside edge to forward short leg

EXTRAS B 13, LB 3, NB 5 — 21

TOTAL (ALL OUT, 72.1 OVERS) 228

BOWLER	O	M	R	W	NB/W
LILLEE	21	5	65	2	3/2
THOMSON	23	7	74	2	1/
WALKER	16	5	46	2	1/
MALLETT	16.5	9	21	4	
I.CHAPPELL	3	2	1	0	

Runs	Mins	Overs	Last50
50	72	13.3	
100	154	26.9	82
150	246	43.9	92
200	354	68.9	108
250			
300			
350			
400			
450			
500			

STUMPS DAY 4: 33-0
11 overs, 367 to win

LUNCH 107-4
31 overs, 293 to win

TEA: 184-8
54 overs, 216 to win

Edrich ret. hurt, 11:38
(70-2) until 3:00 (156-6)

MATCH ATTENDANCE:
178,027

Wkt	Partnership		RUNS
1	Amiss	Lloyd	68
2	Amiss	Cowdrey	2
3	Edrich/Fletcher	Cowdrey	4
4	Fletcher	Greig	29
5	Knott	Greig	33
6	Titmus	Greig	20
7	Edrich	Greig	2
8	Edrich	Underwood	17
9	Edrich	Willis	26
10	Edrich	Arnold	27

FIFTH TEST MATCH

AUSTRALIA v **ENGLAND** at ADELAIDE OVAL on JANUARY 25-27, 29-30 1975

2nd DAY TIME	BOWLERS Cathedral End (N) NAME	BOWLERS City End (S) NAME	BATSMEN UMP: T. BROOKS (N) NAME	B	4/6	BATSMEN UMP: R.BAILHACHE (S) NAME	B	4/6	NOTES Toss ENG	AUSTRALIA 1ST INNINGS TOTALS AT END OF OVER				
									O	R	W	LBat	RBat	Ext
	NO PLAY DAY 1 – RAIN		REDPATH			McCOSKER								
11:00	ARNOLD		. 3	4		. . . L	4		lb1	1	4	0	3	0	1
	1-0-3-0	WILLIS				. . 2	12			2	6	0	3	2	
	ARNOLD	1-0-2-0	. . . .	12					M1	3	6	0	3	2	
	2-1-3-0	WILLIS		13		 3	19			4	9	0	3	5	
	ARNOLD	2-0-5-0	. 1	15		. . . 1 . .	25			5	11	0	4	6	
	3-0-5-0	WILLIS	1	16		. . . . . 4 .	32	1		6	16	0	5	10	
	UND'WOOD	3-0-10-0	. . . . . . 2 .	24						7	18	0	7	10	
	1-0-2-0	ARNOLD	. . .	27		. n 2 . 2 1	38		nb1	8	24	0	7	15	2
	UND'WOOD	4-0-10-0	. . .	30		 1	43			9	25	0	7	16	
	2-0-3-0	ARNOLD	. . . . . .	36		. 3	45			10	28	0	7	19	
	UND'WOOD	5-0-13-0				. . . . . . 2 .	53			11	30	0	7	21	
	3-0-5-0	ARNOLD	. . . .	44					M2	12	30	0	7	21	
	UND'WOOD	6-1-13-0				. . . 2 2 . . .	61			13	34	0	7	25	
	4-0-9-0	ARNOLD	. . . .	52					M3	14	34	0	7	25	
	UND'WOOD	7-1-13-0				. . . . . 4 2 .	69	2		15	40	0	7	31	
12:16	5-0-15-0	GREIG	. . . 2 3	57		. . 4	72	3		16	49	0	12	35	
12:23	UND'WOOD	1-0-9-0	. 3	59		W	73				52	1	15	35	
	6-0-18-2					I.CHAPPELL									
12:25						. . W	3				52	2	15	0	
						G.CHAPPELL									
12:27						. .	2			17	52	2	15	0	
		GREIG	. . . . 1 .	65		2 3	4			18	58	2	16	5	
12:34	UND'WOOD	2-0-15-0				. W	6				58	3	16	5	
	7-0-22-3					WALTERS									
12:35						 4	6	1		19	62	3	16	4	
		GREIG	. 2 1	73						20	65	3	19	4	
	UND'WOOD	3-0-18-0	. . . .	81					M4	21	65	3	19	4	
	8-1-22-3	GREIG	. . . .	85		. . 4 1	10	2		22	70	3	19	9	
	UND'WOOD	4-0-23-0				. . . .	18		M5	23	70	3	19	9	
	9-1-22-3	TITMUS	. . b	88		. . . 4 .	23	3	b1	24	75	3	19	13	3
1:01	UND'WOOD	1-0-4-0	. . . . . 2 W	95							77	4	21	13	
	10-1-27-4		LUNCH			LUNCH									
1:40			MARSH												
			3	1						25	80	4	3	13	
		ARNOLD	2 . . . n . . . 1	10					nb2	26	84	4	6	13	4
1:49	UND'WOOD	8-1-16-0	. . . . . . W	17							84	5	6	13	
	11-1-30-5		JENNER												
1:51						3	24			27	87	5	0	16	
		ARNOLD				. n n . . 4 . . .	33	4	nb4	28	93	5	0	20	6
	UND'WOOD	9-1-20-0	. . 3	3		 3	38			29	99	5	3	23	
	12-1-36-5	ARNOLD	. 2 . 2	7		. . . 1	42			30	104	5	7	24	
	UND'WOOD	10-1-25-0	3	8		1 . 4 4 . . .	49	6		31	116	5	10	33	
	13-1-48-5	ARNOLD	. . 4 4 . . . 4	16	3					32	128	5	22	33	
	UND'WOOD	11-1-37-0	. 3 . 1	20		1 1 . . 4	53	7		33	138	5	26	39	
	14-1-58-5	GREIG	. . . 3 1 1	26		1 1	55			34	145	5	31	41	
		TITMUS	5-0-30-0 2 . . 1	30		. 6 2 .	59	7/1		35	156	5	34	49	
	2-0-15-0	GREIG	. . 1 1 . .	36		1 3	61		50:83min 60 balls	36	162	5	36	53	
2:46	UND'WOOD	6-0-36-0				2 . . W	65				164	6	36	55	
	15-1-67-6		WALKER												
2:48			. 4 3	39	4	.	1			37	171	6	43	0	
		TITMUS	 2	47						38	173	6	45	0	
	UND'WOOD	3-0-17-0	. . .	50		2 . . 1	6			39	176	6	45	3	
	16-1-70-6	TITMUS	 3	56		. (b3)	8		b4	40	182	6	48	3	
	UND'WOOD	4-0-20-0	. . . . . . L .	64					M6;lb3	41	184	6	48	3	8
	17-2-70-6	TITMUS	. 1	66		. 3 . . 2 .	14			42	190	6	49	8	
	UND'WOOD	5-0-26-0	. . . 3	70		. . . .	18		50: 82m 70 balls	43	193	6	52	8	
	18-2-73-6	TITMUS	 1	76		20				44	194	6	53	8	

TIME		BOWLERS		BATSMEN					ENGLAND 1ST			INNINGS	
									O	R	W	LBat	RBat	Ext
		UND'WOOD	6-0-27-0	. . 4	84	5			45	198	6	57	8	
		19-2-77-6	TITMUS				 L	28	M7;lb2	46	199	6	57	8	9
			UND'WOOD	7-1-27-0	1	89		1 . 3	31		47	204	6	58	12	
		20-2-82-6	WILLIS	1	90		. . . . n . 1 1	39	nb5	48	208	6	59	14	10
			UND'WOOD	4-0-13-0	. . .	93		. . 2 . 3	44		49	213	6	59	19	
3:41		21-2-87-6		TEA			TEA							
4:00			WILLIS	. 4 2	96	6	 3	49		50	222	6	65	22	
			UND'WOOD	5-0-22-0	. 4 . . 1	101	7	1 . .	52		51	228	6	70	23	
		22-2-93-6	WILLIS	1	102		. . 2 . . 3	59		52	234	6	71	28	
			UND'WOOD	6-0-28-0				 4	67	1	53	238	6	71	32	
		23-2-97-6	WILLIS	. . . 2 . . 1	110					54	241	6	74	32	
4:27			UND'WOOD	7-0-31-0	. . . W	114					241	7	74	32	
		24-2-98-7		LILLEE											
4:29				. 1	2		. .	69		55	242	7	1	32	
			WILLIS	2 3	9		1	70		56	248	7	6	33	
			UND'WOOD	8-0-37-0	. . . . . .	15		. 1	72		57	249	7	6	34	
4:45		25-2-99-7	GREIG	. 3	17		1 4 . 2 RO	77	2	58	259	7	9	41	
							MALLETT								
4:47			UND'WOOD	7-0-46-0				 2	8		59	261	8	9	2	
		26-2-101-7	GREIG	1 . 1 .	21		1 . . 1	12		60	265	8	11	4	
			UND'WOOD	8-0-50-0				. 4	20	1	61	269	8	11	8	
		27-2-105-7	GREIG	. 3 4	24	1	 1	25		62	277	8	18	9	
			UND'WOOD	9-0-58-0	. 4 .	27	2	2 . . . 1	30		63	284	8	22	12	
		28-2-112-7	GREIG	 2	33		2 1	32		64	289	8	24	15	
			UND'WOOD	10-0-63-0	. . . . .	38		. . 1	35		65	290	8	24	16	
5:28		29-2-113-7	WILLIS	2 W	40		. 2 / . . . 1	41	/new ball	66	295	9	26	19	
				9-0-42-1	THOMSON										
5:29			ARNOLD	. . 4 .	4	1	. . . 1	45		67	300	9	4	20	
			12-3-42-0	WILLIS	. 1	6		. . . 1 . 2	51		68	304	9	5	23	
5:29			ARNOLD	10-0-46-1	. W	8					304	10	5	23	
			12.2-3-42-1												

2nd		BOWLERS		BATSMEN					ENGLAND 1ST			INNINGS	
DAY		Cathedral End (N)	City End (S)	UMP: T. BROOKS (N)			UMP: R. BAILHACHE (S)		NOTES	TOTALS AT END OF OVER				
TIME		NAME	NAME	NAME	B	4/6	NAME	B	4/6	O	R	W	LBat	RBat	Ext
				AMISS			LLOYD								
5:51			LILLEE	. . . .	8					M1	1	0	0	0	0	
		THOMSON	1-1-0-0				. . (L2)	8		M2;lb2	2	2	0	0	0	2
6:01		1-1-0-0		STUMPS			STUMPS			ATTENDANCE: 30,682						
11:01			LILLEE	. . W	11						2	1	0	0	
			2-1-7-1	COWDREY											
11:03				. 2 . 1	4		4	9	1	3	9	1	3	4	
		THOMSON		. 4 1	7	1	. . . . .	14		4	14	1	8	4	
			2-1-5-0	LILLEE	. 1	9		. . . . . .	20		5	15	1	9	4	
		THOMSON	3-1-8-1	. 1	11		. . . . . .	26		6	16	1	10	4	
11:24		3-1-6-0	LILLEE	. 3	13		W	27			19	2	13	4	
			4-1-11-2				DENNESS								
11:26							. . . . .	5			7	19	2	13	0	
		THOMSON		. . . . n . . . 1	22					nb1	8	21	2	14	0	3
			4-1-7-0	LILLEE	. . . 2 . 2 4 .	30	2				9	29	2	22	0	
			WALKER	5-1-19-2	. .	32		 1	11		10	30	2	22	1	
			1-0-1-0	LILLEE				. 2 . . . 4 . 2	19	1	11	38	2	22	9	
			WALKER	6-1-27-2	. . . .	40					M3	12	38	2	22	9	
			2-1-1-0	LILLEE	. . . . 2 . .	47		1	20		13	41	2	24	10	
			WALKER	7-1-30-2				. . . 4	28	2	14	45	2	24	14	
			3-1-6-0	THOMSON	n . 1 . . 1 .	54		4 3 (n1)	31	3	nb3	15	56	2	26	22	4
			WALKER	5-1-17-0	. . . .	58		. . 2 3	35		16	61	2	26	27	
12:30		4-1-11-0	THOMSON	W	59		2 3	42		17	66	3	26	32	
			6-1-22-1	FLETCHER											
12:31		WALKER					. . . 4 . . . 4	50	5		18	74	3	0	40	
			5-1-19-0	THOMSON	. n . 1 .	5		4 . . 3	54	6	nb4	19	83	3	1	47	5
			JENNER	7-1-30-1				. . . . . . 2 1	62		50:79min 62 balls	20	86	3	1	50	
12:49		1-0-3-0	THOMSON	. 3	7		1 . W	65			90	4	4	51	
			8-1-35-2				GREIG								
12:51				.	8		. 1	2		21	91	4	4	51	

369

	JENNER				 2	10		22	93	4	4	3
	2-0-5-0	THOMSON	 2	16				23	95	4	6	3
1:00		9-1-37-2	LUNCH		LUNCH							
	JENNER				. . . 2	18		24	97	4	6	5
	3-0-7-0	LILLEE	1	17	. . . .	25		25	98	4	7	5
	JENNER	8-1-31-2	. . 3 . . 1	23	1 4	27	1	26	107	4	11	10
	4-0-16-0	LILLEE	. . 1	26	2 . 4 . .	32	2	27	114	4	12	16
	JENNER	9-1-38-2	. . 4 4 . 4 . .	34	3			28	126	4	24	16
	5-0-28-0	LILLEE			. . 2	40		29	128	4	24	18
	MALLETT	10-1-40-2	 1	40	. 1	42		30	130	4	25	19
2:13	1-0-2-0	LILLEE			. W	44			130	5	25	19
		11-2-40-3			KNOTT							
2:14					. . . . . .	6	M4	31	130	5	25	0
	MALLETT		. . . . 2 . . .	48				32	132	5	27	0
	2-0-4-0	LILLEE	. 4	50	4	. . . 2 . 3	12		33	141	5	31	5
	MALLETT	12-2-49-3			. . . .	20	M5	34	141	5	31	5
	3-1-4-0	THOMSON	2 . . . 4 . . .	58	5			35	147	5	37	5
2:37	MALLETT	10-1-43-2			. . W	23			147	6	37	5
	4-2-4-1				TITMUS							
2:40					. . . . .	5	M6	36	147	6	37	0
		THOMSON	 1	63	. . .	8		37	148	6	38	0
	MALLETT	11-1-44-2	. . 1	66	2 . 2 . .	13		38	153	6	39	4
2:57	5-2-9-1	THOMSON	. . 1 . W	71	. . 1	16		39	155	7	40	5
		12-1-46-3	UND'WOOD									
3:01	MALLETT		. W	2	. . . 1	20			156	8	0	6
	6-2-10-2		ARNOLD									
3:02			. .	2			M7	40	156	8	0	6
		THOMSON	. . . .	9	1	21		41	157	8	0	7
3:10	MALLETT	13-1-47-3			. 4 . W	25	1		161	9	0	11
	7-2-14-3				WILLIS							
3:11			. . . . .	14				42	161	9	0	0
		THOMSON			. . 4 2 4 . . .	8	2	43	171	9	0	10
	MALLETT	14-1-57-3	. . . .	22			M8	44	171	9	0	10
	8-3-14-3	THOMSON	. . . .	39	1	9		45	172	9	0	11
	MALLETT	15-1-58-3			. . . .	17		46	172	9	0	11
3:32	9-4-14-3	LILLEE	. . . . W	34			M9		172	10	0	11
		12.5-2-49-4										

3rd DAY	BOWLERS		BATSMEN						132 AHEAD AUSTRALIA 2nd INNINGS					
	Cathedral End (N)	City End (S)	UMP: R. BAILHACHE (N)			UMP: T. BROOKS (S)			NOTES	TOTALS AT END OF OVER				
TIME	NAME	NAME	NAME	B	4/6	NAME	B	4/6		O	R	W	LBat	RBat	Ext
			REDPATH			McCOSKER									
3:55	ARNOLD		1 .	3		. n 4 2 . . 1	7	1	nb1	1	9	0	1	7	1
	1-0-8-0	WILLIS	. . . 2 . . .	9		3	8			2	14	0	3	10	
4:09	ARNOLD	1-0-5-0	1	10		. . . 1 W	13				16	1	4	11	
	2-0-10-1					I.CHAPPELL									
4:10						. .	2			3	16	1	4	0	
		WILLIS	1	11		n . 2	10		nb2	4	20	1	5	2	2
	ARNOLD	2-0-8-0	1	12		. n	18		nb3	5	22	1	6	2	3
	3-0-11-1	WILLIS	. . . 4 . 1	18	1	. .	20			6	25	1	11	2	
	ARNOLD	3-0-13-0	. . 1 ,	22		4 2 n . 1	25	1	nb4	7	34	1	12	9	4
	4-0-19-1	WILLIS	. 1 3	25		4 . 3 1 .	30	2		8	46	1	16	17	
	UND'WOOD	4-0-25-0	 3	30		. . .	33			9	49	1	19	17	
	1-0-3-0	ARNOLD	4 . . 1 . .	36	2	. 1	35			10	55	1	24	18	
	UND'WOOD	5-0-25-1				. 2 2	43			11	59	1	24	22	
	2-0-7-0	ARNOLD	3 . n .	40		 1	48		nb5	12	66	1	27	23	5
	UND'WOOD	6-0-29-1	. . . . . .	46		. 1	50			13	67	1	27	24	
	3-0-8-0	TITMUS				. . . .	58		M1	14	67	1	27	24	
	UND'WOOD	1-1-0-0	 1	52		. 1	60			15	69	1	28	25	
	4-0-10-0	TITMUS	1 . 3	55		. . . 1 1	65			16	75	1	32	27	
	UND'WOOD	2-1-6-0	. . . 1 . . .	62		1	66			17	77	1	33	28	
	5-0-12-0	TITMUS	1 . . .	66		. . 1 1	70			18	80	1	34	30	
5:33	UND'WOOD	3-1-9-0	. 1	67		6 . 3 2 W	75	2/1			92	2	35	41	
	6-0-24-1					G.CHAPPELL									
5:35						.	1			19	92	2	35	0	
		TITMUS	. . 4	75	3					20	96	2	39	0	
	UND'WOOD	4-1-13-0				. . . .	9		M2	21	96	2	39	0	
	7-1-24-1	TITMUS	. . 1 . . 3	81		4 1	11	1		22	105	2	43	5	
	UND'WOOD	5-1-22-0	. . . .	89					M3	23	105	2	43	5	
	8-2-24-1	WILLIS	. n 1	92		. . . . 1 .	17			24	108	2	44	6	
		TITMUS	. . 2 1	96		. . . .	21			25	111	2	47	6	
6:01	6-1-25-0		STUMPS			STUMPS					ATTENDANCE; 34,241				
11:00		ARNOLD	2 . 1	103		1	22		50: 127m 99 balls	26	115	2	50	7	
	UND'WOOD	7-0-33-1	. . .	106		. . . 4 1	27	2		27	120	2	50	12	
	9-2-29-1	ARNOLD				. . . .	35		M4	28	120	2	50	12	
	UND'WOOD	8-1-33-1	1	113		1	36			29	122	2	51	13	
	10-2-31-1	ARNOLD	. . . . .	118		2 . 1	39			30	125	2	51	16	
	UND'WOOD	9-1-36-1	. .	120		 1	45			31	126	2	51	17	
	11-2-32-1	ARNOLD	. . . 1	124		. . . 1	49			32	128	2	52	18	
11:32	UND'WOOD	10-1-38-1	W	125							128	3	52	18	
	12-3-32-2		WALTERS												
11:34			(L3)	1		. . . .	55		M5; lb3	33	131	3	0	18	3
		ARNOLD	. . . . . . 2 .	9						34	133	3	2	18	
11:48	UND'WOOD	11-1-40-1				. . . . . . W	61				133	4	2	18	
	13-4-32-3					MARSH									
11:50						. .	2		M6	35	133	4	2	0	
		ARNOLD	. . . 1 . . .	16		1	3			36	135	4	3	1	
	UND'WOOD	12-1-42-1				. . . .	11		M7	37	135	4	3	1	
	14-5-32-3	TITMUS	1 1	18		. . 1 2 . .	16			38	140	4	5	4	
	UND'WOOD	7-1-30-0	. . 4	26	1					39	144	4	9	4	
	15-5-36-3	TITMUS	3	27		1 1	23			40	149	4	12	6	
	UND'WOOD	8-1-35-0	. 2	34		3	24			41	154	4	14	9	
	16-5-41-3	TITMUS	.	35		 1	31			42	155	4	14	10	
	UND'WOOD	9-1-36-0				. . . 4 . 2 2 .	39	1		43	163	4	14	18	
	17-5-49-3	TITMUS	. 1 . 1	39		. 4 . 1	43	2		44	170	4	16	23	
	UND'WOOD	10-1-43-1	. . . 4 6 . . .	47	2/1					45	180	4	26	23	
	18-5-59-3	TITMUS	1 1	49		1 . . 1 . .	49			46	184	4	28	25	
	UND'WOOD	11-1-47-0	. 2 1	56		.	50			47	187	4	31	25	
	19-5-62-3	TITMUS	. 1	58		. . . . . .	56			48	188	4	32	25	
		GREIG	12-1-48-0	1 1 .	61		1 . . . 1	61			49	192	4	34	27	
	1-0-4-0	TITMUS	3	62		. . . L . 2 .	68		lb4	50	198	4	37	29	4
		GREIG	13-1-53-0	2 . 1	65		. . 2 . .	73			51	203	4	40	31	
1:02	2-0-9-0		LUNCH			LUNCH									

371

		ARNOLD	...1 3	70		..1	76		52	208	4	44	32
1:40	UND'WOOD	13-1-47-1	4 1 1	73	3/1	1 .4..	81	3	53	219	4	50	37
		20-5-73-3	ARNOLD	....1 ..	80		1	82		54	221	4	51	38
		UND'WOOD	14-1-49-1			1	90		54	222	4	51	39
		21-5-74-3	ARNOLD	1	81		.....1 ..	97		55	224	4	52	40
	UND'WOOD	15-1-51-1	.4 1 1	85	4/1	2 .1 3	101		• 100p	56	236	4	58	46
		22-5-86-3	ARNOLD	....	89		...1	105		57	237	4	58	47
2:21	UND'WOOD	16-1-52-1				.6 2 .W	110	3/1	50: 110m 107 balls	245	5	58	55
		23-5-94-4				JENNER							
2:24				...	92					58	245	5	58	0
		ARNOLD	1	97		1 .1	3		59	248	5	59	2
	UND'WOOD	17-1-55-1	1	103		1 2	5		60	252	5	60	5
		24-5-98-4	ARNOLD	..3 ...	109		.3	7		61	258	5	63	8
	UND'WOOD	18-1-61-1	...1	113		...1	11		62	260	5	64	9
		25-5-100-4	ARNOLD	....1 ..	119		1	12		63	262	5	65	10
	UND'WOOD	19-1-63-1	1	120		.1	19		64	264	5	66	11
		26-5-102-4	ARNOLD	4 1	127	5/1	.3	21		65	272	5	71	14
3:00		20-1-71-1	DECLARED			DECLARED							

372

4th DAY	BOWLERS		BATSMEN						405 TO WIN ENGLAND 2ND INNINGS					
	Cathedral End (N)	City End (S)	UMP: R. BAILHACHE (N)			UMP: T. BROOKS (S)			NOTES	TOTALS AT END OF OVER				
TIME	NAME	NAME	NAME	B	4/6	NAME	B	4/6		O	R	W	LBat	RBat	Ext
3:12			AMISS			LLOYD									
3:14		LILLEE	...W	4						0	1	0	0		
		1-1-0-1	COWDREY												
3:15			....	4					M1	1	0	1	0	0	
3:22	WALKER		3	5		4 1 W	1	3			8	2	3	5	
	1-0-10-1					DENNESS									
3:23						.2..	4			2	10	2	3	2	
3:30		LILLEE	......W	12						10	3	3	2		
		2-1-2-2	FLETCHER												
3:32			2	1						3	12	3	2	2	
	WALKER		.4....	7	1	.1	6			4	17	3	6	3	
	2-0-15-1	LILLEE	....	11		...3	10			5	20	3	6	6	
	WALKER	3-1-5-2				4....4..	18	2		6	28	3	6	14	
3:50	3-0-23-1		TEA			TEA									
4:10		LILLEE	....4 1	17	2	..	20			7	33	3	11	14	
	WALKER	4-1-10-2	....	25					M2	8	33	3	11	14	
4:22	4-1-23-1	LILLEE				...W	24				33	4	11	14	
		5-1-11-3				GREIG									
4:24			..	27		.1	2			9	34	4	11	1	
	WALKER					....	10		M3	10	34	4	11	1	
	5-2-23-1	LILLEE	b	28		....	17		M4; b1	11	35	4	11	1	1
	WALKER	6-2-11-3	....1 .	34		.3	19			12	39	4	12	4	
	6-2-27-1	LILLEE		35		.....4 1	26	1		13	44	4	12	9	
	MALLETT	7-2-16-3	..3	38		..1 ..	31			14	48	4	15	10	
	1-0-4-0	LILLEE	2 3	40		....	37			15	53	4	20	10	
	MALLETT	8-2-21-3	1	41		....	44			16	54	4	21	10	
	2-0-5-0	WALKER	1	46		...	47			17	55	4	22	10	
	MALLETT	7-2-28-1	....	54					M5	18	55	4	22	10	
	3-1-5-0	WALKER	.1	56		1	53			19	57	4	23	11	
	MALLETT	8-2-30-1	..1 ..n 1	63		L .	55		lb1, nb1	20	61	4	25	11	3
	4-1-7-0	WALKER	3	64		.2..4.1	62	2		21	71	4	28	18	
	MALLETT	9-2-40-1	....	68		...1	66			22	72	4	28	19	
5:35	5-1-8-0	WALKER	..3	71		1 .W	69				76	5	31	20	
		10-2-44-2				KNOTT									
5:36						..	2			23	76	5	31	0	
	MALLETT		..4.....	79	3					24	80	5	35	0	
	6-1-12-0	WALKER				...2....	10			25	82	5	35	2	
	MALLETT	11-2-46-2	L	80		...2...	17		lb2	26	86	5	35	4	4
	7-1-14-0	WALKER	......4.	88	4					27	89	5	39	4	
	MALLETT	12-2-50-2				3	25			28	92	5	39	7	
	8-1-17-0	WALKER				.2......	33			29	94	5	39	9	
6:03		13-2-52-2	STUMPS			STUMPS				ATTENDANCE: 20,771					
	MALLETT		....	96					M6	30	94	5	39	9	
	9-2-17-0	LILLEE	..44.4.	103	7	3	34		50: 139m 102 balls	31	109	5	51	12	
	MALLETT	9-2-36-3	.....	108		2.3	37			32	114	5	51	17	
	10-2-22-0	LILLEE	.1	110		.3 ...4	43	1		33	122	5	52	24	
	MALLETT	10-2-44-3	....	118					M7	34	122	5	52	24	
	11-3-22-0	JENNER	.1 ...	123		2 1 3	46			35	129	5	53	30	
	LILLEE	1-0-7-0				....	54		M8	36	129	5	53	30	
	11-3-44-3	JENNER	.22.....	131						37	133	5	57	30	
	LILLEE	2-0-11-0	.	132		.4....1	61	2		38	138	5	57	35	
	12-3-49-3	JENNER				....	69		M9	39	138	5	57	35	
11:52	LILLEE	3-1-11-0	2.4...W	139							144	6	63	35	
	13-3-55-4		TITMUS												
11:54			.	1						40	144	6	0	35	
		JENNER	....	8		3	70			41	147	6	0	38	
	WALKER	4-1-14-0	.	9		2.....1	77			42	150	6	0	41	
	14-2-55-2	JENNER	..	11		21	83			43	153	6	0	44	
	WALKER	5-1-17-0	2..	14		.4..1	88	3		44	160	6	2	49	
	15-2-62-2	JENNER	..1 ...	20		1 1	90		50: 100m 89 balls	45	163	6	3	51	
		WALKER	6-1-20-0	..1	23		4...1	95	4		46	169	6	4	56	

373

Time													
	16-2-68-2	MALLETT	.... 1 .	29		. 1	97		47	171	6	5	57
	WALKER	12-3-24-0	.. 4 ...	35	1	2 3	99		48	180	6	9	62
	17-2-77-2	MALLETT	... 2 ...	42		1	100		49	183	6	11	63
	WALKER	13-3-27-0	... 2 . 2 .	49		1	101		50	188	6	15	64
	18-2-82-2	MALLETT	..	51		 1	107		51	189	6	15	65
	WALKER	14-3-28-0	2	52		. 2 . 2 .. 1	114		52	196	6	17	70
	19-2-89-2	MALLETT	....	59		1	115		53	197	6	17	71
	I.CHAPPELL	15-3-29-0	.....	64		.. 1	118		54	198	6	17	72
	1-0-1-0	MALLETT				....	126	M10	55	198	6	17	72
1:00		16-4-29-0	LUNCH			LUNCH							
1:40	JENNER		. 2	72					57	200	6	19	72
	7-1-22-0	MALLETT				....	134	M11	58	200	6	19	72
	JENNER	17-5-29-0	....	80				M12	59	200	6	19	72
	8-2-22-0	MALLETT	b2	85		.. 1	137	b3	60	203	6	19	73	6
	JENNER	18-4-30-0				....	145	M13	61	203	6	19	73
	9-3-22-0	MALLETT	....	93				M14	62	203	6	19	73
	JENNER	19-6-30-0	.. 1	96		1	150		63	205	6	20	74
	10-3-24-0	MALLETT	....	104				M15	64	205	6	20	74
	JENNER	20-7-30-0				. 4	158	5	65	209	6	20	78
	11-3-28-0	MALLETT	....	112				M16	66	209	6	20	78
2:16	JENNER	21-8-30-0	... W	116		.. 2 1	162		67	212	7	20	81
2:18	12-3-31-1		UNDERWOOD										
2:23		MALLETT	.. W	3		 L	167	M17;lb3	68	213	8	0	81	7
	22-9-30-1	ARNOLD											
2:25	JENNER					...... 4 .	175	6	69	217	8	0	85
2:30	13-3-35-1	MALLETT	...... W	6						217	9	0	85
	23-10-30-2	WILLIS											
2:31			...	2				M18	70	217	9	0	85
	JENNER					....	183	M19	71	217	9	0	85
	14-4-35-1	MALLETT	1 1	8		1 .	185		72	220	9	2	86
	JENNER	24-10-33-2	. 1	10		... 2 . 1	191		73	224	9	3	89
	15-4-39-1	MALLETT	.	11		.... 2 . 1	198		74	227	9	3	92
	LILLEE	25-10-36-2				/. 2 4 ... 4 4	206	9	/new ball 100:220m 205 balls	75	241	9	3	106
3:00	14-3-69-4	WALKER	.... W	19					76	241	10	3	106
		20-3-89-3	AUSTRALIA WON BY 163 RUNS						ATTENDANCE: 6,707				

AUSTRALIA FIRST Innings

IN	OUT	MINS	NO	BATSMAN	HOW OUT	BOWLER	RUNS	WK	TOTAL	BALLS	4s	6s	N O T E S
11:00	1:01	121	1	IR REDPATH	CT GREIG	UNDERWOOD	21	4	77	95			Edged turning delivery to gully
11:00	12:23	83	2	RB McCOSKER	CT COWDREY	UNDERWOOD	35	1	52	73	3		Edged defensive push to second slip
12:23	12:25	1	3	IM CHAPPELL	CT KNOTT	UNDERWOOD	0	2	52	3			Ball popped and took top edge
12:24	12:34	7	4	GS CHAPPELL	LBW	UNDERWOOD	5	3	58	6			Missed attempted hit to leg side
12:27	2:46	92	5	KD WALTERS	CT WILLIS	UNDERWOOD	55	6	164	85	7	1	Diving behind bowler, leading edge
12:35	1:49	9	6	RW MARSH	CT GREIG	UNDERWOOD	6	5	84	17			Skied drive to deep mid-wicket
1:40	4:27	137	7	TJ JENNER	BOWLED	UNDERWOOD	74	7	241	114	7		Swung across line of flighted ball
1:51	4:45	98	8	MHN WALKER	RUN OUT		41	8	259	77	2		Refused run, Denness toss to bowler
2:48	5:28	59	9	DK LILLEE	BOWLED	WILLIS	26	9	295	40	2		Fast ball on leg stump
4:29	5:41	54	10	AA MALLETT	NOT OUT		23			51	1		
4:47	5:41	12	11	JR THOMSON	BOWLED	ARNOLD	5	10	304	8	1		Full ball, ricochet off pad

EXTRAS B4, LB 4, NB 5   16

TOTAL (ALL OUT, 68.2 OVERS)   304

BOWLER	O	M	R	W	NB/W
WILLIS	10	0	46	1	1/
ARNOLD	12.2	3	42	1	4/
UNDERWOOD	29	3	113	7	
GREIG	10	0	63	0	
TITMUS	7	1	27	0	

Runs	Mins	Overs	Last50
50	82	16.2	
100	145	29.3	63
150	174	34.6	29
200	227	46.1	53
250	283	57.1	56
300	335	66.6	52
350			
400			
450			
500			

LUNCH 77-4
25 overs

TEA 213-6
49 overs

Wkt	Partnership		RUNS
1	Redpath	McCosker	52
2	Redpath	Chappell	0
3	Redpath	Chappell	6
4	Redpath	Walters	19
5	Marsh	Walters	7
6	Jenner	Walters	80
7	Jenner	Walker	77
8	Lillee	Walker	18
9	Lillee	Mallett	36
10	Mallett	Thomson	9

ENGLAND FIRST Innings

IN	OUT	MINS	BATSMAN	NO	HOW OUT	BOWLER	RUNS	WK	TOTAL	BALLS	4s	6s	NOTES
5:51	11:01	11	DL AMISS	1	CT I.CHAPPELL	LILLEE	0	1	2	11	0		Edged defensive shot to first slip
5:51	11:24	34	D LLOYD	2	CT MARSH	LILLEE	4	2	19	27	1		Fended down leg side to keeper
11:03	12:30	87	MC COWDREY	3	CT WALKER	THOMSON	26	3	66	59	2		High one-handed catch at short leg
11:26	12:49	83	MH DENNESS	4	CT MARSH	THOMSON	51	4	90	65	6		Edged back-foot slash to keeper
12:31	12:57	106	KW FLETCHER	5	CT I.CHAPPELL	THOMSON	40	7	155	71	5		Edged uncontrolled back-foot drive
12:51	2:13	42	AW GREIG	6	CT MARSH	LILLEE	19	5	130	44	2		Edged playing at wider delivery
2:14	2:37	23	APE KNOTT	7	CT LILLEE	MALLETT	5	6	147	23			Top-edged pull to square leg
2:40	3:10	30	FJ TITMUS	8	CT G.CHAPPELL	MALLETT	11	9	161	25	1		Caught on mid-wicket boundary
2:59	3:01	2	DL UNDERWOOD	9	CT LILLEE	MALLETT	0	8	156	2			Swept to backward square leg
3:02	3:32	30	GG ARNOLD	10	BOWLED	LILLEE	0	10	172	34			Straight ball, beaten for pace
3:11	3:32	21	RGD WILLIS	11	NOT OUT		11			17	2		

EXTRAS		LB 2, NB 3 5
TOTAL	(ALL OUT, 46.5 OVERS)	172

Runs	Mins	Overs	Last50
50	76	14.4	
100	140	25.3	64
150	200	37.4	60
200			
250			
300			
350			
400			
450			
500			

STUMPS DAY 2: 2-0
2 overs, 302 behind

LUNCH: 95-4
23 overs, 209 behind

BOWLER	O	M	R	W	NB/W
LILLEE	12.5	2	49	4	
THOMSON	15	1	58	3	4/
WALKER	5	1	18	0	
JENNER	5	0	28	0	
MALLETT	9	4	14	3	

Wkt	Partnership		RUNS
1	Amiss	Lloyd	2
2	Cowdrey	Lloyd	16
3	Cowdrey	Denness	47
4	Fletcher	Denness	24
5	Fletcher	Greig	40
6	Fletcher	Knott	17
7	Fletcher	Titmus	8
8	Underwood	Titmus	1
9	Arnold	Titmus	5
10	Arnold	Willis	11

AUSTRALIA SECOND Innings

IN	OUT	MINS BATTED	NO	BATSMAN	HOW OUT	BOWLER	RUNS	WKT	TOTAL	BALLS	4s	6s	NOTES
3:55	11:32	158	1	IR REDPATH	BOWLED	UNDERWOOD	52	3	128	125	3		Played on playing defensive push
3:55	4:09	14	2	RB McCOSKER	CT KNOTT	ARNOLD	11	1	16	13	1		Ball seamed away to find edge
4:10	5:33	83	3	IM CHAPPELL	CT KNOTT	UNDERWOOD	41	2	92	75	2	1	Slog sweep skied off edge of bat
5:35	11:48	74	4	GS CHAPPELL	CT GREIG	UNDERWOOD	18	4	133	61	2		Diving mid-off catch after loose drive
11:34	3:00	168	5	KD WALTERS	NOT OUT		71			127	5	1	
11:50	2:21	113	6	RW MARSH	CT GREIG	UNDERWOOD	55	5	245	110	3	1	Caught on mid-wicket boundary
2:24	3:00	36	7	TJ JENNER	NOT OUT		14			21			
			8	MHN WALKER									
			9	DK LILLEE									
			10	AA MALLETT									
			11	JR THOMSON									
				EXTRAS		LB 4, NB 6	10						
				TOTAL		(5 WICKETS, 65 OVERS)	272 DEC						

BOWLER	O	M	R	W	NB/W
ARNOLD	20	1	71	1	4/
WILLIS	5	0	27	0	2/
UNDERWOOD	25	5	102	4	
TITMUS	13	1	53	0	
GREIG	2	0	9	0	

Runs	Mins	Overs	Last50
50	48	8.5	
100	110	21.4	62
150	200	40.1	90
200	244	50.1	44
250	303	60.7	57
300			
350			
400			
450			
500			

STUMPS DAY 3: 111-2
25 overs, 243 ahead
LUNCH: 203-4
51 overs, 337 ahead
• Walters/Marsh 100 partnership in 103 min

wkt	Partnership		RUNS
1	Redpath	McCosker	16
2	Redpath	Chappell	76
3	Redpath	Chappell	36
4	Walters	Chappell	5
5	Walters	Marsh	112
6	Jenner	Walters	27
7			
8			
9			
10			

ENGLAND SECOND Innings

AUSTRALIA WON BY 163 RUNS

IN	OUT	MINS	NO	BATSMAN	HOW OUT	BOWLER	RUNS	WK	TOTAL	BALLS	4s	6s	NOTES
3:12	3:14	2	1	DL AMISS	CT MARSH	LILLEE	0	1	0	4			Edge to lifting and seaming delivery
3:12	3:22	10	2	D LLOYD	CT WALTERS	WALKER	5	2	8	3	1		Back-foot edge to third slip
3:15	3:30	15	3	MC COWDREY	CT MALLETT	LILLEE	3	3	10	12			Edged to diving catch at gully
3:23	4:22	39	4	MH DENNESS	CT JENNER	LILLEE	14	4	33	24	2		Slashed to fly slip
3:32	11:52	183	5	KW FLETCHER	LBW	LILLEE	63	6	144	139	8		Pinned by inswinging yorker
4:24	5:35	71	6	AW GREIG	LBW	WALKER	20	5	76	69	2		Ball moved in; trapped on back foot
5:36	3:00	227	7	APE KNOTT	NOT OUT		106		212	206	9		
11:54	2:16	102	8	FJ TITMUS	LBW	JENNER	20	7	212	116	1		Beaten by full-pitched googly
2:18	2:23	5	9	DL UNDERWOOD	CT I.CHAPPELL	MALLETT	0	8	213	3			Edge defensive shot to first slip
2:25	2:30	5	10	GG ARNOLD	BOWLED	MALLETT	0	9	217	6			Pushed wrong line to turning ball
2:31	3:00	29	11	RGD WILLIS	BOWLED	WALKER	3	10	241	19			Ball kept low, played wrong line

EXTRAS: B 3, LB 3, NB 1   7

TOTAL (ALL OUT, 76 OVERS)   241

BOWLER	O	M	R	W	NB/W
LILLEE	14	3	69	4	
WALKER	20	3	89	3	
MALLETT	25	10	36	2	1/
JENNER	15	4	39	1	
I.CHAPPELL	1	0	1	0	

Runs	Mins	Overs	Last50
50	83	14.1	
100	157	30.4	74
150	214	41.7	54
200	272	55.2	58
250			
300			
350			
400			
450			
500			

TEA: 28-2
6 overs, 377 to win

STUMPS DAY 4: 94-5
29 overs, 311 to win

LUNCH: 198-6
55 overs, 207 to win

MATCH ATTENDANCE: 92,401

Wkt	Partnership		RUNS
1	Amiss	Lloyd	0
2	Cowdrey	Lloyd	8
3	Cowdrey	Denness	2
4	Fletcher	Denness	23
5	Fletcher	Greig	43
6	Fletcher	Knott	68
7	Titmus	Knott	68
8	Underwood	Knott	1
9	Arnold	Knott	4
10	Willis	Knott	24

SIXTH TEST MATCH

AUSTRALIA v **ENGLAND** at MELBOURNE CRICKET GROUND on FEBRUARY 8-10, 12-13 1975

1st DAY TIME	BOWLERS Southern End (S) NAME	BOWLERS Pavilion End (N) NAME	BATSMEN UMP: T. BROOKS (S) NAME	B	4/6	BATSMEN UMP: R.BAILHACHE (N) NAME	B	4/6	NOTES Toss AUS	AUSTRALIA 1ST INNINGS TOTALS AT END OF OVER O	R	W	LBat	RBat	Ext
			REDPATH			McCOSKER			M1	1	0	0	0	0	
11:00	ARNOLD		....	8							0	1	0	0	
11:09	1-1-0-0	LEVER				...W	4								
		1-1-0-1				I.CHAPPELL									
11:10						....	4		M2	2	0	1	0	0	
	ARNOLD		....	16					M3	3	0	1	0	0	
	2-2-0-0	LEVER				....	12		M4	4	0	1	0	0	
	ARNOLD	2-2-0-1				...1	16			5	2	1	1	1	
11:35	3-2-2-0	LEVER	..W	23		2...1	21			6	5	2	1	4	
		3-2-3-2	G.CHAPPELL												
11:36	ARNOLD		.1 ...	5		21 3	24			7	12	2	1	10	
	4-2-9-0	LEVER	......	11		.1	26			8	13	2	1	11	
	OLD	4-2-4-2	..	13		..2..3	32			9	18	2	1	16	
12:00	1-0-5-0	LEVER	W	14		...1	36				19	3	1	17	
		5-2-5-3	EDWARDS												
12:02			...	3						10	19	3	0	17	
	OLD					...4....	44	1		11	23	3	0	21	
12:13	2-0-9-0	LEVER	.W	5							23	4	0	21	
		6-2-9-4	WALTERS												
12:14			....4.	6	1					12	27	4	4	21	
	OLD					....4...	52	2		13	31	4	4	25	
	3-0-13-0	LEVER	...1 .	11		..3	55			14	35	4	5	28	
	OLD	7-2-13-4				4..4....	63	4		15	43	4	5	36	
	4-0-21-0	ARNOLD	..43	15	2	....	67			16	50	4	12	36	
12:44	OLD	5-2-16-0	.W	17							50	5	12	36	
	5-0-25-1		MARSH												
12:45			..4...	6	1					17	54	5	4	36	
		ARNOLD	1	7		.2.1 22.	74			18	62	5	5	43	
	OLD	6-2-24-0	....4...	15	2					19	66	5	9	43	
1:00	6-0-29-1		LUNCH			LUNCH									
1:40		LEVER	...4	19	3	.4.n 3	79	5	50:118m 79b; nb1	20	78	5	13	50	1
	GREIG	8-2-24-4				4......4	87	7		21	86	5	13	58	
	1-0-8-0	LEVER	...42n1	26	4	.1	89		nb2	22	95	5	20	59	2
	GREIG	9-2-32-4	...	29		1	94			23	96	5	20	60	
	2-0-9-0	OLD	..	31		1	100			24	97	5	20	61	
	GREIG	7-0-30-1	3	36		.3 1	103			25	104	5	23	65	
2:19	3-0-16-0	OLD				.W	105				104	6	23	65	
		8-0-32-2				WALKER									
2:20						.2....	6			26	106	6	23	2	
	GREIG		.....2.4	44	5					27	112	6	29	2	
2:36	4-0-22-0	OLD	W	46		2 1	10				115	7	29	5	
		9-0-35-3	LILLEE												
2:37			...	3						28	115	7	0	5	
	GREIG					....	18		M5	29	115	7	0	5	
	5-1-22-0	OLD	1 ....4.	10	1	1	19			30	121	7	5	6	
	GREIG	10-0-41-3				2..4...1	27	1		31	128	7	5	13	
	6-1-29-0	OLD	.3 .4	14	2	1 ..1	31			32	137	7	12	15	
	GREIG	10-0-50-3	..	16		21	37			33	140	7	12	18	
3:15	7-1-32-0	LEVER	W	17		1	38				141	8	12	19	
		10-2-34-5	MALLETT												
3:17			1	5		.	39			34	142	8	1	19	
	GREIG		.1 1	8		.L ...	44		lb1	35	145	8	3	19	3
3:30	8-1-34-0	LEVER	..4 W	12	1						149	9	7	19	
		11-2-38-6	DYMOCK												
3:31			....	4						36	149	9	0	19	
3:41	GREIG		.... (B2) W	10		1	45		b2		152	10	0	20	2
	8.7-1-35-1														

1st DAY	BOWLERS Southern End (S)	BOWLERS Pavilion End N)	BATSMEN UMP: T. BROOKS (S)			BATSMEN UMP: R.BAILHACHE (N)			NOTES	ENGLAND 1ST TOTALS AT END OF OVER					INNINGS
TIME	NAME	NAME	NAME	B	4/6	NAME	B	4/6		O	R	W	LBat	RBat	Ext
4:00			BAD LIGHT			BAD LIGHT									
			AMISS			COWDREY									
4:38/41		LILLEE	..(b4) W	4					b4		4	1	0	0	4
		1-1-0-1	EDRICH												
4:42			....	4						1	4	1	0	0	
	WALKER					..4....	8	1		2	8	1	0	4	
	1-0-4-0	LILLEE	..2 1	8		...1	12			3	12	1	3	5	
	WALKER	2-1-4-1				....	20		M1	4	12	1	3	5	
	2-1-4-0	LILLEE	....	16					M2	5	12	1	3	5	
	WALKER	3-1-4-1				....	28		M3	6	12	1	3	5	
	3-1-4-0	LILLEE	2..1	20		....	32			7	15	1	6	5	
	WALKER	4-1-7-1	...	23											
5:18	4-1-7-1		LIGHT/RAIN			LIGHT/RAIN					15	1	6	5	
			STUMPS			STUMPS				ATTENDANCE: 32,515					
11:00/03			.1	25		2.W	35			8	18	2	7	7	
						DENNESS									
11:04		LILLEE	.1	27		3	6			9	22	2	8	3	
	WALKER	5-1-11-1				....2...	14			10	24	2	8	5	
	5-1-9-1	LILLEE	.3	29		.....2 1	20			11	30	2	11	8	
	WALKER	6-1-17-1				2 4....4..	28	2		12	40	2	11	18	
	6-1-19-1	DYMOCK	....	37					M4	13	40	2	11	18	
	WALKER	1-1-0-0	...2.2	43		.3	30			14	47	2	15	21	
	7-1-26-1	DYMOCK				4	38	3		15	51	2	15	25	
	WALKER	2-1-4-0	..1	46		.....	43			16	52	2	16	25	
	8-1-27-1	DYMOCK	1	54						17	53	2	17	25	
	WALKER	3-1-5-0	...2..2 3	62						18	60	2	24	25	
	9-1-34-1	DYMOCK	.1 2...	68		.3	45			19	66	2	27	28	
	WALTERS	4-1-11-0	.1 ..1	73		.1 L	48		lb1	20	70	2	29	29	5
	1-0-3-0	DYMOCK	.3	75		.4....	54	4		21	77	2	32	33	
	WALTERS	5-1-18-0	..4....2	83	1					22	83	2	38	33	
	2-0-9-0	DYMOCK	....	87		2..1	58			23	86	2	38	36	
	WALTERS	6-1-21-0				....	66		M5	24	86	2	38	36	
	3-1-9-0	DYMOCK	..1	90		.....	71			25	87	2	39	36	
	WALTERS	7-1-22-0	1	97		1	72			26	89	2	40	37	
	4-1-11-0	DYMOCK				......2.	80			27	91	2	40	39	
	WALTERS	8-1-24-0	...1	101		...3	84			28	95	2	41	42	
	5-1-15-0	DYMOCK				...2..4	92	5		29	101	2	41	48	
	MALLETT	9-1-30-0	4 3 ...	106	2	..3	95		50: 106m 95 balls	30	111	2	48	51	
	1-0-10-0	DYMOCK	...	109		1	100			31	112	2	48	52	
	MALLETT	10-1-31-0	.....	114		.4 1	103	6		32	117	2	48	57	
	2-0-15-0	DYMOCK	..1 .	118		.1 .1	107		•100p	33	120	2	49	59	
1:04		11-1-34-0	LUNCH			LUNCH									
1:40	MALLETT		...2...	125		1	108		50: 163m 122 balls	34	123	2	51	60	
	3-0-18-0	WALKER	...1	129		...3	112			35	127	2	52	63	
	MALLETT	10-1-38-1	...2..1	137						36	130	2	55	63	
	4-0-21-0	WALKER	4.1 .	141	3	..n.1	117		nb1	37	137	2	60	64	6
	MALLETT	11-1-44-1	..1	144		4 3 ...	122	7		38	145	2	61	71	
	5-0-29-0	WALKER	....1 ..	151		1	123			39	147	2	62	72	
	MALLETT	12-1-46-1	.1	153		2 1 ...3	129			40	154	2	63	78	
	6-0-36-0	WALKER				....	137		M6	41	154	2	63	78	
	WALTERS	13-2-46-1	..3	156		.2..2	142			42	161	2	66	82	
	6-1-22-0	WALKER	.1	158		1	148			43	163	2	67	83	
	WALTERS	14-2-48-1	..1	161		.1 ...	153			44	165	2	68	84	
2:33	7-1-24-0	WALKER	2.W	164							167	3	70	84	
		15-2-50-2	FLETCHER												
2:34			.....	5						45	167	3	0	84	
	DYMOCK		..	7		1	159			46	168	3	0	85	
	12-1-35-0	WALKER	.1	9		..1 ..1	165			47	171	3	1	87	
	DYMOCK	16-2-53-2	2	10		1	172			48	174	3	3	88	
	13-1-38-0	WALKER				....	180		M7	49	174	3	3	88	
	DYMOCK	17-3-53-2	....	18					M8	50	174	3	3	88	
	14-2-38-0	WALKER	.1	20		L .24.2	186	8	lb2	51	184	3	4	96	7

	DYMOCK	18-3-62-2	..1 .2.	26		.1	188		52	188	3	7	97
		15-2-42-0	MALLETT	.	27	1	195		53	189	3	7	98
	DYMOCK	7-0-37-0				4	203	9	100:221m 203 balls	54	193	3	7	102
		16-2-46-0	MALLETT	....	35				M9	55	193	3	7	102
	WALTERS	8-1-37-0	..1	38		.1 ...	208		56	195	3	8	103
		8-1-26-0	MALLETT	....	46				M10	57	195	3	8	103
	WALTERS	9-2-37-0	.....	51		..1	211		58	196	3	8	104
		9-1-27-0	MALLETT			....	219		M11	59	196	3	8	104
3:40		10-3-37-0	TEA			TEA							
	WALTERS		.2....3	58		.	220		60	201	3	13	104
		10-1-32-0	MALLETT	....	66				M12	61	201	3	13	104
	WALTERS	11-4-37-0				....	228		M13	62	201	3	13	104
		11-2-32-0	MALLETT	..1 2..3	73		1	229		63	208	3	19	105
	WALTERS	12-4-44-0	3	74		.2.....	236		64	213	3	22	107
		12-3-37-0	MALLETT	....1 .3	81		1	237		65	218	3	26	108
	WALTERS	13-4-49-0	..1 ..1	87		.1	239		66	221	3	28	109
		13-3-40-0	WALKER	../..4..2	95	1			/new ball	67	227	3	34	109
	DYMOCK	19-3-68-2	2	101		.3	241		68	232	3	36	112
		17-2-51-0	WALKER			....	249		M14	69	232	3	36	112
	DYMOCK	20-4-68-2	....	109					M15	70	232	3	36	112
		18-3-51-0	WALKER	.3	111		.1	255		71	236	3	39	113
	DYMOCK	21-4-72-2	3	112		..2...1	262		72	242	3	42	116
		19-3-57-0	WALKER	....	116		.(n2)..3	267		nb2	73	247	3	42	121
	DYMOCK	22-4-77-2				....	275		M16	74	247	3	42	121
		20-3-57-0	WALKER	...1 .1	122		1 .	278		75	250	3	44	122
	DYMOCK	23-4-80-2	.1 ...	127		4.1	281	10	76	256	3	45	127
		21-3-63-0	WALKER	....	131		..2 1	285		77	259	3	45	130
	DYMOCK	24-4-83-2				....	293		M17	78	259	3	45	130
		22-4-63-0	MALLETT	....	139				M18	79	259	3	45	130
	I.CHAPPELL	14-5-49-0	.1	141		....1 ..	298		80	261	3	46	131
		1-0-2-0	MALLETT	....	149				M19	81	261	3	46	131
	I.CHAPPELL	15-6-49-0				....	306		M20	82	261	3	46	131
		2-1-2-0	MALLETT	.1	151		......	312		83	262	3	47	131
	I.CHAPPELL	16-6-50-0	.4 1	154	2	.....	317		50: 174m 153 balls. •100p	84	267	3	52	131
		3-1-7-0	MALLETT	.1	161		1	318		85	269	3	53	132
	I.CHAPPELL	17-6-52-0	3	166		1 ..	321		86	273	3	56	133
		4-1-11-0	MALLETT	....	174					87	273	3	56	133
6:00		18-7-52-0	STUMPS			STUMPS			ATTENDANCE: 43,332					
	WALKER					......2.	329		88	275	3	56	135
		25-4-85-2	MALLETT	3	180		..	331		89	278	3	59	135
	WALKER	19-7-55-0	....	188					M21	90	278	3	59	135
		26-5-85-2	MALLETT	2...	192		...3	335		91	283	3	61	138
	WALKER	20-7-60-0	....	199		1	336		92	284	3	61	139
		27-5-86-2	MALLETT				4	344	11	93	288	3	61	143
	WALKER	21-7-64-0	1	206		.	345		94	289	3	62	143
		28-5-87-2	MALLETT	....	214					M22	95	289	3	62	143
	WALKER	22-8-64-0	.	215		....4.1	352	12	96	294	3	62	148
		29-5-92-2	MALLETT	....	219		...1	356		97	295	3	62	149
	DYMOCK	23-8-65-0				.4....4.	364	14	150:401m 358 balls	98	303	3	62	157
		23-4-71-0	MALLETT	.4..3	224	3	...	367		99	310	3	69	157
	DYMOCK	24-8-72-0	..1	227		4....	372	15	100	315	3	70	161
		24-4-76-0	WALTERS	....	235					M23	101	315	3	69	161
	DYMOCK	14-4-40-0				...4...1	380	16	102	320	3	69	166
		25-4-81-0	WALTERS	..1	238		..1 ..	385		103	322	3	71	167
	DYMOCK	15-4-42-0	.. .1	242		....	389		104	323	3	72	167
		26-4-82-0	WALTERS	...1	246		....	393		105	324	3	73	167
	DYMOCK	16-4-43-0	2.......	254					106	326	3	75	167
		27-4-84-0	WALTERS				.....4..	401	17	107	330	3	75	171
	DYMOCK	17-4-47-0	....	262					M24	108	330	3	75	171
		28-5-84-0	WALTERS	.	263		3	408		109	333	3	75	174
	DYMOCK	18-4-50-0				2	416		110	335	3	75	176
		29-5-86-0	WALTERS	1	268		...	419		111	336	3	76	176

	DYMOCK	19-4-51-0	....2...	276					112	338	3	78	176
		30-5-88-0	WALTERS	...4.	281	4	..3	422		113	345	3	82	179
	DYMOCK	20-4-58-0				2......1	430		114	348	3	82	182
		31-5-91-0	WALTERS	....	285		...3	434		115	351	3	82	185
1:00		21-4-61-0	LUNCH			LUNCH						
						.....2..	442		116	353	3	82	187
		30-5-94-2	I.CHAPPELL	4.......	293	5			117	357	3	86	187
1:51	WALKER	5-1-15-0	.1	295		...1 .W	448		118	359	4	87	188
		31-5-96-3				GREIG						
1:53			I.CHAPPELL	1	302		. 1		119	360	4	88	0
	WALKER	6-1-16-0	4.......	310	6				120	364	4	92	0
		32-5-100-3	I.CHAPPELL	...21	315		3 ..	4		121	370	4	95	3
	WALKER	7-1-22-0	1 ...1	320		.3 2	7		122	377	4	97	8
		33-5-107-3	I.CHAPPELL	4.1	323	7	4	12	1	100:337m 321 balls	123	386	4	102	12
	WALKER	8-1-31-0	1	328		.43	15	2		124	394	4	103	19
		34-5-115-3	I.CHAPPELL			1	23		125	395	4	103	20
	WALKER	9-1-32-0	2....	333		.41	26	3		125	402	4	105	25
		35-5-122-3	I.CHAPPELL	..1 .2	338		43 1	29	4		127	413	4	108	33
	MALLETT	10-1-43-0	...1	342		..1 .	33			128	415	4	109	34
		25-8-74-0	I.CHAPPELL	..1	345		.....	38			129	416	4	110	34
	MALLETT	11-1-44-0	1 ...4	350	8	..1	41			130	422	4	115	35
		26-8-80-0	I.CHAPPELL	.3	352		...1 .2	47			131	428	4	118	38
	MALLETT	12-1-50-0	1	358		.1	49			132	430	4	119	39
		27-8-82-0	WALTERS			4..4..1	57	6		133	439	4	119	48
	MALLETT	22-4-70-0	.1 1 .4	363	9	1 .(n1) 1	61		50:67min 60b; nb3	134	448	4	125	51
		28-8-91-0	WALTERS	,1	365		.4443	67	9	•100p	135	464	4	126	66
	MALLETT	23-4-86-0	1	370		4..	70	10		136	469	4	127	70
		29-8-96-0	DYMOCK	/3 ...	374		...1	74		/new ball	137	473	4	130	71
	WALKER	32-5-95-0	.....	379		..1	77			138	474	4	130	72
		36-5-123-3	DYMOCK	4.1	382	10	4.1 ..	82	11		139	484	4	135	77
	WALKER	33-5-105-0	.2......	390						140	4n 86	4	137	77
		37-5-125-3	DYMOCK	,,(n4)..	395	11	.4.1	86	12		141	495	4	141	82
	WALKER	34-5-114-0	....	402		1	87			142	496	4	141	83
3:40		38-5-126-3	TEA			TEA						
			DYMOCK	3	409		1	88			143	500	4	144	84
	WALKER	35-5-118-0	.....2..	417						144	502	4	146	84
		39-5-128-3	DYMOCK	....	421		.4.1	92	13		145	507	4	146	89
4:16	WALKER	36-5-123-0				.W	94			507	5	146	89
4:17		40-6-128-5				KNOTT						
4:20				.....W	426					507	6	146	0
				OLD								
4:21				.	1				M25	146	507	6	0	0
4:26			DYMOCK	.W	3		..1	3			508	7	0	1
		37-5-126-1	UNDERWOOD									
4:27				..2	3					147	510	7	2	1
4:31	WALKER					4.W	6			514	8	2	5
4:32		41-6-135-7				ARNOLD						
4:34						.W	2			514	9	2	0
						LEVER						
4:35				.	4		2 1	2		148	517	9	2	3
			DYMOCK		6		1	8		149	518	9	2	4
	WALKER	38-5-127-1	1 .4 1	10		1 1 ..	12			150	526	9	8	6
		42-6-143-7	DYMOCK	3	16		..	14			151	529	9	11	6
4:53	WALKER	39-5-130-1	.W	18						528	10	11	6
		42.2-6-143-8											

3rd DAY	BOWLERS		BATSMEN					NOTES	TOTALS AT END OF OVER				
	Southern End (S)	Pavilion End (N)	UMP: R.BAILHACHE (S)			UMP: T. BROOKS (N)							
TIME	NAME	NAME	NAME	B	4/6	NAME	B	4/6		O	R	W	LBat	RBat	Ext
			REDPATH			McCOSKER			M1	1	0	0	0	0	
5:05	ARNOLD		....	8											
	1-1-0-0	LEVER	..2....	15		1	1			2	3	0	2	1	
	ARNOLD	1-0-3-0				....24.3	9	1		3	12	0	2	10	
	2-1-9-0	LEVER	...	18		1	14			4	13	0	2	11	
	ARNOLD	2-0-4-0	1	19		.4.1...	21	2		5	19	0	3	16	
	3-1-15-0	LEVER	......4.	27	1					6	23	0	7	16	
	OLD	3-0-8-0	.....	32		..3	24			7	26	0	7	19	
	1-0-3-0	LEVER	2..1	36		...3	28			8	32	0	10	22	
	OLD	4-0-14-0	....	44					M2	9	32	0	10	22	
	2-1-3-0	UND'WOOD				....	36			10	32	0	10	22	
6:02		1-1-0-0	STUMPS			STUMPS				ATTENDANCE: 15,084					
11:00	ARNOLD		....	52						11	32	0	10	22	
	4-2-15-0	LEVER	...2	56		4..3	40	3		12	41	0	12	29	
	ARNOLD	5-0-23-0	.....	61		...(n3)	44		nb1	13	44	0	12	32	
	5-2-18-0	LEVER				4....44.	52	6		14	56	0	12	44	
	ARNOLD	6-0-35-0	.1	63		.n2....	59		nb2	15	60	0	13	46	1
	6-2-21-0	LEVER	.4..2...	71	2					16	66	0	19	46	
	ARNOLD	7-0-41-0	...	74		..2(n2).1	65		50:97m, 63b;nb3	17	71	0	19	51	
	7-2-26-0	OLD	.1	76		1	71			18	73	0	20	52	
	ARNOLD	3-1-5-0	....	84					M3	19	73	0	20	52	
	8-3-26-0	OLD	....	91		1	72			20	74	0	20	53	
	GREIG	4-1-6-0	..	93		1	78			21	75	0	20	54	
	1-0-1-0	OLD	4......	100	3	1	79			22	80	0	24	55	
	GREIG	5-1-11-0				..(L2)....3	87		lb2	23	85	0	24	58	3
	2-0-4-0	OLD				..24..21	95	7		24	94	0	24	67	
	GREIG	6-1-20-0	......	106		(b4)3	97		•100p; b4	25	101	0	24	70	7
	3-0-7-0	OLD	.3	108		.3 ...1	103			26	108	0	28	74	
	GREIG	7-1-27-0	....1.	114		1 1	105			27	111	0	28	76	
12:40	4-0-10-0	ARNOLD				..W	108			111	1	28	76		
		9-4-26-1				I.CHAPPELL									
12:41						.....	5		M4	28	111	1	28	0	
	GREIG		4.1	117	4	.....	10			29	116	1	33	0	
	5-0-15-0	ARNOLD	.n3	120		.2....	16		nb4	30	122	1	36	2	8
	GREIG	10-4-31-1	....	128					M5	31	122	1	36	2	
	6-1-15-0	ARNOLD				....	24		M6	32	122	1	36	2	
1:03		11-5-31-1	LUNCH			LUNCH									
	GREIG		1	134		.1	26			33	124	1	37	3	
	7-1-17-0	ARNOLD	..	136		2....1	32			34	127	1	37	6	
	GREIG	12-5-34-1				....	40		M7	35	127	1	37	6	
	8-2-17-0	ARNOLD	....4...	144	5					36	131	1	41	6	
	GREIG	13-5-38-1	.	145		...2.21	47			37	136	1	41	11	
	9-2-22-0	ARNOLD				.n..n..4..	57	1	nb6	38	142	1	41	15	10
	GREIG	14-5-42-1	......4.	153	6					39	146	1	45	15	
	10-2-26-0	ARNOLD				...4.2...	65	2		40	152	1	45	21	
	UND'WOOD	15-5-48-1	1	158		...	68			41	153	1	46	21	
	2-1-1-0	OLD	......2.	166						42	155	1	48	21	
	UND'WOOD	8-1-29-0				(b4)........	77		M8; b8	43	159	1	48	21	14
	3-2-1-0	OLD	(L2).3.	170		...1	80		50:239m 169b; lb2	44	165	1	51	22	16
	UND'WOOD	9-1-33-0	....	174		.4.3	84	3		45	172	1	51	29	
	4-2-8-0	OLD	4...n.4.	182	8	3	85		nb7	46	184	1	59	32	17
	UND'WOOD	10-1-44-0	..	184		1	91			47	185	1	59	33	
	5-2-9-0	OLD				....4..1	99	4		48	190	1	59	38	
	UND'WOOD	11-1-49-0				...2....	107			49	192	1	59	40	
	6-2-11-0	GREIG	.1	186		1	113			50	194	1	60	41	
	UND'WOOD	11-2-28-0				....	121		M9	51	194	1	60	41	
	7-3-11-0	GREIG	......4.	194	9					52	198	1	64	41	
	UND'WOOD	12-2-32-0				.4......	129	5		53	202	1	64	45	
	8-3-15-0	GREIG	....	202					M10	54	202	1	64	45	
	UND'WOOD	13-3-32-0				....	137		M11	55	202	1	64	45	
	9-4-15-0	GREIG	....	210					M12	56	202	1	64	45	

377 BEHIND AUSTRALIA 2ND INNINGS

	UND'WOOD	14-4-32-0				...4.....	145	6		57	206	1	64	49
3:40	10-4-19-0		TEA			TEA								
		GREIG	.2......	218						58	208	1	66	49
	UND'WOOD	15-4-34-0	.1	220		.1	151		50: 148m 147 balls	59	210	1	67	50
4:13	11-4-21-0	GREIG	.2.21	225		W	152		•100p		215	2	72	50
		16-4-39-1				G.CHAPPELL								
4:14						..	2			60	215	2	72	0
	UND'WOOD		....	233					M13	61	215	2	72	0
	12-4-21-0	GREIG	2 2	239		.1	4			62	220	2	76	1
	UND'WOOD	17-4-44-1	..4.....	246	10	3	5			63	227	2	80	4
	13-4-28-0	GREIG	......	252		.1	7			64	228	2	80	5
	UND'WOOD	18-4-45-1		253		3	14			65	231	2	80	8
	14-4-31-0	GREIG				.4..4.4.	22	3		66	243	2	80	20
	UND'WOOD	19-4-57-1	..2.....	261						67	245	2	82	20
	15-4-33-0	GREIG	...	264		1	27			68	246	2	82	21
	UND'WOOD	20-4-58-1	1	265		...1...	34			69	248	2	83	22
5:01	16-4-35-0	GREIG	......W	272							248	3	83	22
		21-5-58-2	EDWARDS											
5:03			.	1					M14	70	248	3	0	22
	UND'WOOD		.	2		1	41			71	249	3	0	23
	17-4-36-0	GREIG	1	9		1	42			72	251	3	1	24
	UND'WOOD	22-5-60-2	.2..1	14		...	45			73	254	3	4	24
	18-4-39-0	GREIG	1	21		.	46			74	255	3	5	24
	ARNOLD	23-5-61-2	....	29					M15	75	255	3	5	24
	16-6-48-1	GREIG	...	32		3	51			76	258	3	5	27
	OLD	24-5-64-2	1	33		.1.....	58			77	260	3	6	28
	12-1-51-0	ARNOLD	/1	40		1	59		/new ball	78	262	3	7	29
	OLD	17-7-50-1	.	41		.2....1	66			79	265	3	7	32
	13-1-54-0	ARNOLD	1	42		..4.3 ..	73	4		80	273	3	8	39
	OLD	18-7-58-1	1	47		...	76			81	274	3	9	39
6:02	14-1-55-0		STUMPS			STUMPS				ATTENDANCE: 12,712				
		LEVER	.2 1 ...1	54		1	77			82	279	3	13	40
	ARNOLD	8-0-46-0	2 3 ..	58		...1	81			83	285	3	18	41
	19-7-64-1	LEVER	.	59		3	88			84	288	3	18	44
11:20	ARNOLD	9-0-49-0	W	60		...1	92				289	4	18	45
	20-7-66-2		WALTERS											
11:21			..1	3						85	290	4	1	45
		LEVER	.2......	11						86	292	4	3	45
11:35	ARNOLD	10-0-51-0	.W	13		2...3	97		50:142m 97 balls		297	5	3	50
	21-7-71-2		MARSH											
11:36			b	1					B9	87	298	5	0	50	18
		LEVER	...1 ...	8		1	98			88	300	5	1	51
	ARNOLD	11-0-53-0				.2..4...	106	5		89	306	5	1	57
11:52	22-7-77-2	LEVER	..W	11							306	6	1	57
		12-0-55-1	WALKER											
11:53			2...(+4) .	5					wd4	90	312	6	2	57	22
	ARNOLD					...42...	114	6		91	318	6	2	63
	23-7-83-2	OLD	1	11		.1	116			92	320	6	3	64
	GREIG	15-1-57-0	1	11		3	123			93	324	6	4	67
	25-5-68-2	OLD	1 ..2	16		..41	127	7		94	332	6	7	72
	GREIG	16-1-65-0	L 1	18		.4.1 .1	133	8	lb5	95	340	6	8	78	23
	26-5-75-2	OLD	.1	22		..43	137	9		96	348	6	9	85
	GREIG	17-1-73-0	1	23		2....1 .	144			97	352	6	10	88
	27-5-79-2	OLD	1	30		1	145			98	354	6	11	89
	GREIG	18-1-75-0				....	153		M16	99	354	6	11	89
	28-6-79-2	LEVER	.....4 1	37	1	1	154			100	360	6	16	90
	GREIG	13-0-61-1				.....4..	162	10		101	364	6	16	94
1:00	29-6-83-2		LUNCH			LUNCH								
1:40		LEVER	1	44		2	163			102	367	6	17	96
1:49	GREIG	14-0-64-1	.......W	52					M17	103	367	7	17	96
		30-7-83-3	MALLETT											
1:50		LEVER	.	1		1	170			104	368	7	0	97

	GREIG	15-0-65-1	..	3	.4...1	176	11	100:246m 172 balls	105	373	7	0	102
2:02	31-7-88-3	LEVER			W	177				373	8	0	102
2:03		16-1-65-3			DYMOCK								
2:09					.....W	6				373	9	0	0
					LILLEE								
2:10					.	1			106	373	9	0	0
	GREIG												
2:15	31.7-7-88-4		......W	10						373	10	0	0
			ENGLAND WON BY AN INNINGS AND 4 RUNS							ATTENDANCE: 7,778			

AUSTRALIA FIRST Innings

IN	OUT	MINS	NO	BATSMAN	HOW OUT	BOWLER	RUNS	WK	TOTAL	BALLS	4s	6s	NOTES
11:00	11:35	35	1	IR REDPATH	CT GREIG	LEVER	1	2	5	23			Edged swinging ball to second slip
11:00	11:09	9	2	RB McCOSKER	CT GREIG	LEVER	0	1	0	4			Edged swinging ball to second slip
11:10	2:19	149	3	IM CHAPPELL	CT KNOTT	OLD	65	6	104	105	7		Ruled to have nicked down leg side
11:36	12:00	24	4	GS CHAPPELL	CT DENNESS	LEVER	1	3	19	14			Edged drive to gully
12:02	12:13	11	5	R EDWARDS	CT AMISS	LEVER	0	4	23	5			Glance to leg slip
12:14	12:44	30	6	KD WALTERS	CT EDRICH	OLD	12	5	50	17	2		Lifting ball edged to gully
12:45	2:36	61	7	RW MARSH	BOWLED	OLD	29	7	115	45	5		Beaten between bat and pad
2:20	3:41	81	8	MHN WALKER	NOT OUT		20			45	1		
2:27	3:15	38	9	DK LILLEE	CT KNOTT	LEVER	12	8	141	17	2		Aggressive shot edged to keeper
3:16	3:30	14	10	AA MALLETT	BOWLED	LEVER	7	9	149	12	1		Beaten for pace, middle stump
3:31	3:41	10	11	G DYMOCK	CT KNOTT	GREIG	0	10	152	10			Straightforward edge to keeper
				EXTRAS			5			B2, LB 1, NB 2			
				TOTAL	(ALL OUT, 36.7 OVERS)		152						

BOWLER	O	M	R	W	NB/W
ARNOLD	6	2	24	0	
LEVER	11	2	38	6	2/
OLD	11	0	50	3	
GREIG	8.7	1	35	1	

Runs	Mins	Overs	Last50
50	100	15.4	
100	154	24.2	54
150	237	36.1	83
200			
250			
300			
350			
400			
450			
500			

LUNCH: 66-5
19 overs

Wkt	Partnership		RUNS
1	Redpath	McCosker	0
2	Redpath	Chappell	5
3	Chappell	Chappell	14
4	Edwards	Chappell	4
5	Walters	Chappell	27
6	Marsh	Chappell	54
7	Marsh	Walker	11
8	Lillee	Walker	26
9	Mallett	Walker	8
10	Dymock	Walker	3

ENGLAND FIRST Innings

IN	OUT	MINS	NO	BATSMAN	HOW OUT	BOWLER	RUNS	WK	TOTAL	BALLS	4s	6s	NOTES
4:38	4:41	3	1	DL AMISS	LBW	LILLEE	0	1	4	4			Trapped on back foot
4:38	11:03	41	2	MC COWDREY	CT MARSH	WALKER	7	2	18	35	1		Lifting ball via glove to keeper
4:42	2:33	212	3	JH EDRICH	CT I.CHAPPELL	WALKER	70	3	167	164	3		Flashed and edged to slip
11:04	1:51	492	4	MH DENNESS	CT & B	WALKER	188	4	359	448	17		Back-foot drive, one-handed catch
2:34	4:20	446	5	KW FLETCHER	CT REDPATH	WALKER	146	6	507	426	11		Caught on the run at wide mid-on
1:53	4:16	123	6	AW GREIG	CT SUB (JENNER)	WALKER	89	5	507	94	13		Skied drive to mid-off
4:17	4:31	14	7	APE KNOTT	CT MARSH	WALKER	5	8	514	6	1		Thin-edged on drive
4:21	4:26	5	8	CM OLD	BOWLED	DYMOCK	0	7	508	3			Beaten playing backward defensive
4:27	4:53	26	9	DL UNDERWOOD	BOWLED	WALKER	11	10	529	18	1		Missed swing to leg side
4:32	4:34	2	10	GG ARNOLD	CT MARSH	WALKER	0	9	514	2			Back-foot drive edged to keeper
4:35	4:53	18	11	P LEVER	NOT OUT		0		514	14			
					EXTRAS		7						B4, LB 2, NB 1
					TOTAL		529						(ALL OUT, 151.2 OVERS)

BOWLER	O	M	R	W	NB/W
LILLEE	6	2	17	1	
WALKER	42.2	7	143	8	2/
DYMOCK	39	6	130	1	1/
WALTERS	23	3	86	0	
MALLETT	29	8	96	0	1/
I.CHAPPELL	12	1	50	0	

- Edrich/Denness 100 partnership in 172 mins
- Denness/Fletcher 100 partnership in 175 mins
- Fletcher/Greig 100 partnership in 72 mins

Runs	Mins	Overs	Last50
50	81	15	
100	145	29	64
150	192	39.2	47
200	287	59.7	95
250	359	74.7	72
300	448	98	89
350	523	114.5	75
400	568	125.3	45
450	607	134.2	39
500	649	143	42

STUMPS DAY 1: 15-1
7.3 overs, 137 behind

LUNCH: 120-2
33 overs, 32 behind

TEA: 196-3
59 overs, 44 ahead

STUMPS: 273-3
89 overs, 121 ahead

LUNCH: 359-4
118 overs, 207 ahead

TEA: 496-4
142 overs, 344 ahead

Wkt	Partnership		RUNS
1	Amiss	Cowdrey	4
2	Edrich	Cowdrey	14
3	Edrich	Denness	149
4	Fletcher	Denness	192
5	Fletcher	Greig	148
6	Fletcher	Knott	0
7	Old	Knott	1
8	Underwood	Knott	8
9	Underwood	Arnold	0
10	Underwood	Lever	15

AUSTRALIA SECOND Innings

ENGLAND WON BY AN INNINGS AND 4 RUNS

IN	OUT	MINS	NO	BATSMAN	HOW OUT	BOWLER	RUNS	WK	TOTAL	BALLS	4s	6s	NOTES
5:05	5:01	361	1	IR REDPATH	CT AMISS	GREIG	83	3	248	272	10		Mistimed hook to backward square
5:05	12:40	157	2	RB McCOSKER	CT COWDREY	ARNOLD	76	1	111	108	7		Edged cut shot to third slip
12:41	4:13	155	3	IM CHAPPELL	CT KNOTT	GREIG	50	2	215	152	6		Thin edge down leg side
4:14	2:02	250	4	GS CHAPPELL	BOWLED	LEVER	102	8	373	177	11		Played across the line on back foot
5:03	11:20	79	5	R EDWARDS	CT KNOTT	ARNOLD	18	4	289	60			Fended down leg side to keeper
11:21	11:35	14	6	KD WALTERS	BOWLED	ARNOLD	3	5	297	13			Played inside ball that seamed away
11:36	11:52	16	7	RW MARSH	CT DENNESS	LEVER	1	6	306	11			Edged drive to fourth slip
11:53	1:49	76	8	MHN WALKER	CT & B	GREIG	17	7	367	52	1		Driven back at comfortable height
1:50	2:15	25	9	AA MALLETT	CT EDRICH	GREIG	0	10	373	10			Bat-pad catch at short leg
2:03	2:09	6	10	G DYMOCK	CT KNOTT	LEVER	0	9	373	6			Thin edge playing forward defensive
2:10	2:15	5	11	DK LILLEE	NOT OUT		0			1			
					EXTRAS		5			B9, LB 5, W 4 NB 5			
					TOTAL	(ALL OUT, 106.7 OVERS)	373						

BOWLER	O	M	R	W	NB/W
ARNOLD	23	6	83	3	6/
LEVER	16	1	65	3	/1
OLD	18	1	75	0	
UNDERWOOD	18	5	39	0	1/
GREIG	31.7	7	88	4	

MATCH ATTENDANCE: 111,421

Runs	Mins	Overs	Last50
50	79	13.6	
100	142	24.2	73
150	218	39.3	76
200	284	52.2	66
250	370	71.1	86
300	465	87.6	95
350	518	96.1	53
400			
450			

• Redpath/McCosker 100 partnership in 142 min

STUMPS DAY 3: 32-0
10 overs, 345 behind

LUNCH: 122-1
32 overs, 255 behind

TEA: 206-1
57 overs, 171 behind

STUMPS DAY 3: 274-3
81 overs, 103 behind

LUNCH: 364-6
101 overs, 13 behind

• Redpath/Chappell 100 partnership in 152 min

Wkt	Partnership		RUNS
1	Redpath	McCosker	111
2	Redpath	Chappell	104
3	Redpath	Chappell	33
4	Edwards	Chappell	41
5	Walters	Chappell	8
6	Marsh	Chappell	9
7	Walker	Chappell	61
8	Mallett	Chappell	6
9	Mallett	Dymock	0
10	Mallett	Lillee	0